T0076406

Perspectives on the Future
of Software Engineering

Jürgen Münch • Klaus Schmid
Editors

Perspectives on the Future of Software Engineering

Essays in Honor of Dieter Rombach

 Springer

Editors
Jürgen Münch
University of Helsinki
Department of Computer Science
Helsinki
Finland

Klaus Schmid
Universität Hildesheim
Institut für Informatik
Hildesheim
Germany

ISBN 978-3-642-37394-7   ISBN 978-3-642-37395-4 (eBook)
DOI 10.1007/978-3-642-37395-4
Springer Heidelberg New York Dordrecht London

Library of Congress Control Number: 2013939055

ACM Codes: D.2, K.6

Printed on acid-free paper

Springer is part of Springer Science+Business Media (www.springer.com)

Prof. Dr. Dr. h. c. Dieter Rombach

Preface

Our modern society and technology are built on software. Critical embedded systems such as cars or factories, information systems such as ERP solutions or Internet search engines, or infrastructure such as utilities or telecommunications – none would work for even a second were it not for software. Most innovations today are shaped by software and nearly all businesses and industries are transformed by software. We can be quite sure that this will not change and software will continue to be at the core of major future changes. This relevance and dependence on quality software is what makes *software engineering* a key discipline for modern society. Software engineering is the discipline that aims at providing, evaluating, and improving methods, techniques, processes, and tools for the development of defect-free software that fulfills the needs of customers and users within time and budget constraints. Along with the growing importance of software, software engineering has also become a core field of modern research.

Since its inception in the 1960s, software engineering as a discipline has constantly grown and matured in many areas and in many ways. Today, it is a rich discipline with well-established research methods, consisting of many different subdisciplines. Of key importance to the development of a research discipline is always the underlying scientific approach. Here, the discipline has seen a major shift over the last three decades, as its formal foundations were successively augmented by a focus on empirical work aimed at evaluating whether research approaches do contribute value in real-world situations. This came to be known as empirical software engineering and is an important component of any modern software engineering research. One of the leading protagonists of empirical software engineering worldwide and certainly the leader in Germany in this subject is Dieter Rombach.

Prof. Dr. Dr. h.c. Dieter Rombach dedicated his entire career to furthering the cause of empirical software engineering as a discipline. In particular, his main research interests have always been in developing software with predictable quality. He has done intensive work on quantitative methods, languages, and tools to support software process and project management. This focus already became visible while he was working on his dissertation at the University of Kaiserslautern, Germany, where he conducted one of the largest controlled experiments ever – the development and maintenance of eight operating system kernels – to provide evidence regarding the benefits of a new structuring concept for maintainability. Ph.D. degree in hand, he went to spend several years at the University of Maryland, where he worked with Victor Basili, who can be regarded as one of the founding fathers of empirical software engineering research. During this time, Dieter Rombach also worked as a project leader at the NASA Goddard Space Flight Center. In 1990, he received the Presidential Young Investigator Award of the National Science Foundation (NSF), USA. In 1992, he returned to the University of Kaiserslautern. His strong dedication to industrial cooperation directly led to the foundation of the Software Technologie Transfer Initiative (STTI), which later resulted in the creation of the Fraunhofer Institute for Experimental Software Engineering (IESE). This institute currently has about 200 employees and has been an important contributor to the international software engineering world for more than 15 years, exerting a strong influence in both research and industry. In particular, it has helped to significantly promote the concept of empirical software engineering. Beyond his personal impact and the impact of the institute he leads, he has achieved significant impact indirectly through the many students he has advised and taught over the years, including about 60 Ph.D. students.

For his many and important contributions to the field, Dieter Rombach has received numerous awards and recognitions, like the Service Medal of the State of Rhineland-Palatinate and the Federal Cross of Merit on Ribbon of the Federal Republic of Germany. He has also received an honorary doctorate degree from the University of Oulu, Finland, and was elected a Fellow by both the ACM and the IEEE Computer Society.

His impact on the software engineering landscape is amplified by his role as an expert, reviewer, and consultant to industry and as an advisor to different state, federal, and international bodies. Instead of going into more detail on his many achievements, we refer the reader to his bio.[1] Some things, however, cannot be found there, like his strong dedication to Kaiserslautern, his commitment to his favorite soccer team 1. FC Kaiserslautern, and many other things. They show that, while he spends numerous hours on software engineering, his interests are much broader.

This book is dedicated to Dieter Rombach and his contributions to software engineering in general and to empirical software engineering in particular. In fact, it was written to accompany a symposium in honor of his 60th birthday. But beyond this, its aim is to take stock of the current situation in software engineering and point out some visions for the future. This aim guided the concept of this book throughout. We introduce the book with a paper written by Dieter Rombach that provides a good overview of his vision for the empirical software engineering discipline. The remainder of the book is structured into three main parts: The first part focuses on what are generally considered the classical foundations of software engineering research, such as notations, architecture, and processes. The second part addresses the core part of Dieter Rombach's contribution – empirical software engineering – while the third part discusses the broader vision of the software engineering discipline, described along various dimensions. Contributions to this

---

[1] http://www.iese.fraunhofer.de/en/aboutus/directors/cv_rombach_english.html

volume were collected on a by-invitation basis only. Invitations were sent to selected, internationally renowned researchers who have a relationship with Dieter Rombach's work and history. Due to the enormous network of collaborations that he has created over the years, the latter was hardly a restriction. Most of the authors invited promised a contribution right away, which now forms part of this collection. We are very happy about the numerous internationally acclaimed authors who did not hesitate to contribute to this collection. Without their contributions, this book would just not have been possible!

We augmented the collection with contributions by current members of Fraunhofer IESE to ensure that the research focus of Dieter Rombach, which is embedded in Fraunhofer IESE today, is adequately represented throughout this collection. As a result, we believe that this collection now provides an excellent overview of the current state of software engineering and its future directions and emphasizes the specific influences by Dieter Rombach and the research he cares about most.

A collection like this would never be possible without the help of many people. First of all, we would like to thank the numerous authors for their contributions. We know that it is not easy to make room in a busy schedule to be able to write profound contributions like the ones we received for this book, particularly within a tight schedule. The collaboration was simply exceptional! We would also like to thank Fraunhofer IESE as the sponsor of this book and several of its staff who greatly helped in preparing the book: Mrs. Nicole Spanier-Baro, who worked on the administrative issues and the accompanying symposium; Ms. Sonnhild Namingha, who did a great job of proofreading and editing; and Stephan Thiel, who worked relentlessly to get all the final formatting work done. We would also like to thank Christian Kröher from the University of Hildesheim for supporting us with LaTeX editing and Ralf Gerstner from Springer, who worked on the contract issues and supported us at every turn. Finally, we are grateful to Martin Verlage, who worked with us on the concept of the book and contributed a lot of ideas to our discussions.

Helsinki, Finland   Jürgen Münch
Hildesheim, Germany   Klaus Schmid

Contents

Contributors

Myla M. Archer Naval Research Laboratory, Software Engineering, Washington, DC, USA, archer@itd.nrl.navy.mil

Christian Bartelt Chair of Software Systems Engineering, Department of Informatics, Clausthal University of Technology, Clausthal-Zellerfeld, Germany, christian.bartelt@tu-clausthal.de

Victor R. Basili Department of Computer Science and Institute for Advanced Computer Studies, University of Maryland, College Park, MD, USA

Fraunhofer Center for Experimental Software Engineering, College Park, USA, basili@cs.umd.edu

Steffen Becker Fachgruppe Softwaretechnik, Heinz Nixdorf Institut, Universität Paderborn, Paderborn, Germany, steffen.becker@uni-paderborn.de

Barry Boehm University of Southern California, Los Angeles, CA, USA, boehm@usc.edu

Manfred Broy Institut für Informatik, Technische Universität München, München, Germany, broy@in.tum.de

Madeline Diep Fraunhofer Center for Experimental Software Engineering, College Park, MD, USA, mdiep@fc-md.umd.edu

Oscar Dieste Universidad Politécnica de Madrid, Madrid, Spain, odieste@fi.upm.es

Jörg Dörr Fraunhofer Institut for Experimental Software Engineering (IESE), Kaiserslautern, Germany, Joerg.Doerr@iese.fraunhofer.de

Davide Falessi Fraunhofer Center for Experimental Software Engineering, College Park, MD, USA, dfalessi@fc-md.umd.edu

Carlo Ghezzi Dipartimento di Elettronica e Informazione, Politecnico di Milano, Milano, Italy, carlo.ghezzi@polimi.it

Liliana Guzmán Fraunhofer Institut for Experimental Software Engineering (IESE), Kaiserslautern, Germany, liliana.guzmn@iese.fraunhofer.de

Jens Heidrich Fraunhofer Institut for Experimental Software Engineering (IESE), Kaiserslautern, Germany, Jens.Heidrich@iese.fraunhofer.de

Constance L. Heitmeyer Naval Research Laboratory, Software Engineering, Washington, DC, USA, heitmeye@itd.nrl.navy.mil

Sebastian Herold Chair of Software Systems Engineering, Department of Informatics, Clausthal University of Technology, Clausthal-Zellerfeld, Germany, sebastian.herold@tu-clausthal.de

Michael Jackson Department of Computing, The Open University, Milton Keynes, UK, jacksonma@acm.org

Andreas Jedlitschka Fraunhofer Institut for Experimental Software Engineering (IESE), Kaiserslautern, Germany, andreas.jedlitschka@iese.fraunhofer.de

Ross Jeffery NICTA, Eveleigh, NSW, Australia

School of Computer Science and Engineering, University of New South Wales, Kensington, Australia, ross.jeffery@nicta.com.au

Jessica Jung Fraunhofer Institut for Experimental Software Engineering (IESE), Kaiserslautern, Germany, jessica.jung@iese.fraunhofer.de

Natalia Juristo Universidad Politécnica de Madrid, Madrid, Spain, natalia@fi.upm.es

James Kirby Jr. Naval Research Laboratory, Washington, DC, USA, james.kirby@nrl.navy.mil

Holger Klus Chair of Software Systems Engineering, Department of Informatics, Clausthal University of Technology, Clausthal-Zellerfeld, Germany, holg.klus@tu-clausthal.de

Anne Koziolek Institut für Programmstrukturen und Datenorganisation (IPD), Karlsruhe Institut für Technologie (KIT), Karlsruhe, Germany, anne.koziolek@kit.edu

Heiko Koziolek ABB Corporate Research, Ladenburg, Germany, heiko.koziolek@de.abb.com

Constanza Lampasona Fraunhofer Institut for Experimental Software Engineering (IESE), Kaiserslautern, Germany, constanza.lampasona@iese.fraunhofer.de

Lucas Layman Fraunhofer Center for Experimental Software Engineering, College Park, MD, USA, llayman@fc-md.umd.edu

Elizabeth I. Leonard Naval Research Laboratory, Software Engineering, Washington, DC, USA, leonard@itd.nrl.navy.mil

Peter Liggesmeyer Fraunhofer Institut for Experimental Software Engineering (IESE), Kaiserslautern, Germany, Peter.Liggesmeyer@iese.fraunhofer.de

Robyn R. Lutz Department of Computer Science, Ames, IA, USA, rlutz@cs.iastate.edu

Claudio Menghi Dipartimento di Elettronica e Informazione, Politecnico di Milano, Milano, Italy, claudio1.menghi@mail.polimi.it

Jürgen Münch Department of Computer Science, University of Helsinki, Helsinki, Finland, juergen.muench@cs.helsinki.fi

Dirk Niebuhr Chair of Software Systems Engineering, Department of Informatics, Clausthal University of Technology, Clausthal-Zellerfeld, Germany, dirk.niebuhr@tu-clausthal.de

Leon J. Osterweil Laboratory for Advanced Software Engineering Research, School of Computer Science, University of Massachusetts, Amherst, MA, USA, ljo@cs.umass.edu

Andreas Rausch Chair of Software Systems Engineering, Department of Informatics, Clausthal University of Technology, Clausthal-Zellerfeld, Germany, andreas.rausch@tu-clausthal.de

Ralf Reussner Institut für Programmstrukturen und Datenorganisation (IPD), Karlsruhe Institut für Technologie (KIT), Karlsruhe, Germany, ralf.reussner@kit.edu

H. Dieter Rombach Technische Universität Kaiserslautern, Kaiserslautern, Germany

Fraunhofer Institut for Experimental Software Engineering (IESE), Kaiserslautern, Germany, Dieter.Rombach@iese.fraunhofer.de

Klaus Schmid Software Systems Engineering, Institute of Computer Science, University of Hildesheim, Hildesheim, Germany, schmid@sse.uni-hildesheim.de

Daniel Schneider Fraunhofer Institut for Experimental Software Engineering (IESE), Kaiserslautern, Germany, Daniel.Schneider@iese.fraunhofer.de

Carolyn Seaman Fraunhofer Center for Experimental Software Engineering, College Park, MD, USA

University of Maryland, Baltimore County, USA

Department of Information Systems, Information Technology & Engineering (ITE) Building, Baltimore, MD, USA, cseaman@fc-md.umd.edu; cseaman@umbc.edu

Amir Molzam Sharifloo Dipartimento di Elettronica e Informazione, Politecnico di Milano, Milano, Italy, amir.molzam@mail.polimi.it

Sandeep Shukla Virginia Tech, Arlington Research Center, Arlington, VA, USA, shukla@vt.edu

Forrest Shull Fraunhofer Center for Experimental Software Engineering, College Park, MD, USA, fshull@fc-md.umd.edu

Silke Steinbach Fraunhofer Institut for Experimental Software Engineering (IESE), Kaiserslautern, Germany, silke.steinbach@iese.fraunhofer.de

Mario Trapp Fraunhofer Institut for Experimental Software Engineering (IESE), Kaiserslautern, Germany, Mario.Trapp@iese.fraunhofer.de

David M. Weiss Department of Computer Science, Lanh & Oanh Professor of Software Engineering, Ames, IA, USA, weiss@iastate.edu

Claes Wohlin School of Computing, Blekinge Institute of Technology, Karlskrona, Sweden, Claes.Wohlin@bth.se

Marvin V. Zelkowitz Computer Science, University of Maryland, College Park, MD, USA

Fraunhofer Center for Experimental Software Engineering, College Park, MD, USA, mvz@cs.umd.edu

Andreas Zeller Software Engineering Chair, Saarland University – Computer Science, Saarbrücken, Germany, zeller@cs.uni-saarland.de

Empirical Software Engineering Models: Can They Become the Equivalent of Physical Laws in Traditional Engineering?

Dieter Rombach

Abstract

Traditional engineering disciplines such as mechanical and electrical engineering are guided by physical laws. They provide the constraints for acceptable engineering solutions by enforcing regularity and thereby limiting complexity. Violations of physical laws can be experienced instantly in the lab. Software engineering is not constrained by physical laws. Consequently, we often create software artifacts that are too complex to be understood, tested, or maintained. As overly complex software solutions may even work initially, we are tempted to believe that no laws apply. We only learn about the violation of some form of "cognitive laws" late during development or during maintenance, when overly high complexity inflicts follow-up defects or increases maintenance costs. Innovative life cycle process models (e.g., the Spiral model) provide the basis for incremental risk evaluation and adjustment of such predictions. The proposal in this paper is to work towards a scientific basis for software engineering by capturing more such time-lagging dependencies among software artifacts in the form of empirical models and thereby making developers aware of so-called "cognitive laws" that must be adhered to. This paper attempts to answer the questions of why we need software engineering laws and what they might look like, how we have to organize our discipline in order to establish software engineering laws, which such laws already exist and how we could develop further laws, how such laws could contribute to the maturing of the science and engineering of software in the future, and what challenges remain for teaching, research, and practice in the future.

D. Rombach (✉)
University of Kaiserslautern & Fraunhofer IESE, 67663 Kaiserslautern, Germany
e-mail: dieter.rombach@iese.fraunhofer.de

J. Münch and K. Schmid (eds.), *Perspectives on the Future of Software Engineering*,
DOI 10.1007/978-3-642-37395-4 12. The previous version of this paper was published
in the International Journal of Software and Informatics, 2011,5(3):525–534© 2011
ISCAS-reprinted with permission

1   Motivation and Introduction

Why do we need a scientific basis in software engineering based on some form of "laws", and what could these laws look like? Physical laws provide the scientific basis for scaling up engineering in traditional engineering disciplines. For example, all microelectronics is based on laws in semiconductor physics. These physical laws impose constraints on acceptable solutions and require high degrees of regularity to manage scale-up complexity. Violations of physical laws can be experienced instantly in the laboratory. Software engineering is not constrained by physical laws. Consequently, we often create software artifacts that are too complex to be easily understood, tested, or maintained. As overly complex software solutions may even work initially, we are often tempted to believe that no laws exist in the software domain. We only experience the violation of some form of "cognitive laws" late during development or during maintenance, when overly high complexity inflicts follow-up defects or increasing maintenance costs. Problems are the time lag until violations of software laws occur, and the cognitive nature of software laws. The time lag could mean that an overly complex design might lead to an initially functioning software system, but later during maintenance changes will result in follow-up defects resulting from the maintenance of an overly complex— and therefore badly understood—software system. In the context of this paper, we refer to "cognitive laws" as qualitatively stable models (see Sect. 3.1) relating the characteristics of different software artifacts. They are typically related to the cognitive capabilities of software developers to comprehend software artifacts. The definition is NOT explicitly related to definitions in the field of Cognitive Science. For example, initial work by Barry Boehm (e.g., CoCoMo) related the estimated size of a software product with the costs for its development; this model is widely used today for software project cost prediction and controlling [1]. Furthermore, innovative life cycle process models (e.g., the Spiral model) provide the basis for incremental evaluation and adjustment of such predictions [2]. The empirical nature of our field implies that our "cognitive laws" can only be detected empirically via time-consuming studies and have to be adapted to different project contexts. The proposal in this paper is to work towards a scientific basis for software engineering by capturing these long-term dependencies between construction and behavior as empirical process-product models and thereby making developers aware of so-called cognitive laws that must be adhered to. This paper motivates the need for cognitive laws as software engineering equivalents to physical laws in traditional engineering, introduces existing examples, and suggests a community effort to advance the states of research and practice.

1.1   Engineering

Most traditional engineering disciplines such as mechanical, electrical, or civil engineering depend on physical laws.

1.1.1 Physical Laws

Laws from semiconductor physics guide all microelectronics. They define the packaging density of chips. High packaging density is achieved by the extreme regularity of computer hardware. This law-enforced regularity has been the prerequisite for scaling the engineering of computer hardware.

1.1.2 Benefits

The benefits are that we are limited in our solution space. For example, in order to pack large numbers of functionality on a chip, rules about distances between connections need to be adhered to, and regular patterns are the key to scaling up. As a result, solutions look uniform; there is not much space for unnecessary creativity.

Education in engineering aimed at adhering to physical laws is easy, as violations lead to immediate failures and can be easily experienced in lab projects. This early experience feedback leads to the unquestioned acceptance of regular and complexity-reducing construction principles.

1.2 Software Engineering: Cognitive Laws

Software engineering is not dependent on physical laws. Often it seems we are not dependent on any laws. However, the creation of any complex human-made artifact—especially such immensely complex artifacts as software—must be easily understood, tested, and maintained. So what are the boundaries or "laws" that constrain our ability to understand, construct, test, or maintain? Concepts like "design for testability" are intended to guide design decisions based on their potential impact on testability. Such concepts need to be captured empirically in quantitative terms, and then formalized as "software engineering laws". These software engineering laws are based on the cognitive abilities of individual developers and, therefore, referred to as "cognitive laws". They describe limitations of the human ability to intellectually comprehend software artifacts. Further examples include the relationship between design complexity and the ability to test or maintain well. Every practitioner has experienced that above a certain design complexity threshold, it becomes hard to test systematically. We all know the consequences of not adhering to certain complexity limitations in the form of residual software defects in operational software as a result of inadequate comprehensibility or testability, or the inability to maintain software (presumably its premier advantage over hardware) without introducing new defects or utilizing an unacceptably high amount of resources.

So why do we not adhere to such cognitive laws as engineers adhere to physical laws (see complexity of a typical software system)? The answer is multifold: (1) These laws can only be experienced with a time lag, and most phase-based life-cycle models do not provide feedback, e.g. from testing to design, (2) they can only be determined empirically and are different for different humans, and (3) computer science has not yet established a broad basis of such laws. Whereas an engineering student can experience the violation of physical laws immediately in the lab, a software engineering student may get a software system to run despite some violation of complexity laws, and thereby establish the illusion that there are no boundaries for the construction of software. Very rarely will he/she experience the impact of such violations during maintenance. Physical laws exist and are universally applicable. The establishment of cognitive software engineering laws requires time-consuming empirical effort (even if laws exist in one environment, due to the personalization of cognition they would have to be re-validated empirically for a new environment). Many software engineering organizations shy away from this effort. Computer Science has been mostly created from mathematics, and keeps following mathematical paradigms of optimal answers to problems. Science requires that results must be challengeable. How can we claim to be a science if human-based techniques such as testing are not augmented with some impact statement (e.g., test technique T can be applied with a certain effectiveness Q provided complexity does not exceed a threshold C). Such empirical dependencies can be established by researchers via controlled lab experiments, or by practitioners via field case studies.

1.2.1   Cognitive Laws

The general form of empirical models is

$$Q/P/T\,(A1) == f\,(A2, C) \tag{1}$$

where A1 and A2 are models of software artifacts—both products and processes, Q/P/T is any aspect of quality (Q), cost and productivity (P), or time (T) of artifact A1, f is the function capturing the relationship, C is the context (e.g., developers' experience, project size) for which the relationship holds, and "==" denotes that the relationship is empirical with some uncertainty (e.g., +/−5 %).

This means that we have four kinds of models:

- Product-product models: Examples include the relationship between the complexity of a software design and the quality (number of residual defects) of the final software [3].
- Product-process models: Examples include the well-known CoCoMo model from Barry Boehm [1] where A1 is the effort distribution model of effort over life-cycle phases, A2 is the size model (measured in terms of #LoC), P is effort, C is described in terms of 14 impact factors, f is "a * size (power b)", and the uncertainty is specific to every organization. Other examples exist [4].
- Process-product models: Examples include models describing the effectiveness of methods (e.g., inspections, testing) on cost and quality [5, 6]. These models are especially important for choosing the methods and tools appropriate for a set of project goals and context characteristics during project planning. For example, the effects of a testing technique may be described as follows:
  - Testing technique T identifies 80 % of all defects (+/−5 %) if the code complexity is below a threshold C and testers' experience is high.

- Testing technique T identifies 65 % of all defects (+/−10 %) if the code complexity is above a threshold C and testers' experience is high.
- Testing technique T identifies 50 % of all defects (+/−20 %) if the code complexity is above a threshold C and testers' experience is average or low.
- Etc.

• Process-process models: Examples include effort distribution models that relate the relative project effort across different phases of development.

We call any equation of the form (1) a "law" if for all relevant contexts function f shows the same qualitatively stable effect (e.g., positive or negative). Such a function could, on the one hand, be the result of a controlled test experiment varying software complexity and tester experience. In this case, the significance of any cause-effect relationship would be high, but its scalability to practice would still be questionable. It could, on the other hand, be the result of observations in an industrial environment over a number of projects with varying degrees of software complexity and tester experience. In this case, scalability would be high, but there would a residual risk regarding cause-effect and hence regarding repeatability in future projects.

1.2.2 Challenges

Cognitive laws are based on empirical evidence. Four specific challenges include:

• The choice of study (controlled experiments, case studies)
• The maturing of characterizing models to predicting models
• The accumulation of observations from individual studies into "laws" and theories
• The adaptation/generalization of observations, laws, and theories to other/wider contexts [7]

Model-based hypotheses must be tested by a series of controlled experiments and/or case studies. From a theoretical perspective, it is generally impossible to test all possible combinations of context. Therefore, such laws will never be established purely statistically. From a practical perspective, it is sufficient to test all critical contexts and then generalize based on general knowledge in the field. The same procedure is applied in medical studies where the same constraints apply.

In general, we have to accept the fact that software is designed and not manufactured. The effects of design processes depend highly on context. The challenges regarding the establishment of a science of software engineering include the creation of empirical observations, the aggregation of empirical observations into laws, and ultimately the establishment of theories. Empirical observations are based on individual controlled experiments or case studies. They represent one data point—valid for a limited context (e.g., one project in the case of case studies) and with limited statistical significance. Empirical laws represent generalizations of aggregations of empirical observations with a common qualitative effect trend— valid for a certain context and tested enough to establish community trust. Examples of empirical laws are "use of systematic reading of requirements reduces the number of defects and rework effort" [8]. A large number of experiments and case studies have been performed—all showing a positive trend despite quantitative differences due to context differences. The community seems to have accepted the existing

Fig. 1 Structure of SE
discipline

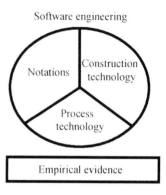

evidence due to its representative coverage of different types of software and contexts. Such evidence should be declared a law—implying that practitioners have to apply it or take the responsibility for possible negative consequences.

The accumulation of observations into laws and theories, in particular, will be discussed further in Sect. 3.1.

2   Software Engineering as a Discipline

How do we have to structure our discipline of software engineering in order to include the development and use of empirical models into research and practice (better: how do we advance towards a true engineering discipline)? What is the state of the art and practice in our discipline? Software engineering—like any other engineering discipline—must address questions related to modeling (e.g., what informal and formal notations are appropriate for modeling software systems?), system technology (what principles for structuring complex software systems are appropriate?), and process technology (what processes must be followed from capturing requirements to delivery and maintenance?). In addition, empirical studies must be performed in order to establish cognitive laws for all of the above.

2.1   Structure of the Discipline

An engineering-style structure of the Software Engineering discipline taking into consideration its human-based cognitive nature is described in Fig. 1.

It is composed of four major sub-areas: notations, construction technology, process technology, and empirical evidence. Examples of notations include programming languages, design and requirements languages, or documentation standards. Examples of construction technology include topics such as architectures, software product lines, software reuse, or general modularization concepts. Process technology addresses life-cycle models and project management practices—everything needed to engineer a software system from the initial needs. Finally, due the nature of software and software engineering, empirical evidence is needed to establish cognitive laws. The methods and tools for performing such empirical studies exist [9–11]. It can be observed that the majority of research in the past has been related to notation and system technology. Limited research has been done in the areas of process technology and empirical studies.

In other technical disciplines, we have a clear separation of science versus engineering. For example in the hardware world, physics represents science, and electrical and mechanical engineering represent engineering. In the software domain, both science and engineering are typically represented by computer science. We need to learn to also distinguish between science (including the creation of cognitive laws) and its application in engineering.

2.2   Characteristics of the Discipline

Engineering can be described as all activities involved in efficiently developing and/or producing human-based artifacts according to plan and with certifiable quality. This requires the existence of explicit models, their use for planning, and their use for early defect prevention and detection. Finally, management of complexity supported by methods and tools—as in other engineering disciplines—is the key to scaling up engineering.

2.2.1   Explicit Models

This includes models of systems and system aspects at all levels of abstraction—including requirements, architecture and design, and coding. Notations can be formal (e.g., programming languages such as JAVA, or requirements languages such as Sequence-Based Specification) or informal (e.g., structured English for requirements) depending on the quality of service guarantees required. Furthermore, models are required for processes (e.g., life-cycle models) or qualities (e.g., defect detection distributions in percentages across life-cycle phases). The current status is that especially for processes and qualities, only few models exist. In the context of model-based development, the importance of sound product models becomes even more evident. A more systematic characterization of models will be listed in Chap. 4.

2.2.2   Planning and Quality Assurance

One important aspect of engineering is the ability to plan and assure adherence to plan throughout a project. Engineering-style planning and quality assurance must be based on models. Existing prediction models include cost and effort predictions based on anticipated system size (e.g., CoCoMo) or requirements size (e.g., Function Points). Both of these prediction models can predict cost and time globally (per project) or locally (per project phase). In the latter case, continuing adherence can be measured. Barry Boehm's CoCoMo model established the first "cognitive law" of type (1) as he established a qualitatively stable relationship between system size and effort, but showed quantitative differences based on context variables. Other planning models include the prediction of residual software defects (so-called reliability models) or defect detection models across development phases based on empirical observations. All of these models allow prediction and quality assurance. Barry Boehm with his risk-based life-cycle models provided the ability to learn and improve within projects.

2.2.3 Early Focus on Prevention and Detection of Defects

Again, Barry Boehm provided the arguments why defect prevention and early defect detection—as in other engineering disciplines—pay off in terms of quality and rework cost reduction. The general law presented by Barry Boehm is that the cost of rework for a given defect increases by a factor of 10 for each development phase it remains in the system. So if the cost for removing a requirements defect during the requirements phase is "1", then its removal or rework cost during design is "10". As a result of this law, systematic inspection or review techniques (based on systematic reading or analysis techniques for software artifacts such as perspective-based reading) have been developed and, in multiple empirical studies, have been demonstrated to always reduce rework in practice.

2.2.4 Complexity Management: Supported by Methods and Tools

The central issue for scaling up engineering is complexity management. The basic principles for managing the complexity of software systems have long been known [12]. The challenges today are the development of model-based software development approaches and their support by tools. The main ideas are to employ either model-based generation or use of patterns [13]. Many empirical studies within the software comprehensibility and maintainability communities show that individual thresholds of complexity represent barriers for good development or maintenance performance.

---

3 Empirical Models

What is the nature of our software engineering laws? How do we mature empirical observations into empirical laws and theories? What is the state of the art and practice in using software engineering laws?

3.1 Empirical Observations, Laws, and Theories

Empirical models have associated levels of significance or trust, which are related to the frequency of observation and the uniformity of result repetition. Single observations are relevant to one single project; no guarantee is given that it can be repeated in future projects. The term "law" refers to a set of observations with representative coverage of a project domain (often attested by experts in technology and domain) and trend-wise (qualitatively stable) identical results. For example, in the area of requirements inspections we have enough replicated studies [14] that cover all relevant variations of software types, experience of inspectors, etc., and all show a positive effect w.r.t. effectiveness and efficiency. Although the quantitative improvements differ (from 5 % to 50 % depending on organizational maturity), we can formulate a cognitive law saying "Use of systematic requirements inspections saves effort and reduces the number of requirements defects!" A law becomes a theory if all independent context factors are known and, therefore, good predictions for future projects become feasible. A detailed discussion regarding the definition of observations, laws, and theories is contained in Ref. [8].

3.2   State of the Practice

In practice, most organizations apply processes, techniques, and methods based on the principle of "we always did it this way", or based on prominent buzz words (e.g., agile) without even knowing whether these approaches benefit the organization or to what degree. The consequences are many project failures, and especially a wide variation of project outcomes (up to 100 % miss of quality, productivity, or time targets). This should not be surprising if approaches are used across projects with differing characteristics. Good engineering should focus on repeating project results under varying project characteristics. This must imply a (often slight) change of process. A German automotive supply company has demonstrated that adequate variation of inspections techniques (ad hoc for experienced inspectors; checklist-based or perspective-based inspections for less experienced inspectors) has resulted in and guaranteed similar project results in terms of defect detection and removal effectiveness.

3.3   State of the Art

There exists a large body of observations, laws, and theories (e.g., [8])—many observations, fewer laws, hardly any theories. These empirical observations, laws, and theories should be known to practitioners (and compliance should be required as good practice, or reasons given for waivers), used as reference for professional behavior in legal disputes, taught to students early on, and complemented by researchers and practitioners.

4   Benefits for Our Discipline

How does this empirical or "cognitive" law-based view of software engineering benefit the science and engineering of software (better: how far are we on the path towards a true science-based engineering discipline)?

4.1   Science

Science requires that software engineering results can be challenged. Therefore, religious claims that new processes (e.g., testing) are better do not qualify as scientific results. Scientific results in the form of (1) do qualify. Therefore, all software engineering researchers must provide such evidence—themselves or in cooperation with others. Although the evidence captured in Ref. [8] provides a good starting point, it is the responsibility of each software engineering researcher to contribute more evidence in his/her respective area of expertise.

4.2   Engineering

Engineering requires that software methods and tools for a project can be chosen based on project goals and project context. In order to do so, we need a pool of best practice methods and tools with empirical effectiveness statements of the form of equation (1). In most organizations, choices are made based on "we always did it this way" or "subjective claims". It is no surprise then that this results in projects being off target by more than 100 %. It should be the responsibility of SEPGs in companies to compile best practice "laws" of the form (1) so that project choices can be made in an engineering-style manner.

5   Future Challenges for the Software Engineering Community

What remains to be done to continue this path in the future? We certainly need to rethink our views regarding education, science, and engineering. All of us need to acknowledge the largely empirical or cognitive nature of our discipline and act accordingly.

5.1   Education

We need to change our education (especially at the freshmen level) from trial- and-error programming to law-based programming. This requires that we initially allow freshmen to self-experience compliance as well as non-compliance with software engineering laws by means of understanding and changing good and bad programs. Equipped with such self-experience, they will be able to appreciate and accept these software engineering laws.

5.2   Science

No science without challengeable results. Results such as "I have defined a useful new testing technique" are evocative of religious claims and can never be challenged or falsified. Results such as "I have defined a new testing technique which in an experiment (detailed description of experimental design, data analysis, and interpretation) yielded 30 % higher defect detection effectiveness" can be challenged by repetition of the specified experiment [14]. We definitely need more experiments including replications [14], apply empirical studies to large-scale development processes [7], and compose individual observations into laws and theories [8].

5.3   Engineering

Practitioners need to accept the existence of best practice laws [9]. They also need to understand that these laws need to be adapted to their specific project contexts [15]. It has to become professional ethics to know and apply those laws. In case of non-compliance, personal responsibility for potential failures must be accepted.

6   Summary

We have started to capture existing observations and laws [9]. However, this can only be the beginning. We as a community must strengthen our activities to build a sufficient body of knowledge regarding key software engineering practices. This would be a starting point for defining a science of software engineering that will enable true engineering of software and prediction of project outcomes with acceptable accuracy.

This paper is an updating of a paper previously published in the International Journal of Software and Informatics [16].

References

1. Boehm, B.W.: Software Engineering Economics. Prentice-Hall, Englewood Cliffs (1981)
2. Boehm, B.W.: A spiral model of software development and enhancement. IEEE Comput. 21(5), 61–72 (1988)
3. Basili, V.R., Briand, L.C., Welo, W.L.: A validation of object-oriented design metrics as quality indicators. IEEE Trans. Softw. Eng. 22(10), 751–761 (1996)
4. Rombach, H.D.: A controlled experiment on the impact of software structure on maintainability. IEEE Trans. Softw. Eng. 13(3), 344–354 (1987)
5. Basili, V.R., Selby, R.W.: Comparing the effectiveness of software testing strategies. IEEE Trans. Softw. Eng. 13(12), 1278–1296 (1987)
6. Travassos, G.H., Shull, F., Fredericks, M., Basili, V.R.: Detecting defects in object-oriented designs: using reading techniques to increase software quality. In: Proceedings of the Conference on Object-Oriented Programming, Languages, and Applications (OOPSLA), Denver (1999)
7. Selby, R.W., Basili, V.R., Baker, F.T.: Cleanroom software development: an empirical investigation. IEEE Trans. Softw. Eng. 13(9), 1027–1037 (1987)
8. Endres, A., Rombach, H.D.: A Handbook for Software and Systems Engineering. Pearson, Harlow (2003)

9. Basili, V.R., Selby, R.W., Hutchins, D.H.: Experimentation in software engineering. IEEE Trans. Softw. Eng. **12**(7), 733–743 (1986)
10. Basili, V.R., Caldiera, G., Rombach, H.D.: Goal question metric paradigm. In: Marciniak, J.J. (ed.) Encyclopedia of Software Engineering, pp. 469–476. Wiley, New York (1994)
11. Basili, V.R., Green, S., Laitenberger, O., Lanubile, F., Shull, F., Soerumgard, S., Zelkowitz, M.V.: The empirical investigation of perspective-based reading. Empirical Softw. Eng. **1**(2), 133–164 (1996)
12. Parnas, D.L.: On the criteria to be used in decomposing systems into modules. Comm. ACM **15**(12), 1053–1058 (1972)
13. Gamma, E., Helm, R., Johnson, R., Vlissides, J.: Design Patterns: Elements of Reusable Object- Oriented Software. Addison-Wesley, Reading (1995)
14. Lott, C.M., Rombach, H.D.: Repeatable software engineering experiments for comparing defect- detection techniques. Empirical Softw. Eng. **1**(3), 241–277 (1996)
15. Humphrey, W.S.: Using a defined and measured personal software process. IEEE Softw. **13**(3), 77–88 (1996)
16. Rombach, H.D.: Empirical software engineering models: can they become the equivalent of physical laws in traditional engineering? Int. J. Softw. Inform. **5**(3), 525–534 (2011)

Part I

Software Development: Notation, Architecture, and Process

Domain Modeling and Domain Engineering: Key Tasks in Requirements Engineering

Manfred Broy

Abstract

Requirements engineering is an essential part of software and systems development. Besides the elicitation, analysis, and specification of the intrinsic system requirements as a basis for these activities, it also involves the elicitation, analysis, and specification of the information about the application domain (also called problem domain or domain for short: includes terminology, concepts, and rules). The result of this activity is an elaborated domain model, which is a model of the relevant parts of the application domain.

Roughly speaking, a domain model for a system or software development task comprises the following parts:

- The domain ontology rules, laws, terminology, and notions describing the relevant terms giving an ontology/taxonomy of the domain and specific rules and principles
  - Concepts, data types, and functions
  - Rules and laws
- The *context model,* which describes the general properties of the system's environment. This includes the operational context such as software systems, physical systems, and actors, encompassing users in the environment, properties of the physical environment in case of cyber-physical systems, as well as the wider business and technological context.

These aspects can be captured by adequate data models.

The domain model collects all the information about the problem domain that must be known and understood to allow capturing requirements for the system, specifying them, implementing and verifying the system. The detailed system requirements, however, are not part of the domain model, but they are based upon it.

M. Broy (✉)

Institut für Informatik, Technische Universität München, 80290 Munich, Germany

e-mail: broy@in.tum.de

J. Münch and K. Schmid (eds.), *Perspectives on the Future of Software Engineering,*
DOI 10.1007/978-3-642-37395-4_2, © Springer-Verlag Berlin Heidelberg 2013

Ultimately, the domain model is a collection of knowledge about the application domain at an adequate level of abstraction—including the use of modeling techniques where useful.

1   Introduction

For developing software and software-intensive systems, a variety of different categories of knowledge is required, including know-how about system and software development processes and methodology, software and hardware technology, and, last but not least, knowledge about the application domain (also called the problem domain). The knowledge about the application domain is captured in a process of domain engineering that develops domain models. The importance of domain modeling has been recognized in the early 1990s (see [1]).

A *domain model* is a conceptual model capturing the topics related to a specific problem domain. Domain theory and domain modeling comprise several aspects. One is the theory of the domain itself. For instance, in domains there exist a number of notions, insights, and rules, which are important when developing domain-specific software. An example would be how to calculate interest in a banking application or how to calculate certain routes in navigation, or speed and acceleration values, in an automotive application Often these tasks require deep insights into the application fields and some understanding of their domain theories and experience.

In domain modeling, we develop different forms of ontologies and taxonomies to capture and document domain knowledge. We may use very logical ontologies related rather to domain-specific terminology and observations (often documented by data dictionaries, glossaries, or meta-models) or very technical ontologies, where we look at technical and physical terms and phenomena.

To capture domain models we have to use quite different kinds of modeling techniques to represent the different parts of domain models. For instance, in cases of domains where we can refer to well-developed theories as in physics, chemistry, or in certain fields of engineering, we can more or less take over these models and domain theories, as they have been worked out in the domain over decades, and import them into the knowledge used in software engineering. At any rate, in many cases it is advisable to import parts of the theory and terminology into the specific models and techniques of software engineering.

If we are dealing with an application domain where no systematic and comprehensive domain models exist yet, we need to work out an adequate domain theory during software and system development. We may only have to represent it in terms of software engineering specific models.

2   Structuring Domain Information

A domain model gathers all the information about a domain as needed to understand and formulate the requirements on a particular application system to be developed in software and systems engineering (see [2, 3]). Domain knowledge and domain properties, in contrast to requirements, cannot be chosen freely (see [4]), but have to reflect facts about the application domain and the operational context of the System or Software under Construction (SuC). This is in contrast to requirements that can be chosen freely according to the stakeholder needs. Domain modeling is part of problem solving and software engineering to develop conceptual models of domains of interest (often referred to as "problem domain") which describes the various notions, entities, their attributes and relationships, plus the constraints that govern the integrity of the model elements comprising that problem domain.

2.1   Domain Models

We consider the following categories of information as part of the domain model:
- *Operational system context*: this comprises all the information about the system's environment such as surrounding systems, properties of users, or sensor input.
- *Application domain model*: general domain terminologies, basic notions, rules, and experiences of the application domain
- *Wider system context*: aspects of business, market, processes, technology, organ- isation, law, sociology, psychology

For these three categories, different forms and degrees of formalizations are advisable. In contrast to system requirements as captured in requirements engineer- ing, the information captured in the domain model is generally not subject to design decisions, but has to be captured as given and valid properties of the problem world.

2.1.1   Domain Modeling and Requirements Engineering

A *domain model* identifies fundamental business- and application-specific entity types and relationships between them, including business processes.

In contrast to the system specification, where the properties of a system are structured and captured in terms of adequately chosen system models, domain models are often quite heterogeneous and diffuse and depend on the particularities of the problem domain. Thus, different modeling techniques should be applied for domain modeling.

Relevant domain information that domain models may include is information about
- Terminology and key notions and concepts
- Operational context: systems and users in the environment and their behavior in terms of interaction with the SuC, including business processes supported by the SuC.
- Application domain concepts and rules
- Business rules

Typically, different areas of information require different techniques for their representation and different kinds of modeling techniques.

Domain knowledge can therefore be roughly structured into the following categories:

- *Background Knowledge* is general knowledge about the application domain, its rules and principles, its terminology as well as its basic notions and concepts. This knowledge is useful for understanding and provides a rationale for decisions and specifications.
- *Operational Context Knowledge* is knowledge about the system's operational environment. It includes the reactions of systems that are part of the environment as well as of users. Formally this knowledge leads to assumptions about the environment, behavior of users and systems in the operational context, and thus about the expected input to the system (see [5]).
- *Direct domain knowledge* in the system refers to knowledge that directly influences the reaction of the system under development. Examples would be how quickly a system has to react to a crash sensor if an airbag is to be activated or how to calculate interest in banking applications (see [6] for an analysis of domain-specific know-how embedded in programs).

Of course, the borderlines between these categories of knowledge are not sharp. Often background knowledge is ultimately used as direct domain knowledge.

The parts and properties of the domain model directly influence the system specification.

- Data model: Typically, the data model for a system reflects terms and notions from the application domain (example: the term and notion of speed may become a data type).
- Operational context model assumptions: In system specifications, we typically find assumptions about the system's operational context (example: the speed cannot increase within one second by more than 10 km/h).

The operational context model describes systems and users in the environment of the system under consideration. For them the same modeling concepts (see Appendix) can be used as for the system under consideration. For the domain model, typical aspects of requirements engineering apply:

- There are different levels of abstraction that we can choose for the individual parts of the domain models.
- We may apply notions of refinement to domain models.
- There might be some uncertainty and disagreement about specific properties of a domain; as a result some information in the domain model may be invalid.

Therefore, domain models have to be validated just like requirements and system specifications.

2.1.2   Domain Knowledge in Context-Aware Systems

The category of context knowledge and direct domain knowledge may overlap in so-called context-aware systems. In this case, context and domain knowledge may be explicitly part of the data states of systems. This means that the system stores information about its operational context, its rules of behavior, as well as the actual

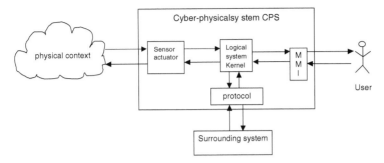

Fig. 1 Two system boundaries: the logical system kernel and the system boundary including sensors

state of its operational context. Then systems may react to specific input depending on the context information stored in the system.

In such cases, excerpts of the domain model are used directly as part of the system state model.

2.2 Scoping: Choosing Boundaries for the System Under Development—Changing System Scope, Interface and Context

Another issue in domain modeling is related to system scoping. In many situations we can choose different scopes for systems under development. Actually, we may consider, in particular, embedded systems having an onion ring structure with a set of onion rings defining operational contexts. If we take the largest scope of the system, then we see the system with its physical surface as a user would see it (Fig. 1). Then we can choose various narrower and more technical scopes and views inside the system, such as the IT systems including sensors and actuators or its IT structure without the sensors and actuators, or just look at the software system itself or only at the CPUs. In every case, we get different scopes and hence different interfaces and relations to domain theories.

Sometimes different system boundaries are considered during system development. We then get systems with different operational context and different boundaries. This means that parts of the context information may become part of the system and vice versa.

We get a formula that describes the interface of the "outer" system and its behavior (for the definition of the operator $\otimes$, see the system model in the Appendix):

$$CPS = S/A \otimes LSK \otimes PRC \otimes MMI$$

The inner system is described by the logical system kernel LSK, the outer one by CPS.

The architecture of the system including the behaviors of the actors in the context PHYC, USER, and SURSYS is described by (for the definition of the operator [×] see the system model in the Appendix):

$$\text{SYS} = \text{PHYC } [\times] \text{ USER } [\times] \text{ SURSYS } [\times] \text{ CPS}$$

In this case, we consider three different system scopes and two different contexts:
1. The empty context for SYS
2. The physical context, the user, surrounding system for the CPS
3. The (sensor/actuator $\otimes$ physical context), the (MMI $\otimes$ User) and the (protocol $\otimes$ surrounding-system) for the logical system kernel

The relationship between the interface behavior of the logical system LSK and the overall system CPS can be understood as vertical refinement (also called a layered system). The behavior of the context PHYC, USER, and SURSYS can be seen as assumptions (see [5], where assumptions are called promises).

2.3 Representing Domain Models

Domain models in terms of operational system contexts should not be modeled much differently than other system models. We can use classical "algebraic" data type specifications to model ontologies and domain-specific data models. Context systems including user behavior can be captured by classical system models but have to be enriched by human factor issues and user models.

Different levels of abstraction can be captured by functions relating levels of abstraction.

General domain knowledge requires different kinds of models, such as
• Ontologies introducing terminology, notions, and their relationships
• Algebraic specifications corresponding to interpreted ontologies

These specifications introduce theories as a basis of software specification and verification.

2.3.1 Domain Models and Their Formalization

Much attention in research has been devoted to so-called formal methods. Their goal is to formalize system properties as part of the specification and support development through formal refinement and verification steps. This form of formalization is justified by the fact that software can be seen as a formal artifact and that software development includes and explicitly or implicitly enforces a step towards formalization.

This is not true for the documentation of the problem domain. Large parts of the problem domain have not to be formalized, since they do not directly relate to software as a formal artifact. Only operational context information has to be formalized since it interacts directly with the software as a formal artifact.

2.3.2   The Integration Problem

Often, there is no homogeneous problem domain. Rather, there are several problem sub-domains with domain models perhaps represented in fairly different description formalisms. The different formalisms are difficult to integrate and to combine into a consistent, coherent problem domain.

2.3.3   The Translation Problem

Sometimes similar or related information is formulated in different languages, using different terms and different levels of abstractions. In these cases the different linguistic frameworks have to be related via translations.

2.3.4   Relating the Problem Domain and the Technical Level: User Input, Sensor Information, and Domain Knowledge

Typically, it is useful to speak about the problem domain independent of the technical implementation—at least in capturing system-level requirements. For instance, a requirement for a car may read as follows:

> In case of a crash, the airbag has to be fully activated within 200 msec.

At the technical level, this reads:

> If the sensor XYZ issues a signal CI, then the signal AA has to be issued within 150 msec.

These two requirements are formulated at completely different levels and have to related to each other.

A famous example is from the development of software for an airplane, where we may ask the question what it means that an "airplane is on the ground and moving fast". Being on the ground is certainly an important logical property in the problem domain of an airplane, which refers to its context, more precisely to the position of the airplane in its physical environment in which the airplane is located. If we are interested in finding out how to detect via sensors that an airplane is on the ground, we need a more technical description for this property. To grasp the property "airplane on ground and moving fast", there are two completely different views of an airplane. One view is a view reflected in a domain model where the plane is seen as part of larger systems. This way we can talk about the position of airplanes and particular aspects of the position, where one would be "the airplane is on the ground and moving fast". Another issue is how to detect and observe this property technically via sensors within the system. One possibility is to consider the torque on the wheels, meaning that if the wheels turn with a certain torque, we may conclude that the plane is on the ground moving at a certain speed.

Sensors capture information about the operational context and its actual state. This information is used as input for the system. For instance, if a sensor measures the speed of a system or its geographical position, then this is operational context information. It is part of the domain model to relate certain sensor information to domain aspects. More precisely speaking, sensors deliver numerical values. To know that these numerical values represent speed with sufficient accuracy for a certain time slot is additional information with reference to the domain model.

In a more general view we can say that with the help of the domain model we interpret the sensor information in terms of the domain model and relate technical requirements to logical requirements (example: "If speed is greater than 20 km/h, the airbags are activated in case of a crash", which is translated into a specification referring to certain sensors, their actual values, and attributes of the state; for details see [7]).

2.3.5   The Validation Problem

The information captured in the problem domain has to be validated. Invalid information in the problem domain leads to invalid assumptions in the requirements and may ultimately result in unsafe, insecure, or unreliable systems.

2.3.6   From Problem Domains to Assumptions in Specifications

The information captured in problem domains serves as assumptions for the requirements. This leads to a specific form of writing requirements specifications (see [5], where assumptions are called promises).

3   Modeling System Context as Part of the Domain Model

For the system model introduced in the appendix, the notion of scope and context is essential. A system has to be clearly separated from its context. The notion of context comprises everything that is not inside the system's boundary. However, we are of course only interested in context aspects in connection with the system requirements that are relevant for the system, its properties, its behavior, and its requirements. In requirements engineering, we capture "facts" about the context—as far as they are relevant for the system under development. They serve as assumptions.

It is helpful to classify the elements of the context further. A straightforward characterization yields the following parts:

- Operational context (Fig. 2): systems, users, and physical environment with which the system under development interacts, possibly as part of business processes in the context
- Usage context: scale of usage, number of users, time ("duration")
- Business context: marketing the system in use
- Development process context: development processes
- Execution context: hardware platform

These context elements have to be captured in sufficient detail during requirements engineering to the extent that they are needed for reflecting and documenting requirements. Strictly speaking, the properties of the context are not requirements but assumptions on which the requirements may rely (Fig. 2).

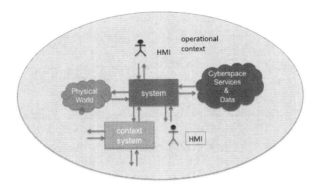

Fig. 2 System and its operational context

The operational context is also described by a syntactic interface and its behavior. There is a rich variety of context aspects:

Business Context: In this business view, we deal with issues of the system related to business and marketing. This may be the number of system instances sold, contract issues, price, and so on. This category may include questions about the cost and value of a system or parts of it.

Development Process Context: In this view, we deal with requirements addressing properties of the development process. Typical examples are the choice of the life cycle model or certain standards of certification.

Execution Context: Platform, runtime environment, and execution hardware—if not part of the system under development—are part of the domain model.

For these different forms of contexts, different modeling techniques are used.

4   Summary and Outlook

Domain modeling is a highly relevant field in software and systems development. Domain modeling must integrate domains, specific techniques for modeling, and modeling techniques and concepts from software and systems engineering. To a large extent, domain knowledge has to be represented by models from software and systems engineering in such a way that domain experts can still validate them and work with them.

At the same time, thorough understanding of a comprehensive problem domain is difficult and requires considerable effort. An example of such a domain approach is [8]. Today, software and systems development is done mainly by domain experts. Software and systems engineers are increasingly becoming domain experts at the same time. This is a very interesting development that has to be taken into account for the role models in software and systems engineering.

The importance of domain modeling will grow even more for several reasons:

- Software systems will be related and integrated into their problem domains tighter and deeper—this cannot be achieved without comprehensive knowledge.
- The development of such software systems calls for deep integration of concepts and modeling techniques from the problem domain and from software and system engineering (see [9]).
- Domain know-how will become an ever greater asset that will be documented and reused and will be essential for the quality of software systems (see [10]).

Last but not least, the process of capturing domain knowledge will increase the knowledge in the problem domain field. The term "computational thinking" (see [11]) is an indication of such approaches where capturing problem domains using computer science methods is claimed to become a new form of scientific method.

A.1   Appendix: The System Model

We use a specific notion of discrete systems in this paper following [12] with the following characteristics and principles.

- A discrete *system* has a well-defined boundary that determines its *interface*.
- Everything outside the system boundary is called the system's *environment*. Those parts of the environment that are relevant for the system are called the system's *context*. Actors in the context that interact with the system, such as users, neighbored systems, or sensor and actors connected to the physical context are called the operational context.
- A system's interface indicates the steps through which the system interacts with its operational context. The syntactic interface defines the set of actions that can be performed in interaction with a system across its boundary. In our case, syntactic interfaces are defined by the set of input and output channels together with their types. The input channels define the input actions for a system, while the output channels define the output actions for a system.
- We distinguish between the *syntactic interface*, also called *static interface*, which describes the set of input and output actions that can take place across the system boundary, and the *interface behavior* (also called *dynamic interface*), which describes the system's *functionality*; the interface behavior is captured by the causal relationship between streams of actions captured in the input and output *histories*. This way we define a logical behavior as well as a probabilistic behavior for systems.
- The logical interface behavior of a system is described by means of logical expressions, called *interface assertions* or by *state machines,* or it can be further decomposed into *architectures*.
- A system has an *internal structure* and behavior ("glass box view"). This structure is described by its state space with state transitions and/or by its decomposition into sub-systems forming its architecture in case the system is decomposed into a number of subsystems that interact and also provide the

interaction with the system's context. The state machine and the architecture associated with a system is called its state view and its structural or architectural view, respectively.

- In a complementary way, the behavior of a system can be described by sets of *traces*, which are sets of scenarios of the input and output behavior of a system. We distinguish between finite and infinite scenarios.
- Moreover, systems operate in time. In our case, we use discrete time, which seems particularly adequate for discrete systems. Sub-systems operate concurrently within the architecture.

This gives a highly abstract and at the same time quite comprehensive model of a system. This model is formalized in the following by one specific modeling theory.

A.2   Data Models: Data Types

Data models define a set of data types and some basic functions for them. A *(data) type* T is a name for a data set for which a family of operations is usually available. Let TYPE be the set of all data types.

A.3   Interface Behavior

Systems have *syntactic interfaces* that are described by their sets of input and output channels attributed by the type of messages that are communicated over them. Channels are used to connect systems to allow transmitting messages between them. Formally, a channel is an identifier for a uni-directional communication link. A set of typed channels is a set of channels with types given for each of its channels.

Definition.   Syntactic interface
   Let I be the set of typed input channels and O be the set of typed output channels. The pair (I, O) characterizes the syntactic interface of a system. The *syntactic interface* is denoted by (I▶O).   □

Figure 3 shows the syntactic interface of a system F in a graphical representation as a data flow node with its syntactic interface consisting of the input channels x_1, ... of types T_1, ... and the output channels y_1, ... of types T'_1, ...

Definition.   Timed Streams
   Given a message set M of data elements of type T, we represent a *timed stream* s of type T by a mapping

$$s : IN\backslash\{0\} \rightarrow M^*$$

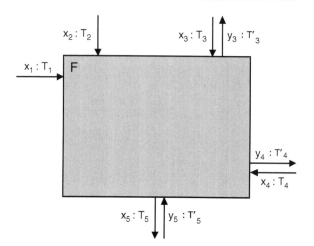

Fig. 3 Graphical representation of a system F as a data flow node

In a timed stream s, a sequence $s(t)$ of messages is given for each time interval $t \in IN\backslash\{0\}$. In each time interval, an arbitrary, but finite number of messages may be communicated. By $(M^*)\infty$ we denote the set of timed streams. □

A (timed) channel history for a set of typed channels C assigns to each channel $c \in C$ a timed stream of messages communicated over that channel.

Definition. Channel history

Let C be a set of typed channels; a (total) *channel history* x is a mapping (let IM be the universe of all messages)

$$x : C \rightarrow \big(IN\backslash\{0\} \rightarrow IM^*\big)$$

such that $x(c)$ is a timed stream of messages of the type of channel $c \in C$. $\vec{C}$ denotes the set of all total channel histories for the channel set C. □

The behavior of a system with a syntactic interface $(I \blacktriangleright O)$ is defined by a mapping that maps the input histories in $\vec{I}$ onto output histories in $\vec{O}$. This way we get a functional model of a system interface behavior.

Definition. I/O-Behavior (see [13])

A causal mapping $F : \vec{I} \rightarrow \wp(\vec{O})$ is called an *I/O-behavior*. By IF$[I \blacktriangleright O]$ we denote the set of all (total and partial) I/O-behaviors with a syntactic interface $(I \blacktriangleright O)$ and by IF the set of all I/O-behaviors. □

Interface behaviors model system functionality. For systems we assume that their interface behavior is total. F behaviors may be deterministic (in this case, the set $F(x)$ of output histories has at most one element for each input history x) or nondeterministic.

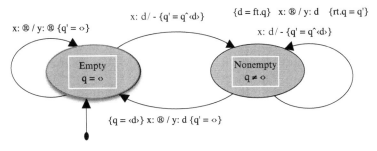

Fig. 4 A simple state machine—described by a state transition graph

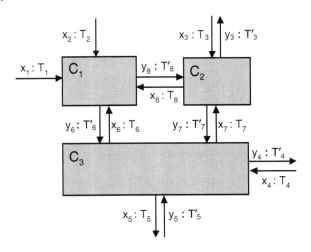

Fig. 5 A simple architecture—described by a data flow graph

A.4   State Machines by State Transition Functions

State machines with input and output describe system implementations in terms of states and state transitions. A state machine is defined by a state space and a state transition.

Definition. State Machine with Syntactic Interface ($I \blacktriangleright O$)
    Given a state space Σ, a state machine (Δ, Λ) with input and output according to the syntactic interface ($I \blacktriangleright O$) consists of a set $\Lambda \subseteq \Sigma$ of initial states as well as of a nondeterministic state transition function   □

$$\Delta : (\Sigma \times (I \to M^*)) \to \wp(\Sigma \times (O \to M^*))$$

For each state $\sigma \in \Sigma$ and each valuation a: $I \to M^*$ of the input channels in I by sequences of input messages, every pair $(\sigma', b) \in \Delta(\sigma, a)$ defines a successor state σ' and a valuation b: $O \to M^*$ of the output channels consisting of the sequences produced by the state transition (Fig. 5).

A.5   Architecture

In the following, we assume that each system used in an architecture as a component has a unique identifier k. Let K be the set of identifiers for the components of an architecture.

Definition. Set of Composable Interfaces
   A set of component names K with a finite set of interfaces (Ik►Ok) for each identifier k ∈ K is called *composable* if the following propositions hold:
*   The sets of input channels Ik, k ∈ K, are pairwise disjoint,
*   The sets of output channels Ok, k ∈ K, are pairwise disjoint,
*   The channels in {c ∈ Ik: k ∈ K } ∩ {c ∈ Ok: k ∈ K } have consistent channel types in {c ∈ Ik: k ∈ K } and {c ∈ Ok: k ∈ K }.   □

If channel names and types are not consistent for a set of systems to be used as components, we can simply rename the channels to make them consistent.

Definition. Syntactic Architecture
   A syntactic architecture $A = (K, \xi)$ with the interface $(I_A \blacktriangleright O_A)$ is given by a set K of component names with composable syntactic interfaces $\xi(k) = (Ik \blacktriangleright Ok)$ for k ∈ K.

$I_A = \{c \in Ik: k \in K \}\backslash\{c \in Ok: k \in K \}$ denotes the set of *input* channels of the architecture,
$D_A = \{c \in Ok: k \in K \}$ denotes the set of *generated* channels of the architecture,
$O_A = D_A\backslash\{c \in Ik: k \in K \}$ denotes the set of *output* channels of the architecture,
$D_A\backslash O_A$ denotes the set of *internal* channels of the architecture
$C_A = \{c \in Ik: k \in K \} \cup \{c \in Ok: k \in K \}$ denotes the set of all channels

   By $(I_A \blacktriangleright D_A)$ we denote the *syntactic internal interface* and by $(I_A \blacktriangleright O_A)$ we denote the *syntactic external inte*rface of the architecture.   □

A syntactic architecture forms a directed graph with its components as its nodes and its channels as directed arcs. The input channels in I_A are ingoing arcs and the output channels in O_A are outgoing arcs for that graph.

Definition. Interpreted Architecture
   An interpreted architecture (K, ψ) for a syntactic architecture (K, ξ) associates an interface behavior $\psi(k) \in IF[Ik \blacktriangleright Ok]$, where $\xi(k) = (Ik \blacktriangleright Ok)$, with every component k ∈ K.   □

An architecture can be specified by a syntactic architecture given by its set of sub-systems and their communication channels and an interface specification for each of its components.
   For an interpreted architecture A with syntactic internal interface $(I_A \blacktriangleright D_A)$, we define the glass box interface behavior $[\times] A \in IF[I_A \blacktriangleright D_A]$ by the equation (let $\psi(k) = Fk$):

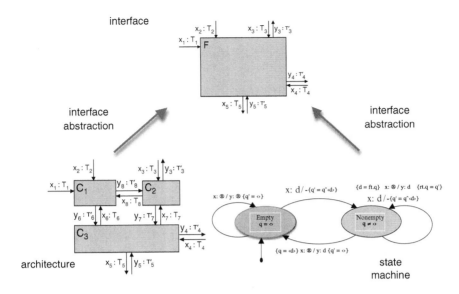

Fig. 6 Abstraction functions between modeling concepts

$$([\times] A)(x) = \Big\{ y \in \vec{D}_A : \exists\, z \in \vec{C}_A : x = z|I_A \wedge y = z|D_A \wedge \forall\, k \in K : z|O_k \in$$

$$F_k(z|I_k)\Big\}$$

$[\times]$ A describes the behavior of the architecture A. For $[\times]\{F_1, F_2\}$ we also write $F_1 [\times] F_2$.

In a black box view $\otimes A \in IF[I_A \blacktriangleright O_A]$ onto the architecture we hide internal channels

$$(\otimes A)(x) = \Big\{ y \in \vec{O}_A : \exists\, z \in \vec{C}_A : x = z|I_A \wedge y = z|O_A \wedge \forall\, k \in K : z|O_k \in$$

$$F_k(z|I_k)\}$$

$\otimes$ A describes the interface behavior of the architecture A. For $\otimes \{F_1, F_2\}$ we also write $F_1 \otimes F_2$ (Fig. 6).

A.6   Relating the Modeling Concepts

The three basic modeling concepts can be related as shown in Fig. 4. Through interface abstractions we can relate state machines and architectures to interfaces.

References

1. Batory, D., McAllester, D., Coglianese, L., Tracz, W.: Domain modeling in engineering of computer-based systems. In: 1995 International Symposium and Workshop on Systems Engineering of Computer Based Systems, Tucson (1995)
2. Gunter, C.A., Gunter, E.L., Jackson, M., Zave, P.: A reference model for requirements and specifications. IEEE Softw. **17**(3), 37–43 (2000)
3. Jackson, M.: Problem Frames: Analyzing and Structuring Software Development Problems. Addison-Wesley, Boston (2001)
4. Kofler, Th., Ratiu, D.: Towards a reusable unified basis for representing business domain knowledge and development artifacts in systems engineering. In: DE@ER2010, Workshop on Domain Engineering (2010)
5. Broy, M.: Towards a theory of architectural contracts:—schemes and patterns of assumption/promise based system specification. In: Broy, M., Leuxner, Ch., Hoare, T. (eds.) Software and Systems Safety—Specification and Verification. NATO Science for Peace and Security Series—D: Information and Communication Security, vol. 30, pp. 33–87. IOS Press, Fairfax
6. Ratiu, D.: Intentional meaning of programs. Dissertation, Technische Universität München, Fakultät für Informatik (2009)
7. Broy, M.: The logic of requirements – formalizing tracing, In: Schnieder, E., Tarnai, G. (eds.) Forms/Format 2012, Technische Universität Braunschweig, Beyrich Digital Service GmbH & Co. KG, pp. 2–4
8. Scholz, G., Scholz, G.: IT-Systeme für Verkehrsunternehmen. In: Informationstechnik im öffentlichen Personenverkehr. dpunkt.verlag, Heidelberg (2012)
9. Broy, M.: Functional safety based on a system reference model. In: Cant, T. (ed.) Australian System Safety Conference (ASSC 2012). Conferences in Research and Practice in Information Technology (CRPIT), vol. 145. Brisbane, 23–25 May 2012
10. Basili, V.R., Rombach, H.D.: Support for comprehensive reuse. Softw. Eng. J. **6**(5), 303–316 (1991)
11. Wing, J.M.: Computational thinking. Comm. ACM **49**(3), 33–35 (2006)
12. Broy, M.: Software and system modeling: structured multi-view modeling, specification, design and implementation. In: Hinchey, M., Coyle, L. (eds.) Conquering Complexity, pp. 309–372. Springer (2012)
13. Broy, M., Stølen, K.: Specification and Development of Interactive Systems: Focus on Streams, Interfaces, and Refinement. Springer, New York (2001)

Towards Agile Verification

Carlo Ghezzi, Amir Molzam Sharifloo, and Claudio Menghi

Abstract

Advances in software verification techniques have been impressive in the past decade. Formal verification of large production software is now increasingly feasible and this is paving the way to transferring these techniques from research to practice. We argue, however, that there is still a serious mismatch between verification and modern development processes, which highly focus on agility and incremental, iterative development. To address this issue, verification has to become agile, and seamless introduction into agile processes has to become feasible. We envision new approaches that will support verification-driven development in the same way as test-driven development is possible today, for example through JUnit within an IDE like Eclipse. In this paper we discuss how agile verification can be achieved, and we show some promising initial steps in this direction.

1 Introduction

Software systems have been pervading every aspect of human life in recent years. Society has become totally dependent on software, both in terms of the functionalities it supports and of its quality, which may ultimately affect its usefulness. It is thus crucial that we can assure that a given software satisfies a set of predefined properties, which represent the functional and non-functional *requirements* the system must fulfill. Functional requirements concern the effect of operations the system is expected to deliver, whereas non-functional requirements concern their qualities, such as performance, availability, usability, energy consumption, and

C. Ghezzi (✉) · A.M. Sharifloo · C. Menghi
Dipartimento di Elettronica e Informazione, Politecnico di Milano, P.zza Leonardo da Vinci 32, 20133 Milano, Italy
e-mail: carlo.ghezzi@polimi.it; amir.molzam@mail.polimi.it; claudio1.menghi@mail.polimi.it

J. Münch and K. Schmid (eds.), *Perspectives on the Future of Software Engineering*, DOI 10.1007/978-3-642-37395-4_3, © Springer-Verlag Berlin Heidelberg 2013

cost [31]. Software *verification* aims at ensuring that a system executes according to some specified, desirable functional and non-functional behavior. Verification is a most important activity performed during software development and evolution. In practice, it is normally achieved by *testing* [33], i.e., by sampling a representative set of behaviors that are deemed to provide useful information about the running conditions that will be encountered by the software once it is operational. *Formal verifiction*, on the other hand, aims at mathematically proving that given properties, which specify the desired requirements, are indeed satisfied by the system.

Model checking is a method that now occupies a prominent role in formal verification. Given a system model $\mathcal{M}$ and a formal property ϕ, model checking systematically and exhaustively checks whether ϕ holds for $\mathcal{M}$ [1]. The model may be an abstraction generated from code, e.g. C or Java; or it may be a high-level specification that is developed during design to support some reasoning about the system under construction (the *system to-be*). It represents the system's behavior in an abstract, yet precise and non-ambiguous, mathematical form. The property specifies instead the requirements the system must satisfy. The overall idea behind model checking is to explore the state space of the model, and ensure that the properties of interest are satisfied by considering all possible behaviors.

Formal verification has now become mature. It has already been used in practice in several application domains and has been adopted in various industrial settings. In particular, model-checking techniques have been substantially improved over the years. Formal verification can, in principle, complement testing to achieve improved assurance. Still, however, its transition into practice has not happened yet. We argue that this is largely due to the fact that no attention has been placed so far on integrating formal verification techniques within practical software development lifecycles.

Most modern development lifecycles are iterative and incremental instead of purely sequential and monolithic. In one word, they are *agile* [13]. Instead of being obsessed with *complete* elicitation of requirements, followed by a waterfall-shaped development based on hierarchical teams of highly specialized engineers, in an agile approach requirements and solutions evolve through collaboration between self-organizing, cross-functional teams. Verification became an intrinsic component of agile lifecycles through *test-driven development* (TDD). TDD is a software development process that relies on the repetition of a very short development cycle consisting of the following stages: first, the developer writes a test case that defines a desired improvement or new function, then he or she produces the minimum amount of code to pass that test, and finally the new code is refactored to improve its quality. This approach has led to the development of automated testing tools, like JUnit, which has been successfully integrated into the Eclipse IDE. The key to the success of TDD is that testing can be efficiently done in increments.

The question we discuss in this paper is the following: Can we do the same for formal verification, leading to *formal verification-driven development* (VDD)? What needs to be done to achieve VDD? What actually makes a VDD approach feasible?

A TDD-based approach focuses on *code* as the artifact that should be subject to continuous verification. A VDD-based approach instead focuses more generally on *models*. We argue that traditional agile methodologies focus on code also because other artifacts—e.g., high-level models—too often only serve for documentation purposes, are expensive to develop, and in practice almost inevitably diverge from the real implementation. We believe instead that models should play a fundamental role in software development because the abstractions they can represent support systematic development and quality assurance. Modeling and model verification, however, need to blend into agile development, in much the same way as coding and testing do.

The rest of this paper focuses on agile verification in the context of models. Programs (code) are just a special case of implementation models that are executed by the running target software. In addition, code verification is normally achieved by translating the code into some state machine model that represents it. We therefore envision an agile software development approach where designers start by developing abstract models and progressively refine these models into executable code, according to a *model-driven* paradigm. Models represent abstractions on which designers can reason, by proving that they satisfy certain properties. For example, an initial high-level model of an application can be checked to see if user requirements on—say—the average response time to certain transactions are satisfied under certain assumptions on user profiles and under a certain high-level architectural decision. At each stage, alternative design decisions should be explored, and models should be progressively transformed, along with the required properties, until the code level is reached and all assurances are checked.

We argue that to support a highly explorative—iterative and incremental—model-driven design approach like the one we have discussed so far, the existing formal verification techniques must be profoundly revisited. They should allow *incomplete specifications*, that is, partial models where some parts are left unspecified, in much the same way as today's verification via testing does not require a complete system to be available. As changes are made, by either adding a part that was previously not specified or by revisiting a previous design decision, we want to ensure that only a minimal part of the system—the one that is affected by the change—needs to be analyzed, thus avoiding re-verifying everything after every change. This would otherwise become intolerably expensive in practice, and would alienate practical interest in incorporating formal verification into agile development processes.

Agile verification is further discussed in Sect. 2. Section 3 shows examples of model specifications that can evolve according to an iterative and incremental design approach. Section 4 shows how verification can be made agile to support dynamic changes in the specification models. It also provides some experimental results that show the potential gains in efficiency we can achieve through agile verification as opposed to using conventional model checkers. Section 5 describes related work. Finally, Sect. 6 draws some conclusions. We explicitly warn the reader that this paper deliberately focuses on the general principles and discusses the practical implications of an agile verification approach, avoiding the technical details of the specific techniques that support the approach. These can be found in the referenced work on which this approach is founded.

2   Agile Verification

Agile verification is intended to support developers throughout all development stages, starting from the early phases of the lifecycle and providing a way to efficiently verify a system in an iterative and incremental way. The principles of agile verification can be applied to any kind of model for which a verification method has been developed, not just to code, as testing necessarily does. In analogy with TDD, the procedure starts by identifying and formally specifying the properties of interest for the part under scrutiny of the system to-be. A model is then designed which is expected to satisfy the properties, and satisfaction is proved by model checking. To cope with the dynamism inherent in iterative and incremental model-driven development, an agile model-checking technique should be able to tackle *evolving* and *incomplete* specifications.

Evolution and incompleteness go together: they are two aspects of the same problem. An incomplete specification evolves into a complete one once the unknown aspects become known. By following the principle of separation of concerns, parts of the system are deliberately left incomplete at a given stage, and their completion is postponed to a later stage. Another kind of evolution regards the support for the exploration of alternative designs. This may be viewed as consisting of two steps: first, the model is put in an incomplete state by deleting parts that are then completed in a second step. By verifying a model vis-a-vis its evolution, designers can assess the impact of changes.

In an agile setting, software development is structured through frequent iterations; hence iterations must be supported efficiently. Since in our framework iterations heavily depend on verification via model checking, it is crucial that its continuous use does not interfere with efficiency. To achieve this purpose, the model-checking procedure should support both *reusability* and *incrementality*. Reusability matters because changes to a model may have a local impact, so re-doing the whole verification after any change would be very inefficient. Let us assume for example that a large-scale workflow successfully satisfies a certain property; a new activity is later added to the workflow, requested by customers. By following most existing model-checking approaches, the new versions of the workflow would need to undergo a complete re-check against the property. If changes are frequent, formal verification becomes a bottleneck of the development process. Furthermore, as we mentioned, in the real world systems are often designed through iterative decomposition, to support prioritization of different parts and separate developments. This approach requires that it should be possible to complete a specification incrementally as the different parts are designed and developed. It would thus be useful to be able to check if an incomplete specification meets the specified requirements. In the likely case that satisfaction of the global property depends on the missing components, it would be desirable to know under which constraints the missing parts should be designed so that the global property holds for the complete specification. Satisfaction of these constraints is later performed by analyzing only the added completion. The benefit of such incomplete model

Fig. 1 Conventional
model-checking process

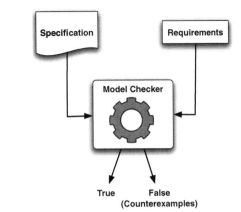

Fig. 2 Agile verification

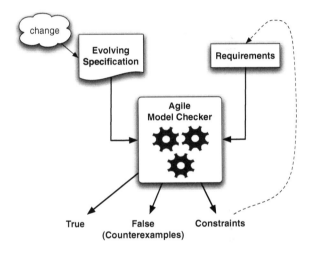

checking is that the unavailable components can be independently developed and verified regardless of the rest of the system.

Figure 1 shows how a conventional model-checking process would behave. A *complete specification* is provided for the system to-be. The specification may consist of several models, which may specify the system under different viewpoints and which would then allow different kinds of requirements to be analyzed for each of them; for example, functional models or performance models. Model checking tools can be used to verify the different kinds of models. A model checker verifies the given properties, and in case a property cannot be proved to hold, it may return a counterexample. Any change to a model requires the model checker to be re-run.

Figure 2 illustrates how model checking should be tailored to support agile verification. Models can be partial. Unknown parts, or parts for which their design is delayed, or for which we would like to explore different design alternatives, are treated as unknown, and if the truth of the desired properties cannot be proved (nor disproved), the model checker derives constraints for the unknown parts, which become requirements to be verified separately.

3   Evolving Specification

An evolving specification is an incomplete specification that contains unknown parts, which denote sub-specifications that are defined and treated separately. In this section we elaborate on this notion of incompleteness and how it can be expressed in a specification. We also briefly present the property languages we use to formalize the requirements our models should satisfy. The next section elaborates then on how incremental verification can be achieved to efficiently support verification-driven development.

In the remainder of this section, we focus on how evolving specifications can be expressed for behavioral notations. Specifically, we consider two high-level notations (*Sequence Diagrams* and *StateCharts*), and two lower-level formal notations (*Labeled Transition Systems* and *Markov Chains*). Next, we briefly illustrate the property languages we use to specify requirements.

We chose *Sequence Diagrams* (SDs) and *StateCharts* (SCs) because they are well-known among practitioners, being part of UML. They are used quite extensively to specify high-level behaviors of software systems throughout the development process, from the early stages to low-level design. They can be used to document design choices and to reason about the satisfaction of functional and non-functional requirements. Hereafter we will discuss how SCs and SDs can be used incrementally in our framework to specify complementary views of the system to-be and to support reasoning on different classes of requirements.

SCs describe *finite-state models*. We use them to model the functional behavior of the sustem to-be. We then verify functional SC models against properties that express functional requirements, such as *safety* and *liveness* properties. SDs, on the other hand, describe *scenario-based models*. We use them to model non-functional parameters of the system to-be and then verify them against properties that express non-functional requirements.

Labeled Transition Systems (LTSs) and *Markov Chains* (MCs) are the two other formalisms for which we wish to be able to express incompleteness. LTSs and MCs are considered because they are the source formalisms for which model-checking algorithms have been defined and verification tools exist. The approach we describe here assumes that the software engineer provides models by using SCs and SDs. These are translated into LTSs and MCs, respectively, and formally verified as we will explain in the next section. Since our approach focuses on agile development and therefore specifications may be incomplete, in the following we discuss how we model incompleteness in the different notations.

3.1 Evolving StateCharts and Incompletely Labeled Transition Systems

StateCharts [19] are a state-based graphical formalism commonly used to describe systems, such as reactive systems, software systems, and digital control units. They provide a flexible and powerful notation to specify a behavioral view of the system being developed. *Functional requirements* may be expressed and verified for them, as we will discuss in the next section. SCs extend finite state machines with hierarchy, concurrency, and communication. Hierarchy is used to model the system at different levels of abstraction, by refining states through a sub-SC or the composition of sub-SCs. Concurrency supports the definition of two or more SCs running in parallel. Finally, communication allows concurrent SCs to be synchronized through the use of global controlled variables.

StateCharts can be formally defined as a tuple $S = \langle Q, q_0, q_F, St, \rho, \tau \rangle$:

- Q is a finite set of states;
- q_0 is the initial state;
- q_F is the final state;
- St is a finite set of StateCharts;
- ρ is the hierarchical relation;
- τ is the transition relation.

In SCs, states can be either basic or composite, and the system operates by performing transitions and moving to different states. Composite states package a component behavior, which can be defined via a SC, thus enabling developers to use SCs in a modular and hierarchical fashion.

We choose to express incompleteness in SCs by extending the way they express hierarchy. We added the notion of a *transparent* state as a subclass of a composite state in which the behavior of the corresponding SC is unknown in the present stage. In the subsequent steps of development and as soon as the transparent states are elaborated, they become a composite state, whose behavior is expressed by the associated sub-SC.

Labeled transitions systems [5] are widely used in computer science as formal behavioral models [1]. LTSs are directed graphs whose states represent the different configurations of the system. Transitions describe how the system can evolve, moving from one state to another. Each state is labeled with a set of atomic propositions that indicate the set of properties true in that state. To model incompleteness, we rely again on the notion of a *transparent state*, which abstracts and encapsulates the notion of a currently unknown behavioral component. A transparent state is a state where the value of the atomic propositions in it may be unknown. This leads to the notion of an Incompletely Labeled Transition System, which is defined hereafter.

Formally, an *Incompletely Labeled Transition System* (ILTS) [29] is defined as a tuple $< S, s_0, s_f, \rightarrow, L >$ over the alphabet A of atomic propositions, where:

- S is a set of states, which is partitioned into two sets: R (Regular) and T (Transparent);
- s_0 is the initial state;

- s_f is the final state;
- $\rightarrow\ \subseteq\ S \times S$ represent the transitions between states;
- $L\ :\ R\ \rightarrow\ \wp(A)$ is the labeling function that associates a subset of atomic propositions to each regular state.

3.2   Evolving Sequence Diagrams and Markov Models

UML Sequence Diagrams (SDs) [3] are an extension of Message Sequence Charts (*MSCs*) [14], which are widely used as a graphical language to specify interaction scenarios among components of distributed systems. The main elements of SDs are lifelines and messages. Lifelines represent the participating components, while messages are used to show both communications and computations. Communication is basically performed by sending and receiving messages between two components. Computation can be shown by adding self-messages. Moreover, SDs support combined fragments, e.g. Option, Loop, etc., which add particular semantics to parts of a behavior. For example, a behavior enclosed by an Option is performed only if the condition imposed by the Option is true. Similarly, a behavior within a Loop is iteratively performed as long as the Loop's condition is true.

SDs are annotated with quantitative information, which can be used to express non-functional attributes according to the UML MARTE Profile [22]. We may, for example, use a MARTE property to express the probability that a message will fail. The operands of a combined fragment can also be annotated with an execution probability. Specifically, the Option fragment, which has only one operand, is annotated with a single execution probability, while each of the alternative behaviors of an alternative fragment is annotated with an execution probability.[1] Further MARTE properties can be used to express quantitative information about the resource usage associated with the message. For example, this may represent such data as average time, power consumption, cost, etc. More details on behavioral modeling by SDs and annotating them with MARTE can be found in [16].

To support incomplete specifications, we introduce the notion of an *abstract message*. This indicates a message where one or more values of its annotations are unknown. Unknown values are indicated by using variable names (e.g., $X, Y, \ldots$) instead of numeric values.

A *Markov Chain* (MC) can be viewed as a finite state machine where each transition is labeled by the probability that the transition is taken to exit the state. Hereafter, we will implicitly refer to the special case of Discrete Time MCs (DTMCs), and we further assume that transitions may also be labeled with a numeric value, representing a benefit (or loss) due to moving along the transition. These values are called *rewards*. Similar to the case of SDs, rewards can represent information such as average execution time, power consumption, number of I/O operations, etc.

---

[1]The sum of the execution probabilities of the alternative behaviors shall equal to *one*.

An MC (with rewards) can be formally defined as a tuple $< S, S_0, P, L, \iota >$ where:

- S is a finite set of states;
- $S_0 \subseteq S$ is a set of initial states;
- $P : S \times S \to [0, 1]$ is a stochastic matrix ($\sum_{s' \in S} P(s, s') = 1 \; \forall s \in S$). An element $P(s_i, s_j)$ represents the probability that the next state of the process will be s_j given that the current state is s_i;
- $L : S \to 2^{AP}$ is a labeling function which assigns to each state the set of *Atomic Propositions* that are true in the state;
- $\iota : S \times S \to \mathbb{R}_{\geq 0}$ is a *transition reward* function assigning a non-negative real number to each transition.

To support incomplete specifications, as we did for SDs, we allow transitions to be labeled by *variables* instead of numeric values. If a variable X is used to denote the probability associated with a transition, it means that the value of that probability is currently unknown. Likewise, variables can be used to represent unspecified rewards. These unknowns are used to represent phenomena that may affect the system to-be's non-functional behavior and which either we do not know yet or about which we have uncertain knowledge.[2]

3.3   Property Languages

According to verification-driven development, whenever a design iteration develops a new model, or evolves an existing model, the relevant properties that specify the functional and non-functional requirements must be checked for validity. As mentioned above, we specify and check *qualitative* properties against SCs and *quantitative* properties against SDs.[3] The property languages we adopted in our work are briefly discussed hereafter in an intuitive and informal manner.

The language for specifying qualitative properties is a (variant of) CTL temporal logic language. This is used to express properties for SCs and LTSs. Details about CTL and its use in the context of SCs and LTSs can be found in [1, 17]. By using this language in the case of a hypothetical traffic control system, we can express *safety* properties like:

> A red light shall always be preceded by a yellow light.

or *liveness* properties like:

> A green light should occur infinitely often.

As for SDs and MCs, the property language is defined as a variant of the language PCTL with Rewards (R-PCTL). Details on R-PCTL can be found in [24]. For its

---

[2]For both SDs and MCs it is possible to also support hierarchical decompositions, where an SC message OR a MC transition is detailed by a sub-SC or a sub-MC, respectively. This is ignored here for the sake of simplicity.

[3]For a discussion of qualitative versus quantitative verification, please refer to [23].

use in the context of SDs and MCs, the reader can refer to [9, 10, 16]. Using this language, we can express properties like:

> The probability of the train eventually entering the intersection with the gate open is less than 10^{-5}.

or

> The total cost of reaching a certain situation cannot exceed a given threshold.

4   Verification

Verification of SC and SD models can be performed by translating them into equivalent models expressed in lower-level mathematical notations for which model-checking algorithms have been developed and implemented tools exist. We do so by mapping into LTSs and MCs, respectively. Furthermore, since to support agile verification, source models can be partial, the corresponding target models can be partial, too, which requires that model-checking algorithms should be extended to support partiality. In the following, we outline both the translation and the model-checking steps for SCs and SDs. We also show how the incremental verification approach can provide benefits in terms of verification efficiency.

4.1   Agile Verification of Evolving StateCharts

Assume that a development increment leads to an initial high-level SC model $\mathcal{M}$, which must satisfy the requirements expressed by property ϕ. Also assume that $\mathcal{M}$ includes two unknown parts $\mathcal{C}_1$ and $\mathcal{C}_2$, which we do not want to deal with at this stage, whose design is postponed to a later stage. This is illustrated in Fig. 3 (Level 1). Level 1 verification generates properties ϕ_1 and ϕ_2, which must be verified by the models that will be developed when the design of components $\mathcal{C}_1$ and $\mathcal{C}_2$ is addressed. The process can, of course, continue if $\mathcal{C}_1$ further includes unknown parts.

To perform verification, a partial SC model is translated into an equivalent ILTS, following the algorithm described in [17]. Without entering into the details on how this is done, we observe that since in SCs transitions are labeled by event/condition/action triples (ECA rules), these must be translated into an equivalent state labeling, which is what LTSs require. Furthermore, since certain states are transparent, the translation generates transparent states also in the target model. Further complications are introduced by the possibility that a state is and-decomposed into parallel substates.

After a SC is converted into the equivalent ILTS, we apply the verification procedure described in [29]. The verification iteratively analyzes the parse tree of the CTL formula to be verified, from the leaves to the root. The leaves of the tree represent the set of atomic propositions, while the inner nodes connect these propositions using Boolean and temporal operators. The idea is to calculate the satisfactory states of each sub-formula. Since transparent states are states in which

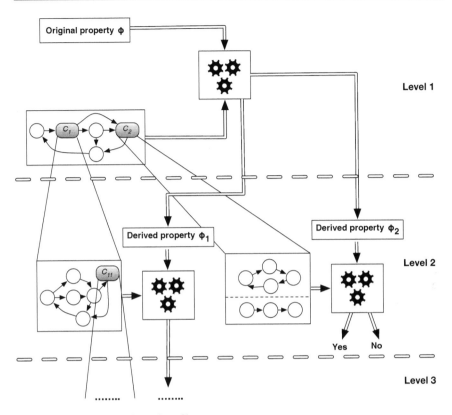

Fig. 3 Verification of evolving StateCharts

the formula can be either true or false, these states are labeled in a way to make the formula ϕ true. When the entire parse tree of the formula has been analyzed, the algorithm terminates. The set of labels generated for the transparent states contains the constraints that must be satisfied.

To show the potential speed-up of an agile verification approach as opposed to a conventional model-checking approach, we report the results of an experiment we did in the hypothetical case of a SC with ten states, where two of these states are transparent. For the sake of simplicity, we considered the situation where transparent states are recursively detailed by the same SC, which is iterated several times. In a conventional model-checking framework, whenever a transparent state is detailed by a SC, a new flattened SC must be generated, which macro-expands the transparent state and arbitrarily labels transparent states. The flattened SC is then model-checked. The results are depicted in Fig. 4a by the plot labeled "classical verification", which shows that the time grows very rapidly as the number of refinement levels increases.[4] The figure also plots the results of the agile approach.

---

[4]Note that in Fig. 4a we use a logarithmic scale.

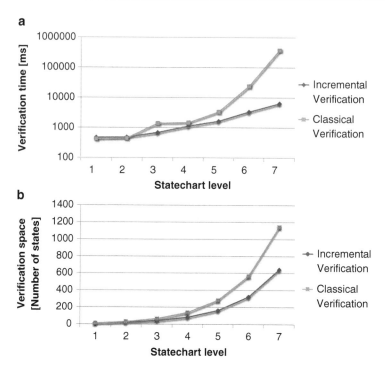

Fig. 4 A comparison between incremental and classic approaches. (**a**) The verification time required for each level of the StateChart. (**b**) The number of states analyzed for each level of the StateChart

In this case, the verification time grows linearly with the number of refinement steps applied to transparent states.[5] In the example, the conventional approach takes 6 min when a 7-level SC is analyzed, while incremental verification only takes 6 s. The speed-up we can achieve, in general, depends on the structure of the SC. Figure 4b shows the number of states analyzed by the two verification algorithms. In the case of conventional verification, the space required is larger, since at each step all the states of the SC must be considered.

4.2   Agile Verification of Incomplete Sequence Diagrams

We now briefly discuss how incomplete (evolving) SDs can be verified. As mentioned above, we assume that incompleteness can concern the annotations describing the non-functional parameters that decorate messages. For example, an

---

[5]Figure 4a shows linear growth on a logaritmic scale because the number of refined states grows exponentially with the number of levels.

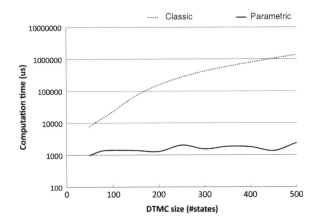

Fig. 5 Classic model
checking versus the
parametric approach to
re-verifying MCs

annotation may indicate the average time needed to execute the operation modeled
by the message, or the probability that a certain message has to be resent due to
a transmission failure. Incompleteness may mean that in the current stage we lack
this information, which may require further analysis investments that are currently
postponed. Or it may mean that we do not know it now, but we want to be able
to explore the effect of possible different values for the parameter on the overall
property of interest for the specification.

As before, the approach we follow here consists of two steps: translation of
an SD into an MC, followed by model checking. The MC into which the SC is
translated is *parametric*, meaning that the probabilities and/or the rewards that label
its transitions may be represented by a variable instead of a numeric value. The
model-checking procedure applied to a parametric MC generally gives as a result a
formula on these variables instead of a constant value. The formula can be evaluated
when all the unknowns become known. This technique, called *parametric model
checking*, was first described in [9, 10].

It can be shown that parametric model checking ensures a very significant speed-
up if we want to explore the effect of different values for the parameters, since it does
not require re-running the model checker for each set of values that materializes
them, but simply requires evaluating the formula. An example of this speed-up
is shown in Fig. 5, which reports the verification time needed to check a set of
parametric MCs against a reachability property [10]. The experiment was performed
on a set of randomly generated models growing from 50 to 500 states, each including
4 variables. Given a set of values for the variables, the classic approach first builds
MCs by replacing the variables with the values, and then runs a classic model
checker (here PRISM [25]). The parametric approach, on the other hand, only
re-evaluates the formula, which substantially reduces the verification time.

5   Related Work

A general approach to breaking verification into manageable units is based on the assume-guarantee approach [12, 20]. This approach views systems as a collection of cooperating components, each of which has to guarantee certain properties. A component is verified independently from the others assuming a certain behavior of the components it is interacting with [27]. The verification methods based on this approach are said to be compositional, since they allow reasoning about each module separately and deducing properties about their integration. If the effect of a change can be localized inside the boundary of a module, the other modules are not affected, and their verification does not need to be redone.

In an assume-guarantee approach the designer has to hypothesize the assumptions a component has to make on the environment to then show that it satisfies certain properties. In contrast, our approach computes the constraints (the assumptions) on the unknown parts so that a required property is satisfied by a component. An approach similar to ours is described by Păsăreanu et al. [6,18]. Given a property, their approach can automatically generate assumptions for the environment, which can be used to facilitate compositional verification. The output of the approach constrains the environment in which a component will satisfy an expected property. Our previous work [29] can also generate assumptions for unspecified components within a specification. However, we consider the unspecified components in pre-determined places within a specification and generate properties for each of them, while the existing assume-guarantee techniques focus on the interaction between a single component and its environment.

Analyzing software models that may contain unknown elements has been recently studied by Salay et al. [28] and Famelis et al. [8]. Salay et al. [28] describes how uncertainty can be specified in requirements specifications. This work focuses on the models used at the early stages (e.g. i*). The same authors later discuss how to reason about them in [8] by expressing them as partial models. They describe how to construct the partial models from possible design alternatives. The main idea is to annotate the elements of models, which exist only in some of alternatives, with Maybe tags and then to apply SAT-based analysis techniques to check First-Order Logic properties. The analysis output produces three possible values: True, False, and Maybe.

Fisler and Krishnamurthi [11], which is extended by Thang and Katayama [30] for CTL properties, present a model-checking technique for verifying the properties of component-based systems. The technique mainly focuses on efficient verification of extensions of a component. The basic idea is to check whether or not an extension violates the properties that hold in the base component. The components are described by a state-based formalism, e.g. state machines, and the extensions are simply introduced by adding states and transitions. The technique basically consists of checking the base component by applying a conventional model-checking technique. When the extension is introduced, it is checked if this addition does not lead to violation in the states of the base component. This approach does not deal with incomplete specifications; it basically uses the intermediate results of the previous verification performed on the base component. Similar to this approach, Cordy et al. [7] studied the verification of extended specifications against LTL properties, and proposes how to use the previous results to speed up the model-checking task.

Other approaches focus on incremental verification, trying to minimize the number of states explored, by "reusing" the program's state space derived from a previous check and not affected by a change in the code. For example, Henzinger et al. [21] analyzed a new version of the program by checking for the conformance of its (abstract) state space representation with respect to the one of the previous version. When a discrepancy is found, the algorithm that recomputes the abstraction is restarted from the location where the discrepancy is found. Depending on where the change is localized in the program text, the algorithm could invalidate—and thus recompute—a possibly large portion of the program state space. Similarly, incremental approaches for explicit-state model checkers, such as [26, 32], analyze the state space checked for a previous version and assess the parts that either do not need to be re-analyzed or can be pruned. In this case, a structural change in the program might invalidate the entire state space, nullifying the optimization.

6   Conclusion and Future Work

In this paper, we discussed the importance of making model checking agile, so that it can be easily plugged into modern iterative and incremental development methodologies, which require fast development cycles. Agile verification is also advocated by recent advances in the development of self-adaptive software, which show that verification needs to be moved to run-time to support adaptation [4]. Run-time verification (and adaptation) must comply with the timing requirements imposed on the software by the environment. Often, this demands very efficient incremental verification.

In this paper our focus has been on a small subset of UML and a subset of temporal logic. Our future work will expand our techniques to deal with other specification notations and property languages. We also plan to optimize our current prototype implementation.

Finally, we are also exploring a general approach to the development of incremental verification based on meta syntactic/semantic analyzers [2, 15].

Acknowledgements This research has been partially funded by the European Commission, Programme IDEAS-ERC, Project 227977-SMScom.

References

1. Baier, C., Katoen, J.-P.: Principles of Model Checking, vol. 26202649. MIT, Cambridge (2008)
2. Bianculli, D., Filieri, A., Ghezzi, C., Mandrioli, D.: A syntactic-semantic approach to incremental verification. In: Submitted for Publication (2013)

3. Breu, R., Hinkel, U., Hofmann, C., Klein, C., Paech, B., Rumpe, B., Thurner, V.: Towards a formalization of the unified modeling language. In: Aksit, M., Matsuoka, S. (eds.) ECOOP'97 Object-Oriented Programming, Jyväskylä. Lecture Notes in Computer Science, vol. 1241, pp. 344–366. Springer, Berlin/Heidelberg (1997)
4. Calinescu, R., Ghezzi, C., Kwiatkowska, M., Mirandola, R.: Self-adaptive software needs quantitative verification at runtime. Commun. ACM 55(9), 69–77 (2012)
5. Clarke, E.M., Grumberg, O., Peled, D.A.: Model Checking. MIT, Cambridge (2000)
6. Cobleigh, J.M., Giannakopoulou, D., Păsăreanu, C.S.: Learning assumptions for compositional verification. In: Proceedings of the 9th International Conference on Tools and Algorithms for the Construction and Analysis of Systems, TACAS'03, Warsaw, 2003, pp. 331–346
7. Cordy, M., Schobbens, P.-Y., Heymans, P., Legay, A.: Towards an incremental automata-based approach for software product-line model checking. In: Proceedings of the 16th International Software Product Line Conference—Volume 2, SPLC '12, Salvador, 2012, pp. 74–81
8. Famelis, M., Salay, R., Chechik, M.: Partial models: towards modeling and reasoning with uncertainty. In: 34th International Conference on Software Engineering (ICSE), Zurich, June 2012, pp. 573–583
9. Filieri, A., Ghezzi, C.: Further steps towards efficient runtime verification: handling probabilistic cost models. In: 2012 Formal Methods in Software Engineering: Rigorous and Agile Approaches (FormSERA), Zurich, pp. 2–8. IEEE (2012)
10. Filieri, A., Ghezzi, C., Tamburrelli, G.: Run-time efficient probabilistic model checking. In: Proceedings of the 33rd International Conference on Software Engineering, Waikiki, Honolulu, pp. 341–350. ACM (2011)
11. Fisler, K., Krishnamurthi, S.: Modular verification of collaboration-based software designs. In: Proceedings of the 8th European Software Engineering Conference Held Jointly with 9th ACM SIGSOFT International Symposium on Foundations of Software Engineering, ESEC/FSE-9, Vienna, pp. 152–163. ACM, New York (2001)
12. Flanagan, C., Qadeer, S.: Assume-guarantee model checking. Technical report, Microsft Research (2003)
13. Fowler, M., Highsmith, J.: The agile manifesto. Softw. Dev. 9(8), 28–35 (2001)
14. Genest, B., Muscholl, A., Peled, D.: Message sequence charts. In: Desel, J., Reisig, W., Rozenberg, G. (eds.) Lectures on Concurrency and Petri Nets. Lecture Notes in Computer Science, vol. 3098, pp. 537–558. Springer, Berlin/Heidelberg (2004)
15. Ghezzi, C.: Evolution, adaptation, and the quest for incrementality. In: Monterey Workshop, Oxford, 2012, pp. 369–379
16. Ghezzi, C., Sharifloo, A.M.: Model-based verification of quantitative non-functional properties for software product lines. Inf. Softw. Technol. 55(3), 508–524 (2013)
17. Ghezzi, C., Menghi, C., Sharifloo, A.M., Spoletini, P.: On requirements verification of evolving models. In: Submitted for publication (2013)
18. Giannakopoulou, D., Păsăreanu, C.S., Barringer, H.: Assumption generation for software component verification. In: Proceedings of the 17th IEEE International Conference on Automated Software Engineering, ASE '02, Edinburgh, 2002
19. Harel, D.: Statecharts: a visual formalism for complex systems. Science Comput. Program. 8(3), 231–274 (1987)
20. Henzinger, T., Qadeer, S., Rajamani, S.: You assume, we guarantee: methodology and case studies. In: Hu, A., Vardi, M. (eds.) Computer Aided Verification. Lecture Notes in Computer Science, vol. 1427, pp. 440–451. Springer, Berlin/Heidelberg (1998)
21. Henzinger, T.A., Jhala, R., Majumdar, R., Sanvido, M.A.A.: Extreme model checking. In: Dershowitz, N. (ed.) Verification: Theory and Practice, pp. 180–181. Springer, Berlin/London (2004)
22. Object Management Group. The UML profile for MARTE: modeling and analysis of real-time and embedded systems. Online at: http://www.omgmarte.org/
23. Kwiatkowska, M.: Quantitative verification: models, techniques and tools. In: Proceedings of the 6th Joint Meeting of the European Software Engineering Conference and the ACM SIGSOFT Symposium on Foundations of Software Engineering, Dubrovnik, pp. 449–458. ACM (2007)

24. Kwiatkowska, M., Norman, G., Parker, D.: Stochastic model checking. In: Bernardo, M., Hillston, J. (eds.) Formal Methods for Performance Evaluation, pp. 220–270. Springer, Berlin/New York (2007)
25. Kwiatkowska, M., Norman, G., Parker, D.: Prism: probabilistic model checking for performance and reliability analysis. ACM Perform. Eval. Rev. **36**(4), 40–45 (2009)
26. Lauterburg, S., Sobeih, A., Marinov, D., Viswanathan, M.: Incremental state-space exploration for programs with dynamically allocated data. In: Proceedings of the 30th International Conference on Software Engineering, Leipzig, pp. 291–300. ACM (2008)
27. Pǎsǎreanu, C.S., Dwyer, M.B., Huth, M.: Assume-guarantee model checking of software: a comparative case study. In: Proceedings of the 5th and 6th International SPIN Workshops on Theoretical and Practical Aspects of SPIN Model Checking, Trento/Toulouse, 1999, pp. 168–183
28. Salay, R., Chechik, M., Horkoff, J.: Managing requirements uncertainty with partial models. In: 20th IEEE International Requirements Engineering Conference (RE), Chicago, Sept 2012, pp. 1–10
29. Shariffoo, A.M., Spoletini, P.: Lover: light-weight formal verification of adaptive systems at run time. In: 9th International Symposium on Formal Aspects of Component Software, Mountain View, 2012, pp. 170–187
30. Thang, N.T., Katayama, T.: Towards a sound modular model checking of collaboration-based software designs. In: Tenth Asia-Pacific Software Engineering Conference, Chiang Mai, Dec 2003, pp. 88–97
31. Van Lamsweerde, A.: Requirements Engineering: From System Goals to UML Models to Software Specifications. Wiley, Chichester (2009)
32. Yang, G., Dwyer, M.B., Rothermel, G.: Regression model checking. In: IEEE International Conference on Software Maintenance, 2009. ICSM 2009, Edmonton, pp. 115–124. IEEE (2009)
33. Young, M., Pezze, M.: Software Testing and Analysis: Process, Principles, and Techniques. Wiley, Hoboken (2008)

On Model-Based Software Development

Constance L. Heitmeyer, Sandeep Shukla, Myla M. Archer, and Elizabeth I. Leonard

Abstract

Due to its many advantages, the growing use in software practice of Model-Based Development (MBD) is a promising trend. However, major problems in MBD of software remain, for example, the failure to integrate formal system requirements models with current code synthesis methods. This chapter introduces FMBD, a formal MBD process for building software systems which addresses this problem. The goal of FMBD is to produce high assurance software systems which are correct by construction. The chapter describes three types of models built during the FMBD process, provides examples from an avionics system to illustrate the models, and proposes three major challenges in MBD as topics for future research.

1 Introduction

A promising approach to obtaining high assurance that software systems satisfy their requirements is Model-Based Development (MBD). In MBD, one or more models of the required system behavior are built, validated to capture the intended behavior, verified to satisfy required properties, and ultimately used as the foundation for the system implementation. Model properties to be verified include completeness (no missing cases), consistency (no non-determinism), and application properties such as safety properties. MBD has many potential advantages, e.g.:

C.L. Heitmeyer (✉) · M.M. Archer · E.I. Leonard
Software Engineering, Naval Research Laboratory, Washington, DC, USA
e-mail: heitmeyer@itd.nrl.navy.mil; archer@itd.nrl.navy.mil; leonard@itd.nrl.navy.mil

S. Shukla
Virginia Tech, Arlington Research Center, Arlington, VA, USA
e-mail: shukla@vt.edu

J. Münch and K. Schmid (eds.), *Perspectives on the Future of Software Engineering*,
DOI 10.1007/978-3-642-37395-4_4, © Springer-Verlag Berlin Heidelberg 2013

- Bugs, often subtle, are discovered early in the development process when they are less costly to fix.
- Understanding and reasoning about the required system behavior is easier at the model level than the code level.
- Simulation and formal verification of models can lead to improved confidence in the model's correctness.
- Models provide a solid foundation for automatic code generation.
- The ability to compose models provides improved potential for interoperability (i.e., plug-and-play) and can also simplify proving properties. Deriving properties of a composed model from properties of its component models is often easier than proving properties about a large model.

In recent years, many powerful tools have been introduced for building models of software systems, for validating the models using simulation, and for verifying properties of the models. Separately, other techniques have been introduced which automatically synthesize source code from models. Integrating these two approaches has the potential for producing software code that is correct by construction. To date, however, synthesis of code from models has been problematic. One major problem is the lack of good formal requirements models. In most cases, system requirements models are unavailable. When they do exist, these models are often expressed in languages without an explicit semantics and at a low level of abstraction.

Moreover, although some techniques for code generation from models are available, these techniques have serious limitations. For example, a developer can automatically generate C and C++ source code from Simulink diagrams, Stateflow models, and MATLAB functions using MathWork's Simulink Coder[25]. However, because Simulink, Stateflow, and MATLAB lack a formal semantics, the source code generated is untrustworthy. Another serious problem is that currently no technique takes into account the supplementary information (e.g., the hardware details) needed to synthesize source code from a formal model. Reference [30], for example, describes a method for automatically generating C code from a formal model, but the method omits relevant details about the hardware and the timing requirements.

In Ptolemy II [4], a popular academic tool for modeling and simulating large systems, many models of computation have been encapsulated, each in a separate *domain*. When the behavior of a system component matches a specific model of computation, e.g., a finite state machine, a model of that component is placed in the corresponding domain. Ptolemy II provides *domain directors* to schedule simulations for specific domains. For a system composed of components from different domains, a *simulation director* coordinates the actions of individual domain directors to execute the simulation. While automatic code generators exist for some Ptolemy II models (e.g., [31]), like the languages in MathWorks, the Ptolemy II modeling languages lack a formal semantics.

This chapter introduces FMBD, a formal MBD process for building high assurance software systems; describes the three different formal models developed during the FMBD process; and concludes by describing three major challenges of MBD—how to obtain formal requirements models; how to validate the translation of a formal model to another formal model or to source code; and how to define and enforce the system's timing requirements.

2   FMBD: A Formal MBD Method for Software Systems

The focus of the FMBD process, an extension of the process in [3], is control systems. The FMBD process flow, illustrated in Fig. 1, is an idealization of the actual real-world process which has more iteration and feedback and may not always proceed top down. The process, which proceeds as follows, begins with formal models of the required system behavior and then applies a sequence of translations to those models, the final translation producing code that is correct by construction:

1. **Create the abstract requirements (AR) model.** The AR model is represented as a state machine model which specifies the required system behavior in terms of (1) environmental quantities that the system monitors and controls and (2) a set of system modes. *Monitored variables* represent the monitored quantities and *controlled variables* the controlled quantities. The AR model defines the value of each controlled variable as a function of modes and monitored variable values. Once specified, the model can be checked mechanically for consistency and completeness, and validated using simulation or animation.

2. **Formulate and prove system properties.** Desired system properties, e.g. security properties, are formulated and verified to hold in the AR model.

3. **Create the concrete requirements (CR) model.** The AR model is transformed into a more concrete model that (1) describes the characteristics of I/O devices, e.g., sensors and actuators, which measure the values of the monitored variables and assign values to the controlled variables and (2) defines algorithms to compute the values of the controlled variables. The CR model must refine the AR model—the set of CR model behaviors must be a subset of the set of AR model behaviors.

4. **Create the code synthesis (CS) model.** The CR model is translated to a code synthesis (CS) model, i.e., a model from which source code can be generated. To perform the synthesis, supplementary information is needed, e.g., the details of the hardware architecture, and thus must be included in the CS model.

5. **Synthesize the source code.** Finally, the synthesis model is translated into executable source code.

2.1   Abstract Requirements (AR) Model

An important construct for defining the AR model is the *mode class*, formally a set of system modes which partitions the system's state space [11]. Thus a mode is an equivalence class of system states, and a mode class can be treated as a variable whose possible values are modes. Modes are important in system requirements models because the system usually behaves differently in one mode than it does

Fig. 1 Process for building high assurance software systems using FMBD (Formal Model-Based Development)

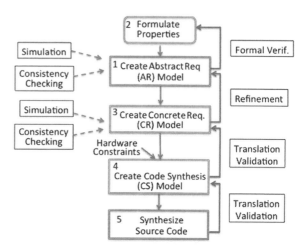

in another mode. A major benefit of using appropriate modes is a more concise, more understandable requirements model. A related benefit is that modes provide an abstract and intuitive structure for organizing the requirements model. This is especially important for control systems, which are often large and complex, and whose requirements models can also be very large and complex.

The AR model defines the monitored and controlled variables, including their types, and the set of mode classes, along with the possible modes and mode transitions for each. It also defines the value of each controlled variable as a function of the current mode and the values of monitored variables and makes explicit assumptions imposed on the system by physical laws and the system environment. In addition, it defines the system's timing requirements, such as the time intervals during which the environmental quantities (e.g., the roll and pitch of an aircraft) must be updated. These definitions, functions, and assumptions taken together form the AR model.

We describe next how the behavior of an avionics system for a version of the ArduPilot (AP) unmanned aerial vehicle [1] can be captured in an AR model. In AP, mSwitchPos and mDesiredRoll are examples of monitored variables, each representing an operator input. AP's controlled variables manage the aircraft's movement by setting the values of the roll, pitch, and throttle. An important mode class in AP is Nav, the navigation mode class, whose modes include TakeOff, Landing, Manual, Loiter, and RTL (Return To Launch site). One example of a mode transition for Nav is Nav $=$ RTL $\land$ mSwitchPos$'$ $=$ loiter $\Rightarrow$ Nav$'$ $=$ Loiter; that is, if the current mode is RTL and the operator moves the switch to the loiter position, then the new mode is Loiter.[1] In AP, the function defining the controlled variable cRoll states that

---

[1] An unprimed variable x represents x's value in the old state of a transition in the state machine model, while x' represents x's value in the new state.

Nav = Manual ⇒ cRoll = mCurrentRoll; that is, if the operator chooses Manual mode, then the roll is the current roll. In contrast, Nav = FlyByWire ⇒ cRoll = F(mCurrentRoll,mDesiredRoll); that is, if the operator chooses FlyByWire mode, then the roll is a function of the current roll and the desired roll specified by the operator. Intuitively, the difference between Manual and FlyByWire is that in Manual mode the operator physically adjusts the roll (represented abstractly by changes to mCurrentRoll), whereas in FlyByWire mode the operator specifies a desired roll and the system adjusts the roll accordingly (perhaps not exactly to the desired roll in order to limit abrupt changes).

2.2   Property Formulation and Checking

A set of application properties, e.g., security, safety, fault-tolerance, and timing properties, is formulated and represented in some logic, e.g., propositional logic or first-order predicate logic. These properties are a more abstract specification of the system requirements. The AR model developed in step 1 of the FMBD process is checked to ensure that it satisfies these properties. The advantage of having two representations of the system requirements, one a state machine model and the other a set of properties, is that finding inconsistencies between them can expose defects: sometimes, the model is incorrect, whereas other times a property is incorrect. In AP, an example of a safety property is Nav = Landing ⇒ cWheels = Down.

2.3   Concrete Requirements (CR) Model

Unlike the AR model, the CR model includes information about the I/O devices. For example, the values of the monitored quantities are typically computed from sensor data; similarly, the values of controlled variables are used to set the values of actuators. The CR model typically uses the same mode classes and mode transitions as the AR model but replaces the abstract specifications of the values of controlled variables with more concrete definitions based on the values read from sensors and written to actuators. In AP, for example, if the operator chooses Manual mode, then the controlled variable cRoll will be set to the actual roll computed from sensor data rather than the value of the abstract variable mCurrentRoll as was done in the AR model.

2.4   Code Synthesis (CS) Model

The CR model is translated to a code synthesis (CS) model from which source code can be generated. To perform the synthesis, additional information, such as the characteristics of the hardware architecture, needs to be captured in the CS model. The translation from the AR Model to the CR model is relatively straightforward given that both models can be expressed in the same language. In contrast, the translation from the CR model to a CS model may be problematic because the two modeling languages are likely to have different semantics. This problem is further discussed in Sect. 4. Another issue, also discussed in Sect. 4, is how to organize and represent the supplementary information needed for code synthesis.

2.5   Source Code Synthesis

In generating source code from the code synthesis model, the timing behavior of different software components must be coordinated so that the system's timing requirements are satisfied. Clearly, the timing behavior of different system components can be vastly different. For example, in AP, the time intervals of the human-system interaction—the time the operator requires to move switches and dials and the timing bounds on system communication to the operator—are very large in comparison to the time intervals between sensor inputs and the timing deadlines the system must satisfy in updating the aircraft's roll and pitch.

3   Techniques and Tools Supporting the FMBD Process

Numerous tools and techniques are available to support the FMBD process described above: many languages are available to specify formal models and a wide variety of techniques and tools are available to analyze the models for critical properties. Moreover, new research is in progress to design languages for specifying code synthesis models and to use the models to synthesize source code. This section briefly summarizes the results of earlier and current research relevant to FMBD.

3.1   Requirements Modeling and Analysis

SCR (Software Cost Reduction) is one example of a method supporting the construction of formal requirements models. These models can be analyzed using the SCR tools—validated using simulation [13], analyzed automatically for consistency and completeness [11], and formally verified using model checking [12], theorem proving [13], composition [17, 18], and automatically generated invariants [23]. Moreover, techniques exist for generating both C and Java source code from formal requirements models expressed in SCR [22, 30]. Among the many other methods which offer similar capabilities for building and analyzing formal models and for automatic code generation are Event-B [32], the Labeled Transition System Analyzer (LTSA) [24], the VDM tools [8], and the FOCUS and AutoFOCUS tools [5].

   One limitation of many of these methods is their focus on software design models rather than requirements models. Two exceptions are the SCR method and the goal-oriented method described in [6], both of which focus on developing and analyzing formal requirements models. A second limitation of all of these methods is the almost exclusive focus on AR models rather than CR models. New research is needed to explore the suitability of current formal modeling languages and tools for specifying and analyzing CR models.

3.2   Code Synthesis Models

As described in Sect. 1, many currently available code synthesis methods have serious limitations. In Ptolemy II, the developer can represent the code synthesis model in a formal language, but code synthesis is not automatic—many compiler passes as well as significant guidance from the programmer are required. While MathWork's Simulink Coder offers automatic code synthesis, the semantics of the modeling language available in the workbench is not defined formally, thus making the synthesized code untrustworthy.

MRICDF (Multirate Instantaneous Channel Connected Data Flow) [19], a variant of SIGNAL [9], is a new methodology designed to specify computation in asynchronous environments, which overcomes these limitations. Not only is the semantics of the MRICDF modeling language defined formally, in addition, once needed supplementary information is provided, synthesis of C source code by MRICDF is automatic. Supplementary information includes the characteristics of the hardware architecture (e.g., the micro-controllers and processors, and the buses, gateways, and networks which connect them); and the behavior of software components such as processes and subprograms.

In contrast to synchronous models, such as Lustre [10] and Esterel [2], which use a totally ordered model of time, MRICDF models are polychronous, that is, use a partially ordered model of time. Formally, a *polychronous model* is made up of components, each with its own clock. In a polychronous model, a set of asynchronous processes execute in parallel and are synchronized intermittently to maintain determinism in certain states of a computation. The advantage of the polychronous model is that it can specify many real-world programs impossible to specify in a synchronous language.

Since a large control system usually contains many micro-controllers and processors, connected via buses, gateways, and networks, the entire distributed architecture and its properties must be specified before code can be synthesized. To accomplish this, MRICDF captures the entire hardware architecture in the Architecture Analysis and Design Language (AADL) [7], where process behaviors are specified with MRICDF. To make processes and subprograms, which are represented as MRICDF models, understandable to the AADL tools, MRICDF is being integrated into AADL as a behavioral annex language in the OSATE toolset.

4   Challenges

Before the FMBD process described above can be used to synthesize correct-by-construction code, a number of challenging problems must be solved. These problems—how to obtain good formal requirements models, how to validate the translation of a model to another model or to source code, and how to represent and enforce timing requirements—are targets for future research. Each of these problems is discussed next.

4.1 Obtaining the Formal Requirements Models

A major problem is how to obtain the system requirements model. As described above, in many cases, system requirements models are unavailable. In other cases, models exist but are expressed in languages without an explicit semantics or are at a low level of abstraction. Ambiguity in the semantics of their specifications makes the models hard to analyze formally, while a low level of abstraction leads to unneeded implementation bias and makes the models hard to understand, validate, and change.

To address these problems, researchers have introduced techniques for synthesizing formal models from scenarios. Informally, scenarios describe how the system interacts with humans and the system environment to provide the required system functions. Because many practitioners already use scenarios to elicit and define requirements, synthesizing formal models from scenarios is promising.

A popular notation for specifying scenarios is that of Message Sequence Charts (MSCs) [16]. Many techniques for synthesizing formal models from MSCs have been proposed but most (see, e.g., [15, 21, 34]) translate MSCs into software design models rather than system requirements models. In contrast, Damas et al. [6] synthesize formal requirements models from MSCs and have techniques for detecting model incompleteness and for generating invariants.

However, capturing the system requirements in scenarios may be unrealistic for many control systems because these systems are often very large and their behavior is highly complex. An alternative is to begin the FMBD process not with scenarios or a formal requirements model, but with a system prototype. Prototypes have often been used by practitioners to explore and to better understand the system requirements. Once stakeholders agree that the prototype captures the intended system behavior, the next step is to elicit the system requirements from the prototype and to represent the requirements as a set of scenarios. We are currently exploring such an approach [14]. In our approach, the system requirements are expressed as MSCs and "mode diagrams"; each mode diagram names a mode class, identifies the modes in the mode class, and describes the mode transitions. A formal requirements model synthesized from MSCs and mode diagrams will most likely be incomplete, because the scenarios captured by the MSCs will not typically cover all of the many exceptional cases. In our experience, however, if the formal model is easy for developers to understand, then they should be able to extend and refine the initial requirements model and ultimately produce a high quality AR model.

4.2   Model Transformations

To produce software that is correct by construction, the translation of one model to another model or to code must be validated. In the FMBD process, three translations must be validated: AR-to-CR, CR-to-CS, and CS to source code. As stated in Sect. 2, the translation from the AR Model to the CR model may be relatively straightforward if both models can be expressed in the same language. This is in contrast to the CR-to-CS translation and the translation of the CS model to source code. As noted above, because the languages used to specify the CR and CS models are likely to have different semantics, showing that the behavior of the CS model refines (or is equivalent to) the behavior of the concrete model is nontrivial. For similar reasons, showing that the source code refines the CS model is also nontrivial.

One approach to validating the translation of a formal model to another more concrete model, or to source code, is to apply *translation validation*, a technique introduced in 1999 by Pnueli et al. [28]. Translation validation provides an alternative to proving the correctness of a compiler by validating translation results on a case by case basis. The objective of the approach proposed in [28] is to validate the translation of an abstract description of system behavior into a more concrete description, each description represented as a synchronous transition system (STS). The translation described in [28] is from the synchronous language SIGNAL to the source code language C, with the C code restricted to a form easily represented as an STS. The goal of the validation is to establish the full correctness of the translation by proving that the concrete STS refines the abstract STS.

A challenge is how to make this approach scale. The approach of Pnueli et al. minimizes the complexity of the analysis by first replacing function applications, including inequalities, with uninterpreted symbols, and later, if necessary, introducing more information about the functions. An alternative approach to managing scale is to focus validation on something less ambitious than proof of full correctness. Such an approach is used in [27], which focuses on correct implementation of clocks and clock relations in the translation of an abstract STS. More general recent methods developed for translation validation of optimizers at the intermediate language level (see, e.g., [26, 33]) do not attempt to prove full correctness, but instead use validation to raise (sometimes false) alarms of possible translation errors.

4.3   Capturing and Enforcing Timing Requirements

To be acceptable, control systems must satisfy their timing requirements. However, obtaining code whose timing behavior is correct by construction is enormously difficult. Even when a formal requirements model exists, a specification of the timing behavior required by the system is rarely available. Further, although some limited research on real-time patterns is available (see, e.g., [20, 29]), how to represent timing requirements in formal requirements models has not been studied. Including timing requirements in the system requirements model could have significant impact on the success of code synthesis. If timing requirements were captured in the code synthesis model, the code synthesis process might use this timing information to generate code that satisfies its timing requirements. Of course, satisfying the timing requirements may not always be feasible. However, the compiler can at least take the timing requirements into account during code generation and perhaps report points in the code where satisfying the timing requirements is infeasible.

5 Conclusions

The described vision of model-based development of software systems overcomes many of the weaknesses of current methods for synthesizing software code from formal models. First, rather than low-level models, the FMBD process starts with abstract requirements models. This approach not only avoids the bias and implementation detail of low-level models, it also simplifies verification: proving properties about an abstract model is usually much easier than proving properties of a larger, more detailed low-level model. Second, some approaches cannot synthesize code automatically. The goal of our approach is to synthesize the software code as automatically as possible. Third, unlike those needed for FMBD, many modeling languages currently used by practitioners do not have an explicit formal semantics. The result is that the synthesized code is untrustworthy. As described in Sect. 4, however, many challenging research issues remain—how to obtain formal requirements models, how to validate translations from one model to another, and how to capture and enforce timing requirements. If these challenges are addressed, software development could 1 day achieve a goal that researchers have sought for decades—code that is correct by construction.

References

1. ArduPilot. http://www.diydrones.com/notes/ArduPilot
2. Berry, G., Gonthier, G.: The Esterel synchronous programming language: design, semantics, implementation. Sci. Comput. Program. **19**(2), 87–152 (1992)
3. Bharadwaj, R., Heitmeyer, C.: Developing high assurance avionics systems with the SCR requirements method. In: Proceedings of 19th Digital Avionics System Conference, Philadelphia (2000)
4. Brooks, C.X., Lee, E.A., Tripakis, S.: Exploring models of computation with Ptolemy II. In: Proceedings of 8th International Conference on Hardware/Software Codesign and System Synthesis (CODES+ISSS 2010), Scottsdale, pp. 331–332 (2010)
5. Broy, M., et al.: Service-oriented modeling of CoCoME with Focus and AutoFocus. In: The Common Component Modeling Example (CoCoME). Lecture Notes in Computer Science, vol. 5153, pp. 177–206. Springer, Berlin/New York (2008)
6. Damas, C., Lambeau, B., Dupont, P., van Lamsweerde, A.: Generating annotated behavior models from end-user scenarios. IEEE Trans. Softw. Eng. **31**(12), 1056–1073 (2005)
7. Feiler, P.H., Gluch, D.P.: Model-Based Engineering with AADL: An Introduction to the SAE Architecture Analysis and Design Language. Addison-Wesley, Upper Saddle River (2012)

8. Fitzgerald, J.S., Larsen, P.G.: Modelling Systems–Practical Tools and Techniques in Software Development. Cambridge University Press, Cambridge/New York (2009)
9. Gamatié, A.: Designing Embedded Systems with the SIGNAL Programming Language–Synchronous, Reactive Specification. Springer, New York (2010)
10. Halbwachs, N.: A synchronous language at work: the story of Lustre. In : 3rd ACM & IEEE International Conference on Formal Methods and Models for Co-Design, Verona, pp. 3–11 (2005)
11. Heitmeyer, C.L., Jeffords, R.D., Labaw, B.G.: Automated consistency checking of requirements specifications. ACM Trans. Softw. Eng. Methodol. 5(3), 231–261 (1996)
12. Heitmeyer, C., Kirby, J., Labaw, B., Archer, M., Bharadwaj, R.: Using abstraction and model checking to detect safety violations in requirements specifications. IEEE Trans. Softw. Eng. 24(11), 927–948 (1998)
13. Heitmeyer, C., Archer, M., Bharadwaj, R., Jeffords, R.: Tools for constructing requirements specifications: the SCR toolset at the age of ten. Int. J. Comput. Syst. Sci. Eng. 1, 19–35 (2005)
14. Heitmeyer, C., Pickett, M., Breslow, L., Aha, D.W., Trafton, J.G., Leonard, E.I.: High assurance human-centric decision systems (2013, Submitted)
15. Hirsch, D., Kramer, J., Magee, J., Uchitel, S.: Modes for software architectures. In: Third European Workshop on Software Architecture, EWSA, Nantes, pp. 113–126 (2006)
16. ITU. Message sequence charts (1996). Recommendation Z.120, International Telecommunications Union, Standardization Sector
17. Jeffords, R.D., Heitmeyer, C.L.: A strategy for efficiently verifying requirements. In: ESEC/FSE-11: Proceedings of 9th European Software Engineering Conference/11th ACM SIGSOFT International Symposium on Foundations of Software Engineering, Helsinki, pp. 28–37 (2003)
18. Jeffords, R.D., Heitmeyer, C.L., Archer, M., Leonard, E.I.: Model-based construction and verification of critical systems using composition and partial refinement. Form. Methods Syst. Des. 37(2), 265–294 (2010)
19. Jose, B.A., Shukla, S.K.: MRICDF: a polychronous model for embedded software synthesis. In: Shukla, S.K., Talpin, J.-P. (eds.) Synthesis of Embedded Software, pp. 173–199. Springer, New York (2010)
20. Konrad, S., Cheng, B.H.C.: Real-time specification patterns. In: 27th International Conference on Software Engineering (ICSE 2005), St Louis, pp. 372–381 (2005)
21. Krüger, I., Grosu, R., Scholz, P., Broy, M.: From MSCs to statecharts. In: Distributed and Parallel Embedded Systems (DIPES), Schloss Eringerfeld. IFIP Conference Proceedings, vol. 155, pp. 61–72. Kluwer, Boston (1999)
22. Leonard, E.I., Heitmeyer, C.L.: Program synthesis from formal requirements specifications using APTS. High. Order Symb. Comput. 16(1–2), 63–92 (2003)
23. Leonard, E., Archer, M., Heitmeyer, C., Jeffords, R.: Direct generation of invariants for reactive models. In: Proceedings of 10th ACM/IEEE Conference on Formal Methods and Models for Co-Design (MEMOCODE 2012), Arlington (2012)
24. Magee, J., Kramer, J.: Concurrency – State Models and Java Programs. Wiley, New York (1999)
25. MathWorks: Simulink Coder. http://www.mathworks.com/products/simulink-coder/
26. Necula, G.C.: Translation validation for an optimizing compiler. In: Proceedings, 2000 ACM SIGPLAN Conference on Programming Language Design and Implementation (PLDI), Vancouver, pp. 83–94 (2000)
27. Ngo, V.C., Talpin, J.P., Gautier, T., Guernic, P.L., Besnard, L.: Formal verification on compiler transformations on polychronous equations. In: Derrick, J., Gnesi, S., Latella, D., Treharne, H. (eds.) International Conference on Integrated Formal Methods (IFM'11), Pisa. Springer (2012)
28. Pnueli, A., Shtrichman, O., Siegel, M.: Translation validation: from SIGNAL to C. In: Correct System Design. Lecture Notes in Computer Science, vol. 1710, pp. 231–255, Springer, New York (1999)
29. Post, A., Menzel, I., Hoenicke, J., Podelski, A.: Automotive behavioral requirements expressed in a specification pattern system: a case study at BOSCH. Requir. Eng. 17(1), 19–33 (2012)

30. Rothamel, T., Heitmeyer, C., Leonard, E., Liu, Y.A.: Generating optimized code from SCR specifications. In: Proceedings of the ACM SIGPLAN/SIGBED Conference on Languages, Compilers and Tools for Embedded Systems (LCTES 2006), Ottawa, June 2006
31. Schoeberl, M., Brooks, C., Lee, E.A.: Code generation for embedded Java with Ptolemy. In: Proceedings of 8th IFIP Workshop on Software Technologies for Future Embedded and Ubiquitous Systems (SEUS 2010), Waidhofen/Ybbs (2010)
32. Su, W., Abrial, J.-R., Huang, R., Zhu, H.: From requirements to development: methodology and example. In: Formal Methods and Software Engineering. Lecture Notes in Computer Science, vol. 6991, pp. 437–455. Springer, Berlin/Heidelberg (2011)
33. Tristan, J.-B., Govereau, P., Morrisett, G.: Evaluating value-graph translation validation for llvm. In: Proceedings, 32nd ACM SIGPLAN Conference on Programming Language Design and Implementation, PLDI 2011, San Jose, pp. 295–305 (2011)
34. Uchitel, S., Kramer, J., Magee, J.: Synthesis of behavioral models from scenarios. IEEE Trans. Softw. Eng. **29**(2), 99–115 (2003)

From Software Systems to Complex Software Ecosystems: Model- and Constraint-Based Engineering of Ecosystems

Andreas Rausch, Christian Bartelt, Sebastian Herold, Holger Klus, and Dirk Niebuhr

Abstract

Software is not self-supporting. It is executed by hardware and interacts with its environment. So-called software systems are complicated hierarchical systems. They are carefully engineered by competent engineers. In contrast, complex systems, like biological ecosystems, railway systems and the Internet itself, have never been developed and tested as a whole by a team of engineers. Nevertheless, those complex systems have the ability to evolve without explicit control by anyone, and they are more robust to dealing with problems at the level of their constituent elements than classical engineered systems. Consequently, in this article we introduce the concept of complex software ecosystems comprised of interacting adaptive software systems and human beings. Ecosystems achieve the demanded flexibility and dependability by means of a kind of higher-level regulatory system. Their equilibrium is continuously preserved through the appropriate balance between the self-adaptation and the self-control capabilities of an ecosystem's participants.

We will outline a methodology to support the engineering of ecosystems by integrating a model- and constraint-based engineering approach and applying it during design- and runtime. The open-world semantics of constraints establish a framework for the behavior of the participants and the ecosystem itself. Violations of constraints can be identified during design time, but also provide knowledge transfer to runtime. Constraints are additionally monitored and enforced during runtime. Thus, we propose an evolutionary engineering approach covering the whole life-cycle for forever active complex software ecosystems.

A. Rausch (✉) • C. Bartelt • S. Herold • H. Klus • D. Niebuhr
Chair of Software Systems Engineering: Department of Informatics, Clausthal University
of Technology, 38670 Clausthal-Zellerfeld, Germany
e-mail: andreas.rausch@tu-clausthal.de; christian.bartelt@tu-clausthal.de;
sebastian.herold@tu-clausthal.de; holg.klus@tu-clausthal.de; dirk.niebuhr@tu-clausthal.de

J. Münch and K. Schmid (eds.), *Perspectives on the Future of Software Engineering*,
DOI 10.1007/978-3-642-37395-4_5, © Springer-Verlag Berlin Heidelberg 2013

1   Can Complex Software Systems Be Engineered?

Software does not stand by itself. It is executed on physical machines and communication channels (*hardware*) and interacts with its *environment*, which includes humans and other software packages. So you might see software as the meat in a hamburger. The bottom of the burger bun is the hardware; the top is the environment.

Based on that analogy, software engineering research might be understood as the research discipline that devotes itself to the improvement of the process for producing perfect hamburger meat. Clearly, that alone is not enough to come up with a better burger. Rather, we have to take the whole system into account, including the hardware executing the software, as well as the environment in which the software is embedded. Therefore we prefer to use the term software systems engineering, resp. software systems engineering research.

Due to the continuous increase in size and functionality of those software systems [1], they are now among the most complex man-made systems ever devised [2]. As already discussed in [3], everyone would agree that a car, with its millions of components, is an extremely complicated system. The same can be said of the European railway system. Both the car and the railway system are human constructions, but there is clearly a significant difference between them. The complicated car was carefully designed and tested by a team of engineers who put every component in its place with the utmost precision, and that is why it works. But no one designed the European railway system as a whole, and no one can claim to entirely understand or control it—and yet it works, somehow!

And whilst the car can be improved only through a careful re-design by competent engineers, the European railway system grows and shrinks on its own, without explicit and overriding control by any one specific person. Moreover, the ability of the car to function is highly dependent on the successful operation of each of its core sub-components, while the efficiency of the European railway system is much more robust to disruptions and failures at the level of each of its constituent elements.

Looking around, one can see many other systems with the same characteristics: communication networks, transportation networks, cities, societies, markets, organisms, insect colonies, ecosystems. These systems have come to be called *complex systems*, not to be confused with merely very *complicated systems* such as cars and aircraft carriers. The definition of complex systems in [4], developed by scientists doing research in the area of complexity theory and its descendants, is as follows:

> Complex systems are systems that do not have a centralizing authority and are not designed from a known specification, but instead involve disparate stakeholders creating systems that are functional for other purposes and are only brought together in the complex system because the individual "agents" of the system see such cooperation as being beneficial for them. (Cited from [4])

The question that we aim to raise and discuss in this paper is as follows: What is it that unites these complex systems, and makes them different from cars and networks? And can something be learned from them that would help us build not only better cars and networks, but also smarter software systems, like safer building infrastructures, more effective disaster response systems, and better planetary probe systems?

2   From Software Systems to Complex Software Ecosystems

In the developed world, software now pervades all areas of business, industry, and society. Public administration, management, organization and production companies are but a few examples. Even day-to-day personal life is no longer conceivable without the use of software and software-controlled devices can be found in every household.

As already mentioned, the software industry currently faces an inexorable march towards greater complexity—software systems are the most complex man-made systems in existence [2]. The reasons for the steady increase in their complexity are twofold: On the one hand, the set of requirements imposed on software systems is becoming larger and larger as their *extrinsic complexity* increases. This includes the following examples: features, depth of functionality, adaptability, and variability. In addition, the structures of software systems, e.g., in terms of size, scope, distribution, and networking of the system, are themselves becoming more complex, which leads to an increase in the *intrinsic complexity* of the system.

The expectations placed upon software systems have been growing, along with their steadily increasing penetration into people's private, social, and professional lives. Users expect:

- A high degree of autonomy, openness, intuitive usability, and timely response to changes in both the software system itself and in the processes for the expected life cycle and demands (*flexibility* [5]).
- A high degree of reliability of the software system and the surrounding development, operation, and administration processes (*dependability* [6]).

As an analogy, let us consider the field of classical engineering: A single (even large) building can still be planned, explained, and implemented centrally; however, the planning, design, establishment, and further development of a city need to be performed using very different methods and models.

Similarly, the ever-increasing complexity of software systems and the rise in user expectations have led to a situation where the classical methods and techniques of software systems engineering have reached their limits. In the long run, the mechanisms required in software systems engineering for developing and controlling software systems are also facing a paradigm shift. To respond to this challenge, we use this paper to put forward the proposal that software systems be interpreted as parts of larger *complex software ecosystems*, thus taking a first step in the direction of the necessary paradigm shift.

Complex software ecosystems are *complex adaptive systems of adaptive systems and human beings* (see outer ring in Fig. 1)—i.e., complex, compound systems consisting of interacting individual adaptive systems, which are adaptive as a whole, based on engineered adaptability. This means that not every large, resp. complicated

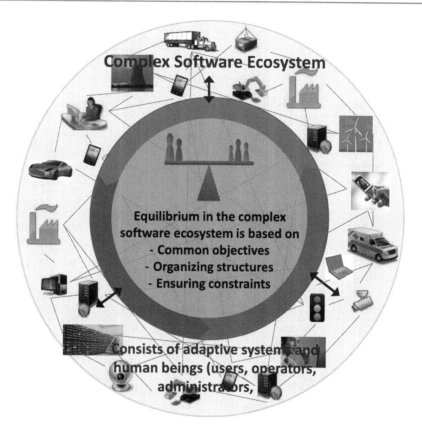

Fig. 1 Structure and equilibrium concepts of complex software ecosystems (Note that this picture is an updated version of the corresponding picture in [7])

system can be considered as a complex software ecosystem: The complexity of the interaction between the elements of the complex software ecosystem and its resulting adaptability is one essential characteristic. It must also take into consideration the different life cycles of the individual adaptive systems.

This is an important difference to the traditional understanding of hierarchical systems: A hierarchical system consists of subsystems whose interactions tend to be globally predictable, controllable, and designable. A complex software ecosystem comprises individual adaptive systems whose behavior and interactions change over time. These changes are usually not centrally planned, but arise from independent processes and decisions within and outside the complex software ecosystem.

In addition, complex software ecosystems are mixed human-machine artifacts: human beings in the complex software ecosystem (see the outer ring in Fig. 1) interact with the individual systems, and in this way they become an integral, active part of the complex software ecosystem. Therefore, human requirements, goals, and behavior must be considered when designing a complex software ecosystem, by modeling them as active system components. Humans act as users, administrators, operators within the ecosystem. The very complex and multifaceted interaction and relationship between people and individual systems of a complex software ecosystem is a further key characteristic. Only by including this aspect can a holistic approach be taken. The requirements, needs, and expectations of humans in the individual systems of a complex software ecosystem are subject to special dynamics and forms of interaction. Thus, the individual systems need to be able to change continuously to meet the changing demands and adapt to the changing behavior of humans. By the same token, the changing expectations of humans will create new demands on the ecosystem.

In analogy to a biological ecosystem, complex software ecosystems achieve flexibility and dependability by means of a kind of higher-level regulatory system, through which equilibrium is maintained between the forces applied by each of the participating individuals. The equilibrium of an ecosystem is based on the following three concepts as shown in the inner ring of Fig. 1:

- *Common objectives*: Communities of adaptive systems and human beings form themselves dynamically. An essential feature of these communities is their common and jointly accepted objectives. Individual participants can be members of several communities simultaneously. These communities may change or dissolve over time, and new ones may be created. This is part of the adaptation in the complex software ecosystem.

- *Organizing structures*: Structures required for organizing and implementing the common objectives of the community form dynamically. These structures define roles, responsibilities, communication channels, and interaction mechanisms in the communities. Like the communities themselves, organizational structures can also change, thus leading to an adaptation of the structures in the complex software ecosystem.

- *Ensuring constraints*: Commonly accepted constraints govern the behavior and interactions of communities and their organizational structures. Control within complex software ecosystems—in the sense of ensuring adherence to these constraints—can be realized by different means. These mechanisms can be explicit, e.g. centralized or federated via dedicated components, or implicit—for example, realized by market mechanisms, local incentives, and preference structures of participants to achieve a specific behavior in the system. Another promising approach to force these constraints is electronic institutions [8].

3   Can We Engineer Those Complex Software Ecosystems?

A key aspect in complex software ecosystems is the establishment of an equilibrium between the forces applied by participating individuals. The equilibrium is continuously preserved through the appropriate balance between *self-adaptation* on the one hand and *self-control* on the other hand. When this equilibrium is disturbed, the complex software ecosystem breaks down and is no longer manageable. For a complex software ecosystem to remain active and continuously evolve, we

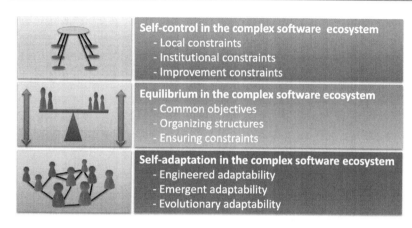

Fig. 2 Appropriate balance between self-adaptation and self-control (Note that this picture is an updated version of the corresponding picture in [7])

must understand this equilibrium and the mechanisms necessary to achieve and preserve it.

A complex software ecosystem is made up of a set of individual adaptive systems interacting with each other. Other than these interactions, the individual systems are considered closed systems that can be created with the classical methods of software systems engineering. However, in the process of designing them, adaptivity, evolution, and autonomy must be taken into consideration. The individual systems themselves may consist of subsystems or components, which are used as sensors, actuators, or the interface to a physical environment.

The compound ecosystem as a whole can no longer be described and controlled by using classical methods due to reasons of complexity. In addition to the complexity caused by the size of the compound ecosystem and its adaptability resulting from the adaptivity of individual systems and their different life cycles, human beings are also considered a part of the complex software ecosystem. The resulting complex software ecosystem can be described and understood only by taking a holistic view. This is a necessary condition for the controllability of the overall ecosystem. However, this holistic approach leads to a very complex ecosystem with a high degree of adaptability, which in turn makes it difficult to control.

This leads us to a dilemma: In order to control the system, we need to treat it holistically, but doing so increases the degree of adaptability, which in turn reduces controllability. To solve this dilemma, we must turn to the notions of self-adaptation and self-control in the complex software ecosystem.

We distinguish three levels of adaptation in a complex software ecosystem (see Fig. 2). It should be noted that the higher the degree of adaptability, the more the human is involved in this adaptation:

- By *engineered adaptability* we are referring to the property of the individual adaptive systems participating within an ecosystem to reconfigure and reorganize themselves at runtime in order to fulfill context-sensitive tasks in the ecosystem. Adaptation is therefore the pre-planned, resp. engineered capability of the individual adaptive systems and their components to adapt themselves and their interaction with the environment. Here, the focus of the adaptability is primarily on functional and quality properties of the individual adaptive systems that are part of the ecosystem. Adaptation is often achieved by modifying component configurations—parameters are set, and this alters the functional behavior of system components.

- By *emergent adaptability* we understand the ability of a complex software ecosystem to provide emergent behavior by modification of the interaction structure between the participating systems and human beings. Complex software ecosystems are open and dynamic systems: new participants may enter into the ecosystem, sometimes with an unknown interface, structure, and behavior. Already known participants may change their behavior (e.g., by engineered adaptation) or leave the complex software ecosystem. Thus, emergent adaptability is in line with concepts in autonomic computing [9] or organic computing [8], respectively. Hence, emergent adaptability is grounded on a decentralized, formed cooperation of individual systems and human beings within the ecosystem. In contrast to engineered adaptability, emergent adaptability is achieved by the autonomy of swarm organization. Such cooperation is not pre-determined and not explicitly designed. Rather, it follows from the interaction structure of the participants.

- *Evolutionary adaptability* is the ability of a complex software ecosystem to evolve itself under changing conditions in the medium to long term, and to sustainably reveal adaptive behavior. It includes the fundamental long-term development of the complex software ecosystem in all its aspects, in particular through change and adaptation of monitoring, configuration, and control mechanisms, including structural and functional aspects. Evolution incorporates the capacity to evolve the individual adaptive systems within the ecosystem as well as the interaction constraints between them. This means that implementing evolution as manual, computer-supported, or (partially) automated further development of the complex software ecosystem poses the biggest challenge with respect to long-term control. Evolution will be triggered by sustainable changes in environmental conditions or by fundamental changes in the expectations of users and operators of the complex software ecosystem. It can be driven by human operators and users, but it also needs to be partly or fully automated in some cases. Evolution can mean either that the management, control, and regulatory mechanisms are altered, or that individual components or entire systems are replaced or modified.

These three levels of self-adaptation have to be supported by all of the participants in the complex software ecosystem. However, at the same time, care must be taken that the complex software ecosystem as a whole remains under control and thus ensures its superordinated goals and functions. For this to be achieved, the participating adaptive systems and humans also have to support three levels of self-control capabilities (see Fig. 2):

- By *local constraints* we are referring to the individual assumptions and guarantees of the ecosystem's participants—the adaptive systems and human beings. In the case of adaptive systems, the local constraints are designed as a self-contained part of the systems, for instance the assumption that a specific database is available within the ecosystem and the guarantee that the database will be accessed as read-only. Moreover, local constraints may define restrictions on the engineered adaptivity capabilities of the adaptive system. Human beings naturally bring their own local constraints to an ecosystem, for instance usage profiles or security demands.

- *Institutional constraints* are, on the one hand, ecosystem-wide constraints that all participants have to obey, for example common traffic rules—stop if a traffic light is red. Moreover, communities in ecosystems share common objectives and organizational structures (see Fig. 1). In order to define and enforce their objectives and structures, institutional constraints can be formulated. Such an institutional constraint could be: All ecosystem participants who wish to use electronic payment have to provide their unique ID.

- By *improvement constraints* we are describing the constraints guiding the ecosystem's own evolution. Those constraints regulate the process for raising new requirements for the ecosystem or its participants and for defining how to react to a disturbed equilibrium within the ecosystem. A high number of new requirements or, frequently, troubles with the equilibrium will force further development of individual participants of the ecosystem or the self-adaptation and self-control capabilities of the ecosystem itself.

An appropriate balance between these self-control and the aforementioned self-adaptation capabilities of all participants of the ecosystem guarantees permanently established equilibrium states. Thereby, we have achieved the goal of providing desirable flexibility, whilst at the same time ensuring dependability.

If the self-adaptation capabilities of the ecosystem's participants prove too high, a risk exists that the ecosystem will evolve in an uncontrolled manner and direction. Consequently, the commonly shared objectives, organizing structures, and ensuring constraints will be lost—the equilibrium is disturbed. Self-control functions will be automatically activated to re-regulate the ecosystem. If the self-control functions are too high, we face an ecosystem standstill. The ecosystem is no longer attractive for the participants and might die off. Hence the self-adaptation functions will be activated.

The concept of equilibrium in complex software ecosystems enables us to provide mechanisms for control, monitoring, and regulation, and to ensure constraint compliance via electronic institutions. If these constraints are violated, the self-adaptation mechanisms provided by the ecosystem and its participants can re-establish the equilibrium. Based on these mechanisms, equilibrium concepts are defined; and approaches for the detection, prevention, and treatment of disorders in the complex software ecosystem are described and implemented (Fig. 3).

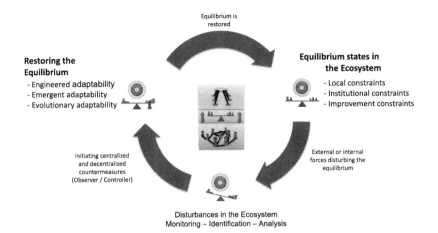

Fig. 3 Ensuring equilibrium states in complex software ecosystems (Note that this picture is an updated version of the corresponding picture in [7])

4 Combining Closed-World Models and Open-World Constraints Towards a Joint Development Approach

Complex software ecosystems contain adaptive software systems and human beings interacting with each other. The constituent parts are independent of each other in terms of functionality and management, are developed evolutionarily, and will show adaptive behavior. These properties distinguish complex software ecosystems from traditional software systems and are the reason why traditional software systems engineering approaches are not sufficiently suitable.

Traditional software development approaches offer various techniques to support software engineers. One of the most fundamental ones is the use of models and modeling. Depending on what is considered relevant to a system under development at any given point, various modeling concepts and notations may be used to highlight one or more particular perspectives or views of that system. It is often necessary to convert between different views at an equivalent level of abstraction facilitated by model transformation, e.g., between a structural view and a behavioral view. In other cases, a transformation converts models offering a particular perspective between levels of abstraction, usually from a more abstract to a less abstract view, by adding more detail supplied by the transformation rules. These ideas of models, modeling, and model transformation are the basis for a set of software development approaches that are well known as model-driven development (MDD). Model-driven architecture (MDA) is a style of MDD that is well-established in research and industry. Four principles underlie the OMG's view of MDA:

• Models expressed in a well-defined notation are a cornerstone to the understanding of systems for enterprise-scale solutions.

- The building of systems can be organized around a set of models by imposing a series of transformations between models, organized into an architectural framework of layers and transformations.
- A formal underpinning for describing models in a set of meta-models facilitates meaningful integration and transformation among models, and is the basis for automation through tools.
- Acceptance and broad adoption of this model-based approach requires industry standards to provide openness to consumers, and foster competition among vendors.

Independent of the specific model-based development approach, they all share a common property: At the end of the day the goal of models and modeling in model-driven development is to drill down to system construction [10]. Consequently, models use the closed-world assumption [11]. A closed-world model directly represents the system under study, meaning that there is a functional relation between the language expressions and the modeled world. Even when modeling is used to create a conceptual model of a domain, the represented knowledge is implicitly viewed as being complete. Note that Reiter [12] distinguishes two kinds of world assumptions: closed-world (CWA) and open-world (OWA). These two different assumptions have fundamental implications on modeling practice [13].

With the increasing scale and complexity of software systems the corresponding models must not automatically grow due to abstraction mechanisms in modeling. However, there is usually a trade-off between the accuracy of the results and the complexity of the model. The more complex the model, the less it may be understood, and often the time taken for analysis and transformation will be increased. The less complex the model, the easier it is to understand and the more efficient it is to evaluate. However, the results may lose their relevance to the real system if too many important details are abstracted.

Due to scale and complexity, engineers in other disciplines such as airplane engineering use a set of different types of models: mechanical models, thermal models, or aviation models. Each model is based on a closed-world assumption. But no closed-world model exists that describes the whole airplane. Such a model would be either too complex to handle or irrelevant due to the required level of abstraction. Although interdependencies between the remaining partial, but closed-world models do exist, they are not explicitly modeled. Instead they are managed through the surrounding engineering process.

The increasing scale and complexity of software systems aiming towards complex software ecosystems will lead us to the same trade-off. A complete closed-world model for a large complex software ecosystem is out of scope. Therefore, we are faced nowadays with a set of closed-world models describing subsystems of the overall complex software ecosystem. Moreover, these subsystems have their own independent life cycles; thus the corresponding models are developed and evolved independently of one another.

Nevertheless, engineers of the overall complex software ecosystem have to take the interdependencies between the models of the subsystems into account. As described in the previous section, software development for complex software

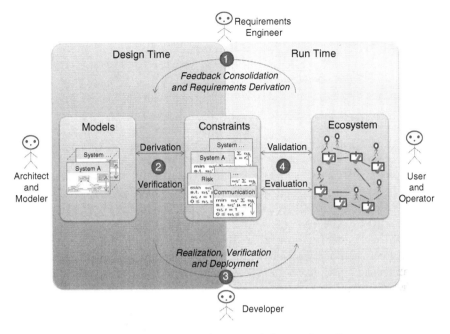

Fig. 4 Model- and constraint-based engineering approach for complex software ecosystems

ecosystems has to be aware of constraints for ensuring adaptability and controllability. Hence, a constraint-based approach based on an open-world assumption is appropriate.

For this reason, we believe that a joint engineering approach combines the best of the two modeling worlds: a model-based approach based on a closed-world assumption for partial system modeling, and a constraint-based approach based on an open-world assumption for modeling the relevant overall system properties.

5   A Model- and Constraint-Based Engineering Approach for Complex Software Ecosystems

The approach combines model-based development with constraint-based development as an efficient way to establish and evolve complex software ecosystems.

As already mentioned, a complex software ecosystem consists of a set of individual adaptive systems. For each individual adaptive system a model, resp. a set of models, based on a closed-world semantic is developed, as illustrated on the right side of Fig. 4.

To restrict the individual adaptive behavior of the adaptive systems, local constraints might be added (cf. the middle column in Fig. 4). In addition, institutional and improvement constraints from an ecosystem's communities or covering common ecosystem objectives and guidelines are added—following an open-world semantic.

All of these constraints can be used to validate the individual models of the adaptive systems as well as to validate the union of models of all adaptive systems, resp. the ecosystem's models. Therefore, constraint validations of individual systems, but also of the interaction between these adaptive systems, can be identified during design time.

However, as changes in these systems are not centrally planned, but rather arise from independent processes and decisions, adaptivity cannot be completely controlled during design time. Consequently, we also have to take the runtime into account. The constraints can therefore be used again. They provide knowledge transfer between design time and runtime. Constraints are additionally monitored and enforced during runtime, and constraints can thus be used during design time as well as during runtime (see Fig. 4).

First, our concept of constraints has to be defined. Constraints are used to express undesired behavior or situations of complex software ecosystems as well as their participants and to define actions describing how to react to them. The constraints defined in this approach thus set up the framework for the behavior of single systems in a complex software ecosystem and the ecosystem itself. Such constraints can be defined at the usual levels of development: requirements elicitation and validation, architectural design, and component implementation. Constraints can be used for verification and validation at design time and at runtime as well.

A constraint consists of various properties and represents crosscutting concerns on the complex software ecosystem. Thus, a uniform formalism is used by requirements engineers, software architects, and component designers, improving their communication as well as documentation of the considered system. We may also distinguish between different kinds of constraints, such as regulation and validation constraints. Regulation constraints are used to actively interact with subsystems of the complex software ecosystem in order to keep it in a useful state. Validation constraints are applied to passively observe the system and log constraint violations that need to be handled manually by a control instance, e.g., a domain expert.

This concept of constraints is now integrated with model-based development. The model- and constraint-based development approach we propose can be thought of as an adaptive but controlled improvement life cycle for forever-young complex software ecosystems [14, 15]. This leads us to an iterative improvement process triggered by end-user feedback as illustrated in Fig. 4.

In order to become widely accepted and used, a software system needs to fulfill the end-users' needs. To accomplish this task in complex software ecosystems, we use end-user feedback and experience to derive new requirements and corresponding constraints. We suggest gathering end-user feedback in-situ at very low effort and cost by using off-the-shelf mobile devices (Step 1 in Fig. 4). Due to the distributed nature of complex software ecosystems, feedback must be forwarded to the responsible addressee to be considered for further development. Analyzing feedback clarifies whether existing subsystems should be changed or whether the feedback demands new requirements or constraints. Moreover, feedback walkthrough facilitates the identification of problems, new ideas, and affected requirements and constraints by the analyst in charge.

Using the feedback received, parallel lines of development start (Step 2 in Fig. 4): In the left column, the relevant systems have to be identified, at first based on feedback. For each identified single system, individual development will be started on the basis of the relevant user feedback, using arbitrary model-driven development approaches. This means that abstract models are transformed and refined to create detailed models, finally leading to executable systems or parts of systems. Common model-driven development techniques, including existing modeling languages (e.g., UML, BPNM, etc.), model transformations (e.g., ATLAS), and frameworks (e.g., EMF), are used.

In the middle column, our concept of constraints, as introduced above, is used. To derive constraints for the requirements affected, the amount of feedback received that can be assigned to a particular domain concept is used. By assembling constraints in topic groups, the complexity of an ecosystem is decreased, and modularized development becomes feasible. Moreover, constraints that are applied to different levels of abstraction are aggregated hierarchically. This means refining requirements constraints down to architectural constraints and component-specific constraints to verify development artifacts against them during design time as well as generating deployable monitoring code for runtime.

Moreover, constraint refinement supports readability and consistency checking, since traceability is assured. If the compositionality of a constraint is guaranteed, the verification of lower-level constraints to ensure overall compliance with higher-level constraints is possible. The overhead of decomposing constraints into lower levels is compensated when parts of the system are modified, since only the modified part has to be re-verified regarding its corresponding constraints.

During execution, constraint monitoring is applied as shown in Fig. 4, Step 4. Valuating systems are continually reported to the runtime environment. Should the constraints change or if a violation is detected within the monitoring framework, then the following escalation strategy is applied:

- First, the individual system tries to adapt its functionality to the new situation in order to comprise all the constraints once again.
- Second, the overall ecosystem tries to re-arrange interaction between the individual participants in the ecosystem to meet the user's needs. Do note that, in certain situations, the ecosystem cannot know what the best option for the user is. Consequently, the user is informed of possible configurations so that he or she can decide which optimization criteria and which configuration best meet his or her needs.
- Finally, if the violation cannot be independently fixed, even after the inclusion of the user, the user is prompted to state his or her needs—a problem report is created. The needs of the user are then evaluated and consolidated and requirements are derived from there. The consolidated feedback and the derivation of the requirements lead to the next improvement stage, starting again with Step 1. Consequently, the problem should be addressed in the next evolution step of the ecosystem.

6   Constraint Satisfaction by Models During Design Time

By using the integrated model- and constraint-based engineering approach during design time, the adaptability of ecosystems can be controlled at the level of single, engineered, adaptable systems, as well as at the level of emergent arising and open interaction structures of the single systems within the ecosystem. To understand the above-explained approach regarding the verification of models based on constraints (cf. Step 2 in Fig. 4), our view on the relation between (software) models and the above-motivated constraint base is introduced first.

Models of (software) systems consist in large parts of notational elements describing elements of the system and their relationships, structural as well as behavioral ones. For example, a class diagram describing the structures of types and interdependencies prescribes that these classes and interdependencies have to be present in a system conforming to the model. Such models can be understood mathematically as relational structures consisting of a universe of entities and relations between them. Since we assume that a model—or at least the complete set of available models for a system—describes the system completely (due to the closed-world assumption), the corresponding relational structure is finite.

In order to express that finite structures have desired properties, we can express such properties as logical formulas, e.g., as first-order logic expressions, that are evaluated on finite structures. A finite structure M satisfying a logical formula C is said to be a model of that formula:

$$M \vDash C$$

Hence, the constraints that we have discussed so far can be understood as first-order logic formulas that are evaluated on the finite structure representing the model(s) of software systems—if, and only if, the finite structure is a model for the formula, the constraint is satisfying in the modeled system. This corresponds to the verification part of step 2 depicted in Fig. 4. This can, of course, only be done at design time if the constraints are available at that time.

In case of constraints related to guarantees in the context of the first level—engineered adaptability—constraints are defined in the design process of the system at hand, and can be (partly) derived from models (Step 2 in Fig. 4., "Derivation"). In this case, the satisfaction of constraints must be considered under the closed-world assumption (CWA). For example, constraints expressing the enforcement of a certain system architecture can be derived from architectural models of the system and can be checked for the detailed design. A detailed research approach regarding the foundations of constraint-based software development was published in [16]. Based on this approach, it can be checked and ensured that constraints are satisfied in a single system, meaning that the desired guarantees expressed by the constraints are fulfilled.

Emergence constraints, which define the collective framework for the emerged adaptability of interacting structures within an ecosystem, have to be defined and adjusted continuously between the system designers of individual autonomous systems, especially when they change in case of evolutionary adaptability.

However, model verification by constraints during the design of a single system differs from the verification of autonomous communities because of the openness of an ecosystem. The validity significance of more general emergence constraints proved at design time is limited in general. For example, even if it has been proved at design time that two time- or mission-critical, independently developed systems each fulfill a global constraint stating that responses are given in less than 8 min (e.g., emergency systems), there is no guarantee that a combination of both will do so. In this case, we have to check whether we can make statements evaluating the formulas under open-world assumptions (OWA)—statements that can give hints that constraints *might* be violated. Therefore, the finite structures (models) of the potentially interacting, individual systems must be joined into a single finite structure. Also, the sets of logical formulas that represent the emergence constraints must be joined into a set of common domain knowledge. To check the validity of potentially arising, emergent structures within an ecosystem during design time, the joining of the different (software) system descriptions $M_1, \ldots, M_n$ must be a model for the joined constraint set of $C_1, \ldots, C_2$ under OWA:

$$M_1 \cup \ldots \cup M_n \vDash C_1 \cup \ldots \cup C_n$$

The theoretical foundations of this kind of verification method are discussed in [17] regarding the verification of joined models during concurrent software development.

In addition to this, such joining of (software) models, resp. constraint sets, can be a challenging task in the case of different description languages. This is a common situation because of the independent development of the participating systems within the open ecosystem. At any rate, the approach is applicable if (software) models, resp. constraint sets, are harmonized regarding their languages before joining of the finite structures, resp. logical expression sets, occurs.

Nevertheless, solely static analyses under OWA at design time are not potent enough to detect constraint violations of emerged structures within an ecosystem. To support more extensive validation, dynamic analyses at runtime are an effective method.

7   Controlled Adaptation During Runtime

After a system has been designed, verified, and developed, it will be deployed and executed within the ecosystem. In order to be useful over time, systems must be able to adapt themselves to changing needs, goals, requirements, or environmental conditions as autonomously as possible. We distinguish three levels of adaptability, namely: engineered adaptability, emergent adaptability, and evolutionary adaptability, as previously mentioned. During runtime, various aspects have to be considered in order to enable and control those kinds of adaptability. In order to discuss these

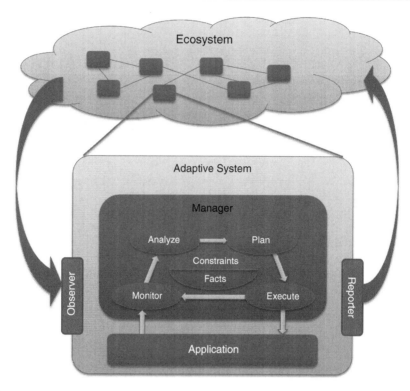

Fig. 5 Architectural blueprint for self-controlled self-adaptation in complex software ecosystems

aspects, we are using an architectural blueprint of a system which is based on the well-known MAPE-K loop [9]. The blueprint is depicted in Fig. 5:

By *engineered adaptability* we understand the ability of a system to react autonomously during runtime to pre-planned events in its environment in order to satisfy certain system-specific constraints. It may be useful to study an adaptive navigation system as an example. One constraint could be that the system should perform routing using road maps in combination with speech output if the user is driving a car. Another constraint could be that it should run in silent mode and use city maps if the user is walking through a town. The system must be able to react to those events automatically during runtime in order to satisfy the constraints at any time.

In our model we distinguish between the application that realizes the actual business logic, such as the navigation functionality, and the manager, which is responsible for performing all tasks necessary to satisfy the given constraints.

For this purpose, the manager has to constantly monitor the application and the environment. It stores the collected information as facts in the internal knowledge base. Furthermore, it analyzes those facts and checks whether they satisfy the given constraints. If this is not the case, it tries to generate a reconfiguration plan with the objective of creating a system configuration that conforms to the given requirements. This is, amongst other factors, achieved by modifying components or application configurations, e.g., by setting parameters that alter the functional behavior of system components and applications. In [18] we presented an approach that enables the specification of certain system constraints. This approach is able to recognize the violation of those constraints and provides mechanisms for reacting autonomously by reconfiguring the system considering the given constraints.

During runtime, situations may occur that were either not foreseen during system development or require the involvement of other systems within the ecosystem in order to satisfy the given constraints. In our model, the interaction between an adaptive system and the ecosystem is done through an observer and a reporter. They are responsible for monitoring the ecosystem and for contacting the internal manager, if required. The manager analyzes the monitored information again, creates plans, and may adapt the application behavior or contact other systems through the reporter.

Certain events may not only lead to adaptation of individual systems, but to structural modifications of the ecosystem, i.e., to connections between systems. On the one hand, certain requirements of individual adaptive systems may require adaptation of the overall ecosystem. On the other hand, the ecosystem must be able to integrate new adaptive systems automatically during runtime and has to be able to deal with failures or behavioral changes of individual systems. We call this ability *emergent adaptability*, as previously mentioned. To realize emergent adaptability, each individual adaptive system must be able to handle events like those mentioned above. If, for instance, a system becomes unavailable for some reason, connected systems may react by automatically reconnecting to another one. The same may happen if a new system becomes available within the ecosystem. In that way, an ecosystem emerges spontaneously. Another reason is the behavioral change of connected systems. It may happen that a system is compatible with another system at one time, and, due to behavioral changes, e.g. caused by engineered adaptation, incompatible at a future date. Therefore, semantic compatibility has to be checked continuously during runtime. In [19] we presented an approach that is based on runtime testing. There, the constraints are specified as test cases, which are executed each time a behavioral change of connected systems is recognized.

In software ecosystems, emergent adaptability cannot be realized by one global authority due to its complexity and size. It is rather achieved through negotiation between equitable systems, where each system focuses on satisfying the given local constraints. This may in turn lead to unbalanced ecosystems and, in the worst case, to a collapse of the whole ecosystem. We call the ability to ensure the balance within the ecosystem over time *evolutionary adaptability*. In our approach, basic conditions for a balanced ecosystem are specified as constraints. The first step in realizing a balanced ecosystem is to recognize an unbalanced ecosystem, i.e., if the constraints are not satisfied anymore. This can be done by the individual adaptive systems themselves or by humans within the ecosystem. If an unbalanced system is recognized, two kinds of reactions are conceivable. The first one is to adapt the ecosystem, or just parts of it. One possibility is to do this by sending appropriate configuration instructions to the observer module of individual adaptive systems. If it is not possible to equilibrate the ecosystem automatically, human intervention is required to prevent a collapse of the ecosystem.

8   Conclusion

In order to be able to answer the question 'Can complex software systems be engineered?', we must be aware that the concept of (software) systems has evolved hugely in the past decade. In the past, it was difficult, but possible to engineer *complicated but closed* systems, such as aircrafts or power plants, with classical *top-down development* methods. Nowadays, and not only as a result of the dissemination of mobile devices, complex systems have an additional *open and flexible character* and face high *dependability* demands.

These complex software ecosystems can no longer be engineered with classical (fully controlled) development methods. In order to engineer these kinds of systems, we need a fundamental extended approach that considers system development from a different view, mixing *top-down* and *bottom-u*p approaches. Therefore, we are proposing an integrated model- and constraint-based engineering approach for complex software ecosystems, which takes into account closed-world models regarding the classical engineering of single (software) systems and open-world constraints to control the adaptability of emergent interaction structures within an ecosystem.

The model- and constraint-based engineering approach separates the specification of structure and behavior by system models from the specification of the allowed behavior through constraints of the overall complex software ecosystem. It therefore clearly distinguishes between the definition of autonomous behavior of system elements and overall control, allowing both to develop and to evolve independently. Both closed-world models and open-world constraints therefore provide the basis for the controllability of the engineering process through static analyses performed at design time and dynamic analyses performed at runtime.

The view on the engineering of complex software ecosystems explained above enables a wide-ranging spectrum of research topics:

Regarding design time, we require a general approach for modeling and constraint specification, which combines both open-world and closed-world aspects. Due to the evolution of complex software ecosystems, an incremental modeling approach must be taken into consideration. Furthermore, specially tailored methods and techniques for the incremental verification and validation at design time must be developed.

To support the controllability of complex software ecosystems *at runtime*, we also require a general approach for constraint verification and validation. In addition, the boundary between automatic machine decisions and human interaction in case of constraint violation needs more investigation. Another ambitious research challenge would be to answer the following open question: 'How can we establish a systematic feedback loop from the detection of constraint violations on the one hand to the evolving system design on the other hand?' To answer this question, amended requirements must be explored and affected system parts must be detected. Subsequently, a suitable impact analysis for evaluating the consequences of incremental design changes has to be researched.

As explained above, the research about the future engineering of complex software systems has created a vast field of open and challenging scientific questions. Therefore, the concept of complex software ecosystems provides a suitable metaphor, and the comprehensive research framework of the proposed model- and constraint-based engineering approach defines a scientific agenda for the coming years.

References

1. Northrop, L., Feiler, P., Gabriel, R.P., Goodenough, J., Linger, R., Longstaff, T., Kazman, R., Klein, M., Schmidt, D., Sullivan, K., Wallnau, K.: Ultra-Large-Scale Systems – The Software Challenge of the Future. Software Engineering Institute, Carnegie Mellon, Technical Report. Available: http://www.sei.cmu.edu/uls/downloads.html (2006)
2. Brown, A.W., McDermid, J.A.: The art and science of software architecture. In: Oquendo, F. (ed.) ECSA, ser. Lecture Notes in Computer Science, vol. 4758, pp. 237–256. Springer, Heidelberg (2007)
3. Braha, D., Minai, A.A., Bar-Yam, Y.: Complex Engineered Systems: A New Paradigm. Springer, Berlin/Heidelberg, ISBN 978-3-540-32831-5, (2006). doi:10.1007/3-540-32834-3_1
4. Sheard, S.A., Mostashari, A.: Principles of complex systems for systems engineering. Syst. Eng. **12**, 295–311 (2009). doi:10.1002/sys.20124
5. Bennett, K., Layzell, P., Budgen, D., Brereton, P., Macaulay, L., Munro, M.: Service-based software: the future for flexible software. In: Proceedings of the Seventh Asia-Pacific Software Engineering Conference (APSEC). IEEE (2000)
6. Laprie, J.C., Avizienis, A., Kopetz, H. (eds.): Dependability: Basic Concepts and Terminology. Springer/New York, Inc., Secaucus (1992)
7. Rausch, A., Muller, J.P., Niebuhr, D., Herold, S., Goltz, U.: IT ecosystems: a new paradigm for engineering complex adaptive software systems. In: 2012 6th IEEE International Conference on Digital Ecosystems Technologies (DEST), pp. 1–6. IEEE (2012)
8. Müller-Schloer, C., Schmeck, H., Ungerer, T. (eds.): Organic Computing a Paradigm Shift for Complex Systems. Springer, Basel (2011)
9. Kephart, J.O., Chess, D.M.: The vision of autonomic computing. Computer. **36**(1), 41–50 (2003). Available: http://dx.doi.org/10.1109/MC.2003.1160055
10. Noy, N.F., Deborah, L.: McGuinness, ontology development 101: a guide to creating your first ontology. Stanford Knowledge Systems Laboratory Technical Report KSL-01-05 and Stanford Medical Informatics Technical Report SMI-2001-0880 (2001)
11. http://subs.emis.de/LNI/Proceedings/Proceedings96/GI-Proceedings-96-3.pdf
12. Reiter, R.: A logic for default reasoning. Artif. Int. **13**(1–2), 81–132 (1980)
13. https://ub-madoc.bib.uni-mannheim.de/1898/1/TR2008_004.pdf
14. Mensing, B., Goltz, U., Aniculaesei, A., Herold, S., Rausch, A., Gartner, S., Schneider, K.: Towards integrated rule-driven software development for IT ecosystems. In: 2012 6th IEEE International Conference on Digital Ecosystems Technologies (DEST), pp. 1–6, 18–20 June 2012. doi:10.1109/DEST.2012.6227951
15. Engels, G., Goedicke, M., Goltz, U., Rausch, A., Reussner, R.: Design for future – legacy-probleme von morgen vermeidbar? Informatik-Spektrum **32**(5), 393–397 (2009)
16. Herold, S.: Architectural compliance in component-based systems, foundations, specification, and checking of architectural rules. Ph.D. dissertation, Clausthal University of Technology (2011)

17. Bartelt, C.: Kollaborative Modellierung im Software Engineering. Dr.-Hut Verlag, Munich (2011)
18. Klus, H.: Anwendungsarchitektur-konforme Konfiguration selbstorganisierender Softwaresysteme. Dissertation, Technische Universität Clausthal, Institut für Informatik (2013). To be published
19. Niebuhr, D.: Dependable dynamic adaptive systems: approach, model, and infrastructure. Dissertation, Clausthal-Zellerfeld, Technische Universität Clausthal, Institut für Informatik (2010)

A Safety Roadmap to Cyber-Physical Systems

Mario Trapp, Daniel Schneider, and Peter Liggesmeyer

Abstract

In recent years, the term cyber-physical systems has emerged to characterize a new generation of embedded systems. In cyber-physical systems, embedded systems will be open in the sense that they will dynamically interconnect with other systems and will be able to dynamically adapt to changing runtime contexts. Such open adaptive systems provide a huge potential for society and for the economy. On the other hand, however, openness and adaptivity make it hard or even impossible for developers to predict a system's dynamic structure and behavior. This impedes the assurance of important system quality properties, especially safety and reliability. Safety assurance of cyber-physical systems will therefore be both one of the most urgent and one of the most challenging research questions of the next decade. This chapter analyzes the state of the art in order to identify open gaps and suggests a runtime safety assurance framework for cyber-physical systems to structure ongoing and future research activities.

1 Introduction

The development of safety-critical embedded systems has to follow strict rules and a rigorous safety assurance case is required before a product can be introduced to the market. Developers therefore avoid using flexible and progressive concepts like dynamic adaptation in safety-critical contexts. Many safety standards such as IEC 61508[1] even prohibit the use of techniques such as dynamic reconfiguration or self-healing.

M. Trapp (✉) • D. Schneider • P. Liggesmeyer
Fraunhofer Institute for Experimental Software Engineering, Fraunhofer-Platz 1,
67663 Kaiserslautern, Germany
e-mail: Mario.Trapp@iese.fraunhofer.de; Daniel.Schneider@iese.fraunhofer.de;
Peter.Liggesmeyer@iese.fraunhofer.de

J. Münch and K. Schmid (eds.), *Perspectives on the Future of Software Engineering*,
DOI 10.1007/978-3-642-37395-4_6, © Springer-Verlag Berlin Heidelberg 2013

Over the last decade, however, new applications have emerged, which are today often subsumed under the popular term cyber-physical systems. In some sense, cyber-physical systems are Open Adaptive Systems, i.e., systems of systems that dynamically connect to each other (openness) and adapt to a changing context at runtime (adaptive). Industry sees huge economic potential in such systems – particularly because their openness and adaptivity enables new kinds of promising applications. Many application domains of cyber-physical systems, however, are safety-critical. This includes, for example, car2car scenarios, plug'n'play operating rooms, or collaborative autonomous mobile machines.

This means that two different worlds, which have intentionally been kept separate in the past, have to grow together in the near future. Using the full potential of Open Adaptive Systems without endangering a product's safety is therefore one of the primary challenges today. Regarding the state of the art, however, there are only a few approaches that explicitly address the safety assurance of Open Adaptive Systems. Whereas the adaptive systems community mostly considers safety as one of many quality properties, the safety engineering community is still mainly concerned with design time variability, and only a few groups focus on the safety of Open Adaptive Systems. Therefore, safety could easily become a bottleneck preventing the successful transition of a promising idea to business success.

This chapter therefore provides an overview on the current state of the art in assuring the safety of open adaptive systems and derives a possible runtime safety assurance framework for open adaptive systems that incorporates ongoing and necessary future research activities.

2   State of the Art

Given that the topic of safety engineering for open adaptive systems is located at the intersection of two different research domains, namely safety and adaptive systems, it is reasonable to investigate the state of the art from these two perspectives.

From the safety engineering perspective, there are two different fields of research that are particularly relevant for safety assurance in open adaptive systems, the fields of modular safety assurance and of runtime safety assurance. Modular Safety Assurance addresses development time system integration only, but it provides different concepts that could be adapted to runtime safety assurance. As regards Runtime Safety Assurance, only a few results are available as of today, but they provide a promising starting point. Both fields of research will be explored in the subsections below.

Regarding the state of the art from an adaptive system's point of view, different approaches are available that address quality assurance in general, but these do not explicitly consider safety assurance. Thus, we only give a brief general introduction regarding this research domain and its safety-related trends and developments.

2.1 Safety Engineering Approaches

From a safety point of view, there are various approaches that could be extended to assure safety in open adaptive systems. For example, some groups are pursuing the idea of safety bags, which detect and handle failures at runtime. By this means, failures that might result from system adaptations would be mitigated so that no additional measures are required. In practice, however, the effectiveness, i.e., the detection rate of such approaches is still very limited. Another alternative would be to assure safety completely at development time by predicting all possible system adaptations and covering the complete adaptation space with traditional safety assurance techniques. Such approaches easily run into a state space explosion problem due to the high number of system variants that must be considered for an adaptive system. For open systems it gets even more difficult, since the safety-relevant characteristics of the system elements that must be integrated at runtime might be completely unknown. This may even lead to a situation where safety assurance at development time is not possible at all. The third class of approaches therefore aims at runtime safety assurance. The core idea of utilizing runtime assurance measures is to shift those aspects of safety assurance into runtime that cannot be tackled at development time due to a lack of information or due to high combinatorial complexity.

2.1.1 Modular Safety Assurance

Modular safety assurance approaches provide a possible basis for runtime safety assurance. Different modular safety assurance approaches are already available in the state of the art since research and industry across various application domains have identified the enormous potential of such approaches for reducing cost and time to market. Even some of the safety standards already reflect first ideas of modular safety assurance. In the avionics domain, for instance, there exist concepts that support modularization, such as the incremental certification principle [2]. Furthermore, some certification bodies describe processes for achieving the acceptance of reusable software components, like the Federal Aviation Administration (FAA) did in its advisory circular (AC[1]) 20–148 [3]. In the automotive domain, the standard ISO 26262 [4] introduces guidelines for the development of a Safety Element out of Context (SEooC) that shall support the safety assurance of reusable components such as operating systems.

In essence, modular safety assurance requires the modularization of different artifacts created in a safety lifecycle. Research has focused on the modularization of safety cases and safety analyses. Research on modular safety cases often refers to the term **modular certification**, which is one of the most important current trends in safety research. This notion is, however, a bit misleading, since corresponding approaches actually do not refer to the certification process itself, but rather focus

---

[1]An AC never contains mandatory instruction, but advice. In this case, the AC provides one, but not the only, possible means for developing reusable software components.

on modular safety cases. The modularization of safety analyses already started in the 1990s and different approaches have since been defined. The principle idea of modularly defining failure propagation from a component's input to its output is often called **failure logic modeling**.

Faller and Gobler [5] propose *Open Certification* in the context of IEC 61508 [1]. Open certification is an application-domain-independent method for vertical modular certification, i.e., it mainly focuses on the modular assurance and composition of hardware and software. The approach is based upon two main documents: (1) a safety case containing a list of all the requirements demanded by IEC 61508 with proof of their fulfillment; (2) an open document serving as a *safety manual* for the integrator of the product.

In the avionics domain, Rushby [6] introduced the use of modular certification for software components in the context of IMA[2] architectures. This work also influenced the safety standard RTCA/DO-297 [7]. The main goal of this approach is to enable incremental assurance for the certification of an IMA system. The process starts bottom-up with the certification of modules, followed by the incremental certification of applications until the system level is reached. Finally, the integration of the system in the aircraft is taken into account.

Under the name of generic safety cases, another important approach was introduced into the field of modular certification by Althammer [8]. The main objective of the modularization concepts introduced as part of the DECOS (Dependable Embedded Components and Systems) project is to facilitate the systematic design and deployment of integrated systems. The method considers the creation of two generic and reusable safety cases on the one hand (one for the core and the other one for the high-level services) and several application-specific safety cases on the other hand.

Due to the increasing complexity of safety cases, graphical notations were introduced. One of the initiators of a graphical description of safety cases was Kelly [9]. In his work, he introduced the concepts and the principles of compositional safety cases. He proposed the Goal Structured Notation (GSN) as a graphical notation for modeling safety arguments, which are the body of the safety case. Bate and Kelly [10] extended the GSN to allow modular construction of the safety case by focusing on the specification of modularized interfaces used for the construction of outgoing and incoming context definitions. In a later publication, Kelly [11] demonstrated that many principles from the field of software architecture can be applied to managing and representing safety cases as a composition of safety case modules. Relationships between modules are recorded as contracts that help to assess whether the requirements are still fulfilled after the system has been changed, e.g., after a module has been replaced. Following Kelly's work, Fenn et al. [12] describe an approach extending the GSN to create modularized safety cases with the use of contracts. Despotou and Kelly [13] investigated the impact of changes on

---

[2]IMA: Integrated Modular Avionics.

a compositional safety case and the assurance communicated by it. They conclude that using modular arguments minimizes the change impact on a safety case.

Zimmer et al. [14] presented the model-based VerSaI language for specifying demanded and guaranteed requirements, which can be used to formalize the definition of contracts between modules in semi-automated safety case reconstruction approaches. VerSaI focuses on the modular assurance and safe integration of different application components with a platform in open integrated architectures like AUTOSAR and IMA.

Safety cases are usually specified quite late in the safety lifecycle as final arguments showing that the safety goals have been reached. There are, however, recommendations to develop a safety case in parallel to system development. ISO 26262 defines the related idea of safety concepts. Safety concepts include all relevant safety requirements and their allocation to functions and components. To this end, the top-level safety goals are refined stepwise into more concrete safety requirements. In later development phases, evidences can be assigned in order to 'prove' that the requirements have been fulfilled. By these means, a safety case can be seamlessly derived from a safety concept. In support of this approach, Domis et al. introduced the idea of *Safety Concept Trees*. As their initial starting point, they used a tree-like notation derived from fault trees [15]. But whereas fault trees model fault combinations that lead to a hazard, safety concept trees specify the requirements that must be fulfilled to achieve the safety goals. This approach has been further refined and extended and now provides a model-based, modular means for describing safety concepts and safety cases [16] using safety contracts at the requirements level.

As described above, **modular safety analysis techniques** usually follow the idea of failure logic modeling as described by Lisagor et al. [17]. A first approach has been the Failure Propagation and Transition Notation (FPTN), which was introduced by Fenelon et al. already in 1994.

Papadopoulos et al. introduced the Hierarchically Performed Hazard Origin and Propagation Studies (HiP-HOPS) in [18]. HiP-HOPS have been the basis of the error annex of EAST-ADL. Based on EAST-ADL, HiP-HOPS have also been integrated into model-driven tool chains [19]. However, HiP-HOPS do not have a model representation; rather, they are mainly included as text annotations.

The drawback of the first failure logic modeling approaches was that they introduced new notations that were not established and thus accepted by neither practitioners nor certification bodies. Therefore, Component Fault Trees (CFT) [20] utilized the well-established fault tree notation as a starting point and extended it with the possibility to decompose the structure of large systems in terms of components. The methodology increases reusability and reduces modeling complexity. Since CFTs do not support the description of dynamic dependencies, there has been a further extension that integrated Markov chains. CFTs have been further advanced to so-called component-integrated CFTs (C^2FT). C^2FTs seize the idea of CFTs and seamlessly integrate the modular fault tree notation with a component-based modeling approach based on established modeling languages like SysML and UML. A practical overview of C^2FTs is given in [21]. A more formal description can be found in [22]. In order to provide more sophisticated support for the incremental development of systems and for hierarchical decomposition, C^{2}FTs have been extended to a *safe component model* supporting abstraction and refinement [23].

2.1.2 Runtime Safety Assurance

The approaches presented so far focus on modular safety assurance during development time. Particularly for cyber-physical systems, however, modular safety assurance at runtime is required. In contrast to modular safety assurance at development time, only a few groups have been addressing runtime assurance explicitly to date. First ideas for certification at runtime were introduced by Rushby [24, 25]. Rushby states that it should be possible to perform formal analyses at runtime, making it possible to formally verify that a component behaves as specified during execution. However, he does not provide concrete solutions. As one possible approach, Schneider et al. introduced the concept of Conditional Safety Certificates (ConSerts) [26–28], which facilitate the modular definition of safety certificates for single components and systems using a contract-like approach. ConSerts have a runtime representation so that the system composition can also take place at runtime. ConSerts do not describe fixed contracts, but support variability. Depending on which demands can be fulfilled by the context, the provided guarantees are adapted. This is essential for providing the necessary flexibility during system integration.

2.2 Dynamic Adaptation Approaches

Some of the first significant research efforts for adaptive systems emerged from the middleware community, where adaptive middleware platforms have been designed to meet the new demands of flexible, distributed heterogeneous systems. Examples in this regard are the solutions proposed by Blair et al. [29] and Capra et al. [30]. A related field of research, where the topic of self-adaptivity also gained momentum quite early, is the field of adaptive quality of service (QoS) assurance. Corresponding research has mostly focused on communication systems and end-to-end consideration of QoS. The results have been platforms, middleware, and frameworks enabling adaptive QoS.

It was soon recognized that quality assurance for adaptive systems is an important topic with significant scientific challenges. Initial corresponding research efforts have mostly focused on the issues of validation and verification (V&V) of adaptive systems. First results were based on development time V&V (e.g., [31]), but recently V&V measures are being increasingly shifted into runtime (e.g., [32, 33]).

In recent years, one main research focus of the community has been on investigating sound engineering methodologies for adaptive systems. Such methodologies ideally span all typical phases of software development (from requirements engineering to the validation of the final product) and explicitly consider important non-functional properties. This methodological research focus has been pushed by community research roadmaps [34] and has been advocated strongly by conferences in the area of adaptive systems, e.g., the SEAMS symposium [35] and the SASO conference [36]. In the context of engineering frameworks, the different fields of adaptive systems research are growing together ever more. The current Models@Runtime research landscape underlines this trend, since researchers from the fields of adaptive middleware, V&V, and engineering methodologies are working together to develop seamless approaches combining all these important aspects under the umbrella of the Models@Runtime topic [37, 38].

Safety assurance as such, however, has been largely beyond the scope of these research communities. As a consequence, safety has typically been treated as 'just another non-functional property', which obviously does not do justice to the special character and the special challenges of safety assurance.

3   Safety Assurance in Open Adaptive Systems

Research on cyber-physical systems has become very popular and quality assurance in cyber-physical systems has often been pointed out as an important research challenge. Nonetheless, almost no explicit safety approaches for open adaptive systems have been proposed as of yet. This impedes the success of cyber-physical systems, since it is not possible to apply conventional approaches to open adaptive systems. This is particularly true due to the unpredictability of open adaptive systems and their dynamic changes. But even if all possible communication partners and system configurations were known at development time already, the resulting adaptation space would be too large to be covered using conventional safety assurance approaches. It is therefore necessary to dynamically assure the safety of the emerging system of systems at runtime.

Regarding current safety standards, runtime safety assurance is obviously not considered and the idea as such violates some basic principles of safety engineering. For example, it is assumed that a system is completely specified and configured prior to a safety assessment and any system change is subject to a rigorous impact analysis and recertification procedure. Consequently, any new runtime safety assurance mechanism requires a proof that it is equivalent or better than the development time mechanisms and methodologies demanded by current standards. Proving this equivalence requires clear traceability between the runtime concept and the corresponding established development-time concept that is to be replaced. For this reason, the following section offers a brief introduction to the principal safety assurance lifecycle as it is used today. The subsequent section then outlines a possible approach to how the established concepts can be evolved into runtime safety assurance.

3.1   Safety Engineering in a Nutshell

The precise definition of a safety engineering lifecycle, and particularly of the terms used, depends on the respective application domain. The principal idea, however, is similar across all safety-related application domains. For the sake of simplicity,

we therefore use the terms as defined in ISO 26262[4], which is the relevant safety standard for automotive systems. It is at the same time one of the most recent safety standards.

The overall goal of safety engineering is to ensure 'freedom from unacceptable risk' [4]. The term risk is defined as the 'combination of the probability of occurrence of harm and the severity of that harm' [4]. Usually, however, it is not possible to directly assess the harm that is potentially caused by a system. Instead, safety managers identify the hazards of a system, i.e., 'potential sources of harm' [4]. In many domains, this vague definition is further refined. In the automotive domain, for example, 'hazards shall be defined in the terms of conditions and events that can be observed at the vehicle level' [4]. Usually, harm is only caused when a hazard, a specific environmental situation, and a specific operation mode of the system coincide. This coincidence is called 'hazardous event' [4].

The identification of these hazardous events and the assessment of the associated risks is the first step in any safety engineering lifecycle, namely the' hazard analysis and risk assessment (HRA)' as shown in Fig. 1. This step is performed during the very early phases of the development process, at the latest when the system requirements are available.

As a result of this step, safety goals are defined as top-level safety requirements, which have to be incrementally refined during the safety engineering lifecycle. Usually, any safety requirement consists of a functional part and an associated integrity level. The functional part defines what the system must (not) do, whereas the integrity level defines the rigor demanded for the implementation of this requirement. The integrity level depends on the risk associated with the hazardous event that is addressed by the safety goal. For example, ISO 26262 defines so-called automotive safety integrity levels (ASIL).

In order to break down the safety requirements, the subsequent steps in the safety engineering process should be performed in parallel to the development activities. To this end, the available development artifacts are used as input to safety analyses in order to identify potential causes of the identified system failures. A wide range of established analysis techniques is available. Failure Modes and Effects Analysis (FMEA) and Fault Tree Analysis (FTA) are certainly the most widely used safety analysis techniques in practice.

Based on these results, a safety manager derives a safety concept. Following the idea of ISO 26262, a safety concept can be defined as a 'specification of the safety requirements, their allocation to architectural elements and their interaction necessary to achieve the safety goals, and information associated with these requirements' [4]. In the same way as the developers incrementally refine the system over the different development phases, the safety manager analyzes the refined development artifacts step by step and refines the safety concept accordingly.

Finally the safety manager has to define a safety case, which forms the basis for certification. A safety case can be defined as an 'argument why an item is safe supported by evidence compiled from work products of all safety activities during the whole lifecycle.'[4]. Actually, a safety case can be derived from a safety concept by extending the latter with evidences proving that the requirements have been fulfilled. Evidence might be anything supporting an argument in the safety case. Evidences of particular importance are the results of validation and verification activities as well as safety analysis results. Since a safety case compiles all evidences that are relevant for proving the system's safety, it is an efficient basis for safety certification.

3.2   Runtime Safety Assurance

In modular certification approaches, a safety expert is responsible for assessing the integrated system. If we want to apply such concepts for runtime assurance, however, there will be no human expert to check the system's safety. Rather, the system must assure its safety on its own. Considering that safety research is still solving the problems of modular certification, safety assurance in open adaptive systems seems to be a very challenging endeavor.

Extrapolating the current developments of safety engineering, it would take much too long until urgently required safety assurance approaches for open adaptive systems would be available. In the same way as open adaptive systems form a new paradigm in system development, there must be a change of paradigms in safety assurance as well. As mentioned earlier, one corresponding aspect would be to shift parts of the safety assurance lifecycle to runtime. At development time, safety engineers use models like safety analysis models, safety concepts, or safety cases to assess and ensure a system's safety. Shifting elements of the safety assurance lifecycle to runtime therefore means making one or more of these models available at runtime and 'teaching' the system how to interpret, utilize, and manage the models at runtime.

To this end, we can use so-called Models@Runtime, which are an upcoming paradigm for the development of adaptive systems. In model-driven development, developers use different model-based analyses to optimize the system with respect to different quality characteristics. To this end, they have to anticipate the runtime context of the system. As this is not possible for adaptive systems, Models@Runtime follow the idea of making important models available at runtime in order to enable the system itself to reason about its current situation in a concrete given runtime context. In contrast to other approaches for the development of adaptive systems, Models@Runtime provide a kind of formal basis for reasoning about the current system state at runtime to analyze or predict the consequences of possible system adaptations. This is how dynamic adaptation becomes reproducible and predictable. Applying the idea of Models@Runtime to safety models therefore seems to be an appropriate approach towards runtime safety assurance. Actually, all models used in a safety lifecycle as described in the previous section could potentially be used as safety models at runtime.

As a first step, it seems to be reasonable to shift the idea of modular certification to runtime. In the same way as modular certificates need to contain all information necessary to safely compose different subsystems, a **SafetyCertificate@Runtime** would enable the safe runtime composition of different subsystems. To this end, they describe a formal safety interface using contract-like interface specifications defining which safety properties can be guaranteed by the system under the assumption that specific safety demands are fulfilled by the integration context. Special negotiation protocols could then ensure that only safe compositions are allowed at runtime. By incorporating variabilities into runtime certificates, they can adapt to changing integration and environment contexts [28].

Sometimes, the flexibility provided by SafetyCertificates@Runtime is not sufficient, however. In such cases it is an option to shift safety cases to runtime. A **SafetyCase@Runtime** is a formalized, modular safety case that can be interpreted and adapted at runtime. Therefore, the system gets runtime access to all arguments and evidences proving that the subsystems' safety goals are met. This means the system is enabled to dynamically check to which extent its safety goals are met in a given runtime context. In case the system adaptations lead to the invalidation of evidences, a revalidation of evidences can be triggered at runtime. This means that (a subset of) predefined verification activities have to be executed at runtime. Sometimes re-verification using predefined tests or analyses is not sufficient. In the same way as system modifications at development often require the modification or creation of new test cases, this might also be necessary after runtime adaptations of a system. This could be realized using **V&V-Models@Runtime** such as those proposed by the adaptive systems research domain. Considering, however, how difficult this step easily becomes for developers at development time, it is obviously a very challenging task to shift these activities to runtime. Particularly for safety-critical systems, V&V models at runtime are more of theoretical than of practical importance.

Some adaptation approaches even include the dynamic adaptation of system requirements. From the safety perspective, if requirements are modified at development time, this requires modification of the hazard analysis and risk assessment (HRA) as well. Therefore, if dynamic requirement adaptations had to be supported, it would be necessary to have **HRA@Runtime**. Assuming a model-based HRA is available, the idea of safety models at runtime could be applied to these models as well. HRA, however, is a very creative process and performing an HRA is a challenging task even for experienced safety experts. It is therefore very unlikely that dynamic adaptation of requirements is going to be accepted in safety-critical systems.

Models@Runtime thus provide a range of possible approaches for the safety assurance of open adaptive systems, and it is certainly not possible to pick out one particular approach that leads to the best trade-off between flexibility and acceptance in general. From a safety engineering point of view, it is obviously reasonable to leave as much responsibility as possible with the safety experts and to reduce the runtime activities to a minimum. Thus, SafetyCertificates@Runtime would be the preferable approach. From an adaptive systems point of view, it is however desirable to have as much flexibility as possible. Therefore we believe that it will be necessary to integrate different approaches into an assurance framework in order to use the advantages and compensate for the disadvantages of the different approaches. Though many mechanisms required for such a framework are not available yet, we nonetheless project a possible runtime safety assurance framework based on the idea of safety models at runtime. This framework incorporates seemingly independent research activities from different research communities into a holistic approach. As such it defines a target scenario enabling us to identify open gaps and to derive a possible roadmap to safety assurance of cyber-physical systems.

Learning from traditional safety engineering, we recommend using modularity as the basic ingredient for a safety assurance framework from the very beginning. First, this obviously reduces complexity. Second, this enables us to use different assurance approaches for different modules. In this context, we use the term module very flexibly to express a modularized entity that can range from a complete system in a system of systems to a single software component. Since the required types of adaptation usually differ widely across the different modules, it is reasonable to limit more complex assurance approaches to those modules that actually have to adapt very flexibly. Following the idea of modular certification, it seems to be reasonable to use SafetyCertificates@Runtime as the basic building blocks to enable the modularization and runtime integration of different subsystems. This means that SafetyCertificates@Runtime are used as a common safety interface. As such they hide the internal safety assurance mechanisms and therefore enable the combination of a wide range of heterogeneous assurance approaches.

If we have a module that adapts to predefined variants only, then the built-in variabilities of a SafetyCertificate@Runtime are sufficient to assure safety at runtime. If we have a module that has too large a configuration space or that also adapts to previously unknown configurations, it might be necessary to have additional safety models at runtime. In this case, for example, the system could use SafetyCases@Runtime to identify invalidated evidences, to revalidate missing evidences, and to adapt the SafetyCase@Runtime and the SafetyCertificate@Runtime accordingly in order to update the system's safety guarantees and demands. Alternatively, it would be possible to use traditional fault tolerance approaches like safety bags (cf. e.g., [1]). Though such approaches are based on traditional mechanisms rather than Models@Runtime, they would nonetheless fit into the framework, as a SafetyCertificate@Runtime can be used to dynamically specify the safety guarantees that can be provided using the safety bag. And the runtime certificates could define demands that are required to use the safety bag. This means that SafetyCertificates@Runtime can be used as a common runtime safety interface independent of the internally used runtime safety assurance mechanism.

If we interpret this framework as a possible roadmap to runtime safety assurance, there are some open gaps that have to be closed. Safety certificates at runtime are obviously an indispensable corner stone and should be in the focus of safety research for cyber-physical systems. First approaches of SafetyCertificates@Runtime are available and provide a good starting point to support a sufficient range of openness and adaptivity for a first generation of cyber-physical systems. In the mid-term perspective, however, cyber-physical systems will require more flexibility than can be supported by runtime certificates. Runtime verification and validation has the potential to allow such flexibility. Today, however, these approaches are of limited use for safety assurance, as systems are neither enabled to identify necessary runtime V&V activities nor to utilize V&V results for ensuring safety at runtime. Regarding the safety assurance lifecycle, the problem becomes obvious: Safety cases at runtime are missing as an indispensable piece of the puzzle that creates the link between safety goals and V&V activities. Before we can utilize research results on runtime verification and validation for runtime safety assurance, it is therefore important to start research on safety cases at runtime. Currently, there is no ongoing research that aims at something comparable to safety cases at runtime. Furthermore, runtime validation and verification is only one source for runtime evidences. In fact, it is very likely that runtime safety analyses will be required as well. Considering the state of the art, this is another open research challenge.

4   Conclusion

Safety assurance of cyber-physical systems poses several challenges, particularly caused by their openness and adaptivity. Even though there are virtually no approaches that could be used right away, there are several research results of different research communities that could be used as a basis for an appropriate safety assurance approach. A corresponding framework based on SafetyCertificates@Runtime as a common safety interface seems to be very promising and has the potential to incorporate different research results. At any rate, runtime safety certificates will form a cornerstone of future safety research for cyber-physical systems. In order to increase the possible flexibility of cyber-physical systems, it will be additionally necessary to utilize runtime validation and verification approaches for runtime safety assurance. To this end, it will further be necessary to provide something comparable to safety cases at runtime, which have been completely out of focus so far.

Whatever future runtime safety assurance will look like, a successful approach will require much more intensive collaboration between the relevant research communities than is found today.

References

1. IEC 61508: Functional Safety of Electrical/Electronic/Programmable Electronic Safety Related Systems. International Electrotechnical Commission (1999)
2. Fenn, J.L., Hawkins, R.D., Williams, P.J., Kelly, T.P., Banner, M.G., Oakshott, Y.: The who, where, how, why and when of modular and incremental certification. In: Proceedings of the 2007 2nd Institution of Engineering and Technology International Conference on System Safety, vol., no., pp. 135–140. 22–24 Oct 2007
3. FAA AC 20–148: Reusable Software Components. AC 20–148 (2004)
4. ISO/CD 26262: Road vehicles, Functional Safety Part 6: Product development at the software level, Part 10 – 'Guidelines' (2011)
5. Faller R., Dr. Goble, W.M.: Open IEC 61508 Certification of Products, exida GmbH (2007)
6. Rushby, J.: Modular Certification. NASA Contractor Report CR-2002-212130. NASA Langley Research Center (2002)
7. RTCA DO-297: Integrated Modular Avionics (IMA) – Development Guidance and Certification Considerations, RTCA/DO-297 (2005)
8. DECOS: Dependable Embedded Components and Systems, Integrated Project within the EU Framework Programme 6, http://www.decos.at. Last visited June 2012
9. Kelly, T.: Concepts and Principles of Compositional Safety Case Construction. University of York (2001)
10. Bate I., Kelly T.: Architectural considerations in the certification of modular systems. In: Proceedings of the 21st International Conference on Computer Safety, Reliability and Security (SAFECOMP'02), pp. 303–324. Springer (2002)
11. Kelly, T.: Using software architecture techniques to support the modular certification of safety-critical systems. In: Proceedings of the eleventh Australian workshop on Safety critical systems and software, vol. 69, pp. 53–65. Australian Computer Society, Inc (SCS'06), Darlinghurst (2006)
12. Fenn, J., Hawkins, R., Kelly, T.P., Williams, P.: Safety case composition using contracts – refinements based on feedback from an Industrial Case Study. In: 15th Safety Critical Systems Symposium. (2007)
13. Despotou, G., Kelly, T.: Investigating the use of argument modularity to optimise through-life system safety assurance. In: 3rd IET International Conference on: System Safety, pp. 1–6. (2008)
14. Zimmer, B., Bürklen, S., Knoop, M., Höfflinger, J., Trapp M. : Vertical Safety interfaces – improving the efficiency of modular certification. In: Proceedings of the 30th International Conference of Computer Safety, Reliability, and Security (SAFECOMP 2011)
15. Domis, D., Forster, M., Kemmann, S., Trapp, M., Safety Concept Trees. In: Reliability and Maintainability Symposium, 2009. RAMS 2009. Annual, vol., no., pp. 212–217. 26–29 Jan 2009. doi:10.1109/RAMS.2009.4914677
16. Adler, R., Kemmann, S, Liggesmeyer, P., Schwinn, P.: Model-based development of a safety concept. In: Proceedings of PSAM 11 & ESREL 2012, (2012)
17. Lisagor, O., McDermid, J.A., Pumfrey, D.J.: Towards a practicable process for automated safety analysis. In: 24th International System Safety Conference, pp. 596–607. (2006)
18. Papadopoulos, Y., McDermid, J.: Hierarchically performed hazard origin and propagation studies. In: Proceedings of the 18th International Conference on Computer Safety, Reliability and Security, Lecture Notes in Computer Science, vol. 1608, pp. 139–152. (1999)
19. Biehl, M., DeJiu, C.,Törngren, M.: Integrating safety analysis into the model-based development toolchain of automotive embedded systems. In Proceedings of the ACM SIGPLAN/SIGBED 2010 Conference on Languages, Compilers, and Tools for Embedded Systems (LCTES '10), pp. 125–132. ACM, New York (2010)
20. Kaiser, B., Liggesmeyer, P., Mäckel, O.: A new component concept for fault trees. In: Lindsay, P., Cant, T. (eds.) Proceedings of the Conferences in Research and Practice in Information Technology, vol. 33, pp. 37–46. ACS (2004)

21. Adler, R., Domis, D., Höfig, K., Kemmann, S., Kuhn, T., Schwinn, J.P., Trapp, M.: Integration of component fault trees into the UML. Model. Softw. Eng. 312–327 (2011), Springer
22. Domis, D., Trapp M.: Integrating safety analyses and component-based design. In: Harrison M.D., Sujan M.-A. (eds.) SAFECOMP 2008, Lecture Notes in Computer Science, vol. 5219. pp. 58–71. (2008)
23. Domis, D., Trapp, M.: Component-based abstraction in fault tree analysis. In: Computer Safety, Reliability, and Security, pp. 297–310. Springer (2009)
24. Rushby, J.: Just-in-Time certification. In: Proceedings of the 12th IEEE International Conference on the Engineering of Complex Computer Systems (ICECCS), pp. 15–24. Auckland (2007)
25. Rushby, J.: Runtime Certification. In: Runtime Verification, 8th International Workshop, RV 2008, Budapest, 30 Mar 2008
26. Schneider, D., Trapp, M.: A safety engineering framework for open adaptive systems. In: Proceedings of the Fifth IEEE International Conference on Self-Adaptive and Self-Organizing Systems, Ann Arbor 3–7 Oct 2011
27. Schneider, D., Trapp, M.: Conditional safety certificates in open systems. In: Proceedings of the 1st Workshop on Critical Automotive applications: Robustness & Safety (CARS), pp. 57–60. ACM, New York (2010)
28. Schneider D., Trapp M.: Conditional Safety Certification of Open Adaptive Systems, To be published in ACM Transactions on Autonomous and Adaptive Systems (TAAS) (2013)
29. Blair, G., Coulson, G., Robin, P.: Papathomas, M.: An architecture for next generation middleware. In: Davies, S.J., N.A.J. Raymond, K. (eds.) IFIP International Conference on Distributed Systems Platforms and Open Distributed Processing (Middleware'98) (1998)
30. Capra, L., Blair, G., Mascolo, C., Emmerich, W., Grace, P.: Exploiting reflection in mobile computing middleware. ACM SIGMOBILE Mobile Comput.Commun. Rev. 6, 34–44 (2002)
31. Zhang, J., Cheng, B.H.C.: Specifying adaptation semantics. In: Workshop on Architecting Dependable Systems (WADS'05), pp. 1–7. ACM, St. Louis (2005)
32. Leucker, M., Schallhart, C.: A brief account of runtime verification. J.Logic.Algebr. Program. 78(5), 293–303 (2009)
33. Goldsby, H.J., Cheng, B.H., Zhang, J.: AMOEBA-RT: run-time verification of adaptive software. In: Giese, H. (ed.) Models in Software Engineering. Lecture notes in computer science, vol. 5002. Springer, Berlin/Heidelberg (2008)
34. Cheng, B.H. et al.: Software Engineering for Self-Adaptive Systems: A Research Roadmap, vol. 5525, pp. 1–26. (2009
35. http://www.self-adaptive.org/. Last visited in June 2012
36. http://www.saso-conference.org/. Last visited in June 2012
37. Gordon Blair et al.: Models@Run.Time. IEEE Comput. (2010)
38. Dagstuhl Seminar on Models@run.time: http://www.dagstuhl.de/en/program/calendar/semhp/?semnr=11481. Last visited June 2012

Modeling Complex Information Systems

Joerg Doerr

Abstract
We are living in an information society. For us it is normal to access relevant information almost immediately. In our world, information systems play an important role in our private as well as in our professional lives. When selecting or developing such systems, especially complex ones, we need to understand and model the requirements on these systems. This paper deals with the modeling of complex information systems. We show which requirements concepts could be modeled, but also argue that it is not necessary to model all concepts. We show empirical studies that make us believe that further empirical research is needed in order to know which requirements concepts are most relevant. Current challenges as well as future challenges with regard to information system modeling are outlined.

1 Introduction

Information Systems have been around for several decades. We are living in an information society, and it is normal for us to access relevant information almost immediately. In our private and professional lives, information systems play an important role. The types of information systems vary from simple mobile applications with very limited functionality to complex information systems with millions of lines of code, such as ERP systems in companies. The complexity of these systems is enormous [1]. Among other reasons, complexity is due to the fact that the systems' scope becomes larger and more and more processes are supported by these information systems. Many stakeholders with varying interests are connected through these information systems. The expectations regarding

J. Doerr (✉)
Fraunhofer IESE, Fraunhofer-Platz 1, Kaiserslautern 67663, Germany
e-mail: joerg.doerr@iese.fraunhofer.de

J. Münch and K. Schmid (eds.), *Perspectives on the Future of Software Engineering*,
DOI 10.1007/978-3-642-37395-4_7, © Springer-Verlag Berlin Heidelberg 2013

functionality increase, as do the expectations regarding the quality characteristics of these systems. And the complexity of information systems will increase even further. Trends like mobile computing, cloud computing, big data, or crowd sourcing will impose additional complexity on information systems in the future.

In the light of this complexity, companies developing software as well as those using software are faced with the challenge to select or build information systems that fit their actual needs. Large information systems are rarely built from scratch. Rather, existing systems are customized and integrated into a solution fitting the requirements of the multitude of stakeholders. Missing services or components are built for the specific functionality needed. In order to start such a selection or development process, the requirements for such kinds of systems need to be determined on a level that is sufficient to make the right decisions. Due to economic constraints, one can rarely model the complete set of requirements for such kinds of systems. Modeling information systems efficiently is therefore a key success factor for the requirements engineering phase.

Technological advances try to reduce and limit this complexity. For example, business process execution engines promise that companies can just model their business processes and execute them immediately. The paradigm of service-oriented architectures promises to reduce complexity by simply orchestrating services from existing service repositories. Still, the fact remains that selecting or building such systems has to start with a thorough requirements analysis and modeling of the expectations regarding such systems.

In practice, Use Case Analysis [2], modeling business processes with notations such as BPMN, EPCs, or activity diagrams [3–5], or just textual requirements can often be found in software requirements specifications (SRS). In academia, one can find additional approaches, such as goal models [6] or scenarios [7]. But more important than single notations for models is to understand which types of information are relevant for modeling in order to select or develop information systems.

In this paper, we outline why the decision on how to model complex information systems is difficult today and how we can improve this situation in the future. The position of this paper is that complete elicitation and modeling of the requirements for these large systems with regard to all possible aspects is often not possible due to system size, complexity, and given economic constraints, and may also not be needed. The paper discusses current challenges in modeling requirements for complex information systems that add to this fact in Sect. 2. In Sect. 3, we outline which concepts of the domain and system could be modeled during the course of requirements engineering. In Sect. 4, we describe that in practice as well as in academia, we have little empirical evidence on why we need certain requirements concepts and for which purposes these requirements models are used. We present the results of first empirical studies that make us believe that not all concepts need to be modeled in all cases and that more (empirical) research needs to be performed in order to understand which concepts are essential for stakeholders of up- and downstream software development roles. In Sect. 5, we conclude and state new challenges that will impact the future modeling of complex information systems.

2   Current Challenges for Modeling Requirements for Complex Information Systems

In this section, important challenges that need to be taken into account to efficiently and effectively model information systems are outlined.

Challenge 1: Integration of Technical, Business and End-User Perspectives   One key challenge in modeling the requirements of information systems is to take into account the different perspectives on information systems: Basically, one can distinguish the requirements from a business, an end-user, and a technical perspective (see Fig. 1). If too much emphasis is given to technical solutions, and modeling focuses on the IT system only, important aspects of the organizational context or the end-user requirements are often neglected. This is one major reason for the perception of insufficient business – IT alignment. Therefore, information system models need to represent information from all three perspectives. During elicitation and integration of this information, the necessary interdisciplinarity of the teams is frequently perceived as a major obstacle for efficient modeling. In practice, smooth interaction between these three perspectives based on integrated requirements modeling is a key success factor for efficient and effective requirements engineering.

Challenge 2: Integration of Quality Requirements and Functional Requirements The stakeholders of today's information systems do not only demand system functionality, but also high quality. As examples we can take the product qualities usability and maintainability. To have a usable system is essential for work performance and for the satisfaction of the end-users. System maintainability is essential as changing markets and business processes demand further advances in system functionality. Therefore, the models of complex information systems need to also address quality requirements, which are sometimes called non-functional requirements. Many state-of-the-art approaches treat quality requirements separate from functional requirements [6]. But it is essential to integrate the modeling of quality requirements with that of functional requirements, also for the sake of giving them the same importance and attention in downstream software development [8].

Challenge 3: Incorporation of Information from Existing Solutions   In the rare situation where we build an information system from scratch, we might want to model all requirements down to a very low abstraction level, especially if we follow a pure waterfall-like process. But in reality, we often want to select existing information systems or integrate a set of existing systems or services. These systems already have capabilities in the sense of functionality and qualities that they provide. The requirements engineering of complex systems can become more efficient if the capabilities of the systems are taken into account early on. One way to do this is to use (functionalities of) existing systems in creativity sessions, for example when business process redesign takes place, or to have vendor presentations early in the requirements process. For the modeling of information systems it is essential

Fig. 1 Stakeholder
perspectives on information
system modeling

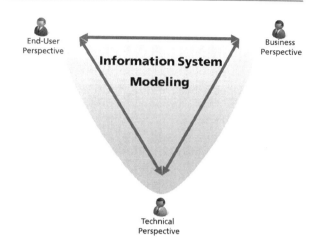

to know how to incorporate this information into the models for the information
systems.

3   Concepts for Modeling Complex Information Systems

About 10 years ago, the TORE (Task- and Object-oriented Requirements Engineering) approach for modeling interactive systems emerged as a result of a systematic
analysis of existing approaches for modeling interactive systems [9, 10]. This
approach was updated in recent years to cope with the challenges of modeling
complex information systems, especially with challenges 1 and 2. The description of
TORE in this paper is an extended version of the description of TORE in [11]. TORE
is a decision framework, which encapsulates decisions on four different levels of
abstraction that typically have to be made during requirements engineering for
information systems (see decision points in the gray area of Fig. 2). The decisions
correspond to requirements concepts that can be modeled for an information system.
They are independent of concretely used processes or notations, allowing high
applicability in many different contexts. For each concept, it is typical that a
requirements specification contains artifacts that model information about these
concepts. The concepts of TORE will be described in detail in the following.

At the Goal & Task Level, the first decision point is *Supported Stakeholders.*
Deciding which stakeholders should be supported by a system to be developed is
usually one of the initial decisions to be made. Typical notations used to model
this decision are stakeholder maps as used in [12], stereotypical user descriptions
such as personas [13], or simple role descriptions. For large information systems
the supported stakeholders can also include the level of complete business units,
whereas for smaller systems, the modeled stakeholders might be on the level of
roles of end-users in business processes. The second decision point is to capture
which *Stakeholder's Goals* exist and shall be supported by the system. Capturing
goals and general strategies of stakeholders in an organization can be supported by

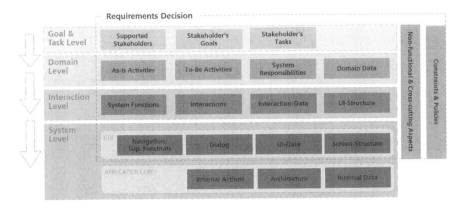

Fig. 2 Concepts in the TORE framework

approaches such as GQM+Strategies [14]. TORE models goals of organizations (business goals) as well as goals of users (individual goals). Typical notations used for modeling goals are notations used in methods such as KAOS [15], i* [16], or simple AND/OR goal refinement trees. Typically, the functional goals are refined into S*takeholder's Tasks*. In a simple information system, the *Stakeholder's Tasks* include the tasks of the users, while in complex business information systems, this decision point is the hierarchy of business processes.

At the Domain Level, each *Stakeholder's Task* is then refined into its *As-Is Activities*, i.e., the description of how tasks and business processes are currently performed without the system to be developed. In contrast to that, the *To-Be Activities* describe the tasks or business processes as they should be carried out when the system to be developed is in place. The typical notation used to model the *As-Is and To-Be Activities* are process modeling notations such as BPMN [5], EPCs [4], or UML Activity diagrams [3]. By modeling the *System Responsibilities,* one then determines which of the *To-Be Activities* are performed automatically, and which are performed only by humans, respectively by humans using system support. Often, the *To-Be Activities* and the *System Responsibilities* are determined at the same time. Information about available systems or system components (see current challenge 3) is often used at this point in time in order to provide and select alternatives for these decision points. Furthermore, *Domain Data* determine which data is handled on the Domain Level, respectively within the *To-Be Activities*. Typical notations for modeling the *Domain Data* are ER Diagrams or UML class diagrams.

At the Interaction Level, the *Interactions* define for all system-supported *To-Be Activities* what the concrete usage of a system by a human should look like. Typical notations used to model decisions of this decision point include Use Cases [2] or other scenario techniques. For all *System Functions* that are identified during the *To-Be Activities* and *Interactions*, the *System Functions* then describe the corresponding details (visible behavior, input, output, etc.). Furthermore, the *Interaction Data* determine the data used in *Interactions* and *System Functions*. Hence, they are typically a refinement of the *Domain Data*, using similar notations. With regard to early UI design, the *UI-Structure* is a first logical grouping of functions and data, but with neither a detailed layout nor a modality decision. Typical notations used to document these decisions are workspaces as proposed in [17]. More detailed information on TORE in general can be found in [9].

The described decision points are the typical concepts that can be modeled for complex information systems during requirements engineering. Sometimes, the different academic software engineering communities discuss quite controversially whether concepts belong to requirements engineering, architecture, usability engineering, or business models. Especially if we take a look at the TORE concepts, people from the architecture and usability engineering communities might wonder why TORE includes concepts that are also typical for their domains. One goal of TORE is to address challenge 1, so it especially aims at including information from usability engineering to satisfy the usability requirements of the end-users. Through integrated modeling of business units, business units' goals, business policies (rules) and constraints, as well as business process, the organizational point of view is also integrated. From our point of view, the definition of Alan Davis [18] is very valuable for explaining our view on requirements models: Davis defines that everything that is visible to the end-users is requirements relevant, independent of the level of detail. He takes an analogy from biology where everything that concerns the phenotype of an insect is part of requirements. This clearly defines that user interface elements are part of the requirements and are therefore included in the TORE framework. This does not mean that we want to exclude usability engineers from these models; rather, we claim that they should be strongly involved in elaborating these models for complex information systems. With regard to the separation from architecture, Davis states – again using the analogy to biology – that the genotype of an insect, i.e., what makes the insect exhibit its phenotype, is architecture and beyond. In the same notion, we intentionally exclude the "application core" decision points from the requirements decisions.

As explained before, TORE already offers strong integration of usability concerns into the requirements models. Nevertheless, requirements for other important qualities such as performance, maintainability, or portability need to be modeled in order to create high-quality information systems. For this purpose, the Fraunhofer IESE non-functional requirements (NFR) method provides support for eliciting and modeling non-functional requirements in an integrated way together with the functional requirements. The IESE NFR method provides basic support for the TORE domain level [8, 19] as well as advanced support for modeling non-functional requirements for the TORE interaction level [8, 20]. We depicted the need for such models with the *Non-Functional & Cross-Cutting Aspects* decision point as an extension of the classical TORE framework in Fig. 2.

We see the concepts described in this Section as the most essential ones for complex information systems and believe them to be the basis for comprehensive requirements models. We use the word "believe" intentionally here. We will outline in the next Section that there is no empirical evidence yet on which concepts are really needed for the subsequent development phases.

4   Usage of RE Models and Concepts in Up- and Downstream Development Activities: Need for Empirical Research

In this section, we outline that current models for information systems are often too general and not targeted at the actual needs of stakeholders of the SRS. Then, we show how we can overcome this situation by performing empirical research on the information needs. The need for such empirical research is described in more detail in [21]. We provide first results from explorative studies that support our claim for more empirical research.

4.1   Missing Evidence on the Real Need for Specific Requirements Models

In the requirements engineering community, a lot of research is going on in the context of requirements modeling, especially for the purpose of specification. Hence, requirements engineers are, for instance, supported by good advice on how to write and structure requirements specifications (like Volere, IEEE 830–1998, or IEEE 1362–1998). But these guidelines are often quite general [22]. And requirements engineering is no end in itself. Rather, in order to know which artifacts are really needed for the development, one has to understand what the specific information need of a role in the upstream or downstream development process is. Upstream roles are, for example, participants in business processes or managers who have a financial interest in the system. Downstream software development roles include the architect, the user interface designer, or the tester [23].

Current approaches often neglect this analysis of the information need and just assume that the concepts documented in the requirements models such as the ones in Sect. 3 are needed by some role in the development. SRS often contain much more information than actually required by a certain role to perform his/her tasks [21], or relevant information is hard to find and analyze in an SRS as it is spread over different chapters and sections. In the worst case, important information is even missing [24] and cannot be found at all because information about a concept is not documented in the SRS. In the state of the art, we can rarely spot papers about which type of information is actually demanded by specific development roles such as [24–26]; even rarer are papers that report empirical evidence for such information needs. A little more common are papers on the acceptance or suitability of new requirements notations [27–30]. The following list summarizes the most common problems that originate from this lack of empirical evidence.

- Important information is missing in the requirements models.
- Important information is spread over different sections and models within a document or is even spread over different documents.
- Important information can't be found, even though it is in the SRS.
- Information is specified that is not interesting at all for a specific role.
- The representation of the information (level of detail, used notation) is not useful.

4.2   Empirical Research on Information Needs

In order to do a more detailed analysis of this situation, detailed and empirically valid knowledge about information needs regarding requirements models and SRS is necessary first. That is, we have to find out by means of suitable studies what the different document stakeholders require from the requirements models dependent on their roles. We carried out some initial research on information needs, especially from the viewpoint of downstream development roles. For our research, we investigated the following research goals and research questions (RQs).

Research Goal G_1: Investigate information needs regarding SRS from the viewpoint of downstream development roles.

According to [31] the term "information need" is characterized as "information seeking towards the satisfaction of needs". Transferring this to the context of requirements engineering means that we have to investigate information that document stakeholders seek in an SRS to satisfy their needs. Typically, information is specified in an SRS by creating artifacts such as persona descriptions of a supported stakeholder or UML activity diagrams visualizing a certain business process, like a business travel process. These artifacts modeling the requirements can basically be categorized into artifact types, such as descriptions of stakeholders, descriptions of business processes, descriptions of goals, etc. These artifact types correspond to the concepts as introduced in Sect. 3.

Hence, to address G_1, we first have to identify and consolidate all important artifact types from the viewpoint of different downstream development roles. The relevance of these artifact types is dependent on the nature of downstream tasks and their characteristics. This is formulated in the following research question:

Research Question $RQ_{1.1}$: What are typical artifact types that should be contained in an SRS from the viewpoint of downstream development roles in order to accomplish their tasks?

In a second step, we have to further investigate the identified artifact types by answering the following RQs:

Research Question $RQ_{1.2}$: On what level of detail should artifacts of a certain type be specified?

$RQ_{1.3}$: Which notation should be used to specify artifacts of a certain type?

Based on the knowledge gained from investigations of these RQs, we would be able to create specifications that model all relevant information required for each of the document stakeholders. However, considering the fact that SRS typically serve as an important source of information for a variety of development engineers with different roles and tasks [22], we claim that there is also a difference in their particular information needs. This means that, even though all relevant information might be modeled in the SRS, the document stakeholders might still be faced with SRS containing "superfluous" information that is not necessary for performing their particular tasks (e.g., artifacts are specified that are relevant for a UI designer but not for an architect). This might also mean that relevant information is still spread over different sections or even over different documents. This motivates a second research goal and related RQs as stated in the following:

Research Goal G_2: Investigate whether there are any differences in the information needs from the viewpoints of different downstream development roles.

Research Questions $RQ_{2.1}$: Is there a difference between different roles regarding information needs?
   $RQ_{2.2}$: Is there even a difference between different persons with the same role?

If the latter RQ were to be answered with "yes", this would mean that there exists a further challenge, as for providing development roles with adequate requirements models, a detailed understanding of the factors that influence these differences within a particular role would become necessary. This is reflected in the next research question:

Research Question $RQ_{2.3}$: What are factors that influence particular information needs from the viewpoint of downstream development engineers with the same role?

Such factors include, for instance, expertise, familiarity with a project domain, motivation, personality, etc.

4.2.1 Related Work
As also outlined in [25], the concept of role-specific viewpoints on SRS has also been successfully applied in the area of inspections, where perspective-based reading techniques are used [24, 26]. However, in contrast to these techniques, which are applied to requirements specifications *after* they have been created, the proposed empirical work considers these perspectives already *during* the process of creating the documents. Furthermore, there also exist several viewpoint requirements engineering techniques such as [27, 28]. They focus, for instance, on specifications from various viewpoints of the system to be specified rather than from the viewpoint of document stakeholders who have to use the specification documents to perform their individual tasks. That is, the empirical research proposed in this paper provides an orthogonal view (one might call it a "filter") on those introduced above, as probably not all system viewpoints are of relevance for each downstream development role. Further related work can be found in the area of aspect-oriented requirements documents [29, 30]. To summarize, none of the existing approaches explicitly addresses role-specific information needs.

4.3   Results and Conclusions from Explorative Studies

In order to investigate the research goals and hypothesis stated in the previous paragraphs, three explorative studies were performed. In the following paragraphs, the main experiences and findings of these explorative studies will be summarized.

Table 1 Summary of ratings in the explorative studies

Artifact Types	A_S	A_E	U_E	U_T
Descriptions of Supported Stakeholder	2.46	2	1	1.78
Descriptions of Stakeholder Goals	2.31	1	2	1.5
Descriptions of Tasks	2.54	2	2	1.6
Descriptions of As-Is Processes	3.69	2	3.5	1.78
Descriptions of To-Be Processes	2.54	2	1.5	1.25
Descriptions of Domain Data	2.69	1.5	2	2.78
Descriptions of Interaction Data	2.75	1.5	2	2.63
Descriptions of Interactions	1.46	1.5	1.5	1.56
Descriptions of System Functions	1.33	1.5	2	2.25
Descriptions of Quality Attributes / NFRs	1.58	1.5	2	-
Descriptions of Technical Constraints	1.77	1	2.5	-
Very important	Important	Rather unimportant	Unimportant	

A_S = Architects SE Course, A_E = Architects Eye-Tracking, U_E = Usability Experts Eye-Tracking, U_T = Usability Experts Tutorial

A more detailed description of the studies and their results can be found in [21]. All material used in the studies can be found in [32].

For the investigation of G_1 ("Investigate information needs towards requirements specifications from the viewpoint of different development engineers"), the main purpose of these studies was to identify important artifact types needed for conducting typical tasks of downstream development roles (RQ_{1-1}), the level of detail at which relevant artifact types should be specified (RQ_{1-2}), and what notation would be preferred (RQ_{1-3}). For all these studies, we used a set of typical artifacts as a baseline. These artifacts are typically created when a goal- and task-oriented requirements engineering approach (see Sect. 3) is applied in software projects in the domain of complex information systems. These artifact types comprise, for example, stakeholder descriptions, goal descriptions, task descriptions, business process and workflow descriptions, interaction descriptions, data descriptions, quality requirements, etc. [1]. Table 1 shows the artifact types that were used and how they were rated in the three studies by the downstream development roles. The studies comprised analyzing a project in a student course, an eye-tracking study with an SRS with professional architects and UI designers, and a study performed at a usability professionals event.

The analysis of the collected data revealed that for example from the viewpoint of software architecture experts, descriptions of goals and technical requirements are considered to be the most important models, directly followed by descriptions of quality requirements, data requirements, interactions, and system functions. Usability experts strongly rely on artifacts specifying detailed information about supported stakeholders, goals, "to-be" processes, and interactions. Regarding notations we found that especially notations that modeled the elements graphically are very useful from the perspective of both software architecture experts and usability experts. Analyzing the ratings of the architecture experts, one might conclude that the study shows that all models are needed for software development, at least from the architects' point of view. However, when we analyze the data from the perspective of the research questions of research goal G_2, we realize that this conclusion would have been too fast and invalid. For example, from the viewpoint of the architects in the student project, As-Is descriptions were considered unimportant, and the usability experts also considered the As-Is descriptions unimportant.

Therefore, a detailed analysis of the data with regard to research goal G_2: ("Investigate whether there are any differences in the information needs from the viewpoints of different downstream development roles") is necessary. We also had to investigate whether there exists any difference between the roles ($RQ_{2.1}$) or even between different persons with the same role ($RQ_{2.2}$). To achieve this, we analyzed the collected data with regard to any differences between different roles and persons. As an example, we repeated the eye-tracking study, which we had initially performed with architects, with usability experts and compared the ratings we collected by means of the questionnaire to the data we collected from the architecture experts. As summarized in Table 1, columns A_E and U_E, there was only one total agreement regarding the rating (for descriptions of interactions). In all other cases, the rating was different – although in most cases only slightly different (i.e., very important vs. important). The biggest difference was detected regarding the rating of "as-is activities": Whereas the architects rated artifacts of this type as being important, the usability experts considered these artifacts unimportant. Another interesting observation was made with regard to the question whether differences exist between different persons with the same role. For this purpose, an analysis of the variances that exist within the data set of a particular group was considered for the study of the student project. The data indicates relatively high variance within the group, which means that the students tended to rate the importance of certain artifact types quite differently. In addition to the calculation of the variances within the student project, we can compare the importance rating of the student architects in Table 1, column A_S, with that of the architecture experts in column A_E and see the differences. Of course, the effect could be attributed to the different settings of the investigations, but it may also indicate that the importance rating, and hence the information needs, might depend on "individual" factors like expertise, project setting, personal motivation, etc.

We can conclude that the analysis of the collected data from the explorative studies regarding differences in the information needs revealed differences both between different roles and between persons with the same role. In the latter case, we assume that "individual" influence factors such as expertise, a particular project setting, or even personality or motivation might have an influence on the importance of artifact types, and hence on information needs.

The results of the explorative studies should not be misunderstood as an answer to the research questions stated in this section. Rather, they are intended to show that empirical research is needed to answer the research questions and that we need to further analyze which requirements models are really needed for a particular project setting. From the indications given by the explorative studies, we can assume that for some projects, various stakeholders do not require the full set of requirements models.

5   Summary and Future Challenges

In this paper, we showed current challenges in modeling requirements for complex information systems. We showed the challenge to integrate end-user requirements, business requirements, and technical requirements in our models. Further, we argued for strong integration of functional and non-functional requirements in information systems models. A further challenge is the integration of the knowledge about the capabilities of existing systems into the requirements models. We discussed which concepts of the domain and system could be modeled. Particularly for complex information systems, requirements models serve as a source of communication and information for a variety of roles involved in up- and downstream activities such as architecture, design, and testing. In order to answer the question of which models are really needed for specifying complex information systems, we need to know the specific information needs of the requirements models' stakeholders. We showed that our research community needs to better understand the particular information needs of up- and downstream development roles. We elaborated key research questions that need to be solved by the community. The results of explorative studies that were performed show that this kind of research can offer valuable insights we can use to improve the models for complex information systems. We presented a summary of the results of these studies, which show that there are differences in the information needs of software development stakeholders that need to be further analyzed in future work. But this is not the only important future work that we see with regard to modeling complex information systems in the future. In this section, we would also like to outline additional future challenges that will have a strong impact on the modeling of complex information systems, may even be disruptive to the modeling of complex information systems, and should guide parts of our future work. These challenges are grounded in observations we see in current trends in the state of the art as well as on technological observations we perceive in industry.

Future Challenge 1: Crowd-Sourced RE   In the information systems domain, we see a class of systems emerge that has a massive number of end-users. Examples from the private domain are social networks. With the advent of so-called smart software ecosystems, we will also see more and more information systems with several thousands of end-users emerge. Examples are information systems in smart cities or networked systems that include data from transportation systems. Potentially, all citizens are end-users of such systems. For requirements engineering, especially for the evolution of such systems, we foresee that crowd-sourcing will take place to support requirements elicitation. In addition to automatic data that will be collected from the end-users and will be (semi-)automatically processed, intentional and direct feedback (e.g., via videos, pictures or textual requirements [33]) will be used in gathering requirements. Finding an efficient way to integrate this information into the models for these kinds of complex information systems will be a huge challenge in future research.

Future Challenge 2: IT as Inspiration, Rather Than Support of Existing Processes This future challenge can be seen as a consequence of the current challenge 3: "Incorporation of information from existing solutions". In a recent Dagstuhl workshop [34], the RE community discussed that we are increasingly moving away from supporting well-known (business) processes with IT to a situation where IT offers support that enables new processes. So IT will provide capabilities to the private and professional communities that cannot be derived via classical RE methods in an elicitation-based manner. Rather, IT inspires communities to live or work differently. In this sense, we have to reason on how this will impact the models of these complex information systems. The information needs of software development roles regarding requirements models might strongly differ from current information needs. In information systems for private life, "trial and error" strategies are often used. For example: New applications for mobile phones emerge, but only few are or remain successful. In the professional environment, companies could make use of this new trend, but they want to make sure that there is a successful business model behind the IT solution. Typically, they are reluctant to use "trial and error" to find out whether a future business model will be successful. We know that prototyping significantly reduces requirements and design errors [35]. Especially for those systems, there is a strong need to offer rapid prototyping also for larger, professional size scenarios. Instead of having the capability to create single prototypes for small information systems in the requirements phase, a rapid prototyping environment for large-scale systems of systems will be needed. In such a setting, the emphasis on requirements models might be less or different.

Future Challenge 3: Importance of User Experience A strong trend that we see for information systems of the future is the need to provide a positive user experience to the end-users [36]. Currently, information systems try to satisfy the classical usability requirements. This is also the reason why we strongly integrated usability aspects into the information systems concepts outlined in Sect. 3. But more and more emphasis is placed on the user experience of the products, for example on whether systems appear trustworthy or whether they motivate the end-users to achieve specific goals. The concepts we use in Sect. 3 do not cover these aspects; they need extensions. We believe that user experience requirements are strongly intertwined with the current concepts of requirements engineering, but more research is needed to find out how to address this challenge.

Acknowledgments We would like to sincerely thank Dieter Rombach for inspiring our RE work. Especially in the area of non-functional requirements, Dieter Rombach has been the author's advisor for this topic. The software engineering fundamentals and the foundations for empirical work he established also had a fundamental influence on the research described in this paper. We would furthermore like to thank all members of the Fraunhofer IESE Requirements Engineering team who performed research on the topics described in this paper together with the author during the last decade.

References

1. Benbya, H., McKelvey, B.: Toward a complexity theory of information systems development. J. Inf. Technol. People **19**(1), 12–34 (2006)
2. Cockburn, A.: Writing Effective Use Cases. Addison-Wesley, Harlow (2000)
3. Rumbaugh, J., et al.: The Unified Modeling Language Reference Manual. Addison-Wesley, Reading (1998)
4. Keller, G., Nüttgens, M., Scheer, A.W.: Semantische Prozemodellierung auf der Grundlage Ereignisgesteuerter Prozeketten (EPK). Universität des Saarlandes, Saarbrücken (1992)
5. Business Process Modeling Notation Version 2.0, Feb 2013, http://www.omg.org/spec/BPMN/2.0/
6. Lamsweerde, A. van: Goal-oriented requirements engineering: a roundtrip from research to practice. In: Proceedings of 12th IEEE International Requirements Engineering Conference, IEEE (2004)
7. Maiden, N., Minocha, S., Manning, K., Ryan, M.: REWS-SAVRE: systematic scenario generation and use. In: Proceedings of IEEE International Requirements Engineering Conference, IEEE (1998)
8. Doerr, J.: Elicitation of a complete set of non-functional requirements. Fraunhofer Verlag, Stuttgart (2011). (Ph. D. theses in experimental software engineering; vol. 34). (Zugl.: Kaiserslautern, Technische Universität. Dissertation 2010). ISBN 978-3-8396-0261-4
9. Paech, B., Kohler, K.: Task-driven requirements in object-oriented development. Perspectives on Software Engineering. Kluwer (2004)
10. Rombach, D., Doerr, J.: Lecture Requirements Engineering. University of Kaiserslautern
11. Adam, S., Doerr, J., Eisenbarth, M., Gross, A.: Using task-oriented requirements engineering in different domains – experiences with application in research and industry, Requirements Engineering Conference, 2009. RE '09. 17th IEEE International Requirements Engineering Conference, pp. 267–272, vol., no., 31 Aug–4 Sept 2009
12. Roberston, S., Robertson, J.: Mastering the Requirements Process. Addison-Wesley, Harlow (2006)
13. Cooper, A., Reimann, R., Cronin, D.: About Face 3.0: The Essentials of Interaction Design. Wiley, Indianapolis (2007)
14. Basili, V.R., Heidrich, J., Lindvall, M., Münch, J., Regardie, M., Rombach, D., Seaman, C., Trendowicz, A.: Linking software development and business strategy through measurement. IEEE Comput. **43**(4), 57–65 (2010)
15. Dardenne, A., van Lamsweerde, A., Fickas, S.: Goal directed requirements acquisition. Sci. Comput. Program. **20**, 3–50 (1993)
16. Yu, E.S.K.: Towards modeling and reasoning support for early-phase requirements engineering. In: Proceedings of the Third IEEE International Symposium on Requirements Engineering, IEEE (1997)
17. Beyer, H., Holtzblatt, K.: Contextual Design: Defining Customer Centered Systems. Morgan Kaufmann, San Francisco (1998)
18. Davis, A.M.: System phenotypes. IEEE Softw. **20**(4), 54–56 (2003)
19. Adam, S., Doerr, J.: Towards early consideration of non-functional requirements at the business process level. In: Khosrow-Pour, M. (ed.) Managing Worldwide Operations and Communications with Information Technology. Proceedings of the 2007 Information Resources Management Association International Conference, pp. 227–230. Igi Publishing, Hershey (2007)

20. Doerr, J., Kerkow, D., Koenig, T., Olsson, T., Suzuki T.: Non-functional requirements in industry – three case studies adopting an experience-based NFR method. In: IEEE Computer Society: 13th IEEE International Requirements Engineering Conference. RE 2005 – Proceedings, pp. 373–382. IEEE Computer Society, Los Alamitos (2005)

21. Gross, A., Doerr, J.: What you need is what you get!: the vision of view-based requirements specifications, Requirements Engineering Conference (RE), 2012 20th IEEE International, vol., no., pp. 171–180. 24–28 Sept 2012

22. Somerville, I.: Software Engineering, 7th edn, pp. 136–140. Pearson Educational Limited, Harlow (2004)

23. Rombach, D., Lecture: Grundlagen des Software Engineering. University of Kaiserslautern (2012)

24. Ciolkowski, M., Differding, C., Laitenberger, O., Munch, J.: Empirical investigation of perspective-based reading: a replicated experiment, ISERN 97–13 (1997)

25. Gross, A.: Perspective-based specification of efficiently and effectively usable requirements documents. In: Proceedings of Doctoral Symposium RE'10, Sydney 2010

26. Basili, V., Green, S., Laitenberger, O., Shull, F., Sorumgaard, S., Zelkowitz, M.: The empirical investigation of perspective based reading. Empir. Softw. Eng.Int. J. **1**, 133–164 (1996)

27. Sommerville, I., Sawyer, P.: Viewpoints: principles, problems and a practical approach to requirements engineering. Ann. Softw. Eng. **3**, 101–130 (1997)

28. Kotonya, G., Sommerville, I.: Viewpoints for requirements definition. BCS/IEE Softw. Eng. J. **7**(6), 375–387 (1992)

29. Araújo, J., Coutinho, P.: Identifying aspectual use cases using a viewpoint-oriented requirements method, In: Workshop on Early Aspects: Aspect-Oriented Requirements Engineering and Architectural Design, in conjunction with AOSD Conference 2003, (2003)

30. Rashid, A., Sawyer, P., Moreira, A., Araújo, J.: Early aspects: a model for aspect-oriented requirements engineering. In: 10th Anniversary Joint IEEE International Requirements Engineering Conference (RE'02), re, p. 199. (2002)

31. Wilson, T.D.: On user studies and information needs. J. Doc. **37**(1), 3–15 (1981)

32. Gross, A., Doerr, J.: Investigating information needs – elicitation guidelines. Fraunhofer IESE-Report, Nr. 033.12/E (2012)

33. Seyff, N., Graf, F., Maiden, N.: Using mobile RE tools to give end-users their own voice. In: Requirements Engineering Conference (RE), 2010 18th IEEE International, pp. 37–46, vol., no., 27 Sept–1 Oct 2010

34. Dagstuhl Workshop: Requirements management – novel perspectives and challenges. http://www.dagstuhl.de/en/program/calendar/semhp/?semnr=12442 (2013)

35. Endres, A., Rombach, D.: A Handbook of Software and Systems Engineering. Empirical Observations, Laws and Theories. The Fraunhofer IESE series on software engineering. Addison-Wesley, New York (2003). ISBN 0-321-15420-7

36. Nass, C., Adam, S., Doerr, J., Trapp, M., et al.: Balancing user and business goals in software development to generate positive user experience. In: Zacarias, M., Valente de Oliveira, J. (eds.) Human-Computer Interaction: The Agency Perspective. Studies in computational intelligence, vol. 396, pp. 29–53. Springer, Berlin (2012)

Continuous Process Improvement

Jens Heidrich

Abstract

Nowadays, a variety of different processes for the development and maintenance of software-intensive systems exists, ranging from agile development processes to classical plan-based approaches. There is no ultimate process that can be applied in each and every situation. It depends on the project goals and environment as well as on the required characteristics of the system under development. Development processes support organizations in developing software-intensive systems with certain quality characteristics, within a certain time span, and requiring a certain amount of effort. Continuous process improvement deals with the establishment and maintenance of high-quality processes, with analyzing their performance and effectiveness, and with initiating corresponding improvement actions if needed. In this chapter, we will take a closer look at how to systematically define and continuously improve development processes based on documented best practices and the use of measurement data collected during the enactment of the development process. The chapter highlights current challenges and presents solution approaches for establishing continuous process improvement in practice.

1 Introduction

There exists a variety of different processes for the development and maintenance of software-intensive systems. For an organization it is challenging to find the "right" process that fits to their specific needs and provides the right balance between the required formalism and the freedom needed for developing innovative software-intensive systems. Processes range from agile development processes such as XP

J. Heidrich (✉)
Fraunhofer Institute for Experimental Software Engineering, Kaiserslautern, Germany
e-mail: Jens.Heidrich@iese.fraunhofer.de

J. Münch and K. Schmid (eds.), *Perspectives on the Future of Software Engineering*,
DOI 10.1007/978-3-642-37395-4_8, © Springer-Verlag Berlin Heidelberg 2013

[1] or Scrum [2] to classical plan-based approaches such as RUP [3] or V-Modell XT [4], and several international and national standards such as ISO/IEC 12207 [5] or ISO/IEC 15288 [6]. Unfortunately, there is no ultimate process that can be applied in each and every situation. It depends on the project goals and environment as well as on the required characteristics of the system under development. Depending on these aspects, different techniques, methods, and tools have to be used as part of the development process to support the product characteristics of interest. For instance:

- Safety-critical systems (such as automobiles or power plants) require different development processes than information systems (such as accounting software and web applications).
- Contractor-subcontractor relationships in a project require a detailed understanding and planning of the interfaces required between all participants and a strong focus on coordinating the different activities and deliverables compared to doing in-house development only.

A process is defined as "a set of partially ordered steps intended to reach a goal" [7]. A development process is thus a means to an end (namely for obtaining that goal) and not an end in itself. It supports organizations in developing software-intensive systems with certain quality characteristics, within a certain time span, and requiring a certain amount of effort. In practice, the impact of a process on quality, time, and cost can only be investigated empirically or, if a formal model can be created, by applying simulation techniques. However, because of certain characteristics of development processes, the latter is often hard to perform. For instance, development processes are typically human-based and involve activities requiring a certain amount of creativity.

In this chapter, we will take a closer look at how to systematically define and continuously improve development processes based on documented best practices and making use of measurement data collected during the enactment of the development process. Continuous process improvement deals with the establishment and maintenance of high-quality processes, with analyzing their performance and effectiveness, and with initiating corresponding improvement actions if needed. There are several approaches to continuous process improvement, such as PDCA [8], Six Sigma [9], or Kaizen [10]. The improvement approaches presented in this chapter are largely based on the Quality Improvement Paradigm (QIP) [11], which describes a generic six-step improvement cycle: (1) characterize the environment and the improvement scope, (2) set goals for improvement, (3) choose procedures and improvement actions, (4) execute the procedures defined, (5) analyze the impact, and (6) package experiences and lessons learned based on the analysis results.

In principle, there are two major strategies for process improvement: First, processes can be improved by using best practices, e.g., elicited from company experts or external sources like standards such as CMMI [12] or ISO/IEC 15504 [13]. Second, processes can be improved by using measurement data for analyzing the characteristics of the activities and artifacts of a development process and generating improvement recommendations. Some typical challenges when dealing with continuous process improvement in these two areas are presented in Fig. 1.

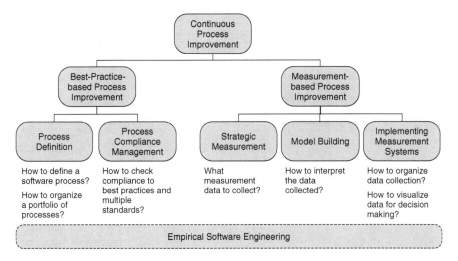

Fig. 1 Challenges in the area of continuous process improvement

Challenges related to best-practice-based process improvement include, but are not limited to, the following aspects:

- Process Definition: Before an organization can continuously improve its development processes, a key challenge is to define efficient and effective processes in the first place and capture the lived processes into reusable models. This is especially important for organizations that must deal with more than one process. For instance, if an organization develops software-intensive systems in multiple domains and environments, a portfolio of different processes with certain communalities and differences among them needs to be managed.

- Process Compliance Management: Nowadays, a variety of best practice catalogues exists on how to develop software-intensive systems. Depending on the application domain, different standards are prescribed that organizations have to adhere to as a precondition for developing a certain class of systems. In practice, it is a challenge to effectively make use of these best practices to systematically improve development processes and prove compliance to the multiple standards and practices required.

Challenges related to measurement-based process improvement include, but are not limited to, the following aspects:

- Strategic Measurement: The major challenge when dealing with measurement for continuous improvement is about what data are actually needed for satisfying the strategic goals behind process improvement.

- Model Building: A second challenge lies in analyzing and interpreting the measurement data for decision-making. Model building is the process of capturing the experience and knowledge of an organization into reusable models, which support practitioners in systematically using the measurement data to analyze the quality characteristics of interest and interpret the results.

- Implementing Measurement Systems: A third challenge is the actual implementation of measurement systems in practice, especially regarding how to present the data so that the different stakeholders involved can use the data for decision-making.

As shown in Fig. 1, the field of Empirical Software Engineering [14] is the foundation for investigating and empirically evaluating the impact of techniques, methods, and tools applied in a specific development context. Its challenges are addressed in different chapters of this book.

This chapter discusses different solution approaches regarding the challenges described above. Section 2 focuses on approaches for the systematic definition of development processes and the management of compliance to process standards and best practices. Section 3 focuses on approaches for the measurement-based improvement of development processes including how to set up measurement systems strategically, how to build models from measurement data, and how to practically implement measurement systems in an organization. The chapter concludes with a brief summary of lessons learned from the approaches presented and an outlook to future work.

2 Best-Practice-Based Process Improvement

This section focuses on process improvement based on best practices, which are either elicited from company experts or external sources like international standards and best practice catalogues. First of all, we discuss the basic definition and maintenance of development processes. Then we take a closer look at managing compliance to standards and best practices.

2.1 Process Definition

2.1.1 Process Selection

Before deciding about the lifecycle and the development philosophy, an organization should clearly define and evaluate the goals and characteristics the development process should accomplish [15] gives some guidance on how to select a suitable development process by investigating the major differences between agile and traditional plan-based approaches. First, it stresses that the development context should be analyzed carefully before deciding about selecting a specific development process. Second, existing experiences and knowledge, especially results from empirical evaluations, should be taken into account and documented transparently. Third, once defined, the process should not be static, but actively monitored, updated, and improved on a continuous basis based on data and feedback collected from enacting the development process.

2.1.2   Process Modeling and Documentation

There are two main approaches when modeling development processes: Prescriptive modeling defines how development activities *should* be done, whereas descriptive modeling defines how development activities *are* actually performed in an organization [16]. When dealing with continuous process improvement, a development process should not be prescribed by selecting a completely new process from scratch, but by considering how development is actually taking place, by analyzing the strengths and weaknesses of a descriptive model, and by introducing improvement changes in an incremental and iterative manner. Continuous improvement describes a cycle between *describing* the actual state and *prescribing* an improved process.

In any case, a process management system is needed to support an organization in modeling and documenting its development process consistently. Such systems use standardized languages for modeling the processes (such as SPEM [17]) or come with their own proprietary built-in modeling language and typically provide support for generating different kinds of representations from a process model (such as an electronic web-based process guide or a process handbook) [18] presents concrete requirements from the Japanese Aerospace Exploration Agency (JAXA) for supporting process management in practice. JAXA has to deal with complex process models in a distributed collaboration context. Figure 2 illustrates an excerpt of the evaluation results. Overall, 11 categories of requirements were defined together with JAXA's process experts and were evaluated for a set of candidate process management tools. For each tool, a summary of the assessment results as well as major advantages and disadvantages were given. Each tool has its individual advantages and disadvantages with respect to the specific requirements of an organization. In general, it is important to have a clear picture of the needs of an organization related to process management before selecting an appropriate tool.

2.1.3   Process Tailoring and Portfolio Management

Large organizations that have to deal with software-intensive systems from different domains, probably delivered from external suppliers, have to cope with managing not a single development process, but a whole portfolio of processes that have certain parts in common and certain discriminators [19] discusses approaches for dealing with this kind of settings exemplified by a typical contractor- supplier relationship in the aerospace domain. JAXA provides a standard development process for all units, which must be tailored to the specific needs of every development project. The SCOPING approach is proposed for analyzing the process needs of development projects and the products produced as well as the capabilities of the existing processes. A recommendation was given on which processes to maintain, which ones to discard, and which ones to apply in projects of a specific type. Figure 3 gives an illustration of the resulting process landscape. Analysis revealed that all project types share 86 % of their activities and 77 % of their work products.

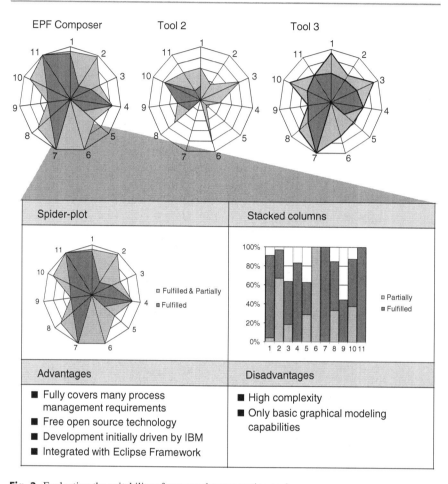

Fig. 2 Evaluating the suitability of process documentation tools

This means that a systematic analysis of the process portfolio helps to achieve a significant reduction in process management effort.

2.2   Process Compliance Management

The motivation for compliance management is manifold. For instance, organizations want to improve their process models by using catalogues of best practices, they want to make sure that the lived processes comply with their internal regulations, or they are forced by their market environment or by legal regulations to prove compliance with national and international standards. Regarding the latter, organizations nowadays must comply with a variety of different practices and standards, like best-practice catalogues, such as PMBoK [21], lifecycle process models, such

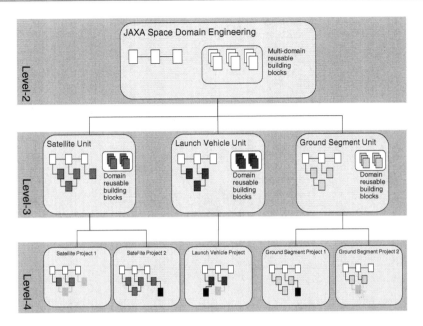

Fig. 3 Process portfolio management at JAXA [20]

as ISO/IEC 12207 [5], process maturity and assessment models, such as ISO/IEC 15504 [13], process standards from certain industry sectors, such as V-Modell XT [4], or domain-specific standards, such as the automotive safety standards ISO 26262 [22]. Checking and proving compliance to all relevant standards is a very effort-consuming process.

Kowalczyk and Steinbach [23] gives an overview of approaches for compliance management and proposes a method for achieving compliance between a company's process models (called process guides) and the requirements from multiple standards. Apart from analyzing the initial compliance of a development process, the focus is on the systematic maintenance of compliance in order to avoid erosion over time. The latter may be caused by an update of one or more of the respective standards or by changes/adaptations of a company's own process models over time. Figure 4 gives an overview of the tool-supported approach for systematic management of process model compliance in multi-standard scenarios. Having such an approach allows an organization to manage compliance more efficiently (requiring less effort) and effectively (detecting more compliance issues).

3   Measurement-Based Process Improvement

This section focuses on process improvement based on the collection, analysis, and systematic usage of measurement data. First, the topic of strategic measurement will be discussed to determine which data is actually needed for monitoring

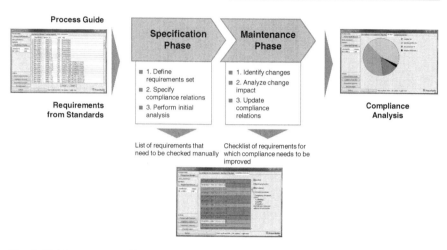

Fig. 4 Multi-process compliance management (cf. [23])

and improving development processes. After that, we will discuss approaches for building models from the data collected in order to support practitioners in making systematic use of the measurement. Finally, we will illustrate approaches for practically implementing measurement systems in an organization.

3.1 Strategic Measurement

Software measurement (see [24]) is used for understanding the current state/ performance of processes (and the corresponding characteristics of development artifacts and activities), for identifying potential areas of improvement, for validating the effects of a change, and for progress monitoring and controlling of development projects. In practice, it is a challenge to determine which data are actually needed to address the strategic goals of an organization. In particular if the data collection process can be automated, there is a tendency towards collecting all data provided via tools instead of focusing on those relevant for the business context. On the one hand, too much unnecessary data is collected, which is not analyzed at all or is analyzed in the wrong environment. On the other hand, important aspects cannot be analyzed because relevant data is actually missing. In general, this leads to wrong conclusions being drawn from measurement data and ultimately to insufficient pay-off for the cost invested into data collection and analysis.

In recent years, several approaches have been developed that address goal-oriented measurement; i.e., deriving metrics from clearly specified measurement needs and goals. One of the most popular ones is the Goal/Question/Metric paradigm (GQM) [25]. Even though GQM supports an organization in specifying their needs with respect to measurement, it is still challenging to combine the different bits and pieces into a meaningful and consistent picture across the whole

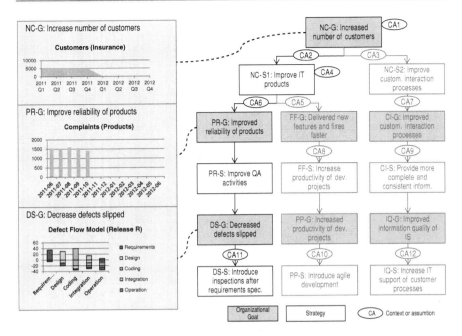

Fig. 5 Example GQM$^+$Strategies® model for strategic measurement

organization and illustrate the connection with organizational goals and improvement strategies. GQM$^+$Strategies® [26] is an extension of the classical GQM approach for strategic measurement. It provides a framework and notation to help organizations define operational, measureable business goals, select strategies for implementing them, communicate those goals and strategies throughout the organization, and translate these goals into lower-levels goals. Moreover, the effectiveness of strategies at all levels of the organization can be assessed by using measurement data and the achievement of business goals can be systematically evaluated. In the literature, a variety of approaches exists for aligning different aspects of goals and strategies of an organization, some even addressing the linkage to measurement data (such as [27], [28], [29], or [30]). The aim of GQM$^+$Strategies® is not to replace these approaches, but to close the existing gaps with respect to strategic measurement.

Figure 5 illustrates excerpts of an example GQM$^+$Strategies® model. The right side shows a hierarchy of organizational goals and strategies. The left side highlights some measurement data that are collected to check attainment of the goals and the success/failure of the strategies used. One important aspect of a GQM$^+$Strategies® model lies in clearly defining the rationale for the connection between goals and strategies. Rationales can be defined as context factors (known facts) or assumptions about certain relationships. Table 1 summarizes context factors and assumptions for the model excerpt shown in Fig. 5. A bottom-level strategy (DS-S) of the highlighted branch may actually be to introduce requirements inspections as one concrete process improvement action in order to find potential defects as early as

Table 1 Overview of context and assumptions

ID	Type	Description
CA1	Context	Company provides banking and insurance services; has a lot of customers in the banking area, but only few in the insurance area
CA2	Assumption	The quality of the IT products has to be improved
CA3	Assumption	The quality of the customer interaction processes has to be improved
CA4	Context	The services are built upon an Enterprise information system
CA5	Context	Customers complain that it takes too long to deliver new releases
CA6	Context	Customers complain that the IT products are not reliable
CA7	Context	Customers complain about customer interaction process
CA8	Assumption	The delay of existing projects is mainly responsible for the inability to deliver new features and bug fixes faster
CA9	Context	Customers complain about inconsistent and incomplete information
CA10	Context	According to the experience from the recently run pilot project, agile development principles will be able to speed up software development
CA11	Context	Too many defects appear in the design and coding stage
CA12	Context	Not all services of X are completely IT supported; some have to be provided manually, which decreases information quality

possible. This in turn will help the organization to decrease the number of defects that slip to later stages of the development process (DS-G). Having less defect slippage is related to the organizational strategy of improving all quality assurance activities (PR-S). This strategy was defined to achieve improved reliability of the organization's IT products (PR-G). Improved IT products (NC-S1) will in turn attract more customers to use the (IT-based) services of the company (NC-G).

The entire model provides an organization with a mechanism for not only defining measurement consistent with larger, upper-level organizational concerns, but also for interpreting the resulting measurement data at each level. Having such a chain of arguments also supports an organization in demonstrating the values of software-related process improvement initiatives, such as introducing a new inspection technique into the development process. The impact of these models can be evaluated directly in terms of higher-level goals of the organization and makes the benefits for an organization measurable.

3.2 Model Building

Model building is the process of capturing an organization's experience and knowledge in reusable models, which support practitioners in systematically using measurement data to analyze process and product quality characteristics of interest and interpret the results. In practice, a variety of usage scenarios for measurement

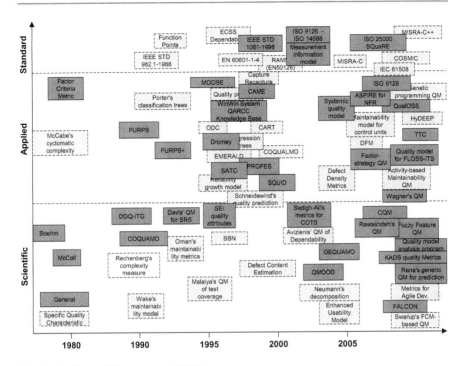

Fig. 6 Quality model landscape (cf. [31])

and analysis models exists, including descriptive models (e.g., for describing current quality characteristics of processes and products), analysis models (e.g., for identifying improvement potential), comparative models (e.g., for internal and external benchmarking), predictive models (e.g., for predicting characteristics of interests such as development effort and error proneness of the system), and prescriptive models (e.g., defining guidelines for proactive process and product improvement). Quality models are a means for defining and operationalizing the term "quality". They support stakeholders in interpreting the measurement data (e.g., by defining thresholds distinguishing between acceptable and not acceptable quality) and aggregating the results in order to obtain an evaluation/assessment of the different quality characteristics of interest. This includes quality characteristics of processes/activities (such as performance, efficiency, or effectiveness) as well as characteristics of products/artifacts created in a development process (such as reliability, maintainability, security, or safety).

Figure 6 gives an overview of the outcomes of a systematic literature review and state-of-the-practice survey in the area of software quality models [31]. It contains 77 quality models ranging from general standards related to software product quality (such as ISO/IEC 25000 [32]) via domain-specific standards (such as MISRA [33]), to quality models from academic research (such as [34]). Some models address quality in general (dark gray boxes), while others address specific quality characteristics (light gray boxes).

3.2.1   Product Quality Models

When it comes to product quality, a mandatory, applicable, and tool-supported quality standard for software development is missing. Product quality models focus on certain quality characteristics of the final product that is delivered to the customer or on intermediate artifacts from the development process. Existing models are hard to use out-of-the-box, because the abstraction level is often too high and it is difficult to come up with reliable and collectable measures. Moreover, there is no universal quality model that can be applied in every environment. Finding the "right" model depends on a clear picture of the goals to be obtained from using the model. Moreover, the model needs to be tailored to company specifics, which is an effort-consuming process. There is also a lack of reliable evaluation criteria and little support for the meaningful aggregation of quality assessment results, which prevents meaningful comparisons and benchmarking.

The Quamoco research project, which aimed at a "Quality Standard for Software-Intensive Systems" [35] provides a comprehensive framework for the cost-efficient specification, adaptation, and practical usage of quality models. Quamoco offers a core model capturing quality characteristics, metrics, and evaluation rules essential for all kind of software-intensive systems and different domain-specific extensions. Moreover, fine-grained customization and quality evaluation processes are defined (see [36, 37]). The corresponding tool suite supports the selection of appropriate domain-specific-models, their tailoring, and connections to the measurement instruments actually collecting and analyzing the data and feeding the analysis results back into the model.

3.2.2   Process Quality Models

Process quality models focus on certain quality characteristics of the overall development process or certain activities thereof, such as performance, efficiency, or effectiveness. Again, there is no standard model that can be used in every environment. It depends on organizational goals and strategies, which should be addressed by the model, as well as on historical measurement data available for building the model. In general, there are three different types of models that can be distinguished: (1) models that are solely based on expert opinion; (2) models that are solely based on historical project data; (3) hybrid models that combine expert knowledge and historical data. For the second type, we may further distinguish between models based upon in-house data and models that come with an external knowledge base containing data from other organizations.

Nowadays, the typical case in practice is that some historical measurement data is available as well as some experts who can provide support in creating a model, but they are only available for a limited amount of time. For that reason, our research focuses on hybrid approaches that try to make use of the data that is actually available in addition to capturing expert knowledge in reusable models.

One such model is the CoBRA® approach for Cost Estimation, Benchmarking, and Risk Assessment [38]. It supports organizations in creating a custom-tailored model for predicting the effort of a development project based on product

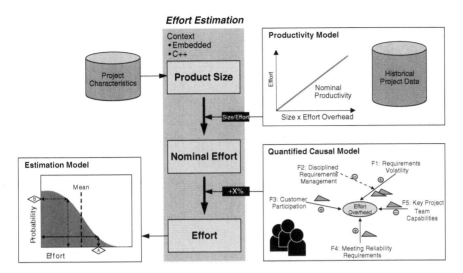

Fig. 7 CoBRA®: prediction model for development effort

requirements and project characteristics. Figure 7 gives an overview of the basic principles. For a certain type of projects within a certain context, historical project data are analyzed in terms of the nominal productivity of these historical projects. Nominal productivity refers to the *ideal* productivity of a development project under optimal environmental characteristics. By using the nominal productivity and an estimate of the size of the product that is going to be developed (e.g., in lines of code or a functional size measure), the nominal effort is estimated. Afterwards, the nominal effort is adjusted according to known impact factors within the context of interest. For instance, volatile requirements and an inexperienced team will certainly increase the development effort significantly. All these factors are captured in a so-called quantified causal model, which stores expert knowledge regarding the impact of these factors. Finally, CoBRA provides a probability-based estimation model including the uncertainty of experts. It basically judges the risk (probability) of exceeding a certain development effort for a given project. The use of these risk profiles allows projects to be benchmarked with respect to their risk of exceeding their budget. The accuracy of such an estimation depends on many factors including, but not limited to, the accuracy of the size estimate of the product under development. However, experiences from practical applications of the CoBRA approach (such as [39]) have shown fairly high estimation accuracy. Moreover, such models are well accepted among company experts because their experience and knowledge can systematically be captured in an estimation model. Finally, identifying the most critical impact factors that drive the effort and cost of a development project allows for systematically introducing improvement actions to cope with these effort drivers.

3.2.3 Combining Process and Product Quality Models

Even though process and product quality models have been discussed separately, there are strong interrelationships and dependencies between process and product quality. For instance, quality models focusing on analyzing process characteristics may use process- *and* product-related data for doing so. The CoBRA effort prediction model uses the product's size as one major input for arriving at an estimate, with the assumption that there is a certain correlation between the size of the product under development and the development effort of a project. In recent years, research has also focused on extending the principles of hybrid approaches, such as CoBRA, to other areas. The HyDEEP approach, for instance, provides a model for estimating the defect content of a development product and the effectiveness of the quality assurance activities [40]. In that sense it is a product quality model (in terms of estimating defect content) and a process quality model (in terms of estimating the effectiveness of quality assurance) as well.

3.3   Implementing Measurement Systems

One aspect that is crucial for integrating measurement sustainably in an organization is how to actually implement measurement systems in practice, especially in terms of how to present the data so that the different stakeholders involved can use the data for decision-making. Nowadays, a broad range of tools exists for collecting measurement data. The first challenge lies in integrating and condensing the data provided along the goals and strategies of interests and the models created. For that purpose, business intelligence tools (such as Pentaho[1]) are typically used, which come with a data warehouse (containing the data of interest) as well as data analysis and presentation capabilities. The second challenge lies in visualizing the data according to the specific needs of the stakeholders to allow intuitive understanding and interpretation of the data as well as mechanisms for interacting with the data (e.g., abstraction and drill-down mechanisms) [41].

The Fraunhofer M-System [42] is a measurement framework that is able to access different software analysis tools and databases containing measurement data, integrate these data, and create different kinds of visualizations. Figure 8 illustrates the general architecture of the framework and presents some sample visualization generated. The measurement framework follows a classical three-layered design: One layer collects data from the different data sources provided. All data, whether from external data sources or provided by the built-in static code analysis capabilities, are mapped to a relational database. A second layer processes the data stored in the relational database and triggers a post-processing process to create different types of visualizations. A set of pre-defined queries may be launched to trigger different kinds of data analysis mechanisms. The third layer provides

---

[1] See http://www.pentaho.com

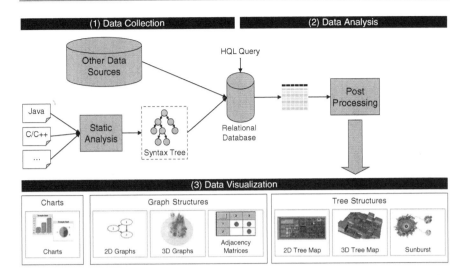

Fig. 8 Fraunhofer M-system measurement framework

interactive data visualizations to the end user and allows for interaction with the second layer (e.g., for launching new queries drilling down into the data).

Different types of visualizations are built into the tool: Standard visualizations (such as simple line, bar, and pie charts) are provided for visualizing measurement data. More advanced graph structures are provided for visualizing the structure and relationships of software-intensive systems. For instance, a 2D/3D graph may illustrate the calling relationships between software components. Measurement data may be integrated by using the size or color of a graph node or edge. Finally, visualization mechanisms are provided for visualizing hierarchical relationships (such as tree maps [43] or sunburst charts [44]) by using visualization metaphors (such as mapping a software system to a city structure). For instance, a tree map may illustrate components of a software system. Each component is represented by a building on the three-dimensional tree map. The base area of a building equals the size of the component (e.g., measured in lines of code); the height is mapped to the complexity of the component (e.g., in terms of interface or algorithmic complexity). Using data visualization mechanisms, outliers and potentially risky software components can be identified and actions can be taken to improve the quality characteristics of interest.

4   Lessons Learned and Future Work

This chapter gave an overview of techniques, methods, and tools for the systematic definition and continuous improvement of development processes based on documented best practices and using measurement data collected during the enactment of the development process. The lessons learned from the practical application of the presented approaches include, but are not limited to, the following aspects regarding the challenges discussed in the first section:

- Process Definition: (a) Clearly define and evaluate the goals and characteristics the development process should accomplish before deciding about the lifecycle and the development philosophy. (b) Introduce process changes in an incremental and iterative manner in order to gain acceptance among all stakeholders. (c) Define and evaluate the needs related to process management before selecting an appropriate process modeling language and corresponding tool. (d) Analyze which processes are suited for which context in order to save process maintenance effort.
- Process Compliance Management: (a) There is no universal set of best practices everybody should follow. Systematically analyze the strengths and weaknesses of the development process regarding the organizational goals and development context and make use of the best practices addressing the weaknesses. (b) Avoid compliance erosion by introducing mechanisms for continuously checking compliance to relevant standards and practices.
- Strategic Measurement: (a) Measurement is a means to an end and not an end in itself. Keep in mind the strategic goals for collecting the data and, consequently, collect the data *needed* instead of all data possible. (b) Measurement should be driven by specific information needs and interpreted in a particular context in order to obtain valid conclusions. (c) Measurement should be aligned to organizational goals and strategies to allow making sound strategic improvement decisions.
- Model Building: (a) Build reusable models for capturing the experience and knowledge of the organization. (b) A model is no oracle. Continuously evaluate its accuracy and improve models over time.
- Implementing Measurement Systems: (a) Measurement needs to be integrated into the organizational processes and procedures in order to make it sustainable in an organization and avoid overhead. (b) More effort should be spent on analyzing and interpreting the data than on collecting the data. (c) Data visualization is crucial for getting acceptance from all stakeholders and for being able to understand and interpret measurement data.

In the future, continuous process improvement will be faced with new challenges that need to be mastered by an organization if it wants to defend and further expand its position on the market. Processes and quality assurance mechanisms must react to ever shorter business and technology lifecycles and must permit flexible adaptation. Moreover, software products and systems are increasingly being developed in a distributed manner in heterogeneous environments. This is particularly true for cyber-physical systems, where organizations from different domains work together on an integrated solution, each with its own special requirements regarding the integration of different processes and quality management mechanisms. In consequence, process improvement approaches must be able to be easy to adapt to new goals and development contexts. Moreover, they must be able to address very heterogeneous requirements from different domains probably using different development processes, and must be capable of integrating all these aspects into comprehensive models for process improvement.

Acknowledgments First of all, we would like to thank Dieter Rombach for providing us with the right environment for doing applied research in the area of continuous process improvement. In addition, we would like to thank the whole team at Fraunhofer IESE that contributed to the development of all techniques, methods, and tools mentioned in this chapter. Finally, we would like to thank Sonnhild Namingha, Andreas Jedlitschka, and Rolf-Hendrik van Lengen for their valuable comments and feedback.

References

1. Beck, K., Andres, C.: Extreme Programming Explained: Embrace Change, 2nd edn. Addison-Wesley, Boston (2004)
2. Schwaber, K., Beedle, M.: Agile Software Development with Scrum. Prentice Hall, Upper Saddle River (2001)
3. Kruchten, P.: The Rational Unified Process: An Introduction, 3rd edn. Addison-Wesley, Boston (2003)
4. V-Modell® XT, Version 1.3 (2009)
5. ISO/IEC 12207: Systems and software engineering – software life cycle processes (2008)
6. ISO/IEC 15288: Systems and software engineering – system life cycle processes (2008)
7. Feiler, P.H., Humphrey, W.S.: Software process development and enactment: concepts and definitions. Software Process pp. 28–40. 25–26 Feb (1993)
8. Deming, W.E.: Out of the Crisis. The MIT Press, Cambridge (2000)
9. Tayntor, C.B.: Six Sigma Software Development. Auerbach Publications, Boca Raton (2007)
10. Brunet, P., New, S.: Kaizen in Japan: an empirical study. Int. J. Oper. Prod. Man. **23**(12), 1426–1446 (2003)
11. Basili, V., Caldiera, G., Rombach, D.: The experience factory. In: Encyclopedia of Software Engineering, vol. 1, pp. 469–476. Wiley, New York (1994)
12. CMMI Product Team, CMMI® for Development – Version 1.3, CMU/SEI-2010-TR-033, Carnegie Mellon University (2010)
13. ISO/IEC TR 15504–6, Information technology – Process assessment – Part 6: An exemplar system life cycle process assessment model (2008)
14. Rombach, D.: Empirical software engineering models: can they become the equivalent of physical laws in traditional engineering? Int. J. Softw.Inform. **5**(3), 525–534 (2011)
15. Armbrust, O., Rombach, D.: The right process for each context: objective evidence needed. In: Proceeding of the Proceedings of the 2011 International Conference on Software and Systems Process (ICSSP), pp. 237–241 (2011)
16. Becker-Kornstaedt, U., Belau, W.: Descriptive process modeling in an industrial environment: experience and guidelines. In: Proceedings of EWSPT, LNCS 1780, Springer, pp. 176–189 (2000)
17. Object Management Group: Software & systems process engineering metamodel specification (SPEM) Version 2.0 (2008)
18. Kowalczyk, M., Armbrust, O., Katahira, M., Kaneko, T., Miyamoto, Y., Koishi, Y.: Requirements for process management support. In: Proceedings of the International Conference on Software and Systems Process (ICSSP), pp. 179–183 (2011)
19. Armbrust, O., Katahira, M., Kaneko, T., Miyamoto, Y., Koishi, Y.: Which processes are needed in five years? Strategic process portfolio management. In: Proceedings of the International SPICE Days 2010, 21–23 June, Stuttgart, Germany (2010)
20. Armbrust, O., Ocampo, A.: Software process lines and standard traceability analysis. In: Proceedings of the 7th Workshop of Critical Software (WSoC), Tokyo, (2009)

21. Project Management Institute: A Guide to the Project Management Body of Knowledge (PMBOK® Guide), 4th edn. Project Management Institute (2008)
22. ISO 26262–2: Road vehicles – Functional safety – Part 2: Management of functional safety (2011)
23. Kowalczyk, M., Steinbach, S.: Managing process model compliance in multi-standard scenarios using a tool-supported approach. In: Proceedings of the 13th International Conference on Product-Focused Software Process Improvement (PROFES), pp. 355–360 (2012)
24. ISO/IEC 15939: Systems and software engineering – Measurement process, (2007)
25. Basili, V., Caldiera, G., Rombach, D.: Goal, question metric paradigm. In: Encyclopedia of Software Engineering, vol. 1, pp. 528–532. Wiley, New York (1994)
26. Basili, V.R., Heidrich, J., Lindvall, M., Münch, J., Regardie, M., Rombach, D., Seaman, C., Trendowicz, A.: Linking software development and business strategy through measurement. IEEE Comp. 43(4)), 57–65 (2010)
27. Object Management Group (OMG): The Business Motivation Model (BMM) V. 1.1. from www.omg.org (2010). Retrieved 6 Aug 2010
28. US Department of Defense and US Army (DoD): Practical Software and Systems Measurement: A Foundation for Objective Project Management. v. 4.0c, from www.psmsc.com. Mar 2003
29. Kaplan, R., Norton, D.: The balanced scorecard – measures that drive performance, Harv. Bus. Rev. 70(1), 71–79 (1992)
30. ISACA: Control Objectives for Information and related Technology (CoBIT®), from www. isaca.org (2007). Retrieved 4 Dec 2007
31. Kläs, M., Heidrich, J., Münch, J., Trendowicz, A.: CQML Scheme: a classification scheme for comprehensive quality model landscapes. In: Proceedings of the 35th EUROMICRO Conference (SEAA), IEEE Computer Society, pp. 243–250 (2009)
32. ISO/IEC 25000–1: Software product Quality Requirements and Evaluation (SQuaRE) – Guide to SQuaRE (2005)
33. MISRA Report 5, Software Metrics (1995)
34. Avizienis, A., Laprie, J. C., Randell, B.: Fundamental Concepts of Dependability. UCLA CSD Report no. 010028, LAAS Report no. 01–256, Newcastle University Report no. CS-TR-73. Online available at: www.malekinezhad.com/FOCD.pdf (2001)
35. Wagner, S., Lochmann, K., Heinemann, L., Kläs, M., Trendowicz, A., Plösch, R., Seidl, A., Goeb, A., Streit, J.: The quamoco product quality modeling and assessment approach. In: Proceedings of the 34th International Conference on Software Engineering (ICSE 2012), pp. 1133–1142. Zurich (2012)
36. Kläs, M., Lampasona, C., Münch, J.: Adapting software quality models: practical challenges, approach, and first empirical results. In: Proceedings of the 37th EUROMICRO Conference (SEAA), pp. 341–348. Oulu (2011)
37. Trendowicz, A., Kläs, M., Lampasona, C., Münch, J., Körner, C., Saft, M.: Model-based product quality evaluation with multi-criteria decision analysis. Proceedings of the Joined International Conferences on Software Measurement (IWSM/MetriKon/Mensura), pp. 3–20. Stuttgart (2009)
38. Trendowicz, A.: Software Cost Estimation, Benchmarking, and Risk Assessment – The Software Decision-Makers' Guide to Predictable Software Development. Springer, Heidelberg (2013)
39. Trendowicz, A., Heidrich, J., Münch, J., Ishigai, Y., Yokoyama, K., Kikuchi, N.: Development of a hybrid cost estimation model in an iterative manner. In: Proceedings of the 28th International Conference on Software Engineering (ICSE 2006), pp. 331–340. Shanghai, China (2006)
40. Kläs, M., Elberzhager, F., Münch, J., Hartjes, K., von Graevemeyer, O.: Transparent combination of expert and measurement data for defect prediction – an industrial case study. In: Proceedings of the 32nd International Conference on Software Engineering (ICSE), pp. 119–128. Cape Town (2010)

41. Liggesmeyer, P., Barthel, H., Ebert, A., Heidrich, J., Keller, P., Yang, Y., Wickenkamp, A.: Quality improvement through visualization of software and systems. Quality Assurance and Management, InTech, pp. 315–334 www.intechopen.com/books/quality-assurance-and-management/quality-improvement-through-visualization-of-software-and-systems (2012)
42. Tanveer, B., Wickenkamp, A., Blersch, M.: Dynamic identification, extraction and reuse of software components in distributed development scenarios. In: Proceedings of the 11th National Conference on Software Measurement and Metrics (MetriKon), pp. 131–150. Kaiserslautern (2011)
43. Johnson B., Shneiderman B.: Tree-maps: a spacefilling approach to the visualization of hierarchical information structures. In: Proceedings of Visualization'91, pp. 284–291. San Diego, Oct (1991)
44. Stasko J., Zhang E.: Focus+context display and navigation techniques for enhancing radial, space-filling hierarchy visualizations. In INFOVIS '00: Proceedings of the IEEE Symposium on Information Visualization 2000, pp. 57–68 (2000)

Part II

Empirical Research and Studies

Paths to Software Engineering Evidence

Ross Jeffery

Abstract
In recent years there has been a call from researchers in empirical software engineering to carry out more research in the industrial setting. The arguments for this have been well founded and the benefits clearly enunciated. But apart from the community's call for empirical goals to be based around business goals, there has been little consideration of the business conditions under which empirical software engineering methods may, or may not, be appropriate for the business. In this paper the empirically derived high-level management practices that are associated with business success are used as initial decision criteria to decide the path to follow: (a) whether empirical software engineering research will be of value to the business, and (b) if it is of value, the form that that research might take. The place of theory is considered in the case of path (b).

1 Introduction

Over a number of years there have been many calls to improve the quantity and quality of evidence collected concerning the software engineering process and product. For example in Endres and Rombach [1], a call is made to carry out "empirical studies in industry". "We believe that this step is due now" they state [p. 285]. In 2012, this call was repeated with the "First International Workshop on Conducting Empirical Studies in Industry" being held at ICSE 2013, at which the aim is to discuss challenges and experiences in conducting these empirical studies. Somewhat related is the call from Sjoberg (in Tichy [2]) who states: "If the goal is to

R. Jeffery (✉)
NICTA, 13 Garden St, 2015 Eveleigh, NSW, Australia

School of Computer Science and Engineering, University of New South Wales,
2052 Sydney, Australia
e-mail: ross.jeffery@nicta.com.au

J. Münch and K. Schmid (eds.), *Perspectives on the Future of Software Engineering*,
DOI 10.1007/978-3-642-37395-4_9, © Springer-Verlag Berlin Heidelberg 2013

build useful knowledge, we cannot run experiments with students on toy systems". The argument is made for the use of software practitioners in experimental settings and the conduct of comparative case studies in industry.

The arguments for industrial studies and practitioner subjects in experiments are, of course, absolutely reasonable. However, I would argue that decisions as to the appropriate method of knowledge acquisition should be subject to a decision scheme in which goals, context, and cost will play a part. For example, if the goal were to develop a new technology, using relatively informal processes, then empirical study of the eventual product, say in terms of product performance might occur at the development and later stages. Similarly, if the development process is not to occur again, or is trial and error based, there would be little argument for extensive empirical study of the process, unless a cost benefit study could show positive business returns. However, once the product exists, then empirical study of the product would be natural, and if a similar activity were deemed useful in the future, then some form of empirical work around the process may have value. The issue of value and cost is of significant importance, and this in turn links to goals and context.

In this paper I contrast two paths concerning software engineering evidence in an industrial setting. One path involves designed evidence collection such as we see in laboratories and field studies, but the other path argues for experiential learning and a "just do it" attitude. The paper structures and contrasts these two paths, the context in which they are applied, and provides a map of research methods linked to question types and variables of interest. The place of theory is considered within these paths and links are made to empirical observations, laws and theories presented in Endres and Rombach [1]. Support for the argument is drawn from prior empirical studies and industrial observation. It is concluded that improving the "quantity and quality of evidence collected" in software engineering will be strengthened by the use of clear research pathways to guide the selection and design of appropriate empirical research methods, and that these pathways will indicate the appropriate point at which to conduct empirical studies in industry.

2   Software Engineering

Definitions of the word "engineering" in Wikipedia and other sources focus on the application of knowledge. "Engineering is the science, skill, and profession of acquiring and applying . . . knowledge" [Wikipedia] and engineering is the "art or science of making practical application of the knowledge" [dictionary.com].

These definitions of the term "engineering" have a common theme concerned with making practical application of knowledge. That knowledge may be scientific, social, economic, experimental or experiential. Endres and Rombach [1] have synthesized a significant collection of knowledge in their book that lists and discusses observed principles, and behaviors that should be known to software engineers and used by them in practice. The authors have synthesized these behaviors from reported experiments, observation and experiences. This is an explicit representation of the result of the application of the scientific method to the field of software engineering through any of the methods of inquiry including experiments (in vivo, in vitro and in silica), case studies, and experience reports.

It has often been the case that this kind of applied scientific knowledge is derived after engineering projects reveal a knowledge acquisition opportunity. The literature on bridge disasters, for example, lists many causes including a very significant number of engineering errors, construction errors, and maintenance errors, quite apart from those caused by occurrences such as earthquakes, cyclones or warfare. The same is true of software engineering, where the opportunity for error similarly occurs in design, construction, and maintenance and thus brings about the opportunity for knowledge acquisition. As Kalinowski et al. [3] report in quoting Petroski [4], "to fail and to learn from failure are essential parts of the engineering discipline". But to derive this knowledge, the empirical software engineering community must have a part in the collection and analysis of the data that derives from experience, and the overriding observation is that the software engineering community has found it difficult to derive deep knowledge, particularly from practice. Analysis of failure is rare. Somewhat like the biological sciences, historically we have gathered significant knowledge from observation in the field and from experimentation in the laboratory. Too little work though has been done in carrying out experimentation in the field and constructing complex models for in silica experiments. The result is that our knowledge is highly situational and a posteriori when derived from observation or case study, or very difficult to generalize when derived from in vitro experiments.

In our 2002 paper [5] we concluded that, in the academic literature, there was a conspicuous absence of "well-formed theories, independent evaluation, replication, theory revision, and empirical software engineering method development". Thus, at this point in history it can be concluded that two futures are possible:

1. To recognize that the knowledge we gather regarding software engineering will likely remain situational and typically of use only within the context from which the knowledge is derived (I will call this case path (a). In this path, the knowledge gathered may be observational and situational.), and/or

2. To accept the larger challenge of responding to the need for theories and models as noted in our 2002 paper [5] (Path b).

These paths are shown below in Fig. 1, where path (a) pursues appropriate organizational means to success with observational knowledge gathering. Path (b) is where the empirical process provides a potentially cost effective means to achieve organizational success criteria.

These two research opportunities are also present in Tichy [2], where in a reported interview with Sjoberg, it is stated that many of the studies we carry out in software engineering are "utilitarian" in that we investigate the merits of a technology, rather than modeling and building theories to provide a "deeper understanding". But of course we need both types of studies, and we need to harness all of the research methodologies in order to satisfy both needs.

I believe that both paths have value and that these paths imply two different approaches for empirical software engineering methods in the organizational

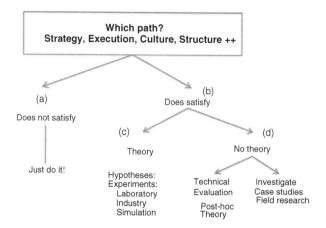

Fig. 1 Empirical software engineering path selection

context. Further I argue and illustrate that each path will be applicable at different times even in the same organization.

3 The Business Case Underlying Empirical Software Engineering in Industry

In the industrial software engineering domain it is the goals of the organization, its context and cost structures that will determine the software engineering processes and products of interest. It may be that the technology being developed has the capacity to reduce operating costs, to provide better customer service, or to facilitate entry to a new market. In this way the factors that drive a successful business in general should be the factors that drive the choices in software engineering technologies. For example, if product quality was critical to customer expectations, then research into software inspections would likely be of interest. If lower cost were a part of the organizational strategy, then software development cost modeling research would be important. But similarly, if the organizational strategy centered on developing new technologies, then there may be very little or even no empirical research activity of interest to that organization. An example of this is provided below.

In the paper entitled "What really works" [6], the authors report on a 5-year study of over 200 management practices used in 160 companies. The conclusions are that there are four primary practices that need to be employed and a further two secondary practices from a list of four that need to be employed in order to achieve a successful organization. It is expected that the implementation of these very high level practices will vary significantly between different organization types. The primary factors are *strategy*, *execution*, *culture*, and *structure*. For the first of these, *strategy*, it was found that it must be "sharply defined, clearly communicated, and well understood" by all stakeholders. *Execution* needed to be "flawless", eliminating excess and waste, meeting customer expectations, and putting decision making close to the front line. *Culture* was all about "holding high expectations" rather than, say, making work "fun", empowering employees, and rewarding achievement. The best *structure* was one that simplifies work, promotes exchange of information, and reduces bureaucracy. The four secondary practices identified were talent of the employees, innovation through disruptive technologies and new process technologies, leadership from the CEO, and mergers and acquisitions where opportune. Any two of the four of these were associated with business success when combined with the four primary practices. Hence it was described as the $4 + 2$ model. Naturally, there may be a number of sub-goals in the organization that are identified as critical to the organization's primary or secondary key management practices.

These factors are used in this paper as the key initial decision criteria for the choice of the appropriate knowledge acquisition path that may be pursued using empirical software engineering methods. A graphical representation of the paths and decision points is provided later in the paper.

4   An Example Case of Path (a): Just Do It

The first case I will use in this paper is that of the L4.verified project within NICTA [7]. This project has delivered "code level formal verification of the full functional correctness of the seL4 embedded systems microkernel". The kernel was composed of 8,700 lines of C code and 600 lines of assembler. Details of the lifecycle model employed in the project are provided in Andronick et al. [8]. Previous work resulted in the creation of the company Open Kernel Labs (OK Labs) [see http://en.wikipedia.org/wiki/Open_Kernel_Labs]. In this example, a new technology, in the sense of its code level formal verification, was developed, tested, and applied to billions of devices, resulting in a very successful business. It is interesting then to investigate the business success and the empirical software engineering applied during this successful software activity.

In terms of the factors revealed by the work of Nohria et al. [6], the activities within NICTA and UNSW reveal excellence in the four primary management factors and the manner in which they were executed. The strategy set for the project had a clear value proposition for the research team (world class research and engineering), the *strategy* was clearly communicated to all of the researchers and engineers, and focus was never lost. The *execution* focused on delivery with decision making at the front line in the hands of the researchers and engineers. The *culture* empowered all of the stakeholders, set high expectations, and rewarded excellence. The organization *structure* was very simple with little bureaucracy and good knowledge sharing. In terms of the secondary practices, the organization satisfied in terms of strong and clear *leadership* and high-level *talent* in the team. The work was all about *innovation* and thus this practice was a goal rather than a management practice. The final practice concerning *mergers* was not relevant.

Based on close knowledge of the project, it is concluded that the $4 + 2$ practices were satisfied in the project.

For this paper the question then concerns the place of empiricism in this software organization. In the development and commercialization of this technology, performance studies of the product were routine for the OKL4 kernel and the seL4 kernel. But almost no empirical work was carried out beyond product performance. Further empirical study simply wasn't seen as relevant for the goals of the organization. To some extent this reflects the comments made by Erdogmus [9] when exploring the importance of evidence. He considered the strength of evidence and the relationship between needed strength and the adoption context. In the case of OKL4, *during initial development* little evidence was needed beyond the success of the verification activity and the performance of the product. Thus the "evidence" in this case was based on logic, qualitative, and yet critical. It was utilitarian in Sjoberg's terms [2] where a new technology was being evaluated. There was no consideration of building models of the process or of developing or evaluating software engineering theory. Empirical software engineering could not contribute to the management practices found by Nohria et al. [6] for business success. This case is an example of path (a) – "Just do it".

Like many engineering fields, there were lessons learned from the development activity and this activity led to new knowledge and research questions that, in turn, lent themselves to subsequent empirical study. The derived knowledge was situational and observational as mentioned above. In the seL4 case, we have since extracted a formal representation of the development process model and used simulation to explore feasible options for change within that model [8]. We have also begun to investigate sizing metrics for the many artifacts used within the process and to look at the question of effort estimation for verification activities [10]. Clear connections between the ongoing empirical work and the business management practices provide the justification for this research. The empirical work links to the business strategy of providing a clear value proposition to customers, who in this case are future adopters of the verified product. The empirical work concerns better estimation to reduce risk in making project commitments. For L4 verified, we are moving from path (a) to path (b).

5   An Example Case of Path (b): Empirical Evidence

In this case I use the work done in Allette Systems, a small software development organization with 20 personnel in Sydney. A description of the company and the study is published in Ruhe et al. [11]. The area of study was software sizing and cost estimation. In the study we succeeded in carrying out empirical data collection and analysis, refinement of the software size metric for this context, refinement of the cost driver definitions relevant to the organization, development of a cost estimation method and toolset, and evaluation of the estimates produced by the toolset. The study is related to the Nelson-Jones law that a multitude of factors

Table 1 Results summary

Estimation method	Min MRE	Max MRE	Mean MRE	Median MRE	Pred (0.25)
Informal Allette method	0.12	0.68	0.37	0.36	0.25
OLS regression	0.00	0.60	0.24	0.23	0.67
Web-COBRA	0.02	0.35	0.17	0.15	0.75

influence developer productivity, and Boehm's third law, that development is a function of product size [1].

In the study we collected data on 12 development projects with measures of development effort in person-hours, size in web objects, peak staffing levels for the project by number of people. In addition, we identified nine relevant cost factors for the organization and used a consensus definition approach to ensure orthogonality of all of the cost drivers. The Web-COBRA model and estimation method and toolset developed and used was based on COBRA [12]. In statistical comparisons, the Web-COBRA model performed statistically better than OLS regression and also better than the informal estimation technique in use by the management at Allette at that time. Table 1 reproduces some of the results found.

It can be seen in this table that the relative error was smallest for Web-COBRA and the prediction level was greatest. In addition, it was noticed that the estimates done by Allette using their informal method generally tended to underestimate development effort, in conformance with the DeMarco-Glass law documented in Endres and Rombach [1].

If we turn to the paper by Sjoberg et al. [13], they argue, amongst other things, for tighter links between academia and industry. This work at Allette was carried out as a part of many studies and activities that involved the researchers and this company. It was a "tight" relationship focused on bringing business value through empirical research. But Allette did not adopt the Web-COBRA method and toolset after these studies, despite the evidence for the improved accuracy of estimates resulting. It was not that the empirically derived evidence was ignored, but rather that the execution method chosen in the company for the knowledge was "back of the envelope" rather than the developed software toolset. The responsible manager stated that he used the results of the study, the cost factors, and the size effort relationship, in an informal manner in future projects.

Some indication of the reasons for this can be derived in the business factors identified in Nohria [6]. Concerning the four primary factors, the knowledge derived and the toolset and methodology delivered had no impact on, or relationship with, the business strategy. But it can be argued that the method, being much more complex than the current estimation method and removed from the informal culture of the organization, would not have improved the primary factors and indeed was likely to be at odds with two or three of them. By applying the knowledge gained from the empirical data collection and analysis to the informal, back-of-the-envelope, estimation technique, the benefits of the study could be gained without the cost of changed structure and culture within the organization that would have been needed to adopt the Web-COBRA toolset. So in this case the empirical research was a designed study which delivered value to the organization in terms of the knowledge derived. Although the study also developed a toolset, this toolset was not in conformance with the management practices, conflicting with the organization's culture and structure; two of the four primary management practices.

6   Empirical Research in Industry

The two cases discussed so far provide one instance where empirical software engineering has little relevance to the goals and success of the organization. In the second instance, the knowledge derived through empirical study was relevant but the implementation of that knowledge occurred by application of the findings, and rejection of the technologies developed and used to derive the findings. In both cases successful primary management practices provided the rationale for acceptance or rejection of the empirical practices and the form of knowledge presentation. But the issues are more complex than these.

In Jeffery and Scott [5], we explore empirical research in industry by looking at the topics of cost modeling and estimation and software inspections. For cost modeling we note that although average programming productivity was consistent across some 30 organizations, reuse had a significant impact. In addition, we note the gradual improvement in cost modeling from the original COCOMO model, through SLIM, and later through relatively complex models containing both increasing and decreasing returns to scale, and incorporation of detailed staffing models with up to 16 variables concerning project size, development rates, overheads, experience, and so on (see Zhang [14]). The findings of this work refine and formalize Brooks law, noted as law 36 in Endres and Rombach [1]. Of course, there are many other studies in cost modeling and estimation, but the conclusion that can be drawn is that there has been focused and successful research, the development and refinement of theory and models, a better understanding of development productivity, and the successful adoption of research outcomes in industry. Kitchenham et al. [15] comment on the accumulation of evidence in the area of cost estimation and show that systematic literature reviews (SLR) are most common in this area of research. But it must be emphasized that evidence shows that successful adoption occurs only when the primary management practices are fulfilled.

When we investigate the research on software inspections, we find a very large number of publications. This is one research area in software engineering in which there are theories and clear models to drive the derivation of research questions. Again in Jeffery and Scott [5], we explore the evidence concerning software inspections and empirical research and conclude that in this area there is "a misdirected focus on the experiment rather than the theory that supports the experiment". Kitchenham et al. [15] report only one SLR in this field of research; that of Petersson et al. [16] concerning capture-recapture in software inspections. However, in this paper it is noted that the challenge ahead is to apply the capture-recapture techniques in industry.

These examples reveal occasions where research is the goal irrespective of industrial use, and occasions where industrial use drives the research goal. In the industrial domain, empirical software engineering methods may, or may not, support the critical business practices. Where the goal is software technology, it is likely that empirical methods will have limited applicability. In the pure software research domain, empirical software engineering methods may be most appropriate in knowledge generation, theory development, and modeling.

7 The Empirical Two-Path Model in Industry

Figure 1 provides a representation of the two-path model developed so far in this paper. In this figure, we see the initial decision point based on the $4 + 2$ model of Nohria et al. [6]. When the proposed empirical research does not address any of the four primary or two secondary practices, it is argued that there is no necessary pre-condition to conduct a designed empirical study. Under these conditions, it is argued that the place of software engineering is to "just do it" (path a). Software engineering may offer significant business advantage, through the development of new technologies which may contribute to the organizational strategy, but empirical software engineering cannot contribute to the management practices critical to the success of the organization. As noted above though, observations made during the "just do it" activities will contribute to the organizational knowledge.

The second path in Fig. 1 (path b) is a representation of the conditions under which empirical software engineering can significantly contribute to the management practices identified by Nohria et al. Thus it may be in the area of improving execution of the software process for a software development organization, for example. In this case, it could be by improving the estimation accuracy or product quality. In turn, this might be achieved by carrying out experiments based on existing theory (path c), or using path (d) in which there is no known theory but a technical evaluation and possible post-hoc theory development, or investigative studies around a proposed technology, which addresses the management practices. Of course, this research will come at a cost; the cost of doing the research itself, and the possible cost of implementing process change in the organization if pursued.

8 Theory in Software Engineering

Hannay et al. [17] found 40 theories used in 24 articles in software engineering. The areas of software engineering that have most-referenced theories are found to be inspections and object-oriented design. They conclude that the theories used in software engineering research to date "incorporate constructs that are endemic to other disciplines" and that "it may be difficult to devise theories . . . endemic to software engineering". In Fig. 2 (taken from Jeffery and Scott [5]), we represent the investigation of a particular phenomenon and the place of theory in that investigation. If very little is known about the phenomenon, or if the overriding

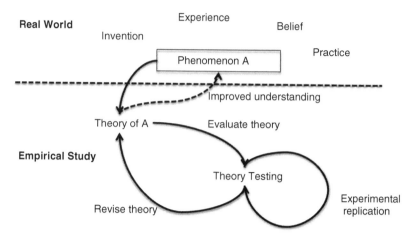

Fig. 2 A scientific inquiry model

business goal is technology evaluation, then understanding might be sought using observation for example (above the line). Once a degree of understanding is available, then a tentative theory might be formulated (below the line), which is then testable and open to evaluation.

This is another way of considering the path (a) and path (b) options. Above the line in Fig. 2 is associated with path (a) or path (d) in Fig. 1. In both paths there is no existing software engineering theory, but a phenomenon that might be implemented. If the phenomenon is associated with key management practices, then it is argued that path (d) is appropriate; if not, then path (a). In the case that some theory and models are available and the phenomenon addresses key management practices, it is argued that path (c) is appropriate. Thus for example, if software inspections are key to execution in the organization, there exists some appropriate theory [18], which could be tested through empirical study in the organization. In this way improvement in the phenomenon and theory revision are possible outcomes.

9   Conclusions

In this paper I have proposed a two-path selection model to guide the use, or non-use of empirical software engineering methods and techniques in an industrial setting. It is proposed that where these empirical research questions do not address the key management practices identified in the 4 + 2 model, the appropriate action is "just do it": implement the planned technology; learn from experience, build beliefs, and practice. However, where the intended action does bear on the practices of 4 + 2, it is appropriate to implement a planned empirical initiative. This initiative may be experimental, say in the case of theoretically based investigations or investigative case studies and field research (subject to cost benefits of the research activity) that may, or may not, derive post-hoc theoretical explanation. This decision tree provides the mechanism to distinguish between those conditions under which empirical analysis is, or is not, warranted within the organizational context. It is not intended as being appropriate for pure research activities in which paths (c) or (d) in Fig. 1 will be appropriate regardless of organizational usage of the phenomenon of interest.

Acknowledgments NICTA is funded by the Australian Government as represented by the Department of Broadband, Communications, and the Digital Economy, and the Australian Research Council (ARC) through the ICT Centre of Excellence Program. This work has also benefited from discussions with Mark Staples, Liming Zhu, Paul Bannerman, and Len Bass.

References

1. Endres, A., Rombach, H.D.: A Handbook of Software and Systems Engineering: Empirical Observations Laws and Theories. Pearson Addison Wesley, Harlow (2003)
2. Tichy, W.: Empirical software research: an interview with Dag Sjoberg, University of Oslo, Norway. Ubiquity ACM Pub. **2011**(June), 1–14 (2011)
3. Kalinowski, M., Card, D., Travassos, G.: Evidence-based guidelines to defect causal analysis. IEEE Softw. **29**, 16–18 (2012)
4. Petroski, H.: To Engineer is Human: The Role of Failure in Successful Design. St Martin's Press, New York (1985)
5. Jeffery, R., Scott, L.: Has twenty five years of empirical software engineering made a difference? In: Proceeding of the 9th Asia-Pacific Software Engineering Conference, IEEE Computer Society, pp. 539–546. (2002)
6. Nohria, N., Joyce, W., Roberson, B.: What really works. Harv. Bus. Rev. **81**(7), 42–52 (2003)
7. Klein, G., Elphinstone, K., Heiser, G., Andronick, J., Cock, D., Derrin, P., Elkaduwe, D., Engelhardt, K., Kolanski, R., Norrish, M., Sewell, T., Tuch, H., Winwood, S.: seL4: Formal verification of an OS kernel. In: Proceedings of the 22nd SOSP, pp. 207–220. ACM (2009)
8. Andronick, J., Jeffery, R., Klein, G., Kolanski, R., Staples, M., Zhang, H.J., Zhu, L.: Large-scale formal verification in practice: a process perspective. In: Proceedings of the 34th ICSE, pp. 1002–1011. ACM (2012)
9. Erdogmus, H.: How important is evidence, really? IEEE Softw. **27**(3), 2–5 (2010)
10. Staples, M., Kolanski, R., Klein, G., Lewis, C., Andronick, J., Murray, T., Jeffery, R., Bass, L.: Formal specifications better than function points for code sizing, to appear Proceedings of the ICSE 2013, San Francisco (2013)
11. Ruhe, M., Jeffery, R., Wieczorek, I.: Cost estimation for web applications. In: Proceedings of the 25th International Conference on Software Engineering (2003)
12. Briand, L. C., El Emam, K., Bomarius, F.: COBRA; A hybrid method for software cost estimation, benchmarking and risk assessment. In: Proceedings of the 20th International Conference on Software Engineering, pp. 390–399. (1998)
13. Sjoberg, D., Dyba, T., Jorgensen, M.: The future of empirical methods in software engineering research. In: Proceeding of FOSE, IEEE Computer Society (2007)
14. Zhang, H., Huo, M., Kitchenham, B., Jeffery, R.: Qualitative simulation model for software engineering process. In: Proceedings of the Australian Software Engineering Conference, IEEE Computer Society (2006)
15. Kitchenham, B., Brereton, O.P., Budgen, D., Turner, M., Bailey, J., Linkman, S.: Systematic literature reviews in software engineering – a systematic literature review. Inform.Softw. Technol. **51**, 7–15 (2009)
16. Petersson, H., Thelin, T., Runeson, P., Wohlin, C.: Capture-recapture in software inspections after 10 years of research – theory, evaluation and application. J. Syst. Softw. **72**, 249–264 (2004)

17. Hannay, J., Sjoberg, D., Dyba, T.: A systematic review of theory use in software engineering experiments. IEEE Trans. Softw. Eng. **33**(2), 87–107 (2007)
18. Sauer, C., Jeffery, R., Land, L., Yetton, P.: The effectiveness of software development technical reviews: a behaviorally motivated program of research. IEEE Trans. Softw. Eng. **26**(1), 1–14 (2000)

An Evidence Profile for Software Engineering Research and Practice

Claes Wohlin

Abstract

Evidence-based software engineering has emerged as an important part of software engineering. The need for empirical evaluation and hence evidence when developing new models, methods, techniques and tools in research has grown in the last couple of decades. Furthermore, industrial decision-making ought to become more evidence-based. The objective here is to develop and present an evidence-based profile, which could be used to divide pieces of evidence into different types and hence create an overall picture of evidence in a specific case. The evidence profile is developed in such a way that it allows evidence to be judged in context. The evidence profile consists of five types of evidence, and it is illustrated for perspective-based reading. It is shown how pieces of evidence can be classified into the different types. It is concluded that this type of approach may be useful for capturing the evidence with respect to a specific topic and in a specific context. Further work will include applying the evidence profile to evidence collected from different types of studies and contexts.

1 Introduction

Evidence is the basis for decision-making. Every day we make decisions based on the information available, and hence we practice informal evidence-based decision-making. In science, decision-making should be more formalized. To do so, we introduce an evidence-based research approach. Evidence-based medicine has been practiced for a long time, as described by for example by [1]. The concept of

C. Wohlin (✉)
School of Computing, Blekinge Institute of Technology, SE-371 79 Karlskrona, Sweden
e-mail: Claes.Wohlin@bth.se

J. Münch and K. Schmid (eds.), *Perspectives on the Future of Software Engineering*,
DOI 10.1007/978-3-642-37395-4_10, © Springer-Verlag Berlin Heidelberg 2013

evidence-based research was introduced into software engineering in 2004 [2] and also presented from a practitioner's point of view by Dybå et al. [3].

A key challenge in all evidence-based research is the synthesis and valuation of the evidence available. In evidence-based medicine, the highest level of evidence is based on randomized controlled trials. However, in software engineering the best evidence is definitively context-dependent. This is not only a concern in software engineering, but is also a criticism raised in evidence-based medicine [4].

Synthesis and valuation of evidence can start from two main standpoints: research or practice. In the former case, researchers are trying to synthesize evidence to capture what we know, in some sense, objectively about a specific model, method, technique, or tool. In the latter case, the evidence must be re-valued and interpreted in different contexts, such as different application domains, process models, or companies. Something that may be perceived as relevant and useful evidence in research or in one context may not be as highly valued in another context. For example, in a contact with a large telecommunication company, they wondered about the available evidence in relation to productivity and quality changes when moving development of software products from one site to another site. The manager asking the question had a gut feeling, but wanted scientific evidence to better argue "his case" when discussing the challenges with higher-level management. Unfortunately, the evidence found was not in the telecommunication domain, and hence perceived as having limited value in the argumentation [5]. This illustrates the need to take context into account when discussing evidence and its value with industry.

The most commonly known use of evidence is probably in law, since it forms the basis for a modern society's juridical system. Thus, a classification of evidence according to the juridical system is taken here as the starting point to introduce levels of evidence for software engineering. A general model is introduced and its use in specific contexts is discussed. To illustrate the model, studies of perspective-based reading are classified into the model first from a "pure" research perspective and then re-valued and interpreted in a specific industrial scenario. The latter is needed given that the evidence must be viewed as being context-dependent as argued above. It is concluded that it is possible to classify evidence and hence package the available evidence using a generic model for research and also into specific cases that are relevant for specific industrial contexts.

The remainder of the chapter is structured as follows. Next, related work on synthesis of evidence in software engineering is presented. This is followed by a description of the generic model for valuation of evidence for software engineering. The model is then illustrated for perspective-based reading. After that the chapter concludes with a summary, including some future work.

2 Related Work

Discussions about the need to synthesize research in software engineering started before the introduction of the concept of evidence-based software engineering. Some examples can be found in literature from the late 1990s [6–8]. Pickard et al.

discuss combining research results [6]. Miller [7] and Hayes [8] both address the issue of combining research results through meta-analysis. The authors stress the need for a systematic combination of research results. They stress the need not only to conduct individual research studies, but also to build knowledge by combining findings from different studies on a topic. Basili et al. [9] present some early work along these lines, addressing how to combine a set of research studies and hence knowledge we have with regard to software inspections. Ciolkowski [10] followed up on this line of research by conducting a meta-analysis of perspective-based reading, which will be used as a starting point for the illustration later in the chapter.

As a response to the need to collate evidence in software engineering, Endres and Rombach [11] systematized and presented a number of empirical observations, theories, and laws in relation to software engineering. The authors collected a number of recurring phenomena in software and systems engineering.

Despite the increased focus on conducting systematic literature studies [12] in software engineering, there is still too little attention on conducting research synthesis. This needs to change and synthesis needs to be an integral part of systematic reviews in order to increase their significance and usefulness for research and practice [13]. According to [13], most synthesis is narrative or thematic. Different steps for conducting thematic synthesis are discussed by Cruzes and Dybå [14]. The lack of or at least limited synthesis in software engineering is a challenge for both researchers and practitioners alike. Researchers need proper synthesis to identify research gaps and to be able to generalize research results. Practitioners need synthesis to obtain evidence for decision-making. The latter challenge is also addressed by Pfleeger [15] when discussing the problems experienced by industry in building knowledge from the evidence available in individual research studies. Thus, it can be concluded that there is indeed a need to support both researchers and practitioners in their decision-making process by providing packaged evidence, and not only pieces of evidence.

Different ways of combining evidence have been proposed, such as meta-analysis and vote counting [6]. Meta-analysis is primarily a statistical method for combining findings from different studies, while vote counting is more a straightforward count of results pointing in a certain direction. The way to combine evidence is far from straightforward; in particular if a specific context needs to be taken into account, such as a specific industrial context.

The objective here is to address the gap in the research literature related in particular to the synthesis and valuation of evidence from both a research perspective and an industrial point of view. This is done by introducing and illustrating a model for valuing evidence of different types and taking the context into account. The combination of evidence is based on a generic model, but the key point is that the evidence must be judged in each specific case. The model should act as a starting point for combining evidence, and should not be perceived as a prescriptive model.

3   Evidence Profile

Based on the above, it is concluded that a model for valuation of evidence is needed. The model presented here is influenced by how evidence is used in criminal law. Thus, the basic conjecture for the work is: Decisions regarding the use of models, methods, techniques, and tools in software engineering could be made as law is practiced, although with a lower level of confidence. The latter is added since the evidence does not have to support the case beyond any reasonable doubt. The key issue is that the evidence is reasonable and it is cost-efficient to act according to the evidence. Cost may be viewed differently depending on whether academia or industry is represented.

Admittedly, criminal law is different in different countries, but the basic levels of evidence are still very similar in terms of strength (the levels and interpretations were discussed with a lawyer with long-term experience in criminal law in Sweden). If we look at evidence and other sources of information from strong to weak, we get the following order (although the actual order between two items could be argued):

3.1   Evidence

1. Physical evidence—for example documentation, digital traces, fingerprints, and genetic information (DNA).
2. Eyewitnesses—statements from trustworthy witnesses.
3. Expert witnesses—statements about the accused person from expert witnesses (typically medical doctors or psychologists).
4. Circumstantial evidence—circumstances that indicate guilt, but this is not proof. It could be having a motive or being at the scene of the crime.

3.2   Other Sources of Information

5. Hearsay—second-hand information.
6. Self-statements—statements from the accused person (typically with vested interest).
7. Suspicion—A feeling of distrust.

The three lowest levels are not evidence. However, even suspicion is important since it may, as in the case with transferring a software product, be the starting point for trying to identify real evidence. Thus, from an industry point of view, suspicion is very close to what is often referred to as "gut feeling".

The main research hypothesis in this work is: *It is possible to systematically structure different types of claims and evidence in software engineering to allow for more informed decisions regarding research gaps and the use of models, methods, techniques, and tools in specific contextual software development practices?*

A key point here is that the claims and evidence must be evaluated and valued in a specific context, either in academic research or in specific industrial settings. A structuring of industrial context factors to take into account can be found in [16]. Some examples of contextual factors include: application domain, size of project, and specific technical factors that are deemed to be relevant, for example a specific programing language or use of a specific process model. Evidence from an agile project using Java may not be viewed as relevant for a more plan-driven development environment using C. Ultimately, each case must be judged separately since it is impossible to state exactly which context factors are important in a specific case.

When it comes to the evidence, several aspects must be taken into account. These aspects are:

- Quality of evidence—an eyewitness may be perceived as very reliable or as not so reliable. This may be due to what exactly a person remembers about a situation. Reliability of evidence comes from triangulation, i.e., different pieces of evidence corroborate each other.
- Relevance of evidence—given a situation, some evidence may be viewed as more relevant than in other cases. For example, the importance of a fingerprint in the case of a murder committed in a house differs depending on whether it was made by the homeowner or by a burglar.
- Aging of evidence—in the juridical system this relates to memory and time. In software engineering, it is more related to technology change, and hence evidence may have aged too much and thus not be perceived as relevant anymore.
- Vested interest—evidence given by a person who has a vested interest in the outcome must be viewed differently than if the person is perceived as being objective.
- Strength of evidence—this refers to the strength of the evidence as such, i.e., along the types of evidence listed above. However, the previous four bullets may affect the perceived strength of the evidence.

Inspired by this list of seven types of evidence and other sources of information, a model of five evidence levels is proposed as a general model for handling evidence in software engineering. The reason for collapsing it into five levels is that levels 5–7 are not really evidence at all and levels 5 and 6 are combined into one level since their level of trustworthiness may be viewed as quite similar. Hearsay is normally not admissible as evidence in court, and statements from the accused person are normally made in self-interest unless it is an admittance of guilt. Independently, both these types must be viewed as weak when it comes to trust and basing decisions on them, and hence they have been combined into one level in the model. Furthermore, the order of levels 3 and 4 is swapped in the proposed model since in a specific field, such as software engineering, the people involved are mostly experts and hence external experts do not exist in the same way as in the criminal courts.

In software engineering, evidence may support, for example, a specific tool or provide evidence against it, and evidence may therefore be positive or negative in the case of scientific evidence. For example, a new tool may be significantly better or worse than the current tool, or the results may be inconclusive.

Table 1 Types of evidence

Positive or negative				
Strong evidence	Evidence	Circumstantial evidence	Third-party claim	First- or second-party claim

The five general levels of evidence suggested are listed in Table 1 and outlined in general guideline terms below. It should be noted that evidence may be for or against a specific model, method, technique, or tool. In an evaluation case, there are then actually eleven cells in the table, i.e., five for positive evidence, five for negative evidence, and one for inconclusive evidence from a study.

The empty line is for listing papers/studies with evidence of that specific strength after having taken the four additional aspects (quality, relevance, aging, and vested interest) into account, and after having combined them with the general descriptions of the area of interest and interpreted them in the context. For example, if we are interested in inspections of research specifications, then inspections of other artifacts are of less importance than if we are evaluating a specific inspection technique (or reading technique such as perspective-based reading) more generally. This distinction is further elaborated below in the discussion about the use of the proposed model or evidence profile for perspective-based reading.

The following descriptions should be interpreted as guidelines for valuing different types of evidence. It is not intended to define each type of evidence exactly. On the contrary, it is important that each single empirical study is judged based on its own merits and in the context of interests. The key issue is that evidence is categorized into one of the five types of evidence (positive or negative), and the placement can be motivated given the context of interest. Some guidelines for the five types of evidence are given below:

Strong evidence: The conditions for judging evidence as strong in general are as follows: well-documented controlled experiment with industrial participants, cross-company multi-case study, studies conducted by researchers who are independent from the inventor of the object of study. The research should be published after peer review.

Evidence: The following are examples of requirements for the evidence level: well-documented controlled experiment with non-representative subjects, or series of case studies within a company, published in a peer-reviewed conference or journal, and published by independent researchers with no vested interest.

Circumstantial evidence: Expectations for this level are: well-documented controlled experiment by anyone having a vested interest, well-documented single case study, cross-company survey, published in a peer-reviewed conference or journal.

Third-party claim: The expectations for this level of evidence are: experience report, lessons learned, single company survey, and published anywhere but not by anyone having a vested interest.

First- or second-party claim: Finally, the lowest level of "evidence" includes: any information published by the inventor or by anyone else having a vested interest (for example tool developer).

The objective is that Table 1 should be used to categorize specific studies, and hence obtain frequency counts of different levels of evidence. Frequency counts allow anyone using the model to generate a bar chart with 11 bars (from strong positive evidence to strong negative evidence with the middle being no evidence, i.e., an inconclusive study). This is referred to as the evidence profile for the object of study in a specific context. The actual studies placed at each level (positive, neutral, and negative) should be presented alongside the evidence profile to enable transparency of the judgments.

The descriptions of each level should be viewed as a guideline for placing studies on the levels. However, all placements of studies should be motivated to make the actual evidence profile transparent and hence allow it to be accepted or challenged. Thus, it is important to provide a characterization of each study together with the motivation for the placement of each study in the table. When presenting the table (and bar chart), all individual studies must be publicly available.

Placement of individual studies may depend on actual usage of the collated evidence. Thus, the placement of studies may change depending on whether studying research in general or a specific application domain or any other specific context. This is illustrated when discussing the actual use of the evidence-profile.

4   Illustration of Model

The descriptions of the five types of evidence support the creation of an evidence profile, where the types of evidence as such help provide weights to the different types of evidence. Not all evidence is equally important and different pieces of evidence may be viewed as being of different importance depending on the actual usage of the evidence. For example, the evidence in a research situation may be different than if we look at the actual use of a model, method, technique, or tool. Furthermore, different pieces of evidence may be viewed differently in different industrial contexts, for example depending on different application domains or different process models being used. Research evidence must be interpreted in context, and hence the evidence profile will become different. Thus, it is only possible here to illustrate the usage of the evidence profile in a specific scenario.

We chose to base the illustration on perspective-based reading in software inspections [17]. The main reason for this decision was that Ciolkowski published a meta-analysis of 12 sources related to perspective-based reading [10], which means that the evidence profile obtained here can be compared with the findings from [10]. It should be noted that Ciolkowski evaluated perspective-based reading in general, i.e., from a general research perspective, while here the evidence profile is created for a general research scenario and is then also discussed for an industry scenario. This is done to illustrate the differences and show how important it is to interpret evidence in context when discussing the usage of different models, methods, techniques, and tools in industry.

Ciolkowski lists 12 sources of information regarding perspective-based reading. The selection of these sources is further elaborated in [10]. The 12 sources contain 22 studies, which are used to create the illustration for the usage of the evidence profile. Based on the listing in [10], the 12 sources were downloaded and evaluated. First, a general profile based on PBR is created, and then a specific industrial scenario is introduced, which leads to a discussion about the placement of the pieces of evidence to obtain a context-dependent evidence profile for the scenario presented.

General research scenario—The focus is on effectiveness, i.e., on the ability to identify defects without taking the time factor into account. Statistically significant results reported in the original study are viewed as positive. When possible, this is based on the p-value and hence independent of the significance level chosen in the original study. Here, results with a p-value below 0.1 are considered as significant from the evidence-profile point of view. The type of artifact inspected is not considered relevant. The type of subject is judged according to the basic description provided above with respect to the evidence types. The authors of the first paper on perspective-based reading are viewed as having a vested interest.

Industry scenario—A telecommunication company is considering changing from their current checklist-based inspection method and plan to start using perspective-based reading with the objective of increasing their effectiveness in detecting defects. They are interested in doing so for inspections of requirements, design, code, and test documentation. The company is collaborating with an academic partner, and has asked for their advice based on the available evidence in the literature. We received questions regarding research evidence related to other topics in our close industrial collaboration [18]. Given that they perceive inspections as not being very domain-dependent, they do not only want findings from their own domain. However, they still want the evidence to be from the development of technical systems. They prefer evidence from industrial usage of perspective-based reading or experiments with industrial participants.

To address the two scenarios, we will go through each source of information with its studies. The sources are discussed in order of publication:

Paper by Basili et al. from 1996 [17]—This paper contains four studies with industry participants inspecting requirements documents. The authors are assumed to have a vested interest given that it is the first paper on perspective-based reading. Three studies provide significant results in favor of perspective-based reading. The fourth study is inconclusive.

Report by Ciolkowski et al. from 1997 [19]—This is a technical report containing one significant and one insignificant study. The significant study was run with students inspecting a requirements document. The author list contains one researcher involved in the original study, and hence the studies were run with a vested interest.

Paper by Laitenberger and DeBaud from 1997 [20]—This paper does not compare perspective-based reading with any other reading technique, hence it is not viewed as relevant for the objective of finding evidence in relation to perspective-based reading in comparison to other reading techniques.

Report by Ciolkowski from 1999 [21]—The report includes four studies and none of them are significant.

Paper by Biffl from 2000 [22]—The paper contains one study with students. The results are significant, although in favor of checklist-based reading.

Paper by Laitenberger et al. from 2000 [23]—The paper includes one study with industry participants inspecting design documents. The study has significant results in favor of perspective-based reading. One author had a vested interest as a co-author of the original paper.

Paper by Lanubile and Visaggio from 2000 [24]—The paper presents two studies and neither one of them has significant results.

Paper by Biffl et al. from 2003 [25]—The paper contains one study with students. The results are significant, although in favor of checklist-based reading. The outcome is very similar to the findings in [22].

Report by Sabaliauskaite from 2004 [26]—The report presents one study and the results are not significant.

Paper by Denger et al. from 2004 [27]—The paper presents one study and the results are not significant.

Paper by Lanubile et al. from 2004 [28]—The paper presents one study and the results are not significant.

Paper by Maldonado et al. from 2006 [29]—The paper presents two studies and the results are not significant. Results are reported for both the combination of the two studies and for the studies separately, and hence the reporting differs slightly between [10] and here. The difference is of little interest given that the results were not significant.

In summary, three studies were removed, given that they lacked a comparison with another reading technique. Twelve studies did not provide any significant results. Four studies provide significant results from experiments with industry participants. Three of these are from the original study where requirements documents were inspected, and one study is from the inspection of design documents. One study with students produced significant results in favor of perspective-based reading. Finally, two studies showed significant results in favor of checklist-based reading in comparison to perspective-based reading. Thus, in reality seven studies had to be evaluated to decide on their placement in the evidence profile. Three studies were removed and the other twelve were placed in "neutral" given their lack of significant results.

For the general case, the seven studies are placed as follows:

- The three studies from the original study and the additional significant study with industry participants are placed in "evidence". It is positive that the studies were conducted with industry participants, but the authors had a vested interest, which brings the placement down from "strong evidence".

Fig. 1 Evidence-profile in the general case (General research scenario)

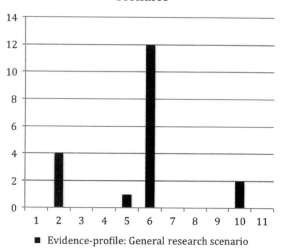

Evidence-profile: General research scenario

• The significant study with student participants is placed in "first- or second-order party claim", since the study was conducted with students including one author who was also an author of the original study and since the source is a technical report.

• The two significant studies favoring checklist-based reading over perspective-based reading are placed in "evidence", although on the negative side, since the significance was in favor of checklist-based reading.

This results in the evidence profile presented in Fig. 1 with 11 classes ranging from positive "strong evidence" being "1" via non-significant results with its bar on "6" to negative "strong evidence" being "11".

From the research profile in Fig. 1 it can be seen that the evidence is quite inconclusive, although more significant results are in favor of perspective-based reading than not. It is noteworthy that all studies with significant results include one or more of the authors of the original paper [17]. Furthermore, both studies significantly in favor of checklist-based reading over perspective-based reading include one joint author [22] and [25]. These observations are aligned with those by Ciolkowski [10].

In this particular case, the industry scenario does not result in any major changes if we look at it in general. However, if we look at the specific phases of interest for the company, there is no evidence at all when it comes to inspections of code and test documentation. Even for design, the evidence is very limited with one significant study. Thus, the company would definitely not change to perspective-based reading for inspections of design, code, and test documentation. The results for using perspective-based reading for requirements documents may be considered if the company is prepared to experiment with a new reading technique.

5   Summary

Evidence-based software engineering has been driven by the need to make informed decisions about which models, methods, techniques, and tools to use in a specific context. Unfortunately, it is a challenge to synthesize the evidence available. If controlled experiments are primarily available, it may be possible to conduct meta-analysis. However, software engineering evidence comes from different types of studies and even synthesizing evidence from controlled experiments is a challenge. Thus, a less formal method is needed. Here an evidence profile has been proposed as a response to the overall research question. It is formulated as a way to capture and visualize evidence. The evidence profile includes five types of evidence, which means that anyone using the approach can classify different pieces of evidence in whichever type found suitable in the specific context. It must be possible to clearly motivate the placement of evidence from different studies to ensure that the final evidence profile is found trustworthy and hence useful.

The use of the evidence profile was illustrated with a set of studies of perspective-based reading. This reading technique was used to make the illustration clear. However, the objective is that the evidence profile should be useful for different types of empirical studies including case studies, surveys, and other types of empirical studies.

Further research will include evaluating the evidence-based profile approach for other areas than reading techniques, and evaluate its usefulness in relation to synthesis of evidence in systematic literature reviews.

Acknowledgment   The Knowledge Foundation in Sweden supported this work under the grant for BESQ + (2010–0311).

References

1. Sackett, D.L., Rosenberg, W.M., Gray, J.A., Haynes, R.B., Richardson, W.S.: Evidence based medicine: what it is and what it isn't. BMJ **312**(7023), 71–72 (1996)
2. Kitchenham, B., Dybå, T., Jørgensen, M.: Evidence-based software engineering. In: Proceedings of the 26th International Conference on Software Engineering, pp. 273–281. Edinburgh (2004)
3. Dybå, T., Kitchenham, B., Jørgensen, M.: Evidence-based software engineering for practitioners. IEEE Softw. **22**(1), 58–65 (2005)
4. Upshur, R.E., van den Kerkhof, E.G., Goel, V.: Meaning and measurement: an inclusive model of evidence in health care. J. Eval. Clin. Pract. **7**(2), 91–96 (2001)
5. Wohlin, C., Smite, D.: Classification of software transfers. In: Proceedings of the 19th Asia-Pacific Software Engineering Conference (APSEC), pp. 828–837. Hong Kong (2012)
6. Pickard, L., Kitchenham, B., Jones, P.: Combining empirical results in software engineering. Inform. Softw. Technol. **40**(14), 811–821 (1998)
7. Miller, J.: Can results from software engineering experiments be safely combined? In: Proceedings of 6th International Symposium on Software Metrics, Boca Raton (1999)
8. Hayes, W.: Research synthesis in software engineering: a case for meta-analysis. In: Proceedings of the 6th International Symposium on Software Metrics, pp. 143–151. Boca Raton (1999)

9. Basili, V.R., Shull, F., Lanubile, F.: Building knowledge through families of experiments. IEEE Trans. Softw. Eng. **25**(4), 456–473 (1999)
10. Ciolkowski, M.: What do we know about perspective-based reading? An approach for quantitative aggregation in software engineering. In: Proceedings of the 3rd International Symposium on Empirical Software Engineering and Measurement (ESEM), pp. 275–284. Orlando (2009)
11. Endres, A., Rombach, D.: A Handbook of Software and Systems Engineering: Empirical Observations, Laws and Theories. Pearson/Addison Wesley, Harlow (2003)
12. Kitchenham, B.A., Charters, S.: Guidelines for performing systematic literature reviews in software engineering. Version 2.3, Technical Report, Software Engineering Group, Keele University and Department of Computer Science University of Durham (2007)
13. Cruzes, D., Dybå, T.: Research synthesis in software engineering: a tertiary study. Inform. Softw. Technol. **53**(5), 440–455 (2011)
14. Cruzes D, Dybå, T.: Recommended steps for thematic synthesis in software engineering. In: Proceedings of the 5th International Symposium on Empirical Software Engineering and Measurement, pp. 275–284. Banff (2011)
15. Pfleeger, S.L.: Soup or art? The role of evidential force in empirical software engineering. IEEE Softw. **22**(1), 66–73 (2005)
16. Petersen, K., Wohlin, C.: Context in industrial software engineering research. In: Proceedings of the 3rd International Symposium on Empirical Software Engineering and Measurement (ESEM), pp. 401–404. Orlando (2009)
17. Basili, V.R., Green, S., Laitenberger, O., Lanubile, F., Shull, F., Sørumgård, S., Zelkowitz, M.V.: The empirical investigation of perspective-based reading. Empirical Softw. Eng. **1**(2), 133–164 (1996)
18. Wohlin, C., Aurum, A., Angelis, L., Phillips, L., Dittrich, Y., Gorschek, T., Grahn, H., Henningsson, K., Kågström, S., Low, G., Rovegård, P., Tomaszewski, P., van Toorn, C., Winter, J.: Success factors powering industry-academia collaboration in software research. IEEE Softw. **29**(2), 67–73 (2012)
19. Ciolkowski, M., Differding, C., Laitenberger, O., Münch, J.: Empirical investigation of perspective-based reading: a replicated experiment. ISERN, Technical Report ISERN-97-13 (1997)
20. Laitenberger, O., DeBaud, J-M.: Perspective-based reading of code documents at Robert Bosch Gmbh. Technical Report ISERN-97-14 (1997)
21. Ciolkowski, M.: Evaluating the effectiveness of different inspection techniques on informal requirements documents. Diploma Thesis, University of Kaiserslautern (1999)
22. Biffl, S.: Analysis of the impact of reading technique and inspector capability on individual inspection performance. In: Proceedings of the 7th Asia-Pacific Software Engineering Conference, (APSEC), pp. 136–145. Singapore (2000)
23. Laitenberger, O., Atkinson, C., Schlich, M., Emam, K.E.: An experimental comparison of reading techniques for defect detection in UML design documents. J. Syst. Softw. **53**(2), 183–204 (2000)
24. Lanubile, F., Visaggio, G.: Evaluating defect detection techniques for software requirements inspections. ISERN, Technical Report ISERN-00-08 (2000)
25. Biffl, S., Halling, M., Koszegi, S.: Investigating the accuracy of defect estimation models for individuals and teams based on inspection data. In: Proceedings of the 2nd International Symposium on Empirical Software Engineering (ISESE), pp. 232–243. Rome (2003)
26. Sabaliauskaite, G.: Investigating defect detection in object-oriented design and cost-effectiveness of software inspection. Dissertation, Osaka University (2004)
27. Denger, C., Ciolkowski, M., Lanubile, F.: Investigating the active guidance factor in reading techniques for defect detection. In: Proceedings of the International Symposium on Empirical Software Engineering (ISESE), pp. 219–228. Redondo Beach (2004)
28. Lanubile, F., Mallardo, T., Calefato, F., Denger, C., Ciolkowski, M.: Assessing the impact of active guidance for defect detection: a replicated experiment. In: Proceedings of the 10th International Symposium on Software Metrics, pp. 269–278. Chicago (2004)

29. Maldonado, J., Carver, J., Shull, F., Fabbri, S., Dória, E., Martimiano, L., Mendonça, M., Basili, V.: Perspective-based reading: a replicated experiment focused on individual reviewer effectiveness. Empirical Softw. Eng. **11**(1), 119–142 (2006)

Challenges of Evaluating the Quality of Software Engineering Experiments

Oscar Dieste and Natalia Juristo

Abstract

Good-quality experiments are free of bias. Bias is considered to be related to internal validity (e.g., how well experiments are planned, designed, executed, and analysed). Quality scales and expert opinion are two approaches for assessing the quality of experiments. **Aim:** Identify whether there is a relationship between bias and quality scale and expert opinion predictions in SE experiments. **Method:** We used a quality scale to determine the quality of 35 experiments from three systematic literature reviews. We used two different procedures (effect size and response ratio) to calculate the bias in diverse response variables for the above experiments. Experienced researchers assessed the quality of these experiments. We analysed the correlations between the quality scores, bias and expert opinion. **Results:** The relationship between quality scales, expert opinion and bias depends on the technology exercised in the experiments. The correlation between quality scales, expert opinion and bias is only correct when the technologies can be subjected to acceptable experimental control. Both correct and incorrect expert ratings are more extreme than the quality scales. **Conclusions:** A quality scale based on formal internal quality criteria will predict bias satisfactorily provided that the technology can be properly controlled in the laboratory.

1 Introduction

According to Kitchenham [1], the SLR process involves: (1) identifying experiments about a particular research topic, (2) selecting the studies relevant to the research, (3) including/excluding studies based on their quality, (4) extracting the data from

O. Dieste (✉) • N. Juristo
Universidad Politécnica de Madrid, 28660 Boadilla del Monte, Madrid, Spain
e-mail: odieste@fi.upm.es; natalia@fi.upm.es

J. Münch and K. Schmid (eds.), *Perspectives on the Future of Software Engineering*, 159
DOI 10.1007/978-3-642-37395-4_11, © Springer-Verlag Berlin Heidelberg 2013

the included studies, and (5) aggregating the data to generate pieces of knowledge. The quality assessment (QA) step acts like a filter during which the quality of primary studies is assessed and the passage of poor quality experiments to the data extraction and synthesis phases is blocked. QA aims to make the review process more efficient and less error-prone.

It is generally accepted that a good-quality experiment is free of bias. Freedom from bias is the result of careful planning and appropriate control during design and operation, which maximises the experiment's internal validity [2]. As bias cannot be measured, quality assurance (QA) instruments are designed to assess the internal validity of experiments and infer the quality of the experiment from this assessment [2]. Checklists and quality scales are generally used for this purpose.

Following the guidelines for other disciplines, Kitchenham [1] and Biolchini et al. [3] recommend a detailed QA of SE studies during the SLR process. These papers were followed by Dybå and Dingsøyr's proposal [4], which they applied in later research [5] and which has been adopted by other researchers in SLR [6]. In all cases, the proposed QA instruments were checklists based on internal quality concepts.

The ability of QA instruments to predict bias is far from clear. There are several studies (primarily in medicine) that were unable to identify a clear relationship between QA instruments and bias [7–10]. In SE, this is also an open debate. We recently reported [11] that bias appeared to be related to only some aspects of internal quality included in QA instruments. More recently, Kitchenham et al. [12] have drawn attention to evaluators having an influence on the QA process. One of their conclusions is that "a quality checklist seems useful but it is difficult to ensure that the checklist is both appropriate and understood by reviewers".

As the relationships between internal quality, bias and ratings by experienced researchers are not well understood, this research aims to further the study of this issue, extending our previous research [11].

The paper is divided as follows. Section 2 describes key related concepts. Section 3 states the research questions and methodology. Section 4 describes how we gathered the empirical data. For simplicity's sake, these data will henceforth be referred to as *datasets*. Section 5 describes the checks run on the datasets, which are analysed in Sect. 6. Finally, we wind up with a discussion and the conclusions in Sects. 7 and 8, respectively.

2 Background

The quality of an experiment can be seen from two different viewpoints. The first is to consider quality as the outcome of a good experiment's internal validity. The second is to operationalise quality as the amount of bias in experimental results.

Internal validity refers to the appropriateness of inferences regarding cause-effect relationships [13]. Internal validity is liable to different threats that need to be minimised when an experiment is run. There are many strategies that can be employed during experiment design to deal with validity threats, such as randomisation, blocking, etc.

In statistics, bias is the departure of an estimator (e.g.: sampling mean) from the corresponding population parameter (e.g.: population mean) [14]. This definition has been adopted rather directly in experimental disciplines, such as medicine [2] or SE [15]. Unlike random error, bias is not cancelled out among subjects; it has a tendency to grow. For example, in the case of experimenter-induced performance bias [2], all the subjects that receive help (even if this assistance is provided inadvertently) will tend to perform better than the subjects that receive no help. Bias, then, is a *systematic error* in the experimental results.

In principle, bias can be quantified if there are enough replications, provided that such replications are not affected by the same systematic error. The usual procedure for determining the bias of an experiment is to compare its outcome with the average for all the replications calculated by means of meta-analysis [7, 16, 17]. However, the number of replications is low (not only in SE, but also in experimentally mature disciplines like medicine [2]), meaning that such calculation is not generally possible in practice.

On this ground, many researchers have tried to assess bias (and therefore experimental quality) using QA instruments based on what is commonly accepted as the source of the bias: experimental design, operation and analysis weaknesses. Typical examples of those weaknesses are: inappropriate concealment, blinding, randomisation, etc.; that is, the same strategies used to maximise internal validity. Due to this equation, it is usually believed that internal validity is a prerequisite for low bias. When bias is high, it means that the experiment has not effectively applied strategies for achieving adequate internal validity [2, 18]. High quality becomes another term for expressing internally valid experiments.

There are several approaches for bias assessment, the most important being *checklists* and *quality scales* [2, 18]. Checklists are based on items that are not scored numerically. Quality scales are based on items that are scored numerically to provide a quantitative estimate of overall study quality. Both checklists and quality scales are applied by experienced researchers or practitioners, usually in groups of two or more [19]. Most checklists and quality scales were devised for the field of medicine (e.g.: [20–22]), although there are also proposals in other disciplines such as the social sciences [23], environment and public health. Also, checklists to assess experimental quality [5, 15] have been proposed in SE.

Finally, another common procedure for evaluating experimental quality is expert opinion. This procedure implies that one or several experts provide an assessment of the quality of an experiment based on its face value [12].

3   Research Questions and Methodology

Our main research goal is to determine whether there is a relationship between the different means of evaluating quality and bias in SE experiments. As there are two main ways to evaluate the quality of an experiment (by expert assessment or using

QA instruments), we have divided this primary goal into three specific research questions:

RQ1. Is it possible to predict experimental bias using a QA instrument?

RQ2. Do expert predictions match the results of a QA instrument?

RQ3. Can experts identify when an experiment has low or high bias?

We used a research methodology similar to what other studies in the field of medicine have used [7, 16, 17]:

- We located meta-analyses published in SE. These meta-analyses provide an estimate of the population effects of certain SE technologies based on which bias can be estimated. The meta-analyses we used were published in the SLRs [24–26]. These SLRs identified a total of 35 experiments.
- We selected a QA instrument to determine the quality of experiments. For the sake of comparability with our previous research, we adopted the same quality scale proposed in [11] with some slight modifications (specifically, item Q01 was omitted because it is only applicable to industry experiments). We respect the names of the items on the original quality scale (Q02–10) for cross-referencing purposes.
- We calculated the bias and scores for the quality scale for each experiment. Additionally, three Empirical SE researchers subjectively assessed the quality of the experiments.

We had to manipulate the data reported in the SLRs [24–26] in order calculate the bias. Most importantly, bias was calculated in two different ways (using effect sizes and response ratios). These dataset manipulations are described in Sect. 4. The analyses conducted on the resulting data are as follows:

- We checked and cleansed the data, as described in Sect. 5. Essentially, we identified and removed the most marked outliers and analysed the convergent validity of the bias measures used.
- We analysed the correlations between the quality scale score, bias and expert opinion, which answer the stated research questions. The calculations were made using SPSS® v.21, and the results are reported in Sect. 6.

4 Datasets

We built three datasets using homogeneous or slightly heterogeneous meta-analyses reported in SE. The first dataset, which we call PAIR, is derived from the SLR on pair programming conducted by Hannay et al. [26]. The second is based on the SLR of inspection techniques conducted by Ciolkowski [24]. However, the meta-analysis reported in [24] has a marked between-study heterogeneity that makes bias more difficult to identify since the population effect size obtained by the set of replications could not be such. On this basis, we ran a separate meta-analysis [27] on homogeneous subsets of the experiments considered in [24]. This allowed us to get a reasonably reliable bias calculation. We call this dataset INSPECTION. We used these two SLRs in previous research [11]. However, this investigation reports more cases (that is, observations) than our previous research because we included meta-analyses on different response variables. Finally, the third dataset, which we call ELICITATION, is derived from an SLR of elicitation techniques conducted by Dieste and Juristo [25]. This dataset was not used in [11].

The three datasets include a total of 35 different experiments. All the data (including the variables mentioned below) were stored in a .sav file (SPSS® format) available at http://www.grise.upm.es/sites/extras/8/ for the purpose of replication of the analyses reported here.

The SLRs [24, 26] use the weighted mean differences method, that is, effect sizes [28], as the synthesis method. Consequently, for the PAIR and INSPECTION datasets, bias was calculated as the difference (in absolute terms) between the effect size reported by the meta-analysis and the effect size of each experiment. The result is stored in the ABSBIASES variable.

Unfortunately, [25] did not use effect sizes, but a version of vote counting. Additionally, although the data of the primary studies are exhaustively reported in [25], not all of these studies report variances. As a result, we cannot use weighted mean differences to re-meta-analyse the experiments. Due to this limitation, we re-meta-analysed the data of [25] using the non-parametric response ratio [29]. In this case, bias was calculated as the difference (also in absolute terms) between the response ratio reported by the meta-analysis and the response ratio of each experiment. The result is stored as the ABSBIASRR variable. As the number of cases in [25] is small (19), we also reanalysed the data in [27] using response ratios. We were unable to do the same with [26] because this study reports neither the measures nor the variances of the primary studies.

Finally, we applied the quality scale to the datasets (the experiments of the three SLR). The rating assigned to each quality scale item is stored in the variablesbreak Q02–10. The total quality scale score (the sum of items Q02–10) is stored in the SCORE variable. Three additional researchers assessed the quality of the experiments in the three SLRs without support. The results are stored in the EXPERT variable. As indicated above, all these data are available at http://www. grise.upm.es/sites/extras/8/.

5   Data Checking and Cleansing

Before proceeding with the analysis, we run three checks that we consider necessary to reduce the risk of flawed findings. First, we examine the datasets in order to identify possible outliers. Next, we check whether the two measures of bias used (ABSBIASES and ABSBIASRR) measure the same construct, that is, have convergent validity [30].

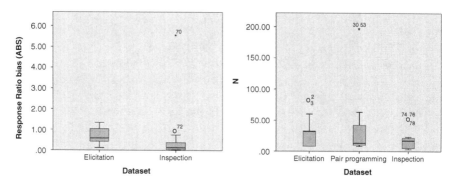

Fig. 1 Outliers detected in the datasets

5.1   Outliers

A visual examination of the datasets reveals that some variables have extreme values, that is, are outliers. Outliers have a harmful influence on all statistical tests, particularly least square based methods like linear correlation and regression [31]. This theoretical indication was confirmed by our preliminary analyses, during which we found that outliers clearly *attracted* any type of tested fitting curve, leading to a reduction in the goodness of fit of the model (R^2) and its statistical significance (*p-value*). Therefore, we removed outliers as suggested by [31].

There is more than one definition of, as well as different methods for calculating, outliers [32], which makes outlier removal a rather subjective process. In order to prevent our decisions influencing the composition of datasets, we adopted a conservative standpoint and only removed the cases with clearly anomalous values. There are four such cases, corresponding to the ABSBIASRR and N variables, as shown in Fig. 1. The case numbers are 70 for ABSBIASRR and 30, 43 and 53 for N. (Note that case number 43 is not charted in the box plot but is displayed by the SPSS® *Show cases* function.)

5.2   Correlation Between Bias Measures

Due to some limitations (mentioned in Sect. 4) of the datasets we used two different measures of bias, one based on effect size (ABSBIASES) and another on response ratios (ABSBIASRR). Now, if both measures were really to represent the underlying bias construct, they should be positively correlated [30]. Otherwise, these measures could not simultaneously represent bias and it would be impossible to decide which (if any) represents this construct.

INSPECTION is the only dataset for which we have both measures of bias. Figure 2 shows a scatter plot comparing ABSBIASES and ABSBIASRR for this dataset. It can be seen that both variables are related to each other more or less

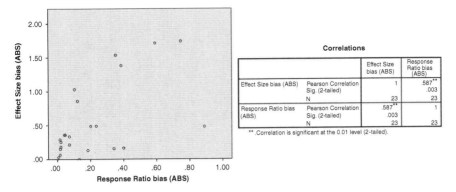

Fig. 2 Correlation between biases measured as effect size and response ratio

linearly, with only one case (no. 71) deviating from this trend. The correlation is highly positive *(r = .587)* and significant *(p-value < 0.01)*. Omitting case 71, the relationship between the two variables is even greater *(r = .746, p-value < 0.001)*.

As the ABSBIASES and ABSBIASRR variables are positively correlated, they can be considered to measure the same underlying bias construct for the INSPECTION dataset, and we can reasonably assume that the same applies to the ELICITATION and PAIR datasets. Therefore, both variables can be used (separately or jointly) as an estimation of bias.

6 Data Analysis

In this section, we present the relationships between internal quality (SCORE), expert opinion (EXPERT) and bias (ABSBIASES and ABSBIASRR) for the three available datasets.

6.1 Relationship Between SCORE and Bias

The SCORE variable is a measure of the quality of an experiment assessed by a quality scale. SCORE is calculated as the sum of the individual items (Q2–Q10) of the quality scale designed in this research. As Likert scales are summative, SCORE is an interval-type measure [33] and can therefore be used with a variety of model fitting methods, in particular least square methods [REF]. In this research, we will use linear regression to study the relationship between SCORE and bias. The model to fit includes the sample size N, because it is well known that sample size affects the estimation of effect size [34]. This model is stated in Eq. 1:

$$Y = N + SCORE + \varepsilon \tag{1}$$

Table 1 Linear regression between N, SCORE and bias (ABSBI-ASES). The datasets using ABSBIASES are PAIR and INSPECTION

Coefficients[a]

Model		Unstandardized coefficients		Standardized coefficients		
		B	Std. error	Beta	t	Sig.
1	(Constant)	−.290	.406		−.714	.479
	N	−.010	.004	−.350	−2.593	.013
	SCORE	.117	.063	.251	1.864	.069

[a]Dependent variable: ABSBIASRR

Table 2 Linear regression between N, SCORE and bias (ABSBI-ASRR). The datasets using ABSBIASRR are ELICITATION and INSPECTION

Coefficients[a]

Model		Unstandardized coefficients		Standardized coefficients		
		B	Std. error	Beta	t	Sig.
1	(Constant)	1.525	.321		4.750	.000
	N	−.003	.003	−.151	−1.044	.303
	SCORE	−.179	.051	−.510	−3.535	.001

[a]Dependent variable: ABSBIASRR

The SCORE-bias relationship has to be determined separately for each of the two bias measures (ABSBIASES and ABSBIASRR). The results of the regression analysis are shown in Tables 1 and 2. The SCORE variable is correlated with bias in both cases, and the coefficient of regression for SCORE is actually significant (the p-value is 0.069 for ABSBIASES, bordering on statistical significance). Therefore, there *appears* to be a relationship between SCORE and bias.

However, a more detailed examination of the results of the analysis reveals two major problems. On the one hand, the goodness of fit for the models is low ($R^2 \approx .200$). This means that the SCORE variable explains bias poorly, or, in other words, there are marked differences between the model predictions and bias. A low goodness of fit means that there are other variables, apart from the variables included in the model (SCORE and N), that explain the observed bias (ABSBIASES and ABSBIASRR).

On the other hand, and probably more importantly, the SCORE coefficient has a positive value ($\beta = .251$) for ABSBIASES, whereas it is negative ($\beta = −.510$) for ABSBIASRR. A negative β coefficient[1] signifies that bias increases as the value of

---

[1]The differences in magnitude between the two coefficients can be attributed to the metrics used (effect size and response ratio); although conceptually interesting, they are less relevant than signs to this discussion.

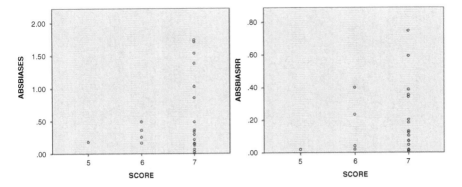

Fig. 3 INSPECTION dataset

SCORE drops (that is, the experiments are rated worse in the questionnaire). This is precisely the relationship that we expected in theory, and it applies to the PAIR and INSPECTION datasets.

Now, we find exactly the opposite to what we expected in the case of datasets that use ABSBIASRR (ELICITATION and INSPECTION) (bias increases as the scores of the experiments increase in the questionnaire). Because the two variables are positively and highly correlated, this can be attributed to the way in which bias has been operationalised (ABSBIASES vs. ABSBIASRR), as specified in Sect. 5.2. Consequently, these results suggest that there is some sort of dependency between the dataset (the experiments used) and the concepts of internal quality/bias. We will examine this dependency in Sect. 6.2.

6.2   Relationship Between SCORE and Bias for Specific Datasets

Figures 3 and 4 show scatter plots comparing the SCORE and bias for the three datasets used. As we calculated bias for the INSPECTION dataset using both ABSBIASES and ABSBIASRR, we present scatter plots for both variables.

The most striking feature of the scatter plots for the INSPECTION dataset is that, as the value of the SCORE variable increases, we observe more experiments with higher bias values (irrespective of ABSBIASES or ABSBIASRR). This shows up in the positive regression coefficients between SCORE and bias for this dataset[2] ($\beta = .234$ for ABSBIASES and $\beta = .148$ for ABSBIASRR). These coefficients are significant ($p\text{-}value = .262$ and $.471$, respectively), although this might be due to the small number of available cases (21). The scatter plots also show that, asalready

---

[2] We use the model stated in Eq. 1 in all cases.

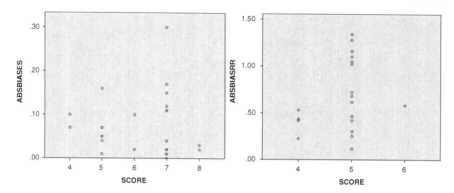

Fig. 4 PAIR (*left*) and ELICITATION (*right*) datasets

mentioned in Sect. 6.1, the goodness of fit of the linear model to the observations is poor, which is confirmed by the low coefficient of determination ($R^2 \approx .150$ in both cases).

In the case of the PAIR dataset, the scatter plot does not show up any systematic relationship between SCORE and bias. The coefficient of regression is near zero ($\beta = -.029$, $p\text{-}value = .887$), which confirms this visual impression. Finally, there is a positive trend for the ELICITATION dataset, similar to our findings for INSPECTION. The coefficient of regression ($\beta = .148$, $p\text{-}value = .471$) confirms this observation. The same arguments apply with respect to statistical significance and goodness of fit of the model ($R^2 = .153$) as for the INSPECTION dataset.

Interpreted with due caution in view of the small number of available cases, the results of the analyses appear to confirm that the relationship between SCORE (evaluation of experiment quality made by experts following a quality scale) and bias depends on the dataset in use. It follows from these results that any analysis should be conducted on separate datasets to make sure that we do not average heterogeneous data. We will follow this procedure in the following sections.

6.3 Relationship Between Expert Opinion (EXPERT) and Internal Quality (SCORE)

The three datasets were evaluated by three different researchers in order to assign a quality level (poor, average, good) to each experiment. This rating was subjective (i.e., the researchers read and rated the experiment). All three researchers are working in the ESE area, and it is reasonable to confide in their good judgement. However, this is a secondary point, as the level of correctness is precisely what we intend to decide in this section.

Expert assessment is commonly assumed to be able to distinguish between good and poor quality experiments [12]. This quality refers to how well an experiment has been designed and executed, that is, to its internal quality. Consequently, expert

Table 3 Correlations between EXPERT and SCORE

Correlations				
		ELICITATION[a]	PAIR[b]	INSPECTION
EXPERT	Pearson correlation	.891[*]	.528[*]	–
	Sig. (2-tailed)	.000	.003	–
	N	19	29	–

[*]Correlation is significant at the 0.01 level (2-tailed)
[a]Bias calculated by means of ABSBIASRR
[b]Bias calculated by means of ABSBIASES

opinion (EXPERT) should correlate positively and highly with the SCORE variable. In order to check whether any such relationship exists, we conducted a correlation analysis between EXPERT and SCORE. Note that, unlike the model examined in Sects. 6.1 and 6.2, this model does not include the N variable, as the expert rating should consider and account for the sample size effect[3].

Table 3 shows the results of calculating correlations, divided by datasets as suggested by the findings reported in Sect. 6.2. As the expert ratings for the INSPECTION dataset were almost uniformly *good*, SPSS® was unable to apply the statistical test and calculate the correlations. With this one exception, however, there was confirmed to be a clear relationship between expert opinion and internal quality or, in other words, experienced researchers are able to distinguish good and poor quality experiments.

6.4   Relationship Between Expert Opinion (EXPERT) and Bias

Following the reasoning explained in Sect. 6.3, that is, if experienced researchers can distinguish between good and poor quality experiments, then they should be able to distinguish between experiments with low bias (high quality) and high bias (low quality).

Table 4 shows the results of calculating the correlations between EXPERT and bias. For the PAIR dataset, the correlation between expert opinion and bias is sizeable ($r = -.418$, $p\text{-}value = .024$) and in the expected direction (negative r).

In the case of the ELICITATION dataset, the correlation is slightly lower and not significant ($r = .375$, $p\text{-}value = .114$). The significance level is likely to be determined by the small number of cases (19), as already specified elsewhere in

---

[3]The coefficients and statistical significance of the EXPERT-SCORE/bias correlation increase when the sample size N is added to the model and are statistically significant in all cases. This would suggest that experienced researchers do not consider sample size as a quality criterion. We did not include the reference to N in the main body of the text so as not to further complicate the discussion.

Table 4 Correlations between EXPERT and bias

Correlations

		ELICITATION[a]	PAIR[b]	INSPECTION
EXPERT	Pearson correlation	.375	−.418[*]	–
	Sig. (2-tailed)	.114	.024	–
	N	19	29	–

[*]Correlation is significant at the 0.05 level (2-tailed)
[a]Bias calculated by means of ABSBIASRR
[b]Bias calculated by means of ABSBIASES

this paper. However, the remarkable thing is that the observed correlation is positive (expert opinion improves as bias increases), contrary to expectations.

7 Discussion

Before discussing the results, we should remove the concept of dataset from the argument. During the analysis, the concept of dataset was useful for unambiguously referencing a subset of observations or cases. Now, dataset has per se no meaning whatsoever, as it is merely a rather arbitrary collection of data. If a specific dataset behaves in a particular manner, this should occur because there is an underlying differential factor causing this behaviour.

We can only identify one factor with any certainty, namely, the SE technology used, which is *elicitation techniques* for the ELICITATION dataset, *pair programming* for the PAIR dataset and *inspection techniques* for the INSPECTION dataset. Of course, there could be other underlying factors, but it would be venturesome to suggest any considering the range of authors, methodologies, techniques, etc. tested in the experiments used. Therefore, we will assume henceforth that a dataset is *primarily* (albeit not exclusively) characterised by the technology used.

The data analysis conducted has provided a multiplicity of results in terms of correlations between all the analysed variables (N, SCORE, EXPERT, ABSBIASES and ABSBIASRR). However, there are three especially noteworthy facts, which we will discuss in the following sections:

1. Expert opinion and the quality scale are highly correlated.
2. The quality scale results (SCORE) and bias correlate as predicted for some technologies (pair programming) and contrary to expectations for others (elicitation techniques and inspection).
3. Expert opinion (EXPERT) and bias correlate as predicted for some technologies (pair programming) and contrary to expectations for others (elicitation techniques). Additionally, expert opinion (EXPERT) and bias are more highly correlated than SCORE and bias.

Table 5 Correlations between EXPERT and quality scale items

Coefficients[a]

Model		Unstandardized coefficients		Standardized coefficients		
		B	Std. error	Beta	t	Sig.
1	(Constant)	−1.273	.370		−3.438	.001
	Q02	.074	.165	0.24	.447	.658
	Q03	.964	.157	.788	6.145	.000
	Q04	.745	.188	.244	3.970	.000
	Q05	−.757	.139	−.537	−5.430	.000
	Q06	1.001	.132	.501	7.589	.000
	Q07	.069	.082	.056	.835	.409
	Q08	.724	.090	.584	8.037	.000
	Q09	−.595	.175	−.433	−3.398	.002

[a]Dependent variable: EXPERT

7.1 Expert Opinion and the Quality Scale Are Highly Correlated

The internal quality of an experiment is usually associated with good practices, such as concealment, blinding or randomisation to mention but three, which mitigate validity threats. These good practices are precisely the aspects to which the items of the quality scale used in this research refer to.

It is generally accepted [2, 18] that when such good practices are applied correctly, the experiment is executed correctly, and therefore its results will be reliable (bias free). Consequently, it is only natural that experienced researchers should use the above aspects, such as concealment, blinding and randomisation, as a basis for rating quality. If this were so, it would mean that expert opinion should be directly related to all (or most) of the quality scale items.

Table 5 shows the result of the linear regression between expert opinion (EXPERT), and the different items of the quality scale. Q10 was excluded by SPSS® because it has constant values or values correlated with other Qs. We find quite clearly that all the items, except Q2 and Q7, are highly correlated with expert opinion. It follows from this relationship that, because it is calculated as the sum of items, the SCORE should also be related to expert opinion, which is precisely what we observed in the analysis reported in Sect. 6.3.

Note, however, that the fact that experienced researchers issue opinions based on aspects similar to the items used in the quality scale does not necessarily mean that these are the *only* criteria they use. We will discuss this point in Sect. 7.3.

7.2 The SCORE-Bias Correlation Depends on the Tested Technology

In our previous research [11], we were unable to identify a clear relationship between SCORE and bias. The results of this analysis explain why: the experiments we used previously mixed different technologies (pair programming and inspection techniques), which, as stated in Sect. 6.2, have a different SCORE-bias relationship.

However, the correlations do not per se explain why different technologies influence experiment quality differently. In the following, we venture an explanatory hypothesis. In this research we used data from three different technologies: elicitation techniques, pair programming and inspection techniques. Let us focus on the first two because there are more results for these two technologies (note that the INSPECTION dataset cannot be used in Sects. 6.3 and 6.4).

Most people would probably agree that requirements elicitation is a complex phenomenon. There are several theoretical recommendations regarding the effectiveness of elicitation techniques (e.g.: [25, 35]), not all of which are compatible. Soft skills are presumed to have a profound impact. Our own research suggests that analyst training and previous experience, as well as customer idiosyncrasies, are all decisive [36]. Consequently, when running an experiment on elicitation, it is far from easy to properly control all the potentially influential variables because they are either unknown or intrinsically linked to the subjects (like experience) and cannot be effectively randomised or blocked.

A priori similar arguments might apply to pair programming, but the programming domain appears to be somewhat better defined than the requirements analysis domain. On the one hand, programming problems can be better defined than requirements problems. On the other, although it is far from clear what distinguishes a good from a bad programmer, a programming task is presumed to require rather "hard" (acquired in training courses) than "soft" skills. From all this we surmise that, despite all its complexity, a programming experiment is controllable, or at least more controllable than an elicitation requirements experiment.[4]

If this were true (note that it is no more than a working hypothesis), good experimental practices (concealment, blinding, randomisation, etc.) would predictably exert a more beneficial influence on pair programming experiments than on elicitation experiments, as the variables are better controlled and the effects produced by the researchers (that is, biases) have a greater quantitative influence. However, the biases in elicitation experiments would be primarily determined by the uncontrolled variables, and good practices would not have such a big impact.

Both predictions can be checked again using linear regression on the available data. Tables 6 and 7 show the relationships between the individual items of the quality scale and the bias for pair programming and for elicitation techniques (using ABSBIASES and ABSBIASRR, respectively). The missing items (e.g., Q03 or Q04 in Table 6, and Q03 and Q05 in Table 7) are either constants or are correlated with the other Qs, and so were excluded from the regression by SPSS®.

Tables 6 and 7 differ primarily as to the statistical significance of the different items (as well as with respect to the missing items, which are not relevant to this discussion). For pair programming, two items (Q06 and Q08) come very close to

---

[4]Inspection techniques are positioned somewhere in-between pair programming and elicitation techniques with respect to controllability.

Table 6 Correlations between quality scale items and bias for pair programming

Coefficients[a]

Model		Unstandardized coefficients		Standardized coefficients		
		B	Std. error	Beta	t	Sig.
1	(Constant)	.127	.127		.998	.329
	Q02	.044	.076	.121	.579	.569
	Q05	.046	.058	.176	.794	.436
	Q06	−.120	.070	−.330	−1.713	.101
	Q07	.020	.036	.129	.548	.589
	Q08	−.045	.033	−.333	−1.368	.186
	Q09	.002	.039	.010	.043	.966
	N	−.001	.001	−.115	−.539	.595

[a]Dependent variable: ABSBIASES

Table 7 Correlations between quality scale items and bias for requirements elicitation

Coefficients[a]

Model		Unstandardized coefficients		Standardized coefficients		
		B	Std. error	Beta	t	Sig.
1	(Constant)	.801	.765		1.047	.313
	Q02	−.005	.421	−.003	−.012	.991
	Q04	−.123	.326	−.102	−.376	.713
	Q06	.177	.266	.196	.665	.517
	Q09	−.272	.231	−.365	−1.179	.258

[a]Dependent variable: ABSBIASES

(although they do not achieve) statistical significance. This means that these items are likely to be related to bias. This claim is also supported to some extent by the preliminary study we conducted [11] where these items were also related to bias (although, as mentioned earlier, that study used a smaller dataset).

7.3 The Correlation Between Expert Opinion and Bias Depends on the Tested Technology

As expert opinion is correlated with the quality scale (SCORE), and SCORE is differentially correlated (depending on the type of technology) with bias, the correlation between expert opinion and bias should obviously also depend on the technology. This is simply a foreseeable purely mathematical effect in a multiple correlation.

However, the fact that the coefficients of the EXPERT-bias correlation, almost significant in all cases, are higher ($r = -.418$ and $.375$) for pair programming and elicitation techniques than the SCORE-bias coefficients of regression ($\beta = -.029$ and $.148$, respectively) is more interesting. To put it plainly and simply, experienced researchers are right (and wrong) more often than the quality scale.

We think that the reason is that experienced researchers base their ratings on other aspects of the experimental design and execution apart from the items on the quality scale. This would explain why, on the one hand, the quality scale and the experts mostly agree, as shown in Table 5. But, on the other hand, it would also explain why experts provide more categorical ratings, which are aligned with bias for technologies that can be controlled in the laboratory (pair programming), but not for less well-known and less controllable technologies (elicitation techniques). Unfortunately we cannot test this hypothesis using the datasets to which we have access.

8   Threats to Validity

We identified several threats during the development of this research that could compromise the reliability of the outcomes:

- The indicator used to measure bias can return imprecise values because it is calculated from a small number of studies. There do not tend to be many experiments, and, at the same time, the sample size of most experiments is small.
- We did not consider all the elements of internal validity that might affect quality. Whereas other disciplines (e.g., medicine) account for multiple experiment characteristics related to internal validity (e.g., drop-outs, concealment, secular changes, etc.), we used only aspects that recur in the literature and are applicable to SE.
- One of the SLRs included in this study was run by researchers of the Universidad Politécnica de Madrid's (UPM) Experimental Software Engineering Research Group. However, this association should not bias this study, as the SLRs were not run for the same purpose as this study, and we have no hidden agenda whatsoever related to the QA of experiments in SLR.
- The researchers who calculated both the quality score and the bias of the experiments used in this study are members of the UPM's Experimental Software Engineering Research Group. As already mentioned, we have no agenda whatsoever regarding the QA of experiments in SLRs, but we do acknowledge that this study needs to be replicated and extended by independent researchers.

9   Conclusions

This paper extends the research reported in [11]. We added a third set of experiments (the ELICITATION dataset), new cases, new bias measures (ABSBIASRR) and quality assessment by researchers experienced in ESE.

The results suggest that there are factors other than external quality that influence bias. The SE technology tested in the experiments is the factor that we identified quite confidently as being related to bias. As the technology per se should not really affect bias, we hypothesised that the underlying reason is how well experimenters can control the technology. The more easily controllable the technology, the more aspects are related to internal quality influence on bias. They are less influential for technologies that are not controllable because either the variables influencing the technology are unknown, or internal quality (defined as standard processes: concealment, blinding, randomisation, etc.) cannot be reliably controlled.

The technology → control → bias relationship is a possible explanation for why quality scales are operational in some cases and not in others: a quality scale based on formal internal quality criteria will accurately predict bias when the technology can be properly controlled in the laboratory. If the quality scale is based on other criteria, the correct prediction of bias will depend on whether such criteria tie in with aspects of the technology that are hard to control.

Finally, note that the above conclusions are preliminary. We are now trying to expand and refine the existing datasets in order to run analyses on a larger dataset and check the consistency of the results.

References

1. Kitchenham, B., Charters, S.: Guidelines for Performing Systematic Literature Reviews in Software Engineering. Version 2.3. EBSE Technical Report, EBSE-2007-01 (2007)
2. CRD, University of York: Systematic Reviews: CRD's Guidance for Undertaking Reviews in Health Care. CRD, University of York, York (2009)
3. Biolchini, J., Mian, P., Natali, A., et al.: Systematic Review in Software Engineering. Technical Report ES 679/05, COPPE/UFRJ (2005)
4. Dybå, T., Dingsøyr, T.: Strength of evidence in systematic reviews in software engineering. In: 2nd International Symposium on Empirical Software Engineering and Measurement (ESEM'08), pp. 178–187. (2008)
5. Dybå, T., Dingsøyr, T.: Empirical studies of agile software development: a systematic review. Inf. Softw. Technol. **50**, 833–859 (2008)
6. Afzal, W., Torkar, R., Feldt, R.: A systematic review of search-based testing for non-functional system properties. Inf. Softw. Technol. **51**, 957–976 (2009)
7. Balk, E.M., Bonis, P.L., Moskowitz, H., et al.: Correlation of quality measures with estimates of treatment effect in meta-analyses of randomized controlled trials. JAMA **287**, 2973–2982 (2002)
8. Deeks, J. J., Dinnes, J., D'Amico, R., et al.: Evaluating non-randomised intervention studies. Health technology assessment (Winchester, England) JID – 9706284, (1030)
9. Emerson, J.D., Burdick, E., Hoaglin, D.C., et al.: An empirical study of the possible relation of treatment differences to quality scores in controlled randomized clinical trials. Control. Clin. Trials **11**, 339–352 (1990)
10. McKee, M., Britton, A., Black, N., et al.: Interpreting the evidence: choosing between randomised and non-randomised studies. BMJ **319**, 312–315 (1999)
11. Dieste, O.: Quantitative determination of the relationship between internal validity and bias in software engineering experiments: consequences for systematic literature reviews. In: 5th International Symposium on Empirical Software Engineering and Measurement (ESEM'11), pp. 285–294. (2011)

12. Kitchenham, B.A., Sjøberg, D.I.K., Dybå, T., et al.: Three empirical studies on the agreement of reviewers about the quality of software engineering experiments. Inf. Softw. Technol. **54**, 804–819 (2012)
13. Shadish, W.R., Cook, T.D., Campbell, D.T.: Experimental and Quasi-Experimental Designs for Generalized Causal Inference. Houghton Mifflin Company, Boston (2001)
14. Montgomery, D.C., Runger, G.C.: Applied Statistics and Probability for Engineers. Wiley, Hoboken (2010)
15. Kitchenham, B. A.: Procedures for Performing Systematic Reviews. Keele University TR/SE-0401 (2004)
16. Jüni, P., Witschi, A., Bloch, R., et al.: The hazards of scoring the quality of clinical trials for meta-analysis. JAMA **282**, 1054–1060 (1999)
17. Schulz, K.F., Chalmers, I., Hayes, R.J., et al.: Empirical evidence of bias. Dimensions of methodological quality associated with estimates of treatment effects in controlled trials. JAMA **273**, 408–412 (1995)
18. Higgins J., Green S.: Cochrane Handbook for Systematic Reviews of Interventions Version 5.1.0. The Cochrane Collaboration (2011)
19. Petticrew, M., Roberts, H.: Systematic Reviews in the Social Sciences: A Practical Guide. Wiley-Blackwell, Oxford (2005)
20. Downs, S.H., Black, N.: The feasibility of creating a checklist for the assessment of the methodological quality both of randomised and non-randomised studies of health care interventions. J. Epidemiol. Commun. Health JID – 7909766, (1028)
21. Jadad, A.R., Moore, R.A., Carroll, D., et al.: Assessing the quality of reports of randomized clinical trials: is blinding necessary? Control. Clin. Trials **17**, 1–12 (1996)
22. Owens, D.K., Lohr, K.N., Atkins, D., et al.: AHRQ series paper 5: grading the strength of a body of evidence when comparing medical interventions – Agency for Healthcare Research and Quality and the Effective Health-Care Program. J. Clin. Epidemiol. **63**, 513–523 (2010)
23. Cook, T.D., Campbell, D.T.: Quasi-Experimentation: Design & Analysis Issues for Field Settings. Rand McNally College Pub. Co., Chicago (1979)
24. Ciolkowski, M.: What do we know about perspective-based reading? An approach for quantitative aggregation in software engineering. In: 3rd International Symposium on Empirical Software Engineering and Measurement (ESEM'09), pp. 133–144. (2009)
25. Dieste, O., Juristo, N.: Systematic review and aggregation of empirical studies on elicitation techniques. IEEE Trans. Softw. Eng. **37**, 304 (2011)
26. Hannay, J.E., Dybå, T., Arisholm, E., et al.: The effectiveness of pair programming: a meta-analysis. Inf. Softw. Technol. **51**, 1110–1122 (2009)
27. Griman, A.C.: Process for the systematic review of experiments in software engineering, Ph.D. thesis, Universidad Politécnica de Madrid, under review process (2013)
28. Hedges, L.V., Olkin, I.: Statistical Methods for Meta-Analysis. Academic, Orlando (1985)
29. Worm, B., Barbier, E.B., Beaumont, N., et al.: Impacts of biodiversity loss on ocean ecosystem services: supplementary online material. Science **314**, 787–790 (2006)
30. Furr, R.M., Bacharach, V.R.: Psychometrics: An Introduction. SAGE, Thousand Oaks (2007)
31. Osborne, J.W., Overbay, A.: The power of outliers (and why researchers should always check for them). Pract. Assess. Res. Eval. **9** http://pareonline.net/getvn.asp?v=9&n=6 (2004)
32. Hodge, V., Austin, J.: A survey of outlier detection methodologies. Artif. Intell. Rev. **22**, 85–126 (2004)
33. Carifio, J., Perla, R.J.: Ten common misunderstandings, misconceptions, persistent myths and urban legends about Likert scales and Likert response formats and their antidotes. J. Soc. Sci. **3**, 106–116 (2007)
34. Richy, F., Ethgen, O., Bruyere, O., et al.: From sample size to effect-size: Small Study Effect Investigation (SSEi). Internet J. Epidemiol. **1** http://archive.ispub.com/journal/the-internet-journal-of-epidemiology/volume-1-number-2/from-sample-size-to-effect-size-small-study-effect-investigation-ssei.html#sthash.9buE8aQx.dpbs (2004)

35. Maiden, N.A.M., Rugg, G.: ACRE: selecting methods for requirements acquisition. Softw. Eng. J. **11**, 183–192 (1996)
36. Aranda, A., Dieste, O., Juristo, N.: Searching for the variables that influence requirements elicitation. Requir. Eng. J. (submitted 2013)

Technical Debt: Showing the Way for Better Transfer of Empirical Results

Forrest Shull, Davide Falessi, Carolyn Seaman, Madeline Diep, and Lucas Layman

Abstract

In this chapter, we discuss recent progress and opportunities in empirical software engineering by focusing on a particular technology, Technical Debt (TD), which ties together many recent developments in the field. Recent advances in TD research are providing empiricists the chance to make more sophisticated recommendations that have observable impact on practice.

TD uses a financial metaphor and provides a framework for articulating the notion of tradeoffs between the short-term benefits and the long-term costs of software development decisions. TD is seeing an explosion of interest in the practitioner community, and research in this area is quickly having an impact on practice. We argue that this is due to several strands of empirical research reaching a level of maturity that provides useful benefits to practitioners, who in turn provide excellent data to researchers. They key is providing observable benefit to practitioners, such as the ability to tie technical debt measures to business goals, and the ability to articulate more sophisticated value-based propositions regarding how to prioritize rework. TD is an interesting case study in how the maturing field of empirical software engineering research is paying dividends. It is only a little hyperbolic to call this a watershed moment for empirical study, where many areas of progress are coming to a head at the same time.

F. Shull (✉) • D. Falessi • C. Seaman • M. Diep • L. Layman
Fraunhofer Center for Experimental Software Engineering, 5825 University Research Court, Suite 1300, College Park, MD 20740-3823, USA
e-mail: fshull@fc-md.umd.edu; dfalessi@fc-md.umd.edu; cseaman@fc-md.umd.edu; mdiep@fc-md.umd.edu; llayman@fc-md.umd.edu

J. Münch and K. Schmid (eds.), *Perspectives on the Future of Software Engineering*, DOI 10.1007/978-3-642-37395-4_12, © Springer-Verlag Berlin Heidelberg 2013

1   Introduction

Software engineering is an exceedingly dynamic field. Since the term "software engineering" was coined at the 1968 NATO conference, the field has seen an explosion in terms of the number of applications and products that use software, an immense growth in the sophistication and capabilities of those products, multiple revolutions in the way software relates to the hardware and networks over which it runs, and an ever-changing set of technologies, tools, and methods promising more effective software development.

Similarly and not surprisingly, the field of empirical software engineering has been dynamic as well. In the decades in which empirical studies have been performed, we have seen evolutions in the objects of study, study methodologies, and the types of metrics used to describe those study objects. Also, as with software engineering in the large, empiricists have seen our own fads come and go, with different types of studies being introduced, becoming (over-)popular, and then settling into a useful niche in the field. Articles elsewhere in this book [1] have reflected on some of these trends. In this chapter, we discuss some recent progressions and opportunities in the area of empirical software engineering by focusing on a particular technology, Technical Debt, which ties together many recent developments in the field. We use Technical Debt to discuss recent advances that are providing empiricists the chance to make more sophisticated recommendations and to have more of an impact on practice. We also use this concept as a launching point to look at how some of these recent progressions may extend into the future.

2   Technical Debt: What Is It?

Before describing the opportunities that TD brings to empirical software engineering, let's try to understand what TD is. First coined in 1992 [2], the underlying ideas come from the mid-1980s and are related to Lehman and Belady's notion of software decay [3] and Parnas' software aging phenomenon [4]. TD is a metaphor, and while it lacks a formal definition, it can be seen as "the invisible results of past decisions about software that negatively affect its future" [5]. The reference to financial "debt" implies that the notion of tradeoffs between short-term benefits and long-term costs is central to the concept.

Because TD is a metaphor, it can be applied to almost any aspect of software development, encompassing anything that stands in the way of deploying, selling, or evolving a software system or anything that adds to the friction from which software development endeavors suffer: test debt, people debt, architectural debt, requirement debt, documentation debt, code quality debt, etc. [6]. Research into TD often bears a superficial resemblance to earlier empirical work on defect identification; TD identification often takes the form of identifying deficiencies in software development artifacts (requirements, architecture, code, etc.).

While TD research builds upon many of the empirical lessons learned from defect identification, we argue that TD research introduces an important new dimension into empirical studies of software defects and software quality: context-dependent short-term versus long-term quality tradeoffs. Consider the progression of empirical work in software quality:

- *Approximating quality via defect counts:* Many studies of software quality have used defect counts as a proxy for a technique's impact on software quality. For example, in studies of software V&V methods, it is often assumed that the more defects identified by a technique, the bigger the resulting improvement to software quality that can result from its application. Some examples include [7, 8].

- *Value-Based Software Engineering:* It was always recognized that defect counts were simply a proxy for software quality, but the Value-Based Software Engineering (VBSE) paradigm gave the community more tools required for a sophisticated view of the problem. VBSE articulated the idea that value propositions in software development need to be made explicit, so that software engineers can determine whether stakeholder values are being met and, indeed, whether they can be reconciled [9]. Studies reflecting a VBSE point of view tend to weight defects differently in terms of their severity for different stakeholders, or according to the operational scenarios under which those defects would be detected. In short, the studies were designed on the assumption that the true impact on quality can vary greatly from one defect to another.

- *Quality is relative in time and context:* Work on TD extends the VBSE considerations even further. First, in TD, the issues needing rework are more tightly coupled to the team's specific quality goals. For example, deficient documentation may not represent a "defect" in the sense that it will lead to incorrect software, but this deficiency may represent TD for teams that prioritize reuse and maintainability. In contrast, deficient documentation would not be considered as TD by a team that is developing a throw-away prototype. Second, TD instances do not automatically represent deficiencies in the system; rather they represent a tradeoff that was made in order to achieve some other short-term goal. TD may even be healthy in the short term, such as trading off a perfectly maintainable design to add quickly a feature needed immediately by an important customer. The TD metaphor stresses that other considerations need to be taken into account by teams contemplating rework of a TD issue, such as how much effort it would take to correct that instance and how much it is "costing" to have that instance in the system.

TD research has inherited much from prior generations of empirical studies that looked at software quality: approaches to counting discrete instances of items for potential rework (whether they be instances of defects or TD); the need for taxonomies to categorize those instances and provide insights regarding root causes; and the goal of characterizing various manual and automated techniques in terms of the number and type of instances that they uncover.

TD encapsulates new aspects of empiricism by providing **a context-dependent way of thinking about software quality across lifecycle phases, and in a way**

tractable to quantitative analysis and hence objective observations. Thus, the primary contribution of TD to the empirical community is useful guidance for: (1) analyzing the cost tradeoffs of software engineering decisions; and (2) effectively transmitting the results of empirical research to practitioners by recognizing the existence and management of these tradeoffs.

3   Technical Debt: A Boundless Challenge

One important distinction is between unintentional and intentional debt [10]. Unintentional debt occurs due to a lack of attention, e.g., lack of adherence to development standards or unnoticed low quality code that might be written by a novice programmer. Intentional debt is incurred proactively for tactical or strategic reasons such as to meet a delivery deadline. Intentional debt has been further broken down into short-term debt and long-term debt, which represent, respectively, small shortcuts like credit card debt, and strategic actions like a mortgage. Based on this classification, Fowler created a more elaborate categorization composed of two dimensions—deliberate/inadvertent and reckless/prudent [11]. These dimensions give rise to four categories: deliberate reckless debt, deliberate prudent debt, inadvertent reckless debt, and inadvertent prudent debt. This classification is helpful in finding the causes of technical debt, which lead to different identification approaches. For example, to identify reckless and inadvertent debt, especially design debt, source code analysis may be required.

Technical debt can also be classified in terms of the phase in which it occurs in the software lifecycle—design debt, testing debt, defect debt, etc. [12]. Design debt refers to the design that is insufficiently robust in some areas or the pieces of code that need refactoring; testing debt refers to the tests that were planned but not exercised on the source code. This type of classification sheds light on the possible sources and forms of technical debt, each of which may need different measures for identification, and approaches for management. For example, comparison to coding standards may be required to identify and measure design debt, while testing debt measures require information about expected testing adequacy criteria. Other types of debt, based on the lifecycle phase or the entity in which the debt occurs, have been suggested in the literature, e.g., people debt, infrastructure debt, etc. Some types of TD grow organically, without any actions on the part of developers, because software and technology inevitably become out of date with respect to their environment.

Another important dimension along which instances of TD can be categorized is visibility to the customer and end-users. Instances of visible TD include poor usability and low reliability. Instances of invisible TD include violations of architectural rules and missing documentation. Some, but not all, definitions of TD exclude debt that is visible to the end-user.

TD has been recognized to exist in every sector of the software industry, and the research community has been active on this topic. Formal, scholarly investigation of TD is just beginning and is starting to produce usable improvements. The number of TD research outputs is increasing rapidly. There have been to date three Workshops on Managing Technical Debt, the first one resulting in a joint research agenda [13] and the remaining two co-located with ICSE 2011 and 2012. Two more workshops are planned for 2013. A recent *IEEE Software* special issue contains several articles on the multifaceted concept of TD [5]. Unfortunately, these workshops and published papers have to date failed to produce a universally agreed-upon and used definition of TD. Thus, there are signs that the term TD has been overloaded and is losing its meaning. Every new software engineering technique or empirical investigation has (to a greater or lesser extent) an impact on, or is affected by, TD. For instance, an empirical study comparing the effectiveness of two V&V techniques could support mitigation of TD because future TD decisions about which V&V activity to implement can be based on such an observation. There is a noticeable trend in titling software engineering papers to relate them to TD, even if that relationship is tenuous. However, the lack of a concrete definition of TD makes it difficult to argue against such titling. Such broad labeling of published studies makes aggregation of results hard. Clearly, an ongoing challenge for the TD research community is to find a way to define the term broadly enough to encompass all relevant research, but concretely enough to draw a useful boundary and give guidance to authors.

4 Technical Debt Brings Empirical Opportunities

The concept of technical debt is one that resonates strongly with the developer community as evidenced by the number of practitioner-authored blog posts, presentations, and webinars conducted on the topic. It has been our experience that practitioners desire research results on this topic more so than on many other subjects of empirical research. What is the reason for this surge of interest? We argue that an important reason is maturity of the empirical research methods applied to TD—many of the most powerful and mature empirical methods have come together in a mutually-supportive way to study TD, to engage real-world problems, and to communicate useful results to practitioners.

4.1 Identifying and Predicting TD Costs Is Improved by Empiricism

In general, managing TD consists of estimating, analyzing, and reasoning about: (1) where TD exists in a system so that it can be tagged for eventual removal, (2) the cost of removing TD (i.e., the principal), and (3) the consequences of not removing TD (i.e., the interest). Regarding point (1), there is a large body of software engineering literature [6, 14] related to how to identify TD. Points (2) and (3) require a more careful discussion. In the context of TD, the term "principal" refers to the cost of fixing the technical problem (i.e., removing the debt). For instance, the principal related to the debt affecting a component of a system with high coupling and cohesion refers to the effort necessary to refactor the component to achieve a lower level of coupling and cohesion (e.g., refactoring the component is estimated to cost $500). Principal needs to be estimated, and the principal estimate will be more accurate and the resulting decisions more sound with a reliable knowledge base. However, in the absence of historical data, a rough estimate (e.g., high, medium, low) based on expert opinion is more helpful than no estimate at all.

In the context of TD, the term "interest" refers to the cost that will be incurred by not fixing the technical problem (i.e., the consequences of not removing the debt). For example, the interest related to a component of a system with high coupling and cohesion refers to the extra effort that will be necessary to maintain the component in the future. We note that, unlike the principal, the interest is not certain but has an associated probability of occurrence. In other words, you can be sure that refactoring a component will cost you something (i.e., $500), but you cannot be certain about the consequences of not refactoring it. Therefore, estimating interest means estimating both the amount and its probability of occurrence. These estimates are difficult to make, and in practice a rough estimate of high, medium, and low is the best that can be obtained. Even these rough estimates are more reliable if they are based on historical data.

Managing TD encompasses several estimation activities that are clearly of an empirical nature. In practice, it is difficult to predict anything without a reliable knowledge base.

4.2   The Pivotal Role of Context and Qualitative Methods

TD concepts like principal and interest are context-specific. In fact, the same TD in one organization (e.g., a specific level of coupling and cohesion) can have a low or high principal (i.e., can be easy or hard to eliminate) and a low or high debt (i.e., can have a low or high impact in the future) depending on the project or even the subsystem within a project. Thus, there is a need for quantitative methods to elicit meaningful representations of interest and debt in context.

Unfortunately, we do not yet know how to determine when one project is similar enough to another to experience similar results. Even when working in the same exact context, the future will always differ from the past. For example, when working with the same industrial partner, they may experience employee turnover that threatens the applicability of past results. Even if employees do not change, their experience and performance inevitably changes over time. Moreover, almost every software engineering technique is dependent on others. Thus, it is questionable if the assessment of a given technology still holds when the related technologies changed.

In the context of TD, principal and interest clearly vary among environments and there is a need to know one's customers and collaborate closely with them. Context factors can be elicited in a number of ways. Qualitative methods are needed when it is not clear which factors are relevant, or when there is a desire to discover new unknown context factors. Given the appropriate prompts, developers, managers, and other stakeholders can all provide important context information through interviews, focus groups, or observation.

There was a time when the software engineering research community debated whether qualitative research methods are appropriate, and proponents had to advocate for more adoption [15, 16]. These qualitative methods are now an integral part of the TD work and one of the reasons why TD tech transfer has been so effective.

When managing or studying TD in particular, two important elements of context are: (1) the software qualities of interest (i.e., what are the most important success criteria?); and (2) the "pain points" (i.e., where has the interest on TD been felt most acutely?). For example, if an organization is most concerned with on-time delivery, then they would be most interested in dealing with TD that causes late-lifecycle surprises, such as inadequate testing. If an organization has a history of damaging cost overruns during maintenance on a large legacy system, then they would be most interested in controlling design debt by refactoring code that is brittle, overly complex, or hard to maintain. Such subtle elements of context are often not documented, and can only be discovered through asking the right questions.

As an example, in [17], practitioners were interviewed and shared a variety of long-term pains resulting from TD. These pains varied from fragile code to poor performance to the added complexity of problems found at the customer site. They also shared varying contexts that influence decisions made about TD, such as the difference between short-lived, non-critical software and software whose longevity is uncertain. The open-endedness of the interviews made it possible to elicit elements of context that had not previously been reported in the literature, and also to gain a richer understanding of previously-known factors.

Sometimes, context information that relates to quality goals and to "pain points" can be found by mining the data archives of a project. In [18], the authors used archival data to conduct an in-depth retrospective study of a particularly high-interest instance of TD. The interest was incurred due to a decision to delay an upgrade in the infrastructure software, then a decision to make a substantial change in the architecture, which then necessitated a greatly increased amount of work later when the upgrade could no longer be delayed. The data analysis revealed the historical sequence of events and decisions that made this TD more expensive in the long run than it initially appeared.

In another study [19], we examined the use of reference architecture across projects in a mid-sized software development company that focuses on database-driven web applications. By collaborating with practitioners, we found that technical debt arises when developers design their own solutions and avoid reuse, and that designing the system to be in compliance with the reference architecture leads to greater understandability and maintainability over time in the future. In this same context, we also observed that code smells and out-of-date documentation can be realistic indicators of technical debt.

Finally, by observing a team developing high-performance code for supercomputers, we noticed that they solve the challenge of optimizing the use of the parallel processors by strongly separating calls to the parallelization libraries from the code doing scientific simulation, thereby allowing both the computer scientists and the domain experts to focus on what they know best [20]. In this context, the instances where this separation of concerns breaks down should be treated as technical debt— by detecting and fixing where the planned architecture of the system is not followed, we can help the developers create a more maintainable and flexible system.

We note that in all these industry collaborations, discussions with the whole team were essential to validating our concepts of TD in that context. For example, the idea of separation of concerns may not be applicable on a more homogeneous team that does not have to deal with multiple types of specialized complexity, and we do not expect that specific rules for identifying "code smells" would be applicable for every development team.

4.3   Tool Support Enables Empiricism

Much of the measurement "infrastructure" that is our legacy from the empirical software engineering research community (e.g., GQM, QIP) was originally defined as a set of methodologies without an explicit tool-supported component. Contemporary empirical studies, in contrast, rely heavily on tool support and automation in order to deal with the size and complexity of today's software engineering products when collecting, analyzing, and exploring metrics data. Moreover, automated or computer-assisted approaches are necessary to get buy-in from project teams who are used to doing all of their other project activities online. TD is no exception.

To date, several methods and tools for detecting anomalies in source code (automated static analysis, code smell detectors, etc.) have been developed, and these tools show promise for the task of identifying TD [19]. However, these tools have not yet been integrated with developers' day-to-day work practices and tools and, more importantly, with management's day-to-day decision-making processes. These shortcomings have led to limited adoption of existing methods to manage TD in industry and a lack of understanding about what can be gained from managing debt.

A long-term vision for tool support for TD decision-making, which will always by necessity include a human component, is a set of integrated tools that continually monitor and diagnose the forms of TD that are accumulating and that threaten the goals of the project, providing a continual stream of actionable information to human decision-makers. Such a toolkit must be integrated so that one single, seamless interaction is available to practitioners for all steps involved in choosing and applying TD identification techniques, aggregating the results, analyzing the choices available for a particular decision, and recording the outcome of the decision itself. The toolkit must also be extensible to incorporate new technical debt identification techniques as well as other decision approaches as they mature. The toolkit must be accompanied by a methodology that describes not only the process of applying the toolkit and choosing among the available options, but also how the use of the toolkit should fit into software maintenance project management practices already in place.

Such tool support is necessary for technology transfer in this area, not only because industry adoption depends on effective tools, but also because such tools will allow experimentation with our findings in development environments and assist in the collection of necessary data to support further research.

4.4   Smarter Dashboards

The idea of dashboards to provide an aggregated view over key metrics is not a new one. The recent trend in this area, however, is the development of a set of principles that exploit the typical data-rich development environment to provide more effective and useful guidance. Across a number of different software domains, some of these common principles include the need for metrics dashboards to be:

- *Built on automated data collection*: Making the collection of measures an extra step for developers who are already overloaded is rarely a recipe for success. Metrics programs with staying power use metrics that are already available for other reasons, e.g., the use of timesheet or time accounting systems to track effort and tasking, or the use of JIRA and other bug tracking tools to measure defect backlog and closure rate. Effective dashboards are those which are built upon integrating data streams from these existing sources, and tying these measures to the questions of interest.
- *Easily Changeable*: In software acquisition environments, data comes from a number of different sources and may change from period to period (within contractually mandated limits). Effective dashboards are those which can easily be adapted to new data schemas as necessary.
- *Trustability:* The data used by the dashboard must be checked to help provide confidence in the results presented. Usually, the quantity of data requires at least some level of automation to verify the quality of the data and the dashboard results.
- *Allowing details-on-demand:* The ability to roll-up low level data, such as data measured at the subsystem level, separate components, or external sources, is necessary if the dashboard is to provide high-level status monitoring. If not done properly, however, roll-up data may camouflage valuable insight. Recent advances in reusable graphical libraries ensure that data exploration can happen quickly and efficiently.

Having a dashboard that pulls together and visualizes TD information would be beneficial during the decision-making process, and hence work has been ongoing in this area [21]. The dashboard should present information that is relevant to both engineers and managers, at varying levels of abstraction. For example, the dashboard could show how many TD instances have been identified, and provide capability for the engineers to drill down to the source of each TD tied to the development work products, e.g., location of the source code that could benefit in refactoring, problematic requirement statements, etc. Such information enables traceability between each TD instance and the affected documentation, as well as allowing the engineers to understand the extent and context of the TD. Additionally, business-level information, such as comparison between the principal cost and estimated interest of the TD, may be more relevant for the managers. The cost can be rolled up to show the collective impact of TD for the whole system/program. At the same, on demand, managers could drill down and understand how the impact of TD is distributed across the subsystems or program modules or other development work products.

More ambitiously, we envision future TD dashboards that include what-if analysis capability, where managers could play out various scenarios corresponding to the removal of one or more TD instances. For each scenario, the dashboard could visualize how the removal of a source of TD impacts the landscape of the remaining TD (the principal and the interest). Additionally, the dashboard could offer the view of the TD landscape over time—one TD instance's cost may increase at a more significant rate than others as the cost of principal and interest (likelihood and additional effort) may vary over time. All these different perspectives could assist in the prioritizing of TD removal effort.

5   Conclusion

In this chapter, we have shown how research in one of the fastest-growing areas of empirical study, Technical Debt, relies on a variety of results and methods from past empirical software engineering research. This represents an important development in its own right, since software engineering research has long suffered from an inability to build on previous results. We have also shown how the success of TD research is indebted to recent trends in all of those areas. In this sense, TD makes an interesting case study in how the current level of maturity in empirical studies is paying dividends—it is perhaps only a little hyperbolic to call this a watershed moment for empirical study, where many areas of progress are coming to a head together.

The TD metaphor itself is an important focus of further work since it provides a framework that is both compelling to practitioners and ties together research results on many different topics. This chapter provided our vision of where the research can go: producing an improved and context-specific approach to software measurement that provides tighter feedback loops and more information to developers when they can best use it. Just as importantly, the refinements to empirical research methodologies and principles in the TD work (e.g., accounting for context and business value) will be crucial to other areas of software engineering research by strengthening the ability to influence software development practice.

References

1. Basili, V.R.: A personal perspective on the evolution of empirical software engineering. In: Münch, J., Schmid, K. (eds.) Perspectives on the Future of Software Engineering: Essays in Honor of Dieter Rombach. Springer (2013)
2. Cunningham, W.: The WyCash portfolio management system. ACM SIGPLAN OOPS Messenger **4**(2), 29–30 (1993). doi:10.1145/157710.157715
3. Lehman, M.M., Belady, L.A.: Program Evolution - Processes of Software Change, APIC Sudies in Data Processing No. 27, Academic (1985)
4. Parnas, D.L.: Software aging. In: Proceedings of 16th International Conference on Software Engineering, pp. 279–287. IEEE Computer Society Press. doi:10.1109/ICSE.1994.296790 (1994)
5. Kruchten, P., Nord, R.L., Ozkaya, I.: Technical debt: from metaphor to theory and practice. IEEE Softw. **29**(6), 18–21 (2012). doi:10.1109/MS.2012.167
6. Sterling, C.: Managing Software Debt: Building for Inevitable Change. Agile Software Development Series. Addison-Wesley Professional (2010). ISBN-10: 0321554132
7. Basili, V.R., Selby, R.W.: Comparing the effectiveness of software testing strategies. IEEE Trans. Softw. Eng. **SE-13**(12), 1278–1296 (1987). doi:10.1109/TSE.1987.232881
8. Basili, V.R., Green, S., Laitenberger, O., Shull, F., Sørumgård, S., Zelkowitz, M.V.: The empirical investigation of perspective-based reading. Retrieved from http://dl.acm.org/citation.cfm?id=241252 (1995)
9. Biffl, S., Aurum, A., Boehm, B., Erdogmus, H., Grünbacher, P.: Value-Based Software Engineering (Google eBook), p. 388. Springer. Retrieved from http://books.google.com/books?id=CAlM6nNPcsgC&pgis=1 (2006)
10. McConnell, S.: 10x software development. Retrieved from http://forums.construx.com/blogs/stevemcc/archive/2007/11/01/technical-debt-2.aspx (2007)
11. Fowler, M.: Technical debt quadrant. Retrieved from http://www.martinfowler.com/bliki/TechnicalDebtQuadrant.html (2009)
12. Rothman, J.: An incremental technique to pay off testing technical debt. Retrieved from http://www.stickyminds.com/sitewide.asp?Function=edetail&ObjectType=COL&ObjectId=11011&tth=DYN&tt=siteemail&iDyn=2 (2006)
13. Brown, N., Ozkaya, I., Sangwan, R., Seaman, C., Sullivan, K., Zazworka, N., Cai, Y., et al.: Managing technical debt in software-reliant systems. In: Proceedings of the FSE/SDP Workshop on Future of Software Engineering Research – FoSER'10, p. 47. ACM Press, New York. doi:10.1145/1882362.1882373 (2010)
14. Zazworka, N., Shaw, M. A., Shull, F., Seaman, C.: Investigating the impact of design debt on software quality. In: Proceeding of the 2nd Working on Managing Technical Debt – MTD'11, p. 17. ACM Press, New York. doi:10.1145/1985362.1985366 (2011)
15. Dybå, T., Prikladnicki, R., Rönkkö, K., Seaman, C., Sillito, J.: Qualitative research in software engineering. Empirical Softw. Eng. **16**(4), 425–429 (2011). doi:10.1007/s10664-011-9163-y
16. Dittrich, Y., John, M., Singer, J., Tessem, B.: For the special issue on qualitative software engineering research. Inf. Softw. Technol. **49**(6), 531–539 (2007). doi:10.1016/j.infsof.2007.02.009
17. Lim, E., Taksande, N., Seaman, C.: A balancing act: what software practitioners have to say about technical debt. IEEE Softw. **29**(6), 22–27 (2012). doi:10.1109/MS.2012.130
18. Guo, Y., Seaman, C., Gomes, R., Cavalcanti, A., Tonin, G., Da Silva, F. Q. B., Santos, A. L. M., et al.: Tracking technical debt – an exploratory case study. In: 2011 27th IEEE International Conference on Software Maintenance (ICSM), pp. 528–531. IEEE. doi:10.1109/ICSM.2011.6080824 (2011)
19. Schumacher, J., Zazworka, N., Shull, F., Seaman, C., Shaw, M.: Building empirical support for automated code smell detection. In: Proceedings of the 2010 ACM-IEEE International Symposium on Empirical Software Engineering and Measurement – ESEM '10, p. 1. ACM Press, New York. doi:10.1145/1852786.1852797 (2010)

20. Hochstein, L., Shull, F., Reid, L.B.: The role of MPI in development time: a case study. In: 2008 SC – International Conference for High Performance Computing, Networking, Storage and Analysis, pp. 1–10. IEEE. doi:10.1109/SC.2008.5213771 (2008)
21. Zazworka, N., Basili, V.R., Shull, F.: Tool supported detection and judgment of nonconformance in process execution. In: 2009 3rd International Symposium on Empirical Software Engineering and Measurement, pp. 312–323. IEEE. doi:10.1109/ESEM.2009.5315983 (2009)

An Empirical Investigation
of the Component-Based Performance
Prediction Method Palladio

Ralf Reussner, Steffen Becker, Anne Koziolek, and Heiko Koziolek

Abstract
Model-based performance prediction methods aim at evaluating the expected response time, throughput, and resource utilization of a software system at design time, before implementation, to achieve predictability of the system's performance characteristics. Existing performance prediction methods use monolithic, throw-away prediction models or component-based, reusable prediction models. While it is intuitively clear that the development of reusable models requires more effort, the actual higher amount of effort had not been quantified or analyzed systematically yet. Furthermore, the achieved prediction accuracy of the methods when applied by developers had not yet been compared. To study this effort, we conducted a controlled experiment with 19 computer science students who predicted the performance of two example systems applying an established, monolithic method (Software Performance Engineering) as well as our own component-based method (Palladio) in 2007. This paper summarizes two earlier papers on this study. The results show that the effort of model creation with Palladio is approximately 1.25 times higher than with SPE in our experimental setting, with the resulting models having comparable prediction accuracy. Therefore, in some cases, the creation of reusable prediction models can already be justified, provided they are reused at least once.

R. Reussner (✉) · A. Koziolek
Karlsruher Institut für Technologie (KIT), Institut für Programmstrukturen und Datenorganisation (IPD), Am Fasanengarten 5, D-76131 Karlsruhe, Germany
e-mail: ralf.reussner@kit.edu; anne.koziolek@kit.edu

S. Becker
Fachgruppe Softwaretechnik, Heinz Nixdorf Institut, Universität Paderborn, Zukunftsmeile 1, 33102 Paderborn, Germany
e-mail: steffen.becker@uni-paderborn.de

H. Koziolek
ABB Corporate Research, Wallstadter Str. 59, 68526 Ladenburg, Germany
e-mail: heiko.koziolek@de.abb.com

J. Münch and K. Schmid (eds.), *Perspectives on the Future of Software Engineering*,
DOI 10.1007/978-3-642-37395-4_13, © Springer-Verlag Berlin Heidelberg 2013

1   Introduction

As current applications always ask for maximum performance, performance problems are continuously prevalent in many software systems [20]. Model-based prediction methods [1] try to tackle these problems during early design phases to avoid the problem of implementing architectures that are unable to fulfill certain performance goals. They counter the still popular "fix-it-later" attitude towards performance problems. Many of these methods use designer-friendly UML-based models for software developers, and transform them into formal models (e.g., queueing networks, stochastic Petri nets, stochastic process algebras), from which performance measures (e.g., response times, throughput) can be derived analytically or via simulation.

During the last decade, researchers have proposed several monolithic prediction approaches (such as SPE [20], uml2LQN [17], umlPSI [2], survey in [1]) and several component-based (CB) prediction approaches (such as CB-SPE [7], ROBOCOP [8], and Palladio [6], survey in [5]). CB approaches try to leverage the benefits of componentry in the sense of Szyperski [21] by reusing well-documented component specifications. This is of particular interest for performance prediction methods, as CB software designs limit the degree of freedom for implementation by (at least partially) reusing existing components. This can also lead to higher performance prediction accuracy. In addition, reusable component prediction models can be composed isomorphically to the software architecture, thereby lowering the effort of performance modelling.

Palladio features highly parametrized component performance specifications, which are better suited for reuse than those of other approaches because they include more context dependencies (i.e., dependencies on external service calls, usage profile, resource environment). The effort for creating such parametrized CB models is naturally higher than that for throw-away models. However, until now this higher effort has not been investigated systematically. Therefore, how to determine when it is justified is an open question.

Based on this observation, we conducted a controlled experiment in 2007 comparing the effort of applying SPE (as an example of a method with throw-away models) and Palladio (as an example of a method with reusable models). In this paper, we summarize the results from two earlier papers [13, 14], which answer the following questions: (Q1) "What is the duration of modelling and predicting with the two methods?" and (Q2) "What is the quality of the models in terms of prediction accuracy?". A more recent paper [15] furthermore investigated the effort reduction achieved by reusing component-based models and found that reusing Palladio models can save time because the effort for reuse can be explained by a model that is independent of the inner complexity of a component.

In our 2007 experiment, we let 19 computer science students apply the methods in an experimental setting. They analyzed two CB software systems and assessed the performance impact of additional five design alternatives (e.g., introducing caches, replication, etc.). By using the tools accompanying the methods

(SPE-ED and PCM-Bench), they predicted response times for two different usage profiles. Therefore, we assessed the effort for the combination of applying the method and the corresponding tools.

Our results for question (Q1) show that modelling the whole task (that is, the initial system and five additional design alternatives) took an average of 1.25 times longer with Palladio than with SPE.

For question (Q2), we found that the models created with both approaches allowed reasonable prediction accuracy to correctly assess the performance of the design alternatives.

This paper is organized as follows. Section 2 presents the basics of model-driven performance prediction and briefly introduces SPE and Palladio. Afterwards, Sect. 3 explains the experimental design, before Sect. 4 describes the results. Section 5 discusses the validity of the empirical study. Related work is summarized in Sect. 6, while Sect. 7 concludes the paper and sketches future work.

2   Model-Driven Performance Prediction

2.1   Background

Several model-driven performance prediction approaches have been proposed [1], all of which follow a similar process model (Fig. 1). First, developers annotate plain software design models (e.g., UML models) with estimated or already measured performance properties, such as the execution time for an activity or the number of users concurrently issuing requests.

Second, model transformations automatically convert the annotated software models into established performance formalisms such as queueing networks (QN), stochastic Petri nets (SPN), or stochastic process algebras (SPA). Existing analytical or simulation-based solution techniques then automatically derive and report performance measures, such as response times for specific use cases, maximum throughputs, or the utilization of resources, which is crucial for identifying performance bottlenecks. Developers compare the predicted results to their requirements and decide whether to change their design or to start implementation. Only a few approaches implement an automated feedback of the prediction results into the software design model.

For our experiment, we compared our component-based Palladio method [6] with the mature, monolithic Software Performance Engineering (SPE) method [20]. We chose SPE as it has been applied in practice and provides a reasonably usable tool support, unlike many other approaches [11] solely proposed by academics. The following two sections briefly describe the two approaches, which both follow the process model sketched above.

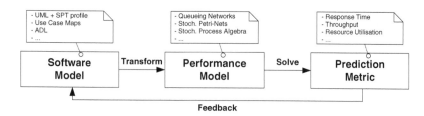

Fig. 1 Performance prediction process

2.2 SPE

The SPE method was the first elaborated, practically applicable comprehensive approach for early, design-time performance prediction for software systems [19]. SPE primarily targets software architects and performance analysts during early development stages. They identify key scenarios (i.e., use cases critical to the overall system performance) and set performance goals for the scenarios (e.g., max. response time) based on the requirements.

Afterwards, developers use a software execution model (Execution Graph, EG) to describe steps within such a performance-critical scenario. EGs are similar to UML activity diagrams and allow annotating each step with resource requirements, for example the number of needed CPU instructions.

With a so-called overhead matrix, software resource requirements in EGs (e.g., a database access) can be mapped to system resources (e.g., 10 ms for a hard disk access per database access). Several scenarios and the corresponding user arrival rates on different machines can be combined to form a system execution model.

EGs do not necessarily reflect actual componentization of a system, but provide an abstraction of the most performance-relevant steps in a scenario. This is useful for conducting performance analyses as early as possible during the life-cycle of a system, when many details are still unknown. It also limits the developers' effort for initial modelling. However, dependencies on the specific project context are not made explicit, but are mixed with component specifics. Thus, it is usually not possible to readily reuse the resulting performance models when reusing the software components. Additionally, the models cannot be used for model-driven development, as their performance-related abstraction does not provide enough information for other purposes like code generation.

The SPE methodology has been applied in industrial settings. Several anonymized case studies are provided in [20].

2.3 Palladio Component Model

The Palladio Component Model (PCM) [6] is a meta-model for specifying and analyzing component-based software architectures with focus a on performance prediction.

This meta-model is divided among the separate developer roles of a component-based development process: The component developer produces independent, reusable component specifications. The other roles (software architects, system deployers, domain experts, and quality-of-service analysts) provide information on the project-specific context, such as binding of the components, their allocation to hardware, and their usage. The meta-model provides each role with a domain-specific language suited to capture its specific knowledge [6].

To support the creation of reusable component performance models, the component specifications are parametrized by influence factors whose later values are unknown to the component developer. In particular, these are the performance measures of external service calls, which depend on the actual binding of the component's required interfaces (provided by the software architect), the actual resource demands that depend on the allocation of the components to hardware resources (provided by the system deployer), and performance-relevant parameters of service calls (provided by the domain expert).

The parametric behavioral specification used in the PCM as part of the software model is the *Resource Demanding Service Effect Specification* (RD-SEFF) which is a control and data flow abstraction of single component services, also similar to UML activity diagrams. It specifies control flow constructs such as loops or branches only if they affect external service calls. Additionally, they abstract component internal computations in so-called *internal actions*, which only contain the resource demand (e.g., reading 100 bytes from a hard drive) of the action but not its concrete behavior. Calling services and parameter passing are specified using *external call actions*, which only refer to the component's required interfaces in order to remain independent of the component binding. Hence, unlike EGs, RD-SEFFs reflect the componentization of the system and allow creating component specifications that can be reused in other project contexts. In this experiment, we thus measure the additional effort required to reflect the componentization in the Palladio models (in contrast to the SPE models).

3 Empirical Investigation

For the empirical investigation, we formulated a goal and two questions and derived metrics using the Goal-Question-Metric approach [4]. The goal of this work is:

Goal: Empirically validate the applicability of the performance prediction approach Palladio from a user's point of view.

The questions and metrics are presented in Sect. 3.1. Section 3.2 presents the experiment's design and Sect. 3.3 describes the preparation of the participants. The tasks and the experiment execution are presented in Sects. 3.4 and 3.5, respectively.

Table 1 GQM plan overview

Goal	Empirically validate the applicability of the performance prediction approach Palladio from a user's point of view.
Question 1	What is the duration of predicting the performance?
Metric 1.1	Average duration of a prediction.
Hypothesis 1	A Palladio prediction needs 1.5 times longer than an SPE prediction.
Question 2	What is the quality of the created performance prediction models?
Metric 2.1	Relative deviation of predicted mean response times of the participants and of the reference model.
Metric 2.2	Percentage of correct design decisions.
Metric 2.3	Normalized deviation in design decision rankings.
Hypothesis 2	The created models are similar to the reference model.

3.1 Questions and Metrics

For the applicability of the performance prediction models under study, two important factors are (1) the duration of a prediction and (2) the quality of the created models, which is reflected by the two questions presented below. Where appropriate, we compare Palladio to SPE as a baseline. For each metric, we formulated hypotheses to support the evaluation of the metrics and answer the questions. Due to space limitations, only informal explanations of the metrics are given here. The formal definitions can be found in [12, p. 35]. Table 1 summarizes goal, questions, metrics, and hypotheses.

Q1: What is the duration of predicting the performance? To evaluate the effort for making a prediction, we looked at the time needed, i.e. the duration, because time (in terms of person-days) is the major factor affecting effort and costs. For an empirical study of the effort of any software development technique, it is indispensable to include the tools. Thus, we measured the effort for the combination of applying the method (SPE and Palladio) and the corresponding tools (SPE-ED and PCM-Bench).

Metric 1.1 is the average duration of making a performance prediction. The duration includes reading the specification, modelling the control flow, adding resource demands, modelling the resource environment, modelling the usage profile, searching for errors, and analyzing.

Q2: What is the quality of the created performance prediction models? First, a performance model should enable predictions that are similar to the reference performance model (i.e., the sample solution) when analyzed. Here, the predicted response time was an important performance metric. Thus, we defined metric 2.1: *Relative deviation of predicted mean response times of the participants and of the reference model* (percentage).

To assess different design alternatives when designing or changing a system, the relation of the respective response times is also of interest. We let the participants evaluate several design alternatives and measured how many participants correctly identified the best design alternative in terms of its response time by stating metric 2.2: *Percentage of correct design decisions.*

As a software architect does not necessarily choose the design alternative with the best performance, but might consider other quality attributes or cost, the results for the lower-performing design alternatives are also important. Thus, after identifying the best design alternative, the participants had to rank all alternatives. The ranking of the design alternatives by the participants was compared to the ranking of the design alternatives of the reference solution in metric 2.3: *Normalized deviation in design decision rankings.* For this metric, we counted how many ranks lie between the position of a design alternative in the ranking of a participant and the correct position of this design alternative in the ranking for the reference solution. We normalized this metric so that a correct ranking has a deviation of 0 % and the reversed ranking a deviation of 100 %. Additionally, we recognized very similar response times as virtually equal design alternatives and did not punish rankings that permuted them.

Our hypothesis is that the created models are similar to the reference model. This can be broken down to (H2.1) that the average deviation as measured with metric 2.1 is not larger than 10 %, (H2.2) that 80 % of the participants can choose the correct design decision, and (H2.3) that the rankings deviate no more than 10 % on average for both Palladio and SPE.

3.2   Experiment Design

The study was conducted as a controlled experiment and investigated the effort with participants who were not the developers of the approaches. The participants of this study were students of a master's level course (see Sect. 5 for the discussion of the student subjects). In an experiment, it is desirable to trace back the observations to changes of one or more independent variables. Therefore, all other variables influencing the results need to be controlled. The *independent variable* in this study was the approach used to make the predictions. Observed *dependent variables* were the duration of making a prediction and the quality of the prediction to ensure minimum quality.

The experiment was designed as a changeover trial as depicted in Fig. 2. The participants were divided into two groups, each applying an approach to a given task. In a second session, the groups applied the other approach to a new task. Thus, each participant worked on two tasks during the course of the experiment (inter-subject design) and used both approaches. This allowed collecting more data points and balanced potential differences in individual factors such as skill and motivation between the two experiment groups. Additionally, using two tasks lowered the concrete task's influence and increased generalizability.

We balanced the grouping of the participants based on the results in the preparatory exercises: We assigned the more successful half randomly to the two groups, and did so with the less successful half as well, to ensure that the groups were equally well skilled for the tasks. We chose not to use a counter-balanced

Fig. 2 Experiment design

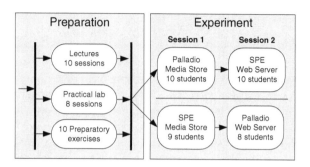

experiment design, as we would have needed to further divide the groups, which would have disturbed the balancing between the groups. We expected a higher threat to validity from the individual participants' performance than from sequencing effects.

Before the participants handed in their solutions, these were checked for minimum quality by comparing the created models to the respective reference model. This acceptance test included the comparison of the predicted response time with the reference model's predicted response time as well as a check for the models' well-formedness.

3.3   Student Teaching

The 19 computer science students participating in the experiment were trained in applying SPE and Palladio during a one-semester course covering both theory and practical labs. For the theory part, there was a total of ten lectures, each of them 1.5 h in duration. The first three lectures were dedicated to the foundations of performance prediction and CBSE. Then, two lectures introduced SPE, followed by five lectures on Palladio. The three additional lectures on Palladio in comparison to SPE were due to its more complex meta-model, which allows for reusable prediction models. Note that this also shows that reusable models require more training effort. In parallel to the lectures, eight practical labs took place, each again taking 1.5 h. During these sessions, solutions to the accompanying ten exercises were presented and discussed. SPE and Palladio were practiced in five exercises each.

The exercises had to be solved by the participants as homework. We assigned pairs of students to each exercise and shuffled frequently to get different combinations of students to work together and exchange knowledge. This was assumed to lower the influence of individual performance in the experiment. Each exercise took the students 4.75 h on average to complete.

Overall, the preparation phase was intended to ensure a certain level of familiarity with the tools and concepts because participants who failed two preparatory exercises or an intermediate short test were excluded from the experiment.

3.4   Experiment Tasks

To be applicable for both SPE and Palladio, the experiment tasks could only contain aspects that can be realized with both approaches. For example, the tasks could not make use of the separate roles of Palladio because these roles are not supported by SPE. Thus, each participant needed to fulfill all roles.

For reasons of compatibility, both experiment tasks had similar set-ups. The task descriptions contained component and sequence diagrams documenting the static and dynamic architecture of a CB system. The sequence diagrams also contained performance annotations. The resource environment with servers and their performance properties was documented textually. The detailed task description is available online in [12]. For each system, two usage profiles were given to reflect both a single-user scenario (*UP1*) and a multi-user scenario leading to contention effects (*UP2*). Additionally, they differed in terms of other performance-relevant parameters (see below).

In addition to the initial system, several design alternatives were evaluated. This reflects a common task in software engineering. Four design alternatives were designed to improve the system's performance, and the participants were asked to evaluate which alternative was the most useful one. Three of these alternatives implied the creation of a new component, one changed the allocation of the components and the resource environment by introducing a second machine. With the final fifth alternative, the impact of a change of the component container, namely the introduction of a broker for component lookups, on the performance should be evaluated.

The two systems were prototypical systems specifically designed for this experiment. In the first session, a performance prediction for a web-based system called **Media Store** was conducted. This system stores music files in a database. Users can either upload or download sets of files. The size of the music files and the number of files to be downloaded are performance-relevant parameters. The five design alternatives were the introduction of a cache component that keeps popular music files in memory (v_1^{MS}), the usage of a thread pool for database connections (v_2^{MS}), the allocation of two of the components to a second machine (v_3^{MS}), the addition of a component that reduces the bit rate of uploaded files to reduce the file sizes (v_4^{MS}), and the aforementioned usage of a broker (v_5^{MS}).

In the second session, a prototypical **Web Server** system was examined. Here, only one use case was given, a request of an HTML page with further requests of potential embedded multimedia content. Performance-relevant parameters were the number of multimedia objects per page, the size of the content, and the proportion of static and dynamic content. The five design alternatives were the introduction of a cache component (v_1^{WS}), the aforementioned usage of a broker (v_2^{WS}), the parallelization of the **Web Server**'s logging (v_3^{WS}), the allocation of two of the components on a second machine (v_4^{WS}), and the usage of a thread pool within the **Web Server** (v_5^{WS}).

The participants using the Palladio approach were provided with the initial repository of available components without RD-SEFFs. It made the tasks for SPE and Palladio more comparable because the participants still had to create the RD-SEFFs with the performance annotations, which is similar to the creation of an EG in SPE.

3.5   Experiment Execution

The group of 19 computer science students was divided into two groups as shown in Fig. 2. We conducted two sessions, each with a maximum time constraint of 4.5 h. One participant did not attend the second session due to personal reasons; thus, only 18 students took part.

The participants were asked to document the duration of the activities given in metric 1.2 and to fill in a questionnaire with qualitative questions at the end of the session.

Four members of our chair were present to help with tool problems, the exercise, and the methods, as well as to check the solutions in the acceptance tests. This might have distorted the results because they might have influenced the duration. The more problems were solved by the experimenters, the less time the participants might have spent on solving them themselves. To avoid this effect, the participants were asked to first try to solve problems on their own before consulting the experimenters. To be able to assess any possible influence of this help, we documented all help and all rejections in the acceptance test [12].

Because many participants did not finish the task within 4.5 h in both sessions, the time restriction was loosened afterwards and they were allowed to work for another 2.5 h (session 1), respectively 2 h (session 2). In both sessions, three (session 1), respectively two (session 2) participants were not properly prepared, as they needed a lot of basic help or were not able to finish even the initial system prediction. Thus, the results of these three/two participants could not be used. All other participants modelled the initial system and at least one design alternative. Because two participants failed using both approaches, omitting their results does not benefit either of the approaches. Additionally, the time constraints did not distort the results for the initial system prediction because every remaining participant finished the initial prediction well before the end of the experiment.

Overall, in session 1, three of the remaining seven participants using Palladio and seven of the nine participants using SPE were able to finish all design alternatives. In session 2, the eight participants using SPE finished all design alternatives, as did six of the eight participants using Palladio. The acceptance test ensured that the created models were meaningful. As a result, the average deviation of the predicted response time from a reference solution was only about 10 %.

4   Results

In this paper, we only present the evaluation of the metrics for Palladio. The results for SPE can be found in [12, p. 83]. The metrics are evaluated for both tasks. Finally, the hypothesis of each question is checked based on the measured metrics.

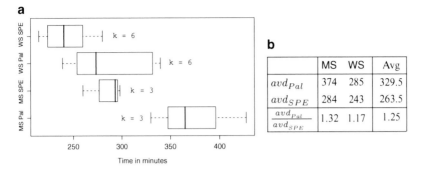

Fig. 3 Metric 1.1: Duration of making a prediction in minutes. (**a**) Boxplot. (**b**) Average

4.1   What is the Duration of Predicting the Performance?

Metric 1.1: Average duration of making a prediction. First, we evaluated metric 1.1 for the whole experiment task (=: scope *wt*), thus the duration d_p includes the duration of analyzing the initial system and all design alternatives. In neither session were all participants able to finish the respective task within the extended time constraints, especially for Palladio. We first looked at those participants who finished the whole task with one approach a: Let k_a be this number of participants. To not favor one approach, only the results of the $k = max(k_{Pal}, k_{SPE})$ fastest participants from both groups were evaluated for metric 1.1, so that for both groups, the slower participants were left out.

Figure 3a shows the results of metric 1.1 for the four combinations of approaches and systems in a boxplot, showing the minimum, the lower quartile, the mean, the upper quartile, and the maximum for all groups and systems. The number of evaluated results is $k = 3$ for the Media Store (MS) and $k = 6$ for the Web Server (WS).

Figure 3b shows the average metric 1.1. Additionally, we compared how much longer it took on average to make the Palladio prediction compared to making the respective SPE prediction. These factors are shown as avd_{Pal}/avd_{SPE}.

We tested our initial hypotheses using Welch's t-test [22], as we cannot assume identical variances for the distributions, and chose a significance level of 0.05. Hypothesis 1.1 is rejected (p = 0.009). The students using Palladio needed significantly less than 1.5 times the time needed by students using SPE, as the opposite is rejected with p = 0.004. The statistical power of these two tests is 0.65 and 0.78, respectively, and barely sufficient [18]. Still, the students using Palladio needed significantly more time than the students using SPE for the whole task as well, as the opposite is rejected (p = 0.01, power 0.78).

Table 2 Metric 2.1: Relative deviation of the predicted response times for Palladio

		v_0^s (%)	v_1^s (%)	v_2^s (%)	v_3^s (%)	v_4^s (%)	v_5^s (%)	Avg (%)
Media Store	UP1	1.93	0.90	0.49	20.08	3.02	1.69	4.69
($s = MS$)	UP2	13.21	2.20	4.15	13.23	4.42	3.51	6.79
Web Server	UP1	1.00	11.07	1.94	4.23	4.55	9.40	5.47
($s = WS$)	UP2	15.92	20.35	10.87	10.67	2.57	3.64	10.67
Overall $propDevMeanResp_{Pal}$								6.90

4.2   What is the Quality of the Created Performance Prediction Models?

Metric 2.1: Relative deviation of predicted mean response times between the participants and the reference model. Table 2 shows the results of metric 2.1 for Palladio.

We first consider the average deviation for each task. Overall, the deviation is lower using the Media Store and for UP1. The overall average is low with 6.9 %. Interestingly, the deviation varied a lot between the different design alternatives. For the Media Store and Palladio, the alternative v_3^{MS} (second server) has a high deviation, and v_0^{MS} for UP2 does, too. For the Web Server and Palladio, the deviations for v_2^{WS}, the broker alternative, v_0^{WS}, v_1^{WS} (Cache), and v_3^{WS} (Logging) are also high.

For SPE, we measured a slightly higher average deviation of 8.3 % and also strong variations for the different design alternatives.

Metric 2.2: Percentage of correct design decisions. For metric 2.2, we compared the results of the reference model (cf. Sect. 3.1) with the participants rankings and assessed the percentage of correct identifications of the best-performing design alternative. Some participants did not manage to model all alternatives in the given time and thus, their rankings were incomplete and their results cannot be used (see Fig. 2 for the total numbers of participants).

As the predicted response time of the best and second-best alternatives of the Media Store were close to each other, we made no distinction between these two. Thus, all participants chose correctly because all of them identified either the bit rate (v_4^{MS}) or the cache option (v_1^{MS}) as the best design alternative and ranked the respective other one second-best.

For the Web Server, UP1 and Palladio, 4 out of 6 participants who ranked all alternatives identified the second server v_4^{WS} as the best alternative. Of the two others, one actually predicted a lower response time for the cache (v_1^{WS}), the other one seemed to have other reasons or could not correctly interpret the CDF, as the second server v_4^{WS} is faster for his model, too. We get $perc_{WS,UP1,Pal} = 0.67$. All eight SPE participants chose the correct alternative: $perc_{WS,UP1,SPE} = 1$.

For usage model 2, all five Palladio participants who ranked all alternatives identified the second server v_4^{WS} as the best alternative. For SPE, 7 out of 8 participants who ranked all alternatives did so: $perc_{WS,UP2,SPE} = 0.88$.

Combined[1] we get $perc_{SPE} = 0.97$ and $perc_{Pal} = 0.85$.

Metric 2.3: Normalized deviation in design decision rankings. Not all participants ranked all alternatives because they did not complete all predictions or missed the time to complete the ranking, even if they completed the predictions. We still used the incomplete rankings for the evaluation of the metrics, but were careful to weight complete rankings stronger (cf. [12, p. 86f]).

For Palladio, the ranks were wrong by 6.5 % of the maximum possible permutation. For SPE, the ranks were wrong by 7.3 % of the maximum possible permutation. Thus, the SPE rankings were more permuted by a factor of 0.12 compared to the Palladio rankings.

Hypothesis 2 With both approaches, the mean response time predicted by the participants only deviates an average of 6.9 % (Palladio) and 8.3 % (SPE) from the mean response time predicted for the reference model. Thus, the deviation of the average is within the limit of 10 %. However, for single alternatives, the deviation was higher (see Table 2). These pose a threat to hypothesis 2.

Most participants were also able to identify the correct design decisions, in particular 85 % for Palladio and 97 % for SPE, which is both within the bounds of 80 %. Finally, the deviation of the ranking is also low (not more than 10 % on average).

Overall, the results indicate that hypothesis 1 cannot be rejected for the average case. However, the high variation of the deviation of the predicted mean response time between the different design alternatives hampers assessing hypothesis 1. As the alternatives have differing results, it is unclear how the metrics would be evaluated for different design alternatives.

5   Threats to Validity

To enable the reader to assess our study, we list some potential threats to its validity in the following. We look at the internal, construct, and external validity (a more thorough discussion can be found in [12]).

Internal validity states whether changes of an experiment's independent variables are, in fact, the cause for changes of the dependent variables [23, p. 68]. Controlling potential interfering variables ensures high internal validity. In our experiment, we

---

[1]Note that the percentages for the two systems do not equally influence the results, but are weighted by the number of decisions by definition of the metric (cf. [12, p. 41]).

evaluated the pre-experiment exercises and assigned the students to equally capable groups based on the results to control the different capabilities of the participants. A learning effect might have been an interfering variable in our experiment, as the students finished the second experiment session faster than the first one.

A potential bias towards or against Palladio was threatening the internal validity in our experiment, as the participants knew that the experimenters were involved in creating this method. However, we did not notice any strong bias from the collected data and the filled-out questionnaires, as the participants complained equally often about the tools of both approaches.

Construct validity states whether the persons and settings used in an experiment represent the analyzed constructs well [23, p. 71]. Palladio and SPE are both typical performance prediction methods involving UML-like design models. The SPE approach has no special support for component-based systems, and was chosen for the experiment due to its higher maturity compared to existing CBSPE approaches. To allow a comparison, we designed the experimental tasks such that not all specific component-based features of Palladio (e.g., separation of developer roles in component-based development, performance requirements using quantiles) were used.

While our experiment involved student participants, we argue that their performance after the training sessions was comparable to the potential performance of practitioners. Most of the students were close to graduating and will become practitioners soon. Due to the training sessions, their knowledge about the methods was more homogeneous than the knowledge of practitioners with different backgrounds. With a homogeneous group of participants, the significance of the results is even improved. Studies, such as [10], suggest the suitability of students for similar experiments.

External validity states whether the results of an experiment are transferable to settings other than the specific experimental setting [23, p. 72]. While we used medium-sized, self-designed systems for the students to analyze, we modelled these system designs and the alternatives after typical distributed systems and commonly known performance patterns [20], which should be representative of systems usually analyzed.

We tried to increase the external validity of our study by letting the participants analyze two different systems, so that differences in the results could be traced back to the systems and not the prediction methods. Effects observed for both tasks are thus more likely to be generalizable to other settings.

Still, the systems under study were modelled on a high abstraction level due to the time constraints of such an experiment. More complex systems would increase external validity, but would also involve more interfering variables, thus decreasing internal validity. Furthermore, the information available at early development stages is usually limited, which would be reflected by our experimental setting.

6   Related Work

Basics about the area of *performance prediction* can be found in [16, 20]. Balsamo et al. [1] give an overview of about 20 recent approaches based on QN, SPN, and SPA. Becker et al. [5] survey performance prediction methods specifically targeting component-based systems. Examples are CB-SPE [7], ROBOCOP [8],and CBML [24].

Empirical studies and controlled experiments [23] are still under-represented in the field of model-based performance predictions, as hardly any studies comparable to ours can be found. Balsamo et al. [3] compared two complementary prediction methods (one based on SPA, one on simulation) by analyzing the performance of a naval communication system. However, in that study, the authors of the methods carried out the predictions themselves. Gorton et al. [9] compared predicted performance metrics to measurements in a study, but only used one method for the predictions.

Koziolek et al. [11] conducted a study similar to this one. They compared predictions with SPE [20], Capacity Planning [16], and umlPSI [2] with measurements of an implementation. Their study attested SPE the highest maturity and suitability for early performance predictions and influenced our decision to compare Palladio to SPE.

7   Conclusions

We conducted an empirical investigation to quantify the higher effort needed for creating reusable, component-based models for performance prediction compared to creating throw-away models. After substantial training, we let 19 computer science students apply the SPE method and the Palladio method to predict the response times of two example systems. We found that the effort for applying Palladio on the whole task was an average of 1.25 times higher than the effort for applying SPE. Our results indicate that in some cases, the effort for creating reusable models for performance prediction can already be justified if the models are reused at least once, provided the costs for the reuse itself are low. If the models are reused more often, the additional upfront effort pays off even more. A more recent study [15] does indeed confirm that reusing Palladio models can save time because effort to reuse can be explained by a model that is independent of the inner complexity of a component. Furthermore, we found that the quality of the models and predictions created by the students deviated less than 10 % from the predictions achieved with a reference model created by the experimenters. We learned that more than 80 % of the students were able to rank the given design alternatives correctly.

The results are useful for both practitioners and researchers. Practitioners such as software architects and performance analysts get a first quantification of the higher effort needed to create reusable, component-based models, which they could use in dealing with management to justify higher upfront costs for modelling. Researchers obtain a reusable experimental setting, which is the basis for future replications of the experiment. The results suggest that it is worthwhile investing more research effort into creating reusable models because their creation can pay off quickly. However, our study cannot give a definite, overall answer to the questions raised, as the results are also confined to our specific experimental setting.

Our investigation opens up future directions for research. The study could be repeated with a larger sample size to allow better quantification of the additional effort as well as validation of the results. Moreover, the analysis of factors influencing the effort, especially the nature of the systems under study, is an issue for future research.

Acknowledgments We would like to thank Walter Tichy, Lutz Prechelt, and Wilhelm Hasselbring for their kind review of the experimental design and fruitful comments. Furthermore, we thank all members of the SDQ Chair for helping to prepare and conduct the experiment. Last, but not least, we thank all students who volunteered to participate in our experiment.

References

1. Balsamo, S., Di Marco, A., Inverardi, P., Simeoni, M.: Model-based performance prediction in software development: a survey. IEEE TSE **30**(5), 295–310 (2004)
2. Balsamo S., Marzolla, M.: A simulation-based approach to software performance modeling. In: Proceedings of ESEC/FSE, Helsinki, pp. 363–366. ACM (2003)
3. Balsamo, S., Marzolla, M., Di Marco, A., Inverardi, P.: Experimenting different software architectures performance techniques. In: Proceedings of WOSP, Redwood Shores, pp. 115–119. ACM (2004)
4. Basili, V.R., Caldiera, G., Rombach, H.D.: The goal question metric approach. In: Marciniak, J.J. (ed.) Encyclopedia of Software Engineering – 2 Volume Set, pp. 528–532. Wiley, Chichester (1994)
5. Becker, S., Grunske, L., Mirandola, R., Overhage, S.: Performance prediction of component-based systems: a survey from an engineering perspective. In: Architecting Systems with Trustworthy Components. Volume 3938 of LNCS, pp. 169–192. Springer, Berlin/New York (2006)
6. Becker, S., Koziolek, H., Reussner, R.: Model-based performance prediction with the Palladio component model. In: Proceedings of WOSP, Buenos Aires, pp. 54–65. ACM Sigsoft, 5–8 Feb 2007
7. Bertolino A., Mirandola, R.:CB-SPE tool: putting component-based performance engineering into practice. In: Proceedings of CBSE, Edinburgh. Volume 3054 of LNCS, pp. 233–248. Springer (2004)
8. Bondarev, E., Muskens, J., de With, P.H.N., Chaudron, M.R.V., Lukkien, J.: Predicting real-time properties of component assemblies: a scenario-simulation approach. In: Proceedings of 30th EUROMICRO-Conference, Rennes, pp. 40–47 (2004)
9. Gorton I., Liu, A.: Performance evaluation of alternative component architectures for enterprise JavaBean applications. IEEE Internet Comput. **7**(3), 18–23. Rennes, France (2003)
10. Höst, M., Regnell, B., Wohlin, C.: Using students as subjects – a comparative study of students and professionals in lead-time impact assessment. Empir. Softw. Eng. **5**(3), 201–214 (2000)
11. Koziolek, H., Firus, V.: Empirical evaluation of model-based performance predictions methods in software development. In: Proceedings of QoSA, Erfurt. Volume 3712 of LNCS, pp 188–202, Sept 2005
12. Martens, A.: Empirical validation of the model-driven performance prediction approach Palladio. Master's thesis, Carl-von-Ossietzky Universität Oldenburg (2007)

13. Martens, A., Becker, S., Koziolek, H., Reussner, R.: An empirical investigation of the applicability of a component-based performance prediction method. In: Thomas N., Juiz, C. (eds.) Proceedings of the 5th European Performance Engineering Workshop (EPEW'08), Palma de Mallorca. Volume 5261 of Lecture Notes in Computer Science, pp. 17–31. Springer, Berlin/Heidelberg (2008)

14. Martens, A., Becker, S., Koziolek, H., Reussner, R.: An empirical investigation of the effort of creating reusable models for performance prediction. In: Proceedings of the 11th International Symposium on Component-Based Software Engineering (CBSE'08), Karlsruhe. Volume 5282 of Lecture Notes in Computer Science, pp. 16–31. Springer, Berlin/Heidelberg (2008)

15. Martens, A., Koziolek, H., Prechelt, L., Reussner, R.: From monolithic to component-based performance evaluation of software architectures. Empir. Soft. Eng. **16**(5), 587–622 (2011)

16. Menascé, D.A., Almeida, V.A.F., Dowdy, L.W.: Performance by Design. Prentice Hall, Upper Saddle River (2004)

17. Petriu, D.C. Wang, X.: From UML description of high-level software architecture to LQN performance models. In: Nagl, M., Schürr, A., Münch, M. (eds.) Proceedings of AGTIVE'99, Kerkrade, vol. 1779. Springer, Berlin/New York (2000)

18. Sachs, L.: Applied Statistics: A Handbook of Techniques. Springer, New York (1982)

19. Smith, C.U.: Performance Engineering of Software Systems. Addison-Wesley, Reading (1990)

20. Smith, C.U., Williams, L.G.: Performance Solutions: A Practical Guide to Creating Responsive, Scalable Software. Addison-Wesley, Boston (2002)

21. Szyperski, C.: Component Software: Beyond Object-Oriented Programming. ACM,New York/Addison-Wesley, Reading (1998)

22. Welch, B.L.: The generalization of student's problem when several different population variances are involved. Biometrika **34**, 28–35 (1947)

23. Wohlin, C., Runeson, P., Höst, M., Ohlsson, M.C., Regnell, B., Wesslén, A.: Experimentation in Software Engineering: An Introduction. Kluwer Academic, Norwell (2000)

24. Wu X., Woodside, M.: Performance Modeling from Software Components. SIGSOFT SE Notes **29**(1), 290–301 (2004)

Can We Trust Software Repositories?

Andreas Zeller

Abstract

To acquire data for empirical studies, software engineering researchers frequently leverage *software repositories* as data sources. Indeed, version and bug databases contain a wealth of data on how a product came to be. To turn this data into knowledge, though, requires deep insights into the specific process and product; and it requires careful scrutiny of the techniques used to obtain the data. The central challenge of the future will thus be to combine both automatic and manual empirical analysis.

1 Introduction

The idea of engineering is to *use insights to solve problems*—or more precisely, to design and develop solutions by applying scientific, economic, and social knowledge. With software engineering, the goal is the same: We want to acquire and apply established knowledge such that we can craft well-designed solutions to given problems. But what is the "established knowledge" in software engineering? This is a challenge both for researchers, who look out for principles and laws, and for practitioners, who need to apply them to the problem at hand.

The aim of *empirical software engineering* is to systematically acquire laws and theories on software engineering. It works by means of *studies,* whose observations help build hypotheses; and *experiments,* which help to verify, falsify, or establish the validity of such hypotheses. By using scientific methods, we can refine the hypotheses until they become *theories* and *laws* with predictive power for a wide range of software engineering challenges. In their pioneering book from 2003 [3],

A. Zeller (✉)
Software Engineering Chair (Prof. Zeller), Saarland University – Computer Science,
Campus E1 1, 66123 Saarbrücken, Germany, http://www.st.cs.uni-saarland.de/zeller/
e-mail: zeller@cs.uni-saarland.de

J. Münch and K. Schmid (eds.), *Perspectives on the Future of Software Engineering,* 209
DOI 10.1007/978-3-642-37395-4_14, © Springer-Verlag Berlin Heidelberg 2013

Endres and Rombach compiled a number of such software engineering laws—rules of wisdom pertaining to any software engineering project. The Compiled laws include *Glass' law:* "Requirement deficiencies are the prime source of project failures", *Lehman's law:* "A system that is used will be changed", or *Pareto's law:* "Approximately 80 percent of defects come from 20 percent of modules".

Of course, these laws do not come out of thin air; each of them is supported by a number of empirical studies. The problem, however, is that conducting such studies can be very costly. Already talking to developers and managers eats into valuable time. Asking them to record data on their doings is worse. And running systematic, repeated experiments to find out how individual factors influence a specific development question is limited by the high hourly wages of the experiment subjects. Finally, there is a goal conflict: Whereas the scientist is interested in general knowledge, his industrial partners want specific answers for their problem at hand. The problem of high cost—combined with little specific gain—seriously hampers the progress of empirical software engineering.

About 10 years ago, researchers discovered a cheap alternative to manually gathering data—namely *mining development data that is already there.* The source of this data is *software repositories;* that is, databases that record events and actions of developers while the software is developed. Such databases had long been used to organize and coordinate the software development process; a version database, for instance, contains every single change to the software ever made—with information on who made the change, when, where, how, and why. Rather than collecting insights from the participants, one could simply collect the data from the repository, by means of simple database queries. However, just having data does not mean having insights; and as much as the field of mining software archives has fueled empirical research all over the place, it is now time to take a critical look at the field—and see how much it constitutes an alternative to classical data gathering.

2   The Sources of Mining

To understand how mining works, let us consider a standard goal: We want to know *where the bugs are*—or to be more precise, which parts of our software had the highest number of bugs in the past. This is a classic setting in mining software repositories, because the defect distribution in a system allows correlating defects with other software properties, and thus making predictions on where future defects will be. To mine such information, the central repositories to be mined are:

Version archives.   Version histories track every change ever made to a software module since its creation. The motivation is to track and organize the trail of changes that is being made during development. Each change comes with the text inserted or deleted, the date and author of the change, as well as a *commit message* in which the author motivates the change.

Bug databases.   A bug database contains information about every problem ever reported for the software. The motivation is to keep track of pending issues and to guide development decisions; for instance, a new release could be made when no serious open bugs remain. Each entry comes with a problem description, steps to reproduce, as well as the severity and importance of the bug; as problems are worked on by developers, they also change their status from "open" via "assigned" to "fixed".

In addition to these main sources, other data sources come in handy. *Automated tests* allow assessing software quality automatically. *Crash databases* are automatically filled with failure data from the field. *Developer databases* allow finding out more about individuals, e.g., relating their experience or team to defect densities. And of course, the *source code* itself is used to determine properties—from simple metrics to full-fledged data-flow or control-flow analysis.

It should be stressed that all of these archives are used on a day-to-day basis for the sole purpose of organizing software development. They are *not* meant to support empirical studies. This is an advantage for studies, as there is no Hawthorne effect; any interaction between researchers and study subjects would take place after the fact. But this is also a disadvantage, as the data is not collected with the aim of being automatically analyzable. This is a challenge—and a risk.

3   The Perils of Mining

For practitioners, just knowing where the bugs have been is already valuable knowledge. The general idea is straightforward: For every module in a system, we analyze its change history from the version database. A *fix* in the change history implies that a bug has been fixed in this very module. The more fixes, the lower the reliability of the module. So far, so good. The central challenge, however, is to tell that *a fix actually is a fix* that addresses a real defect—and not a regular change which adds new features, refactors the code for better maintenance, or adds comments for better readability. Telling fixes from other changes and mapping bugs to changes are central issues in automated mining [4]:

- One might use the *commit message* to tell fixes from changes—for instance, by looking for indicator words such as "bug", "problem", or "fix". This requires that changes come with meaningful commit messages, and that these are organized consistently.
- One might use *bug identifiers* to refer to a bug database. If a commit message refers to a "bug id 38468", and 38468 is actually a valid entry in the bug database, then one may assume that the change is related to the problem in the bug database—which allows associating it with severity, description, and others. In particular, one may want to differentiate between *pre-production bugs*, i.e., those found during development and in-house testing, and *post-production bugs*, i.e., those found and reported by customers.

The crucial point here is that if the commit message of the change does not allow relating it to a bug, then the change cannot be associated to a particular problem; likewise, there will be problems that are reported as fixed, but cannot be associated with a particular change that fixed it. In an analysis of the ECLIPSE history, for instance, Bird et al. found that out of 24,119 fixed bugs, only 10,017 could be linked to an entry in the bug database, causing bias in the dataset [1].

But not only can the association of changes and bugs be missing; it can also be overly imprecise. If a developer has a habit of committing all pending local changes before the weekend in one single transaction, then all changes will effectively form one single blob, addressing multiple problems at once, while adding a few changes somewhere else. If this blob of changes is now classified as a fix (because one of the contained changes refers to a bug report, among others), then all contained modules will be marked as having had a defect in the past—even if only one of them was actually defective.

The situation is actually worse because the *data can be wrong to begin with.* In a recent study [5], Kim Herzig and Sascha Just analyzed and reclassified more than 7,000 issue reports into a fixed set of issue report categories clearly distinguishing the kind of maintenance work required to resolve the task. They found that more than 40 % of issue reports are inaccurately classified in the first place, with 33.8 % of all "bug reports" not referring to corrective code maintenance—that is, the bug database misclassified the reports in the first place. Due to such misclassifications, 39 % of files marked as defective actually never had a bug.

Fortunately, there are ways to avoid such issues. First and foremost comes *discipline* in organizing changes and commit messages. If fixes and features end up in separate *branches* of the version control system, they are much less likely to cause confusion; the best situation occurs if each logical fix forms its own set of logical changes (say, its own branch). This is the case in several industrial studies on mining software repositories, in particular those at Microsoft [7] and SAP [6]. Second, one can validate fixes through *tests:* If a test fails on the original version, and passes on the changed version, then the change must be a fix. The *iBugs* repository [2] of fixes and bugs, for instance, is validated this way. All in all, the message is clear:

> *Automated quantitive analysis should always include human qualitative analysis of the input data.*

4   Insights and Correlations

The limitations that noisy source data imposes were always known to the pioneers of mining software archives. As a consequence, their research turned from "findings" to "recommendations"; the general idea was to have tools that first learn patterns and correlations from software archives, and then make recommendations for future decisions—for instance, which modules to focus upon during testing. The term "recommendation" carries a connotation of insecurity, and is just appropriate in light of the noisy data. Furthermore, the given recommendations would always be project-specific, and not necessarily generalize to all software projects. But even so, any such recommendation should be taken with a grain of salt; as the following stories indicate, taking a correlation at face value may be totally misleading:

Fig. 1 The IROP
keyboard [8]

- In early work, Thomas Zimmermann and I correlated the average bug density of changes with individual developers, and found that across all ECLIPSE developers, Erich Gamma's contributions had the second-highest bug density. Does this mean that Erich Gamma has low coding skills? On the contrary: As a team lead, he had no one to delegate difficult tasks to; and thus worked on the most failure-prone parts of ECLIPSE. His code was failure-prone, yes—but every other team member would have performed worse.
- In a study with an anonymous client, we correlated bug density and testing coverage, assuming that low testing coverage would result in higher bug density. Interestingly, what we found was the opposite: The higher the coverage, the higher the bug density. The reason was simple: The test managers had a good idea of where to find the bugs, and thus focused their tests on these modules. It is just that despite all the testing, a number of bugs still remained.

In both examples, just relying on the quantitative findings could have led to drastic misinterpretations of the situation at hand. Where human checks are not in place, empirical findings can be trivial to outright misleading; in any case, they will be overblown. To express my disdain of the various "findings" researchers claim to have extracted from open source archives, ignoring the noise that is there in the first place, and ruthlessly overgeneralizing their correlations, Tom Zimmermann, Christian Bird, and I wrote a paper entitled "Failure is a Four-Letter Word" [8], a parody in empirical research, where we report our finding that the letters I, R, O, and P have a stronger correlation to defect density than others in some ECLIPSE data set (which is true), and where our consequences range from rewriting source code to avoid "the letters of failure" to designing a special keyboard where these letters are missing (Fig. 1). Keep this in mind:

> *Automated quantitive analysis should always include human qualitative analysis of the findings.*

5   The Next Big Challenges

So can we trust the data and findings from software repositories? Despite all reservations, my answer is yes. We must be aware of the noise and faults in the originating data, and carefully document our assumptions and processes. When it comes to interpretations, we must be sure to check our findings with project insiders, who will give us insights into what is actually going on. These are standard practices in any empirical research, and the fact that plenty of data is available for automatic processing does not make these practices obsolete. Mining data from software archives is a tool for conducting empirical research. It is a powerful tool, a tool that saves time and other resources, a tool that brings great insights and impact, but it is a tool in the hand of humans.

The biggest challenge in the future will therefore be to further integrate these tools into the portfolio of empirical research techniques, combining both automatic and manual analysis. This requires being aware of the strengths as well as the weaknesses of automatic mining tools; but also to be aware of the many standard practices of empirical research in software engineering. It means being aware of risks due to noisy data and misclassifications; it means being aware of risks such as overfitting and overgeneralization.

The best way to avoid this is to build a vibrant community of empirical researchers who keep on refining and cross-checking data and techniques. The more and better empirical findings we have, the better we can improve the practice of software engineering and make it an engineering discipline worthy of its name; and this is where the legacy of empirical pioneers such as Barry Boehm, Victor Basili, or Dieter Rombach will live on.

References

1. Bird, C., Bachmann, A., Aune, E., Duffy, J., Bernstein, A., Filkov, V., Devanbu, P.: Fair and balanced? bias in bug-fix datasets. In: Proceedings of the 7th Joint Meeting of the European Software Engineering Conference and the ACM SIGSOFT Symposium on the Foundations of Software Engineering, ESEC/FSE '09, Amsterdam, pp. 121–130. ACM, New York (2009)
2. Dallmeier, V., Zimmermann, T.: Extraction of bug localization benchmarks from history. In: Proceedings of the Twenty-Second IEEE/ACM International Conference on Automated Software Engineering, ASE '07, Atlanta, pp. 433–436. ACM (2007)
3. Endres, A., Rombach, H.D.: A Handbook of Software and Systems Engineering: Empirical Observations, Laws, and Theories. Addison-Wesley, Harlow (2003)
4. Fischer, M., Pinzger, M., Gall, H.: Populating a release history database from version control and bug tracking systems. In: Proceedings of International Conference on Software Maintenance, ICSM 2003, Amsterdam, pp. 23–32. IEEE (2003)
5. Herzig, K., Just, S., Zeller, A.: It's not a bug, it's a feature: how misclassification impacts bug prediction. In: Proceedings of the International Conference on Software Engineering (ICSE 2013), San Francisco. ACM (2013)
6. Holschuh, T., Pauser, M., Herzig, K., Zimmermann, T., Premraj, R., Zeller, A.: Predicting defects in SAP Java code: an experience report. In: 31st International Conference on Software Engineering-Companion Volume, ICSE-Companion 2009, Vancouver, pp. 172–181. IEEE (2009)

7. Nagappan, N., Ball, T., Zeller, A.: Mining metrics to predict component failures. In: Proceedings of the 28th International Conference on Software Engineering, Shanghai, pp. 452–461. ACM (2006)
8. Zeller, A., Zimmermann, T., Bird, C.: Failure is a four-letter word: a parody in empirical research. In: Proceedings of the 7th International Conference on Predictive Models in Software Engineering, Banff, p. 5. ACM (2011)

Empirical Practice in Software Engineering

Andreas Jedlitschka, Liliana Guzmán, Jessica Jung,
Constanza Lampasona, and Silke Steinbach

Abstract

Experimental software engineering has been defined as the scientific approach to systematically evaluating software technologies by referring to predefined hypotheses using sound empirical methods.

The purpose of this chapter is to give an overview of the history, current practice, and future of empirical practice in Software Engineering. In particular, based on what we have learned from 20 years of research in empirical software engineering, we describe the empirical approach we are currently using in terms of a scientific approach to applied research and as a means for systematic evaluation.

1 Introduction

1.1 The Origins of Experimentation in Software Engineering

Since the very beginning, empirical Software Engineering (SE) has been considered a rigorous discipline intended to help industrial decision makers. In 1986, Basili published his fundamental paper on Experimentation in SE and stated [1]: "... experimentation is performed to help us better evaluate, predict, understand, control and improve the software development process and product". Wohlin et al. [2] define: "Experimentation provides a systematic, disciplined, quantifiable and controlled way of evaluating human-based activities". Bringing Basili's statement and Wohlin's et al. definition together with the IEEE definition of SE, the potential

A. Jedlitschka (✉) • L. Guzmán • J. Jung • C. Lampasona • S. Steinbach
Fraunhofer Institut for Experimental Software Engineering (IESE), Fraunhofer-Platz 1,
Kaiserslautern 67663, Germany
e-mail: andreas.jedlitschka@iese.fraunhofer.de; liliana.guzman@iese.fraunhofer.de;
jessica.jung@iese.fraunhofer.de; constanza.lampasona@iese.fraunhofer.de;
silke.steinbach@iese.fraunhofer.de

J. Münch and K. Schmid (eds.), *Perspectives on the Future of Software Engineering,*
DOI 10.1007/978-3-642-37395-4_15, © Springer-Verlag Berlin Heidelberg 2013

of experimentation becomes clear, especially with regard to a systematic and quantifiable approach [3]: "Software Engineering means application of a systematic, disciplined, quantifiable approach to the development, operation and maintenance of software." Juristo and Moreno reformulate Basili's claim in the following way [4]: "The aim of SE experimentation is to provide facts for the suppositions, assumptions, speculations and beliefs that abound in software construction".

This means that experimentation is the scientific approach to systematically evaluating software technologies by referring to predefined hypotheses using sound empirical methods.

Therefore, experimentation is considered a major concept in organizational learning and an important means for supporting decision making at the management level, especially in case of software process improvement (SPI). It is widely accepted that experimentation provides deeper insights into understanding and establishing cause-effect relationships than any other evaluation method [5].

1.2   Establishing Empirical Software Engineering

The first Dagstuhl Seminar on Experimental SE was held in 1992 [6]. Researchers from both SE and experimentation in SE came together to discuss the state of the art and practice of experimentation in SE and to propose a future research agenda. They concluded that the empirical methods applied in SE were mostly restricted to quantitative studies, i.e., controlled experiments. Since then, a range of qualitative studies has been introduced, from observational to ethnographical studies. Thus the field moved from experimental to empirical SE.

In 1996, D. Rombach founded the Fraunhofer Institute for Experimental Software Engineering IESE [7]. Over time, Fraunhofer IESE has become one of the most important research institutes in empirical SE, contributing with multiple empirical studies to the knowledge base of SE. Additionally, it has contributed to educating SE researchers in empiricism, to encouraging software organizations to get involved in empirical studies, and to adapting empirical methods the SE context [8].

In 1993, the International Software Engineering Research Network (ISERN) [9] was initiated by D. Rombach, V. Basili, R. Jeffery, G. Cantone, M. Oivo, and K. Torii. Since then, ISERN has grown to about 60 members (2012) around the world. ISERN members commit themselves to using the experimental paradigm in their research. The aim of ISERN has been supported by many authors. Fenton et al. [10] claimed repeatedly that rigorous experimentation is needed to evaluate new software technologies and their effects on organizations, processes, and products. Moreover, Pfleeger stated that [11]: "As a software manager, it is important to make key decisions or assessments in an objective and scientific way".

After the first Dagstuhl Seminar on Experimental SE and the foundation of ISERN, several (some of them independent) initiatives have been performed to increase the acceptance and use of empirical methods in SE.

In the context of the DESMET project in the U.K. [12], Kitchenham and colleagues developed a methodology for evaluating SE technologies by using empirical methods. The commonly used/published types of evaluations are post-mortems, surveys, case studies, and both controlled and quasi experiments.[1]

The growing interest in empirical methods also required rigor in performing studies as well as in reporting their results. Consequently, the discussion about guidelines for the empirical work in SE started. In 1999, Singer [13] described how to use the "American Psychological Association (APA) Styleguide" [14] for publishing experimental results in SE.

In parallel, the first text books regarding experimentation in SE were published starting in 2000. Wohlin et al. [2] provide an introduction to experimentation with the focus on the evaluation of methods, techniques, and tools in software engineering. They describe the whole experimental process starting with the definition and ending with the presentation. Juristo and Moreno [4] provide the basics for experimentation in software engineering, especially for planning, conducting, and analyzing experiments. Because at the time, surveys were among the most commonly employed research methods, Pfleeger and Kitchenham started a series on the principles of survey research [15].

Also in 2001, a first version of the initial guidelines on how to perform, report, and collate results of empirical studies in SE based on medical guidelines as well as on the personal experience of the authors was published [16].

In 2003, Shaw [17] provided a tutorial on how to write scientific papers, including the presentation of empirical research as a special case.

1.3   Maturing Empirical Software Engineering

With the increasing maturity and understanding of empirical SE, further requirements were formulated. For instance, in 2003 Ruhe [18] argued that empirical SE has to prove its industrial value by its contribution to decision support.

Moreover, several attempts were initiated to build a common body of knowledge based on the synthesis of existing empirical evidence. Until then, empirical SE research had yielded a rather large number of scientific publications ranging from controlled experiments to countless case studies and surveys. However, attempts to combine the knowledge gained in single studies is reported to be extremely effort consuming [19, 20], if not impossible [21]. Consequently, a body of knowledge was built only for a few areas of SE (i.e., inspections and testing). Besides the individual efforts to build a common body [19, 20, 22], projects like the European ESERNET [23], the American CeBASE, and the Norwegian SPI Programmes [24] aimed at providing such knowledge.

However, at that time, there was clearly no concise answer to R. Glass' [25] request that software managers should be supported by research. Glass, taking the standpoint of software managers, wrote: "Here's a message from software managers

---

[1]In this chapter, we use the word study for all kinds of empirical studies. We use experiment as the generic term for controlled and quasi-experiments.

to software researchers: We (software managers) need your help. We need some better advice on how and when to use methodologies".

At the same time, Turner [26], acknowledging the difficulties in really responding to these demands, stated that empiricism (if applied in a goal-oriented manner and not for the pure sake of quantification) can help to answer the following important questions regarding the "value" of a technology: what are the real costs, what is the benefit, what is its origin, in which context can it be applied, what is the latency, and what might be the barriers.

Also in 2004, a new trend, namely evidence-based SE, arose, which originated mainly in evidence-based medicine. The evidence-based paradigm "... proposes the use of currently best empirical evidence from research integrated with practical experience and human value judgment to support decision-making processes in the development and maintenance of software." [27].

Based on the evidence-based paradigm, Kitchenham [28] proposed guidelines for conducting and reporting systematic reviews.

Following up on that, researchers in empirical SE investigated to which extent the measures implemented in evidence-based medicine can be transferred to and adopted by SE. One issue arises in SE, for example, from the difference in the numbers of publications, especially on controlled experiments. A systematic literature review of experiments in SE [29] identified 103 controlled experiments for the years 1993 to 2002; however, for medicine, 97,467 randomized controlled trials were published for the same period in PubMED. Despite the availability of text books and guidelines, Sjøberg et al. [29] confirm our earlier findings [21] that the reporting of results from studies is often still vague, unsystematic, and lacking consistent terminology. In their conclusion, Sjøberg et al. recommend that researchers should accurately report " ... the type and number of subjects, including the mortality rate; context variables such as general software engineering experience and experience specific to the tasks of the experiments; how the subjects were recruited; the application areas and type of tasks; the duration of the tasks; and internal and external validity of the experiments, including being specific about the sample and target population of the experiment."

Standards for reporting results were asked for to facilitate the review of articles, ease replication of experiments and any kind of synthesis as well as theory building. Based on existing guidelines, requirements from the field and feedback from the community, we iteratively developed a guideline for reporting results from controlled experiments [30].

The 2006 Dagstuhl Seminar on Empirical SE [31] revealed that since 1992, the topic of empirical SE has been adopted more widely by academia as an interesting and promising research topic, and by industry practice as a necessary infrastructure technology for goal-oriented, sustained process improvement. At the same time, the spectrum of methods applied in empirical SE had broadened. Participants acknowledged empirical SE as a positive evolution. However, various issues were identified as still open, among them the need for better support for the reuse of empirical knowledge (combination of results) and for further standardizing the way empirical studies are performed and reported.

Since then, the number of (systematic) reviews has significantly increased, addressing several topics such as elicitation techniques [32] and agile development [33]. However, researchers often use narrative summaries for synthesizing[2] the results from individual studies [35].

In addition, guidelines for reporting experiments [36], case studies [37], and replications [38] have been further discussed and consolidated.

Current research on empirical methods in SE is dedicated to understanding and extending existing quantitative [35, 39] and qualitative synthesis [40] methods to better address the specific needs in SE, and learn how to derive laws and theories from empirical evidence [41].

2   Empirical Research Process at Fraunhofer IESE

In 1997, D. Rombach described an "experimentally-based software technology transfer" concept [42] based on the Goal/Question/Metric (GQM) method [43], the Quality Improvement Paradigm (QIP) [44], and the Experience Factory (EF) [44].

In 2013, applied research and technology transfer at Fraunhofer IESE is enriched by an evolved understanding of a goal-oriented research process, e.g., of what has to be done and what alternatives are available at the different stages of the QIP.

In the following subsections, we present the Fraunhofer IESE applied research process, which is defined on the basis of the QIP. It includes the following steps (cf. Fig. 1):

1. Characterize: Characterize the problem, i.e., identify and specify what the problem is. Experience from previous projects is incorporated.
2. Set goals: Define the research goal, i.e., what, why, and how. This comprises the selection of appropriate solution strategies for achieving the predefined goals.
3. Choose process: Choose and describe the process for implementing the strategies, i.e., establish a plan for how the research will be conducted, in particular, what will happen during the execution, incl. the design of empirical studies.
4. Execute: Perform the research according to the plan, i.e., build technologies or models, introduce them into the organization, collect data regarding goal achievement and models enhancement.
5. Analyze: Perform a summative analysis of the results and evaluate the degree of goal achievement.
6. Package: Document, report, and disseminate the results of all previous phases. If appropriate, integrate the results with the existing body of knowledge.

The steps of the process support us in focusing our research on problems that are relevant for SE practice and thus support our mission of applied research. The process is applicable to all kinds of projects, e.g., customer projects, research projects, and individual projects. Furthermore, each step is enriched by empirical

---

[2]Synthesis is the umbrella term covering different strategies for combining empirical evidence [34].

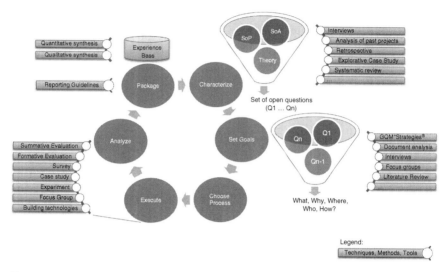

Fig. 1 The empirical research process

studies and methods. The theory of empirical research processes and methods can be found in several text books, such as [2, 45–47].

2.1 Characterize

For both customer and research projects, the first activity is to profoundly formulate the problem of interest, in particular the what, why, and how [48]. While customer projects are driven by more or less explicitly defined organizational goals and context, thus providing well-defined starting points at different stages of the process, research projects have a large degree of freedom in terms of specifying the scope of interest. Nevertheless, the general process remains the same.

According to our process, the first step is to identify and characterize problems in SE practice. This can be done, e.g., by interviewing or surveying experts in the field such as [49–51] or by analyzing past projects via data analyses [52], project retrospectives, or strengths and weaknesses analyses.

For the retrospectives, which we have successfully used in projects with several customers, we adapted the approach proposed by Kerth [53]. The scope varies from single-shot identification of a project's improvement potential to long-term organizational learning. The final results of a retrospective provide valuable feedback to our customers (e.g., identification of improvement potential) and important input for our research agenda. Our approach for performing retrospectives is supported by empirical methods including, e.g., small-sized surveys, document analysis, and focused workshops.

To analyze the current situation at an organization, we employ strengths and weaknesses analyses based on maturity and capability reference models enriched with an analysis of the work products. We also gain rich insights into the state of the practice here, even if it is restricted to the specific context of the organization. Our experiences have shown that semi-structured interviews and document analysis are effective empirical methods for supporting this kind of analysis [51].

If applicable, we additionally review the state of the art in SE by performing systematic reviews. Here we usually focus on: (1) identifying existing solutions, i.e., software technologies, (2) synthesizing empirical evidence regarding the effects of those software technologies in the context of interest (i.e., identifying existing theories), and (3) identifying questions that research does not have an answer for yet. Especially for research projects, this is an important task because the research has to be linked to existing theories. An introduction to the topic of theories in SE is given, e.g., in [54].

In order to obtain deeper insight into a problem and its context, we perform quantitative or qualitative studies. In the former case, we use surveys, explorative pilot studies, or available data, and in the latter, we use structured questionnaires, observational studies, or focus groups.

At this point we have identified a set of open questions (i.e., problems to be solved).

2.2   Set Goal

Together with the experts, we prioritize the open questions (i.e., problems) and define the scope (i.e., number of problems addressed).

Then we translate the problems into related goals, and elicit first improvement suggestions (this is typically part of our retrospectives). Within the target scope, problems are translated into initial goals. Then goals are further refined, prioritized, and specified. Afterwards appropriate strategies are chosen.

In general, we derive appropriate goals and related strategies together with rationales by using the GQM$^+$Strategies$^®$ approach [55]. With the GQM$^+$Strategies$^®$ approach, we ensure that goals and strategies are relevant and coherent. For example, in customer projects, we ensure that the chosen goals and strategies are both relevant for the whole organization and not in conflict with other organizational goals and strategies. Strategies towards the solution of the problem may include: (1) understanding the impact of a technology,[3] (2) comparing alternative technologies, (3) building new technologies, and (4) adopting them in a given context.

The GQM$^+$Strategies$^®$ grid describes the relationships among goals and strategies with rationales. This provides an initial theory for the solution approach. Theory means a set of coherent assumptions (or hypotheses) that describe the expected

---

[3]We use the term technology to refer to technique, method, and tool, following Basili et al. [44].

relations between the selected strategies and the targeted goals. The theory can be built on both the individual experience of involved experts and empirical evidence.

In addition, we define success criteria, i.e., metrics and target objectives (quantified hypotheses) that allow us to judge whether the selected strategies were successfully implemented.

The motivation for using the GQM$^+$Strategies$^®$ approach is to make the relationships between problems, goals, and solution strategies transparent and to provide a starting point for evaluating the solution when it is finally implemented.

Now we are able to describe the overall research question, in particular: What is the problem? Where does it occur? Who has observed it? Why it is important? How to address it (i.e., strategy or solution)? What results to expect?

2.3   Choose Process

After specifying the goals and selecting strategies, the research plan referring to the implementation of the strategies is created. This encompasses, among others, the order and contexts in which the technologies (i.e., strategies) will be implemented, steps for implementing the technology, associated resources, time schedule for achieving the related goals, and the process for collecting measures. For empirical studies, this means that we select an appropriate design according to the research question (e.g., [56]). Concerning the understanding and comparison of technologies, we use a large range of empirical methods for evaluating these technologies depending on the research question and context of the study. The plans for corresponding empirical studies have to be described.

While developing the research plan, we consider the following aspects: Implementation is preferably performed in iterations using formative evaluations to obtain feedback already in early stages. Regarding the adoption of a strategy in an organization, we usually first perform an early evaluation aimed at getting feedback from relevant stakeholders. This evaluation focuses, e.g., on the feasibility of the selected strategy or part of it. For instance, we use focus groups, scenario-based interviews with end users, or small-scaled, well-focused experiments. The collected feedback is used for improving the strategy iteratively. A concrete example of this approach is reported in [57].

In several customer projects, we have observed that industry is reluctant to share necessary data for publications, so we either have to deal with relative numbers or we must generally change the measurement approach to a more qualitative approach. In those cases, questions regarding, e.g., acceptance and perceived increase in effectiveness are used [58, 59] to obtain valuable feedback [60].

Depending on the nature of the selected strategies, the execution phase may comprise: building models or technologies, understanding the impact of a technology, comparing technologies, introducing them into an organization, collecting and analyzing data regarding goal achievement, and further improving the technology.

Models are built to describe reality, respectively a small part of it, and either to explain, predict, or prescribe what is, will, or has to be going on.

Building technologies include, e.g., defining a process model, developing a new software technology, or enhancing an existing one.

It has to be mentioned that the procedure described below accounts for all empirical studies performed in the course of the empirical research process.

According to [48], any empirical study has to start with a profound formulation of the research question, which is the basis for any subsequent evaluation step. If the empirical study is part of a larger project, the research question for the study is derived from the overall research question (cf. process step: set goals). A first decision has to be made as to whether the research question is of an explorative or explanatory nature. In contrast to an explanatory research, explorative research is conducted in a less fixed environment; many aspects, e.g., variables and their cause-effect relationships, are not yet known. The objective is to identify hypotheses which can then be used in explanatory research. For explanatory research, a clear formulation of the research questions with regard to the evaluation object (e.g., a safety method) and its impact on a certain quality aspect (e.g., consistency of system- and failure model) within a specific context (e.g., avionic domain) from the perspective of the relevant target group (e.g., safety engineer) helps to focus the work and supports a systematic, traceable approach to reaching conclusions.

The next step is to further elaborate the underlying theory and investigate related work. A combination of research question, underlying theory, and related work is used to derive hypotheses. There are three types of hypotheses: describing a relationship, a difference, or a change in variables. Different types of variables are used to give a model-based description of the environment of interest: independent variables, dependent variables, and confounding variables. In the context of an empirical study, we assess whether the variation of the independent variable(s) (e.g., safety analysis method) causes an effect in the dependent variable(s) (e.g., consistency). In addition to the independent variable, unknown variables – the confounding variables (e.g., participants' experience in safety analysis) – may influence the dependent variable(s). To measure the outcome in the dependent variable(s) requires operationalization of all variables.

Next, the appropriate empirical research method has to be selected according to the research question, hypotheses, variables, and given context. Typically, empirical methods such as experiments, case studies, and surveys are used. Experiments are used to measure and analyze the effect of systematic variations in the independent variable on the dependent variable. Often an experiment includes an experimental group (treatment applied) and a control group (no treatment applied) to prove the effect of the treatment. For further details on several experimental designs, we refer to [46].

If the results of the experiment show that the solution solves the target problem satisfactorily, then we focus on evaluating its potential in real settings, for example by performing case studies in industry.

According to Yin [47], "a case study is an empirical inquiry that investigates a contemporary phenomenon within its real-life context, especially when the boundaries between phenomenon and context are not clearly evident". Often case studies have small sample sizes and do not allow for controlling confounding variables. Case studies include feasibility studies, observatory single-subject design, longitudinal single-subject design, and semi-structured feedback sessions. Surveys are used to collect information from a large target group. They provide the data "to describe, compare or explain knowledge, attitudes and behavior" [15]. Typically used methods are interviews and online questionnaires.

Furthermore, the target population has to be defined and a (representative) sample has to be drawn. In our example, the target population consists of software and system engineers.

Then, necessary materials, apparatus, and instruments have to be derived and developed; those are the main tools for inducing a treatment (e.g., performing a specific task with a given technology) and for measuring the dependent variables (e.g., a questionnaire for measuring technology acceptance).

The procedure for running the study has to be fixed. This includes describing precisely what will happen to the participants from the moment they arrive to the moment they leave the experiment site [61].

A plan for the summative evaluation of the implemented strategy concludes this phase. Now, we have the plan to execute the research.

2.4   Execute and Analyze

The execution aims at implementing the selected strategies according to the specified plan.

For instance, in recent customer projects, we built generic models for quality and cost estimation using a two-step survey approach. We first interviewed a sample of practitioners to get input on how they characterize quality and costs. The results were used for building initial models. In parallel, we performed a systematic review on the topic. Its results were used for enhancing the initial models. Second, we interviewed the same sample of practitioners to discuss the developed models e.g., [62].

In research projects, we used a series of empirical studies such as interviews, focus groups, systematic reviews, and experiments for building information models to support decision makers in the selection of software technologies [63], for developing a hybrid method for cost estimation [64], or for analyzing the seamless integration of processes with tools [65].

After implementing the chosen strategies or developing a technology, we usually perform a summative evaluation for assessing to which extent the goals were accomplished.

After a study has been conducted and all data have been collected, the results have to be analyzed and interpreted. Feedback sessions with the participants help to better explain the results.

At this point we gain empirical evidence regarding the appropriateness and suitability of the selected strategy in the context at hand. On the basis of this empirical evidence, a better decision regarding whether the technology (i.e., the strategy) will be piloted or introduced in the organization or whether it needs to be further improved or changed (new iteration) can be made [66].

For example, in a large German research project, in the context of system safety analysis in the avionics domain, we were asked to compare the currently used state-of-the-practice method for describing a system's safety in terms of a failure model with a model-based method for the same purpose. The focus of the evaluation was on the consistency of the system model with the resulting failure model from the viewpoint of safety engineers. Because of the complexity of the task, the study had to be performed with people having appropriate technical and domain knowledge. In fact, the study was performed with practitioners and replicated with PhD students working on projects with a focus on system safety [67]. The results of the studies were well perceived by the industry partner and led to further research questions, which are currently being investigated.

Now we have completed the implementation of the strategy and gained empirical evidence regarding its impact in the context of interest.

2.5   Package

We distinguish between the packaging of individual studies, the project, and the synthesis of individual empirical studies.

Individual empirical studies are reported in parallel to the Fraunhofer IESE applied research process. For this purpose, we provide guidelines for different types of empirical studies, e.g., controlled experiments [36], surveys [15, 49], case studies [37], systematic literature reviews [28], and replications [38]. Each empirical study has to be placed into the body of knowledge and assessed with regard to the implications of the findings and validity threats.

In the context of the Fraunhofer IESE applied research process, the scope of a project can address a subset or all steps above. The methods and procedures followed during a project as well as its results and lessons learned are summarized in technical reports and project deliverables. These are made available in the Fraunhofer IESE internal repository and are published in accordance with confidentiality agreements signed with the project stakeholders.

Now all empirical studies and their results as well as the project are documented and accessible in the Fraunhofer IESE internal repository. If applicable, empirical studies are synthesized to increase the body of knowledge of SE.

Once several individual empirical studies have been published regarding a software technology, we emphasize the need to synthesize them in order to systematically build knowledge in SE. Thus, we have adopted existing quantitative and qualitative synthesis methods. For quantitative synthesis, meta-analysis was extended with an approach to incremental aggregation based on aggregation states, which represent the aggregated knowledge of a set of studies, and which allow deriving the required quantitative key information (e.g., effect existence and magnitude) [39].

At this point, all empirical studies and their results as well as the project are documented and accessible in the Fraunhofer IESE internal repository. If applicable, empirical studies are integrated into the body of SE knowledge.

3   Discussion and Outlook

We described an empirical process for applied research that (1) aligns our research with problems that are relevant for industry, (2) ensures involvement of relevant sources of information, (3) makes the contribution of the solution towards the problem at hand transparent, and (4) provides us with empirical evidence regarding the appropriateness of the solution. The results are used to support customers in making informed decisions [39, 63].

Although the request for studies in industry existed from the beginning, the number of publications did not reflect it. Most published studies report on studies with students. The reasons are manifold; among them are: ease of accessing participants, ease of planning, control of the complexity of material and procedures, ownership of the results, ability to publish. The trade-offs, as often criticized, comprise limited realism (external validity) and hence acceptability of the results by practitioners [50]. Several authors, aiming at better "marketing" research results, discuss the pros and cons of studies in artificial settings or with student participants [37] as well as how to better address the information needs of practitioners [66]. Strategies leading to more studies in industry are frequently discussed in the empirical SE community, e.g., at the Dagstuhl 2006 Seminar [31] and subsequent ISERN meetings. Those discussions aim at learning from success stories and identifying feasible models of research-industry collaboration. In addition, individual authors report on organizational set-ups for successful technology transfer [8] and models for research-industry collaborations [31, 68], as well as aspects and lessons learned that have to be taken into account [69], such as building trust, confidentiality, and generating a win-win situation.

In our projects with industry, we currently apply the following approaches:

- Individual studies with practitioners: In close cooperation with an industry partner, we involve practitioners from the business units in a study. This approach is often supported by publicly funded projects. The major success factor is to motivate the participating organization by convincing them of the potential to gain knowledge. They need to be able to identify a win-situation.
- Research Lab: We invite practitioners to collaborate on a solution to a problem at hand in an environment at the research organization that is close to what they know but can easily be enriched with new technology.
- Consultancy and service provision: We provide services to our customers in terms of supporting them in planning and running empirical studies, analyzing the results, and feeding them back into the organization.
- Bi-directional exchange: This approach is similar to sabbaticals; in the first phase, a practitioner visits a research organization and takes part in the daily work on a topic of his interest. In the second phase, the researcher visits the company and works together with the practitioner on the transfer into practice of the solution obtained during the research.

Involving practitioners in studies is also achieved by either paying them [70] or by organizing large coding contests [71].

3.1   Outlook

Aiming at supporting efficient and informed decision-making, from a research perspective we still see the necessity to better understand how and under which circumstances we can synthesize available empirical evidence on particular SE techniques.

Empirical evidence in empirical SE is often created through mixed methods, i.e., the combination of qualitative and quantitative research methods. It can be observed in several research areas that quantitative research and qualitative research are no longer seen as rivals [72] but rather as being complementary. The discussion mainly concerns individual studies, where integration takes place, e.g., by employing triangulation or mixed-method approaches [73]. To build a comprehensive body of knowledge in empirical SE, synthesizing evidence implies the integration of quantitative and qualitative evidence, which is still an open question in other fields of research [74, 75].

As for the discussion regarding the applicability of methods for primary studies, the question regarding whether and why empirical SE is different from other empirical disciplines and consequently requires its "own" methods has not been answered sufficiently yet.

In addition, we see the people factor as being particularly important and deserving further investigation. For instance, what is the impact of experience, knowledge, motivation, and cultural background on the performance in empirical studies? Researchers often claim to have these factors under control by using pre- and post-questionnaires and testing whether they had any significant influence on the results. However, we have experienced issues in some of the studies we did, especially with practitioners, who seem to underestimate their level of experience for several reasons. We acknowledge that knowledge tests might require too much effort, but we think that the way experience is characterized needs to be revisited, and if we go further ahead, a standard for the people factors must be defined.

Acknowledgments First of all, we thank Dieter Rombach, who provided us with the inspiring environment that Fraunhofer IESE is. In addition, we would like to acknowledge the contributions of current and former colleagues as well as friends within the ISERN community to the evolution of empirical SE at Fraunhofer IESE. Since there are so many we are unable to list all of them, but we are particularly grateful to Vic Basili, Marcus Ciolkowski, Natalia Juristo, and Carolyn Seaman, with whom we closely collaborated and walked the path of empirical SE for the past 10 years.

References

1. Basili, V., Selby, R., Hutchens, D.: Experimentation in software engineering. IEEE Trans. Softw. Eng. **12**(7), 733–743 (1986)
2. Wohlin, C., Runeson, P., Höst, M., Ohlsson, M.C., Regnell, B., Wesslén, A.: Experimentation in Software Engineering: An Introduction. Kluwer (2000). ISBN: 0-7923-8682-5
3. IEEE Computer Society: IEEE: standard glossary of software engineering terminology. IEEE Standard 610.12-1990

4. Juristo, N., Moreno, A.: Basics of Software Engineering Experimentation. Kluwer, Boston (2001)
5. Schulz, W.: Kausalität und Experiment in den Sozialwissenschaften – Methodologie und Forschungstechnik. V. Hase & Koehler Verlag, Mainz (1970)
6. Rombach, H.D., Basili, V.R., Selby, R.W. (eds.): Experimental Software Engineering Issues: Critical Assessment and Future Directions. International Workshop Dagstuhl Castle, Germany. Lecture Notes in Computer Science, vol. 706. Springer (1992)
7. http://www.iese.fraunhofer.de. Last visited 14 Feb 2013
8. Rombach, D.: Fraunhofer: the German model for applied research and technology transfer. In: Proceedings of International Conference on Software Engineering 2000, Limerick, pp. 531–537. (2000)
9. http://isern.iese.de. Last visited 14 Feb 2013
10. Fenton, N.E., Pfleeger, S.L., Glass, R.: Science and substance: a challenge to software engineers. IEEE Softw. **11**(4), 86–95 (1994)
11. Pfleeger, S.L.: Design and analysis in software engineering. Part 1: the language of case studies and formal experiments. ACM SIGSOFT Softw. Eng. Notes **19**(4), 16–20 (1994)
12. Kitchenham, B., Linkman, S., Law, D.: DESMET: a methodology for evaluating software engineering methods and tools. Comput. Contr. Eng. J. **8**(3), 120–126 (1997)
13. Singer, J.: (APA) Style guidelines to report experimental results. In: Proceedings of Workshop on Empirical Studies in Software Maintenance, pp. 71–77. Oxford, UK (1999)
14. American Psychological Association: Publication Manual of the American Psychological Association, 5th edn. American Psychological Association, Washington, DC (2001)
15. Pfleeger, S.L., Kitchenham, B.A.: Principles of survey research. Part 1: turning lemons into lemonade. ACM SIGSOFT Softw. Eng. Notes **26**(6), 16–18 (2001)
16. Kitchenham, B.A., Pfleeger, S.L., Pickard, L.M., Jones, P.W., Hoaglin, D.C., El Emam, K., Rosenberg, J.: Preliminary guidelines for empirical research in software engineering. IEEE Trans. Softw. Eng. **28**(8), 721–734 (2002)
17. Shaw, M.: Writing good software engineering research papers. In: Proceedings of the 25th International Conference on Software Engineering (ICSE'03), pp. 726–736. IEEE CS, Portland (2003)
18. Ruhe, G.: Software engineering decision support – a new paradigm for learning software organizations. In: Henninger, S., Maurer, F. (eds.) Advances in LSO. 4th International Workshop, LSO 2002, Chicago, 6 Aug 2002: Revised papers, Lecture Notes in Computer Science, vol. 2640, pp. 104–115. Springer (2003)
19. Aurum, A., Petersson, H., Wohlin, C.: State-of-the-art: software inspections after 25 years. Softw. Test. Verif. Reliab. **12**(3), 133–154 (2002)
20. Juristo, N., Moreno, A., Vegas, S.: Reviewing 25 years of testing technique experiments. J. Empirical Softw. Eng. **9**(1–2), 7–44 (2004)
21. Jedlitschka, A., Ciolkowski, M.: Towards evidence in software engineering. In: Proceedings of International Symposium on Empirical SE 2004 (ISESE2004), pp. 261–270. Redondo Beach (2004)
22. Wohlin, C., Petersson, H., Aurum, A.: Combining data from reading experiments in software inspections. In: Juristo, N., Moreno, A. (eds.) Lecture Notes on Empirical Software Engineering, pp. 85–132. World Scientific Publishing, River Edge (2003)
23. Conradi, R., Wang, A.I. (eds.): Empirical Methods and Studies in Software Engineering – Experiences from ESERNET. Lecture Notes in Computer Science, vol. 2765. Springer, Berlin (2003)
24. Conradi, R., Dybå, T., Sjøberg, D., Ulsund, T.: Lessons learned and recommendations from two large Norwegian SPI programmes. In: Oquendo, F. (ed.) 9th European Workshop on Software Process Technology (EWSPT 2003), Helsinki, 1–2 Sept 2003, Lecture Notes in Computer Science, vol. 2786, pp. 32–45. Springer (2003)
25. Glass, R.L.: Matching methodology to problem domain. Column Pract. Programmer Commun. ACM **47**(5), 19–21 (2004)

26. Turner, R.: Why we need empirical information on best practices. CROSSTALK – J. Defense Softw. Eng. **17**(4), 9–11 (2004)
27. Kitchenham, B.A., Dybå, T., Jørgensen, M.: Evidence-based software engineering. In: Proceedings of 26th International Conference on Software Engineering (ICSE'04), pp. 273–281. Edinburgh (2004)
28. Kitchenham, B.A.: Procedures for performing systematic reviews. Keele University Technical Report TR/SE-0401; ISSN 1353-7776.1 (2004)
29. Sjøberg, D., Hannay, J., Hansen, O., By Kampenes, V., Karahasanovic, A., Liborg, N.-K., Rekdal, A.: A survey of controlled experiments in software engineering. Trans. Softw. Eng. **31**(9), 733–753 (2005)
30. Jedlitschka, A., Pfahl, D.: Reporting guidelines for controlled experiments in software engineering. In: Proceedings of International Symposium on Empirical SE 2005 (ISESE2005), Noosa Heads, Australia, Nov 2005, pp. 95–104. IEEE CS (2005)
31. Basili, V.R., Rombach, D., Schneider, K., Kitchenham, B., Pfahl, D., Selby, R.W. (eds.): Empirical Software Engineering Issues: Critical Assessment and Future Directions. International Workshop Dagstuhl Castle, Germany. Lecture Notes in Computer Science, vol. 4336. Springer (2007)
32. Dieste, O., Juristo, N.: Systematic review and aggregation of empirical studies on elicitation techniques. IEEE Trans. Softw. Eng. **37**(2), 283–304 (2011)
33. Dybå, T., Dingsøyr, T.: Empirical studies of agile software development: a systematic review. Inf. Softw. Technol. **50**(9–10), 833–859 (2008)
34. Chalmers, I., Hedges, L., Cooper, H.: A brief history of research synthesis. Eval. Health Prof. **25**(1), 12–37 (2002)
35. Ciolkowski, M.: What do we know about perspective-based reading? An approach for quantitative aggregation in software engineering. In: Proceedings of ESEM 2009, Lake Buena Vista, pp. 133–144
36. Jedlitschka, A., Ciolkowski, M., Pfahl, D.: Reporting controlled experiments in software engineering. In: Shull, F., et al. (eds.) Guide to Advanced Empirical Software Engineering. Springer, New York (2008)
37. Runeson, P., Höst, M.: Guidelines for conducting and reporting case study research in SE. J. Empirical Softw. Eng. **14**(2), 131–164 (2009)
38. Carver, J.: Towards reporting guidelines for experimental replications: a proposal. In: Proceedings of the 1st International Workshop on Replication in ESE Research (RESER) @ ICSE, Cape Town, 4 May 2010
39. Ciolkowski, M.: An approach for quantitative aggregation of evidence from controlled experiments in software engineering. Kaiserslautern University, Dissertation, 2011, 231 pp, Fraunhofer Verlag, Stuttgart (2012)
40. Cruzes, D.S., Dybå, T.: Recommended steps for thematic synthesis in software engineering. In: Proceedings of ESEM 2011, Banff, pp. 275–284
41. Rombach, D.: Empirical software engineering models: can they become the equivalent of physical laws in traditional engineering? Int. J. Softw. Inf. **5**(3), 525–534 (2011)
42. Linkman, S., Rombach, D.: Experimentation as a vehicle for software technology transfer – a family of software reading techniques. Inf. Softw. Technol. **39**(11), 777–780 (1997)
43. Basili, V.R., Caldiera, G., Rombach, H.D.: Goal question metric paradigm. In: Marciniak, J.J. (ed.) Encyclopedia of Software Engineering, vol. 1, 2nd edn, pp. 528–532. Wiley-Interscience, New York (2001a). doi:10.1002/0471028959. ISBN 10: 0471377376
44. Basili, V.R., Caldiera, G., Rombach, H.D.: Experience factory. In: Marciniak, J.J. (ed.) Encyclopedia of Software Engineering, vol. 1, pp. 511–519. Wiley-Interscience, New York (2001b). doi:10.1002/0471028959. ISBN 10: 0471377376
45. Creswell, J.W.: Research Design: Qualitative, Quantitative, and Mixed Methods Approaches, 2nd edn. Sage, Thousand Oaks (2003)
46. Shadish, W.R., Cook, T.D., Campbell, D.T.: Experimental and Quasi-experimental Design for Generalized Causal Inference. Houghton-Mifflin, Boston (2002)
47. Yin, R.K.: Case Study Research. Design and Methods, 3rd edn. Sage, Thousand Oaks (2003)

48. Chen, H.T., Rossi, P.H.: Evaluating with sense: the theory-driven approach. Eval. Rev. **7**(3), 283–302 (1983). doi:10.1177/0193841X8300700301
49. Ciolkowski, M., Laitenberger, O., Biffl, S.: Software reviews: the state of the practice. IEEE Softw. **20**(6), 46–51 (2003)
50. Jedlitschka, A., Ciolkowski, M., Denger, C., Freimut, B., Schlichting, A.: Relevant information sources for successful technology transfer: a survey using inspections as an example. In: Proceedings of the International Symposium on Empirical SE and Measurement 2007 (ESEM2007), pp. 31–40. Madrid (2007)
51. Jedlitschka, A., Hamann, D., Göhlert, T., Schröder, A.: Adapting PROFES for use in an agile process: an industry experience report. In: Bomarius, F., et al. (ed.) Proceedings of 6th International Conference on Product Focused Software Process Improvement. Profes'2005. Lecture Notes in Computer Science, vol. 3547, pp. 502–516. (2005)
52. Kläs, M., Nakao, H., Elberzhager, E., Münch, J.: Support planning and controlling of early quality assurance by combining expert judgment and defect data – a case study. J. Empir. Softw. Eng. **15**(4), 423–454, Springer (2010)
53. Kerth, N.: Project Retrospectives: A Handbook for Team Reviews. Dorset House Publishing, New York (2001)
54. Sjøberg, D.I.K., Dybå, T., Anda, B.C.D., Hannay, J.E.: Building theories in software engineering. In: Shull, F. et al. (eds.) Guide to advanced empirical software engineering. Springer (2008)
55. Basili, V., Heidrich, J., Lindvall, M., Münch, J., Regardie, M., Rombach, D., Seaman, C., Trendowicz, A.: Linking software development and business strategy through measurement. IEEE Comput. **43**(4), 57–65 (2010)
56. Easterbrook, S.M., Singer, J., Storey, M., Damian, D.: Selecting empirical methods for software engineering research. In: Shull, F., et al. (eds.) Guide to Advanced Empirical Software Engineering. Springer, New York (2008)
57. Kleinberger, T., Jedlitschka, A., Storf, H., Steinbach-Nordmann, S., Prueckner, S.: An approach to and evaluations of assisted living systems using ambient intelligence for emergency monitoring and prevention. In: Universal Access in HCI. Intelligent and Ubiquitous Interaction Environments. Lecture Notes in Computer Science, vol. 5615, pp. 199–208. (2009)
58. Venkatesh, V., Bala, H.: Technology acceptance model 3 and a research agenda on interventions. Decis. Sci. **39**(2), 273–315 (2008)
59. Venkatesh, V., Morris, M.G., Davis, G.B., Davis, F.D.: User acceptance of information technology. MIS Q. **27**(3), 425–478 (2003)
60. Nunnenmacher, S., Jung, J., Chehrazi, G., Klaus, A., Lampasona, C., Webel, C., Ciolkowski, M.: A preliminary survey on subjective measurements and personal insights into factors of perceived future project success. In: Proceedings of 5th International Symposium on Empirical SE and Measurement, pp. 396–399, IEEE CS, Los Alamitos (2011)
61. Harris, P.: Designing and Reporting Experiments in Psychology, 2nd edn. Open University Press, Berkshire (2002)
62. Wagner, S., Lochmann, K., Heinemann, L., Kläs, M., Trendowicz, A., Plösch, R., Seidl, A., Goeb, A., Streit, J.: The Quamoco product quality modeling and assessment approach. In: Proceedings of 34th International Conference on Software Engineering (ICSE 2012), pp. 1133–1142. ACM/IEEE, Zurich, 2–9 June 2012
63. Jedlitschka, A.: An empirical model of software managers information needs for software engineering technology selection. Kaiserslautern University Dissertation, 435 pp. Fraunhofer Verlag, Stuttgart (2009)
64. Trendowicz, A.: Software Cost Estimation, Benchmarking, and Risk Assessment. The Software Decision-Makers' Guide to Predictable Software Development. The Fraunhofer IESE Series on Software and Systems Engineering. Springer, Berlin (2013)
65. Lampasona, C., Rostanin, O., Maus, H.: Seamless integration of order processing in MS outlook using SmartOffice: an empirical evaluation. In: Proceedings of International Symposium on Empirical SE and Measurement, pp. 165–168. ACM Press, New York (2012)

66. Jedlitschka, A.: Evaluating a model of software managers' information needs: an experiment. In: Proceedings of ACM-IEEE International Symposium on Empirical SE and Measurement (ESEM'10). ACM, Bozen, No. 19, 10 pp (2010)
67. Jung, J., Höfig, K., Hiller, M., Jedlitschka, A., Domis, D.: Are Ph.D.-Students with Domain Knowledge Appropriate Subjects for Experiments? Kaiserslautern, IESE-Report; 037.12/E (2012)
68. Rombach, D., Achatz, R.: Research collaborations between academia and industry. In: Proceedings of WS on future of Software Engineering, Minneapolis, pp. 29–36. (2007)
69. Jedlitschka, A., Pfahl, D.: Experience-based model-driven improvement management with combined data sources from industry and academia. In: Proceedings of International Symposium on Empirical SE ISESE 2003, pp. 154–161. Roman Castles (2003)
70. Tichy, W.: Empirical software research: an interview with Dag Sjøberg, University of Oslo, Norway. Ubiquity 2011, June, Article 2, 14 pp (2011)
71. http://www.catalysts.cc/contest/. Last visited 14 Feb 2013
72. Lincoln, Y., Guba, E.G.: Naturalistic Inquiry. Sage, London/Thousand Oaks/New Delhi (1985)
73. Pope, C., Mays, N., Popay, J.: Synthesizing Qualitative and Quantitative Health Evidence. A Guide to Methods. Open University Press, Berkshire (2007)
74. Dixon-Woods, M., Agarwal, S., Jones, D., Young, B., Sutton, A.: Synthesising qualitative and quantitative evidence: a review of possible methods. J. Health Serv. Res. Policy 10, 45–53 (2005)
75. Miles, M.B., Huberman, A.M.: Qualitative Data Analysis: An Expanded Sourcebook. Sage, Thousand Oaks (1994)

Part III

Visions on the Future of Software Engineering as a Discipline

What Is Software? The Role of Empirical Methods in Answering the Question

Leon J. Osterweil

Abstract
This paper explores the potentially pivotal role of Empirical Methods in addressing existential questions about the nature of software. Building upon an earlier paper that asked the question "What is software?", this paper suggests that a key way to gain such understanding is to ponder the question of how to determine the size of a software entity. The paper notes that there have been a variety of indirect approaches to measuring software size, such as measuring the amount of time taken to produce software, and measuring the number of lines of code in a software entity. But these assume implicitly that such measures correlate positively with the inherent size of the software entity, broadly construed to include the entire panoply of code and non-code artifacts and their interconnections that comprise this entity. As in the original paper, this paper makes the case that entities such as recipes, laws, and processes are types of software, and that learning about their natures illuminates the nature of computer software—and conversely. This paper discusses possible approaches to measuring the size of these other types of artifacts, and uses observations about these approaches to suggest a possible approach to measuring the size of computer software entities. All of this is aimed at making progress in gaining understandings about the nature of software, broadly construed.

Preface: This paper is an updating of a paper previously published in Automated Software Engineering, entitled "What is Software?" [1]. That previous paper, written over 5 years ago, made a case for the importance of understanding the essence of what "software" is, noting that computer software is one of a number of different kinds of intellectual products that can and should be considered to be closely related to each other. The paper noted that laws,

L.J. Osterweil (✉)
Laboratory for Advanced Software Engineering Research, School of Computer Science,
University of Massachusetts, Amherst, MA 01003, USA
e-mail: ljo@cs.umass.edu

J. Münch and K. Schmid (eds.), *Perspectives on the Future of Software Engineering*,
DOI 10.1007/978-3-642-37395-4_16, © Springer-Verlag Berlin Heidelberg 2013

processes, and recipes all seem to be closely related in fundamental ways to computer software, and suggested that all might be considered to be subtypes of a type of intellectual product that might be called "software". That being the case, the earlier paper suggested that studying any of these might well produce results of interest and value to the others, and studying the relations among these types of artifacts might ultimately provide insight into the fundamental nature of the type of thing of which all might be considered to be subtypes.

The main addition that this paper makes to the previous version is to note a potentially key contribution that Empirical Methods could make to these understandings. In the paper we argue that the understanding of an object (physical or non-physical) is greatly enhanced by the ability to measure that object. Indeed, Lord Kelvin suggested, over 100 years ago, that

> ... when you can measure what you are speaking about, and express it in numbers, you know something about it; but when you cannot measure it, when you cannot express it in numbers, your knowledge is of a meagre and unsatisfactory kind; it may be the beginning of knowledge, but you have scarcely in your thoughts advanced to the state of Science, whatever the matter may be.

That being the case, Empirical Methods research should be viewed as being essential to gaining knowledge and establishing the science of the nature of software, in that it addresses issues of how to measure various aspects of software. This paper focuses as a case in point on how to define one particular basic measure of software, namely its size. This would seem to be a basic measure and yet we note that no such satisfactory measure of software size seems to exist. Grappling with this and related questions has been a focus of the Empirical Methods community. The community's success in understanding how to establish such measures of computer software is clearly important to progress in being more effective in computer software engineering, but might indeed also have important ramifications for improvements in the engineering of other kinds of software, such as processes and laws, as well. For that reason the ongoing efforts of the Empirical Methods research community should be viewed by the entire "software" community as being of fundamental importance.

1   Apologia

When the words "software" and "engineering" were first put together [2] it was not clear exactly what the marriage of the two into the newly minted term really meant. Some people understood that the term would probably come to be defined by what our community did and what the world made of it. Since those days in the late 1960s a spectrum of research and practice has been collected under the term. Journals, magazines, conferences, and workshops have used it in growing numbers. From time to time some have questioned whether or not the second word of the term, "engineering", is properly applied to what it is that "software engineers" do (e.g. [3]). The debate has been sporadic, but it has probably been good for the community. It seems odd, however, that there has been hardly any discussion of the first word of the term, namely "software". When, on infrequent occasion, the meaning of this term has been questioned, mostly in informal conversation, the question has been met with visible discomfort, and some attempt to dismiss it. The purpose of this paper is to try to address the question head-on.

What is software? If our community feels comfortable in believing that it is engaged in the practice of engineering "software", it seems that the community should show some curiosity about what it is that is the subject of its ministrations. But, when asked to ponder what "software" is, computer software engineers seem to assume that the only kind of software is computer software. They provide answers that roughly equate software with code to be executed on a computer. When prodded, most will readily agree that the software they produce consists of more than just the code, but also somehow incorporates specifications of various kinds, designs, and perhaps testing regimes and results as well. But when it is suggested that there might be types of software other than computer software, some computer software engineers have questioned the value of considering the possibility. Here we suggest that considering this possibility might lead to an understanding of what these various kinds of software have in common, and thus what the nature of "software" is. Some have suggested that the quintessential nature of "software" may be imponderable and unknowable. This may indeed be the case, but it seems worth noting that humans have in the past asked many "unanswerable" questions, about the nature of such things as love, God, truth, and reality. While the answers often have not been very satisfying, the pondering and discussion of them has typically been interesting, revealing, and sometimes ennobling. For these reasons, and others, it does not seem inappropriate to offer this short essay, hoping that it may help to start a debate that turns out to be, at least, interesting.

1.1   Why Ask the Question?

In addition to the sheer intellectual joy of pursuing a hard, fundamental, and potentially unanswerable question, there are additional more pragmatic reasons for thinking about the essential nature of software. One such reason is that if there are others who work with software then it might be possible that their experiences in doing so might be of value to those of us who work with computer software. Other software practitioners might have encountered problems and issues that are analogous to those that concern us. In doing so they may have found some effective approaches to some problems that frustrate us. At the least, their struggles with analogous problems might at least underscore the universality and importance of the problems. Indeed, idiosyncrasies of the problems posed in these analogous domains might well provide new perspectives on the problems that might be useful to us in our own work.

1.2   The Importance of Measurement

As noted above, and following Lord Kelvin, it seems promising to suggest that a path to understanding the nature of software might be through grappling with questions about how to measure it. The Empirical Methods community has been a key focal point of ongoing efforts to measure software. A central challenge the community has faced is the continuing effort to measure the size of a piece of software. Some attempts have focused on how to count the number of "lines" of computer code; others have grappled with trying to measure the size of non-code artifacts, and the complexity of any and all of these artifacts. Other attempts have instead focused on process issues, suggesting that measuring the time, money, and effort taken to develop a piece of software might also be a good way to measure the size of the software item itself. These ongoing efforts do not yet seem to have led to universal agreement about how to measure the size of software, but they have demonstrated correlations between many of the suggested measures. The magnitude of this ongoing challenge suggests the profundity of the question, and also suggests that growing understandings of how to measure size may well be leading to important deep understandings about the nature of software as an entity. We now suggest that these attempts and preliminary successes might be of value and interest to practitioners in other computer-software-like areas. And it indeed raises the question of whether these other practitioners might have had some success in measuring their own artifacts that could be of interest and value to computer software engineers.

2   Other Kinds of Software

It is worth noting that the word "software" is applied to artifacts from domains other than computing. In entertainment, for example, software is sometimes used to describe programmatics, such as videos and television productions. The term seems to be used to contrast this sort of product with "hardware", which refers to physical devices such as VCRs, CD players, and television sets. There are other domains that seem to be very much about "software", but some of these domains may not ever use the word, nor be very conscious of the relevance of what is known about computer software to what they do. Thus, we guide our search for an understanding of what "software" is by searching for other disciplines that seem to deal with "software", even if they may not use that term in describing their work. Thus, for example, it might suffice to simply identify points of similarity between what computer software engineers do and what is done by practitioners of these other disciplines.

2.1   Processes Are (Like?) Software

In a previous paper [4] it was suggested that "Software Processes are Software Too", intending to suggest that those who focus on the engineering of computer software might perhaps widen the scope of their attention to address processes for developing computer software as well. The point here was that processes seem as though they might be items of software that execute on virtual machines that consist of more kinds of devices than only computers. Subsequent work has tended to confirm the plausibility of that suggestion [5–7].

Process research has suggested that process software has strong similarities to computer software. In particular, experience has shown that many processes are highly concurrent, and that software concepts such as locking and synchronization can help the understanding and control of such processes. It has also been observed that exceptions are common in processes, and that exception management approaches that are analogous to those taken by modern programming languages also facilitate the understanding and control of processes. As with computer software, process software needs to address requirements that should be carefully thought out, should have an architecture, and should be designed prior to implementation. In addition, process software is subject to continuous need for change and evolution, which is highly problematic. Attempts to define real world processes have typically resulted in surprisingly large, repetitive, and ungainly process definitions. Experience has shown, however, that judicious use of formal declarations can help avoid dangerous confusions. Moreover, notions of abstraction, modularity, and hierarchy can lead to process definitions that are clearer, more concise, and demonstrate better reuse than those that do not attempt to exploit abstraction.

Thus, it seems that there is growing evidence that those who deal with the development and use of process definitions face and deal with many of the problems encountered by those who develop computer software. This seems to suggest that there could be value in considering processes to indeed be a type of software. On the other hand, experience has also shown that real world processes often raise other issues less commonly dealt with by computer software developers. Processes, for example, make use of resources in ways that are often quite complicated. The prevalence and centrality of this complex usage of very diverse resources in many processes seems to be less analogous to what is typically found in contemporary computer software. This suggests that computer software engineers might consider the relevance of resource specification and utilization to their own work.

2.1.1   Measurement of Processes

It seems that, while there are strong intuitions about the size of processes, there has been relatively little effort to specify rigorously-defined measures of process size. It is certainly not uncommon to see some processes referred to as "large" or "comprehensive", and even as "ungainly" or "clumsy", suggesting that people have strong intuitions about the size and suitability of processes. But there seem to have been few attempts to try to back up these intuitions with definitions and rigor.

Instead, efforts to be quantitative about processes have focused on measuring the execution characteristics of processes. Thus, for example, as noted above, Empirical Methods researchers have suggested that measures of the amount of time and resources required to develop a computer software product seem to provide some useful sense of the size of the product. And so, analogously, there has been a considerable amount of effort devoted to measuring execution parameters of software development processes. Similarly, practitioners in other areas such as healthcare and management are typically concerned to measure and improve the running time of their processes. In some cases, this has caused these practitioners to seek to materialize these processes in the form of process models, in the hope that study and analysis of these models might facilitate the improvement of the execution characteristics of their processes. But even in such cases there seems to have been relatively little attention devoted to measuring the size of these processes themselves.

Interestingly, in our own work, where we think of processes as being a kind of software, we, accordingly, define processes using a programming-like language. Thus we "measure" the size of a process by the number of steps (the analog of statements in a programming language), thereby pushing the problem of measuring size back onto the software development community.

Thinking more directly about the meaning of "size" in the process domain, however, has caused us to ponder whether the size of a process might be measured by the inherent ability of the process to change the state of the real-world situations to which it is applied. It seems, perhaps, more promising to consider how to measure the size of the state of the domain in which a process operates, and to then use this size as the basis for measuring the magnitude of the change(s) the process might effect, and thus the size of the process itself.

2.2   Legislation Is (Like?) Software Development

We also suggest that laws are a form of software, and that legislation is a form of software development. Laws provide rules that govern the execution of governmental and societal activities. Many laws are proscriptive in this way and seem not unlike the rules that could be written using a rule-based language (e.g., see [8, 9]). Other laws are more prescriptive, some even describing the ways in which various institutions are to be established, organized, and operated. Such laws sometimes prescribe the ways in which such institutions and their activities are to be coordinated with each other. Thus laws seem to define processes in many cases, and in these ways they resemble process definition vehicles. The languages used to define laws may seem to be informal, and may seem to be written in natural language. But this is apparently something of an illusion. Most legislative bodies mandate that their laws incorporate reserved words and phrases that have meanings that are often much more precisely defined than words used in natural language. Thus the text of a law is typically peppered with words that are relatively precisely defined, interspersed with words that are used colloquially. It typically impossible for a novice to tell which words are of which type.

It is interesting to note, moreover, that laws and legal documents (e.g., leases) often begin with a prefixed section in which additional terms may be defined, and in which the bindings of values may be made. Thus, for example, a lease typically begins with a paragraph containing words that bind names (i.e., instances of types) to the terms "lessor" and "lessee" (which are essentially types). The similarity to the declaration sections that precede bodies of computer code seems noteworthy.

Additional parallels can be found in, for example, the organizational structure of the government of countries such as the United States. This structure mandates three principal branches: the legislative, which creates software (i.e., laws), the executive, which executes the software (e.g., by creating bureaucratic machinery), and the judiciary, which analyzes bodies of software (e.g., an entire corpus of laws) to determine the extent to which it is, or is not, consistent. Thus these three branches correspond to computer software development notions of development, execution, and analysis.

We note moreover that laws, like computer software, typically need to be evolved as the needs and perceptions of their users change. As with the case of computer software, laws change the way in which the world works (not uncommonly in unexpected ways), thereby changing the context in which the laws work, thus changing the underlying requirements for the laws and creating the need for evolution. Thus, legal software, like computer software, seems to operate in a closed loop with the real world, each both inducing and reacting to change in the other. As a consequence, laws are typically amended, and at times entire bodies of law (e.g., tax codes) are completely discarded and replaced. All of this should be quite familiar to computer software engineers.

Further parallels between laws and computer software are not hard to identify. We thus suggest that laws are also a form of software and that legislation is a form of software development. We note in passing that this observation might cause computer software engineers to have a bit more sympathy for legislators. More to the point, however, it suggests that software engineers might learn something from studying legislation as an activity, and conversely that legislators might perform better if they were to study computer software engineering.

2.2.1 Measurement of Laws

As noted above, people often have strong intuitions about the "size" of a law. Some laws are characterized as being "omnibus", suggesting that they are very broad in scope; others are sometimes characterized as being "landmark", suggesting that they have been placed in a new or different societal domain or interest area. Most typically, however, the size of a law is described in terms of the number of pages of documentation it takes to describe the law and its workings. As in the case of using lines of code to describe the size of an item of software, this measure seems facile and unsatisfying. Counting the articles, clauses, etc. is perhaps something of an improvement, but not a particularly satisfying one, as these lexical measures do nothing to account for the complexity, substance, or reach of the law.

Here, too, it seems interesting to note that a more satisfying measure might be based more upon some quantification of the capacity for the operation of the law to change the state of affairs in the world. Some laws are capable of moving large amounts of money from one place (e.g., the taxpayer) to another (e.g., the government). Some laws are capable of incarcerating large numbers of people for long periods of time. Some laws cause large corporations to make major changes in their processes. Here, too, measuring the magnitude of the changes in state that can be effected by this type of software would seem relatively more measurable, and perhaps a better basis for measuring the "size" of a law.

2.3 Recipes Are Software

Cooking recipes seem to be a form of software as well. Recipes typically begin with a specification block that usually identifies the ingredients that are needed, a form of input parameter specification, and the equipment that is to be used, a sort of abstract machine specification. The steps in a recipe are often the names of procedures (e.g., "fold in" an ingredient, "bring [something] to a 'rolling boil'", and so forth) that are defined elsewhere. Sometimes these steps are defined in the cookbook that contains the recipe, but often it is assumed that the execution agent (i.e., the cook) will access them from some sort of cooking process asset library (e.g., a cookbook intended for beginners).

Most recipes have rather straightforward sequential control flow between their steps, but it is not uncommon for complicated recipes to specify threads of control that are to be executed in parallel, often with synchronization conditions. In addition, many such steps also incorporate exception management. In the preparation of some sauces that use eggs, for example, an exception arises when the eggs start to curdle. There are clearly specified predicates used to identify such exceptions (i.e., what the appearance of the sauce is), and clearly stated exception handling procedures for dealing with them (e.g., remove from heat, rapidly stir in some other ingredient). Experienced cooks will recognize that the concurrent execution of several recipes (e.g., in preparing a complicated dinner party) can create severe resource contention problems (e.g., not enough ovens or burners), and that a more rigorous and thorough approach to resource specification and scheduling could help avoid serious difficulties such as deadlocks, races, and starvation (of both cooking processes and diners).

Note that while many recipes lack explicit requirements, some do indeed specify requirements such as, "this recipe is a good way to deal with leftover chicken". In addition, note that recipes are a particularly good example of time-critical real-time software. Timing specifications such as "boil for 5 minutes", and "cook in a 450 degree oven for 30 minutes" are common, and quite analogous to specifications found in real-time computer software. More interesting, perhaps, is the instruction, "stir occasionally for the next hour", which does not seem to be something that is easily specified using commonly available computer software language primitives.

2.3.1 Measurement of Recipes

In the domain of recipes there also seems to be a great deal of intuition about size. Thus, for example, some recipes are regarded as being "difficult", "complex", etc. Often this refers to the presence in the recipe of techniques that seem to require a lot of experience or practice (e.g., the making of certain sauces). But notions of size and complexity can also arise from recipe features that are quantifiable and quantified. Thus, many recipes incorporate specifications of the amount of time required for completion. Virtually all recipes incorporate ingredients lists with precise quantities specified. In that sense, a dimension of the size of the recipe is implied by the size of the ingredients (both quantity and diversity), and the size of the finished product. Many such recipes also feature concurrency and the need for careful synchronization of parallel threads. In such cases, the number of parallel threads is easily quantifiable, and the tolerances required in synchronizing these threads are often specified as well. It is interesting that the quantification of recipe software seems to be better developed than the quantification of most other kinds of software.

2.4   Other Types of Software

Kit-building, assembly instructions, and driving directions seem to be other examples of software in different domains. Considering the ways in which these endeavors have features that are analogous to computer software development is an exercise that is left to the reader. In addition, the reader is strongly encouraged to think about other domains and endeavors that also seem analogous to computer software and its development. The prevalence of these domains in modern society is striking, suggesting that computer software engineering has much to study, and perhaps much to contribute, in these domains. In most of these domains measurement and quantification seem relatively poorly developed, suggesting the need for progress in all, and the possibility that progress in any (e.g., computer software engineering) could be of significant value to many.

Rather than dwelling upon the specifics of these diverse types of software, it seems more useful to examine the ways in which they address their fundamental problems to see what this might teach us about the nature of "software".

3   What Makes These Different Types of Software Like Each Other?

The foregoing sections suggest that there are many features that these different types of entities have in common. As an aid and a prelude to suggesting what the nature of software might be, this section enumerates some of these features.

3.1   They Are Non-tangible, and Non-physical, but Often Intended to Manage Tangibles

Perhaps what is most immediately noticeable is that all of these types of entities are non-tangible and non-physical, but often are intended to support the handling of entities that are tangible and physical. Thus, for example, recipes are intended to specify the preparation and management of food items, but the recipes themselves are intangible. Similarly, laws are intended to provide guidance, structure, and control of such tangibles as citizens and property, but the laws themselves are intangible.

3.2   Hierarchical Structure Is a Common Feature

Hierarchy seems to be a common vehicle for addressing the complexity that is inherent in all of these products. Laws are usually structures of larger sections (articles, chapters, etc.), and lower levels (e.g., clauses), aimed at providing needed elaborative details. Recipes may also be divided into section or phases, each aimed at the production of a different component. Processes are usually divided into phases as well.

3.3   They Consist of Components Having Different Purposes

In legislation, cooking, and process, as with software development, there seems to be a primary focus on the executable component of the end-product. But the end-product also incorporates other types of components that are often at least as important. Thus, the actual law that results from legislation typically receives much attention. But the law itself typically is drafted only after hearings and conferences aimed at identifying precise requirements, and agreeing upon the design and architecture of the institutions and processes that are to be implemented by laws. Indeed, many laws begin with a preamble of some sort that is intended to state the requirements for the law. Thus, for example, the Constitution of the United States of America begins with a preamble, " ... in order to form a more perfect union, ... promote the general welfare, ... secure the blessings of liberty ... " that is clearly an, admittedly very high level, requirements specification.

Good cooking recipes also are more than just sequences of instructions for the cook. As noted above, the recipe often begins with a specification of what the recipe is good for, and what needs it is intended to address. In addition, the cooking instructions are typically supplemented by explanations of why the cook is being asked to perform certain steps. Thus, for example, a recipe for risotto instructs the cook to coat rice grains with oil in a particular way. But a superior recipe also explains that this is done to foster the slow incorporation of liquid into the rice to impart a particular desirable texture. Note that good recipes also incorporate incremental evaluation steps. Cooks are instructed to test ingredients (usually by tasting them) as the production of the end-product proceeds. Typically this is intended to improve the quality of the final result by supporting the early identification of errors, leading to more prompt and effective correction of the errors.

3.4   All Are Expected to Require Modification/Evolution

Modification and evolution are expected for all of these types of entities. Thus, for example, laws are typically amended and replaced as internal defects are discovered, and as judicial processes demonstrate their incompatibility, either internally, or with respect to other laws. Evolution also takes place as there are changes in the problems that a law is intended to address. Recipes are updated from time to time to accommodate the availability of new kitchen devices, and changes in the availability of certain ingredients. Processes also need to be changed as defects are discovered, efficiency improvements are identified, and as there are changes in the problem that a process is intended to address.

Because all of these types of software are non-physical and intangible, there seems to be a shared belief that needed evolution and change are relatively easy. In all of these cases, this belief is largely illusory. The reasons have much to do with another feature shared by these different types of software, namely their interconnectedness.

3.5   Interconnections Are Key

While the interconnections among the various components of physical and tangible products may be more visible, the quantity and variety of interconnections among the various components of software seem to be no less either in number or in importance. It is relatively easy to see the way in which columns hold up floors and roofs in buildings, and the way the cables hold up the roadway of a suspension bridge. The way in which the structure of clauses and chapters of a law address the need for equity and justice, however, is no less real and important, although it may be far less clear. Similarly, the process of qualifying a voter directly supports the need for an election to assure the "one vote per voter" fairness requirement, although here, too, the way in which this is done may not be immediately clear.

As noted above, these different forms of software all consist of components of different types (e.g., requirements, architecture) in addition to the actual executable component of the software. But in all of these cases, these different types of components must satisfy very specific relationships with each other. The need to maintain these relationships complicates the modification and evolution of these components. Thus, a change to a specific clause in a law, much like a change to a computer software module, must be done in consideration of how that change will affect all of the other software components to which the changed component relates. A changed law must not cause inconsistency with other related laws, and must continue to be responsive to all of the requirements for the law.

The invisibility and intangibility of these constraints seems to be at least largely responsible for perpetuating the illusion of easy modifiability of all of these types of software. But the actuality of these constraints defies the illusion.

3.6   Analysis and Verification Are Universal Underlying Needs

The existence of the relations just described is, in all cases, useful as the basis upon which various approaches to analysis and verification rest. As noted above, the judicial system exists to carry out analyses aimed at determining the con- sistency of various laws with each other, and with stated requirements to which specific laws must adhere. Thus, for example, American courts often decide the "constitutionality" of laws, namely the extent to which the laws may or may not be in violation of the constraint that they conform to the Constitution of the United States (n.b. including the statement of requirements embodied in its Preamble).

Cooking recipes are typically also analyzed, for example, in trial kitchens where their performability is studied. This is in addition to the more usual verification done by tasters who determine whether execution of the recipe does indeed result in the creation of a product that meets requirements for tastiness, colorfulness, and servability.

Processes are also typically verified by executing their executable component(s) and then determining the extent to which they meet requirements for speed, efficiency, and the production of desired results. Processes are sometimes used as the basis for simulations aimed at the same kinds of determinations, but using simulated, rather than actual, situations. Recent work has shown that static analyses are also useful in verifying the effectiveness of processes (Clarke 2008).

4   Characterizing Software

The preceding set of characteristics that seem to be shared by a few notable software domains suggests that these characteristics might be taken as an, at least initial, set of properties of a type of entity that we might refer to as "software". Instances of this entity seem to be characterized by being non-physical and intangible, and yet structured by potentially large and complex sets of constraints that complicate what seems to be a frequent need for modification and evolution. While software is itself non-physical and intangible, a principal goal for instances of the type software is for them to contain one or more components whose execution effects the management and control of tangible entities. Computer software is characterized by the fact that it is intended to execute on a computer. Other types of software execute on different physical manifestations. Thus, for example, laws are executed by government bureaucracies, and recipes are executed on cooking paraphernalia such as ovens, bowls, measuring devices, and mixers.

As a structured entity, software is characterized at least in part as being a collection of constraints and relations that define what it means for it to be well-formed. These constraints are then available for use in determining whether and how the entity may be inconsistent and thus in need of correction. In the case of computer software, there has been considerable effort directed towards creating formal notations for defining these relations, and thus supporting rigorous analyses. Other software domains seem to rely more heavily upon less formal approaches.

The evolutionary forces that act upon all forms of software are also most strikingly universal. Software's role in managing physical and tangible entities that are part of the real world thereby connects software to the vagaries of change that are constant in the real world. The needs and requirements that have been shown to be part of all types of software are rooted in the real world. Thus the constraints between the executing component of software and its requirements component thereby induce the need for change in all components of a software entity as responses to changes in the real world. The need for all of these changes to be consistent with respect to the substantial number of constraints that characterize all types of software is what makes software change difficult. In software domains (e.g., legislation) where the constraints are not particularly rigorously defined or explicitly stated, change is correspondingly problematic.

This informal description of some key characteristics of software is but an early suggestion of the nature of this entity. More formal and rigorous definitions would be far more satisfying. One approach might be to use object-oriented technologies to try to specify the class "software", perhaps starting by defining its attributes and methods. An entity-relation approach might be used to place more emphasis on the relations that structure and constrain a software entity. The use of a type hierarchy might help to distinguish among the various kinds of software (e.g., legal, computer, cooking, etc.). Another approach might be to consider a software entity to be representable by a hyper-multigraph, with the different relations constraining the software entity being represented by different edges and hyper-edges between nodes that have different "colors" corresponding to the different types of the components that they represent.

A key reason for studying the applicability of these formalisms might be as a way to evaluate them as vehicles for measuring and quantifying items of software. Software size might be parameterized, for example, by the number and diversity of constraints used to define its well-formedness, or by the number of software product entities that are actually constrained by these constraints. We note that constraints often have the effect of broadcasting or propagating changes, both to different software product elements and to the tangible real-world entities that they affect.

Accordingly, our suggestion that software size might be measured by the potential of a software product to cause change in the state of its domain could be a definable function of the number and diversity of these constraints. The Empirical Methods community would seem to be in an excellent position to explore such possibilities for establishing cogent and useful measures of these sorts.

5   What Can Computer Software Engineering Contribute to Other Forms of Software Engineering?

The foregoing suggests that computer software engineering may have technologies and approaches that could be of considerable value to those who engineer other types of software. As noted above, a key characteristic of software seems to be that it is highly structured, with its structure being defined by a potentially large and diverse collection of relations and constraints. The utility and evolvability of software entities seems to rest importantly upon how effectively these constraints can be evaluated and brought into consistency with each other. As just noted, computer software engineering has evolved a formal discipline aimed at supporting this need, but other software engineering disciplines such as law may not have been as successful in doing so. As noted, this discipline might be a useful basis for establishing useful and intuitive measures and quantifications of computer software. There have indeed been some attempts to apply computer software engineering formalisms and approaches to laws. Perhaps work on measuring computer software size could lead to better measures of the size of laws. More such work seems clearly indicated. There is also a great deal of interest in applying computer software engineering approaches to the engineering of processes. Workflow languages and systems are examples of this (e.g., see [10]). They support facilitating the creation of processes for coordinating the efforts of humans in areas such as clerical paperwork processing. Other more ambitious efforts have aimed at developing process definition languages and applying analysis approaches borrowed directly from the domain of computer software engineering [4, 5, 11]. Useful measures of the size of processes would come directly from success in defining useful measures of the size of application computer software.

Computer software engineering approaches could presumably add value to such other software domains as cooking and kit-building instruction development. As scheduling is a serious problem in the parallel execution of large numbers of complex recipes (e.g., in the kitchen of a large restaurant), recipe analysis could be applied to study superior utilization of such resources as ovens and burners. This might reduce the size and cost of kitchen facilities and lead to faster delivery of meals. Kit-building and driving instructions could also be improved by the application of such computer software engineering technologies as exception management. Most kit-building, assembly, and driving instructions ignore the possibility of errors in their execution, even though such errors are not uncommon, and can lead to serious problems. Computer software engineers are evolving approaches to assuring robustness that are based upon identifying the symptoms of incorrect execution, and the fashioning of handlers to deal with the consequences. Applying such disciplines to driving instructions would help drivers to recognize when they have gone astray and would guide them back on course. Clearly, early detection of such errors is, as in the case of computer software development, most desirable.

The application of automation is another particularly promising contribution that computer software engineering might make to the engineering of other kinds of software. Computer software engineers have over the past decades shown that computers can themselves be invaluable aids in developing computer software that is of higher quality, and yet has been built more rapidly and more inexpensively. Computer automation can facilitate the analysis of software, as well as its testing, documentation, distribution, installation, and evolution. It seems natural to consider how these benefits of automation could be applied to other forms of software as well. Indeed, one notes that computer automation is beginning to be applied to the storage and retrieval of legal and cooking software, and automated analysis and testing is beginning to be applied to process software. Automated creation of driving instructions from requirement specifications, and constrained by the architecture of road networks is now also beginning to gain prevalence and acceptance. All of this suggests that a systematic investigation of automation needs in non-computer software domains could lead to important applications of automation in those domains, perhaps mirroring the use of automation in computer software engineering.

6   What Can Computer Software Engineers Learn from the Study of Other Forms of Software?

It is clearly gratifying to contemplate how the technologies that have been developed by our computer software engineering community may have the potential to improve the workings of other important communities. But it is potentially even more important for our community to see what we can learn from doing so. Some examples of potentially valuable learning are suggested here.

6.1   Resources

The large and complex systems that are being built today are increasingly attempting to support and coordinate the activities of various kinds of agents, using various kinds of resources. Yet the languages and notations that computer software engineers use to model, design, and implement such systems seem to pay scant attention to how resources are required and utilized in such systems. In the domain of process software, for example, resources often play an important role. In designing and specifying systems for such domains as hospital care, many key issues revolve around the utilization of such resources as doctors, beds, MRI devices, and surgery suites. Modeling of the way such resources participate in hospital processes is complicated, for example, by the existence of various substitution rules. For example, a nurse may not provide certain services such as prescribing medications, and a doctor will prefer not to provide other services, such as drawing blood for testing. But under certain circumstances, these rules and preferences are overridden. Specification of the circumstances can be difficult, and challenging. Resources are modeled in other domains such as management and networking. But the formalisms used in those domains do not seem to provide the semantic power needed to specify all of the complex substitution rules relating to very diverse types of resources that are required in order to model hospital resources in a way that supports the definition of medical processes sufficiently precisely.

In short, the way in which the real world uses resources poses challenges that seem to stress existing approaches to resource specification and management. Applying computer software engineering technologies to the process software domain underscores these challenges and suggests the need to address them with new research.

6.2   Timing

As noted above, attempts to specify processes and recipes (for example) emphasize the need to improve capabilities for dealing with time. All processes impose timing constraints, and thus process languages require facilities for specifying them. Existing languages and real-time systems offer some capabilities that are undeniably useful. But, as noted above, specification of some processes seems to require more. Thus, for example, cooking recipes specify that sauces need to be stirred "occasionally" for some period of time. Medical processes specify that nurses should monitor a transfusion patient "from time to time" for adverse reactions. These concepts are well-understood in the real world, but not well modeled in languages that computer software engineers would offer for use by process software engineers and recipe software developers.

6.3   Verification and Analysis of Legislation

While we may like to believe that legislative software engineers have much to learn from computer software engineers, it may well be the case that the reverse is true as well. As noted above, the judicial system seems to have as its focus the verification and analysis of legal software (laws). It is interesting to note that laws, like computer software, are typically put into use before their consistency with other laws has been definitively and exhaustively determined. Certainly the details of a new law are debated and studied, but at some point the law is enacted without the completion of the analysis. In some sense, the experiences of those subjected to the enacted law pick up at that point, and serve as test cases for an ongoing regime of testing. When the dictates of a new law seem to a legal subject to be inconsistent with another law, a trial may be used to resolve the consistency question.

Computer software engineers seem to have adopted a roughly analogous approach. New computer software is analyzed statically, and with a certain amount of dynamic testing. The computer software is then installed and delivered, at which time users continue the testing process. Thus, legal systems seem to have arrived at a sense of how much analysis is needed before testing begins. As legal software engineers have been doing this for at least hundreds of years longer than computer software engineers, it is quite possible that they have learned something about this that could be of value and use to computer software engineers.

Moreover, legal software engineers have also evolved the notion of "case law" whereby a persuasive body of legal precedents and interpretations eventually assumes the power of law, even though no legislation governing these cases has ever been passed. In some sense it seems that a sizeable body of test cases can eventually comprise an item of software, or at least a component of an item of software. Computer software engineers do not currently seem to have an analogous practice, although recent work aimed at determining invariants by studying execution traces through computer software may perhaps indicate the beginnings of development of such an analog.

7   Conclusion

It is interesting to contemplate the premise that computer software engineers may not be the only people who engineer software. There seems to be considerable evidence that the hard problems that computer software engineers address with their work may have strong analogs to other problem domains, and indeed to the practices of these other domains. This paper suggests that careful examination of these other domains seems warranted, as the approaches of one could be of interest and value to others. In particular, computer software engineering may be of considerable value in improving the state of the practice in such areas as law and process. Moreover, application of automation approaches taken in computer software engineering may deliver particularly good benefits to these other software engineering domains. Conversely, however, some of these other domains are much older and have longstanding approaches and traditions that could be of value and interest as possible areas of study and beneficial application to computer software engineering.

This paper has also suggested that cogent, useful measures of software of all kinds seem to be lacking. Following Lord Kelvin, it seems that deeper and firmer knowledge of the nature of all of these different sorts of software would follow from the ability to measure and quantify such software. And, indeed, one is struck by the observation that virtually all of these sorts of software suffer from analogous inabilities to do such measurement. This paper has taken as an example of this, the lack of cogent measures of software size. A possibility that has been advanced here is that software size might be measured by the potential for an item of software to change the state in the domain in which the software operates. The Empirical Methods community seems to be in an excellent position to address the evaluation of this specific proposal, and the evaluation in general of different ideas for quantification and measurement of software. This would seem to offer considerable prospects for good progress in the development of the many disciplines that are appropriately viewed as software disciplines.

Ultimately, careful examination of these various software engineering domains, aided by effective approaches for measuring in these domains, may lead us to a clear understanding of the elusive nature of the entity that we call "software".

References

1. Osterweil, L.J.: What is software? Automat. Softw. Eng. **15**(3–4), 261–273 (2008)
2. Naur, P., Randell, B. (eds.) Software engineering, report on a conference sponsored by the NATO SCIENCE COMMITTEE, Garmisch, 7–11 Oct 1968. Scientific Affairs Division NATO, Brussels. Also available at http://homepages.cs.ncl.ac.uk/brian.randell/NATO/nato1968.PDF (1968)
3. Parnas, D.L.: Software engineering: an unconsummated marriage. Commun. ACM **40**(9), 128 (1997)
4. Osterweil, L.J.: Software processes are software too. In: ACM SIGSOFT/IEEE 9th International Conference on Software Engineering (ICSE 1987), pp. 2–13. Monterey (1987)
5. Clarke, L.A., Avrunin, G.S., Osterweil, L.J.: Using software engineering technology to improve the quality of medical processes. In: ACM SIGSOFT/IEEE 30th International Conference on Software Engineering (ICSE'08), pp. 889–898. Leipzig (2008)
6. Osterweil, L.J.: Software processes are software too, revisited. In: ACM SIGSOFT/IEEE 19th International Conference on Software Engineering (ICSE 1997), pp. 540–548. Boston (1997)
7. Simidchieva, B.L., Marzilli, M.S., Clarke, L.A., Osterweil, L.J.: Specifying and verifying requirements for election processes. In: Chun, S.A., Janssen, M., Gil-Garcia, J.R. (eds.) In:

DG.O 2008: Proceedings of the 9th Annual International Conference on Digital Government Research, pp. 63–72. Digital Government Society of North America, Montreal (2008)

8. Breaux, T.D., Anton, A.I.: Analyzing regulatory rules for privacy and security requirements. IEEE Trans. Softw. Eng. **34**(1), 5–20 (2008)

9. Sergot, M., Sadri, F., Kowalski, R., Kriwaczek, F., Hammond, P., Cory, T.: The British Nationality Act as a logic program. Commun. ACM **29**(5), 370–386 (1986)

10. Georgakopoulos, D., Hornick, M.F., Sheth, A.P.: An overview of workflow management: from process modeling to workflow automation infrastructure. Distrib. Parallel Databases **3**(2), 119–153 (1995)

11. Chen, B., Clarke, L.A., Avrunin, G.S., Osterweil, L.J., Henneman, E.A., Henneman, P.L.: Analyzing medical processes. In: ACM SIGSOFT/IEEE 30th International Conference on Software Engineering (ICSE'08), pp. 623–632, Leipzig (2008)

A Personal Perspective on the Evolution of Empirical Software Engineering

Victor R. Basili

Abstract

This paper offers a four-decade overview of the evolution of empirical software engineering from a personal perspective. It represents what I saw as major milestones in terms of the kind of thinking that affected the nature of the work. I use examples from my own work as I feel that work followed the evolution of the field and is representative of the thinking at various points in time. I try to say where we fell short and where we need to go, in the end discussing the barriers we still need to address.

1 Introduction

I presented an earlier version of this work in a keynote at ISESE 2006 and published it in the Journal of the Brazilian Computer Society (JBCS) [1]. At the time I had been asked to offer a 40-year perspective on the evolution of empirical software engineering, from the past to the future. That was an arduous task. So I decided to simplify the task by making it a personal perspective, as I have worked in the field for 40 years. My hypothesis is that my work followed the evolution of the field. So, I offer my own opinions on how the field has evolved using mostly examples from my own work to support those opinions. I have some thoughts on how the field started, where we fell short, and where we need to go.

But first, I would like to discuss what makes Software Engineering uniquely hard to research, i.e., to build a body of usable knowledge for the discipline of software engineering [2]. Software engineering has several characteristics that distinguish it from other disciplines. Software is developed in the creative, intellectual sense,

V.R. Basili (✉)
Fraunhofer Center for Empirical Software Engineering, University of Maryland,
College Park, USA
e-mail: basili@cs.umd.edu

J. Münch and K. Schmid (eds.), *Perspectives on the Future of Software Engineering*,
DOI 10.1007/978-3-642-37395-4_17, © Springer-Verlag Berlin Heidelberg 2013

rather than produced in the manufacturing sense, and so the processes we need to study are development processes, not production processes. This unique aspect of the discipline, that each product is created rather than replicated, is probably the most important one, and greatly affects how we build models, evolve, and learn about the software discipline. It means that the context variables for different software developments greatly affect how we develop software, i.e., there will always be variation in study results and we will never be able to control or maybe even identify all the context variables. The discipline creates a need for continual experimentation, as we explore how to modify and tailor processes for different environments, i.e., different sets of context variables.

One consequence of this is that process is a variable, goals are variable, and environment is a variable. That is, we need to select the right processes for the right goals for the environment we are analyzing. So, before we decide how to study a technique and its effects, we need to know something about the environment and the characteristics of the product we are about to build. The environment specifies the collection of context variables.

A second distinguishing characteristic of the software engineering discipline is software's intangibility, or one might say, the invisibility of its structure, components, and forms of development. This is compounded by a third characteristic, the field's immaturity, in the sense that we haven't developed sufficient models that allow us to reason about processes, products, and their relationships. These difficulties intensify the need to learn from the application of ideas in different situations and the requirement to abstract from what we see.

A final problem is that developing models of our experiences for future use (that is, reuse) requires additional resources in the form of money, organizational support, processes, people, etc. Building models, taking measurements, experimenting to find the most effective technologies, and feeding back information for corporate learning cost both time and money. These activities are not a by-product of software development. If these activities are not explicitly supported, independent of the product development, they will not occur and we will not make quality improvements in the development process. This turns out to be a major burden in the evolution of our understanding of the software engineering discipline. How is the large expanse of knowledge being captured, evolving with each new application, and being maintained in a form that is easy to integrate?

All this makes good experimentation difficult and expensive. Controlled experiments are expensive and can be confirmatory only in the small. They do not deal well with scale-up, the integration of one process with another, the understanding of the effect of context variables, etc. It also makes it difficult to build on past work and see where new work fits in the tapestry we are building of problem/solution bounds and limits.

So, let us discuss the evolution of empirical software engineering over the past four decades. I will try to characterize the nature of the discipline in each decade and map the changes across several *key variables*: the *kinds of studies* that were being performed, the set *of methods being used*, the nature of *publications*, the *community of researchers*, the status of *replications and meta-analysis*, and the role of *context variables*.

This article is organized in sections, each section representing a phase, roughly broken down into decades. Section 2 covers the early days (~1971–1979), running isolated studies for a particular purpose. Section 3 focuses on the building of software process and technique knowledge in a single domain and environment, (~1980–1989). Section 4 deals with expanding our observations across environments by limiting the technologies being studied (~1990–1999). Section 5 focuses on tying different types of studies together to create some form of replication by taking advantage of different study types (~2000–2009). In each section, I will try to cover what I saw as the main changes in the approach that was introduced during that decade, giving related personal experiences within that decade and summarizing with a discussion of the key variables. Finally, Sect. 6 focuses on summarizing where I think we are, what we have learned, and the problems with progressing further.

2   Phase I: Isolated Studies (~1971–1979)

The very first software engineering experiment I was aware of was performed by Gerry Weinberg [3]. It was the genesis of a series of controlled experiments on the study of programmers. It was an interesting example of how people tried to follow the goals set out for them, e.g., code readability, code efficiency, etc. And when not given any advice, the self-imposed goal appeared to be performance.

These were the early days when researchers ran isolated independent studies for a particular purpose, using case studies or controlled experiments as the means to analyze a particular question of interest. It was a time when people were developing and using measures in general. The focus was on trying to identify an appropriate set of metrics. Many of us were learning about running an experimental study, and the need for baselines as a basis for evaluation. There were attempts to run a small number of controlled experiments but they were done mostly in isolation, not as part of a larger study.

Personal Examples Two isolated studies I was involved in were the Iterative Enhancement product evaluation [4] and a methodology evaluation [5]. The motivations for the studies were specific to the work we had been doing. The former was a case study with Joe Turner where we used quantitative observations over time, measuring the product, and comparing the product with itself, using prior versions as baselines. The object of study was a compiler we were building for a family of languages [6]. This was a single isolated study aimed a demonstrating that a software product was improving using a particular measurement-driven incremental development approach. The latter was a controlled experiment analyzing the effects of a collection of methods centered on chief programmer teams, including structured design and structured coding. The experimental method applied was a replicated study (controlled experiment) with three treatments: teams using the methods, teams not using the methods, and single programmers, all performing the same task. The study, performed with Robert Reiter, was a single painstakingly designed study in a classroom environment using advanced software engineering students. The purpose was to identify an effective set of methods to use in our software engineering class. These kinds of studies were rare but were typical of the state of the art.

Summary With respect to our key variables, the *kinds of studies* were mostly in vitro controlled experiments analyzing the effects of a particular variable within one environment, typically with students, or a report on some in vivo measurement study of a project. The *publications* mostly consisted of project studies and reviews were mixed. It was hard to get controlled experiments published. Although I remember one published review of our controlled experiment which said "I already knew that methodology was good so what was the point of running the controlled experiment", even though the study won the TSE best paper award for that year. The *community of researchers* was very small with little or no interaction and consisted of mostly model builders, product metric developers, and some scattered set of individual experimentalists. The set of *methods* for experimental studies was mostly quantitative analysis, using nonparametric statistics. The *context variables* were taken as a given, not measured. There was no replication or meta-analysis.

3   Phase II: Multiple Studies in ONE Domain (~1980–1989)

This early work made it clear that experiments can be run in the software engineering domain that provide empirical support for various beliefs, insights into what and how to measure, evidence that we can use measurement to abstract what is occurring in software development. It stimulated the realization that experimentation and measurement were important aspects of software development and that the design of experiments is an important part of improvement (something Deming had been preaching in manufacturing for many years [7]), that evaluation and feedback are necessary for learning, and that we need to experiment with technologies to reduce risk, tailor the technique to the environment, and make improvements.

The study of the software engineering discipline is exploratory and evolutionary; it is an application of the scientific method. Controlled experiments are not always possible or useful in isolation, so we needed to focus more attention on informal exploratory studies using pre-experimental and quasi-experimental studies, i.e., experiments that lack the element of random assignment to treatment or control [8]. These less formal studies are more common in social science disciplines, like education, and can provide useful insights into the effects of processes on product characteristics in large projects. We should couple these informal, exploratory studies with more formal empirical studies such as controlled experiments, when possible, to provide more evidence that what we are observing is valid. This combination of methods takes advantage of what is possible to do given the nature of the software development discipline. It became clear to me at least, that the study of software engineering is a laboratory science requiring collaborating research groups. Understanding the discipline requires exploratory study, confirmatory study if possible, identification and understanding of the effects of context variables, replications of various forms, and meta-analysis creating an integrated tapestry of information.

We need to take advantage of all opportunities we can find to explore various ideas in practice, e.g., test their feasibility, find out if humans can apply them, understand what skills are required to apply them, and test their interactions with other concepts. Based upon that knowledge, we need to refine and tailor each idea to the application environment in which we are studying it so it can be easily transferred into practice. We build and evolve models by trying out our ideas in practice and changing based upon what we have learned. Since the nature of the software engineering discipline is more exploratory than other disciplines, we are more dependent on the empirical application of methods and techniques.

Personal Example The break from the mold of isolated studies for me was the development of the Software Engineering Laboratory (SEL) [9] at NASA Goddard Space Flight Center. The goals were to understand ground support software development for satellites and improve the process and product quality using observation, experimentation, learning, and model building [10].

In 1976, the idea of creating a laboratory environment to study software development was perhaps unprecedented. But it provided an excellent learning environment where potential solutions to problems were proposed, applied, and examined for their effectiveness evolving into more effective solutions. Characteristics that made this setup a good place for empirical research included the limited domain of the application, the use of professional developers, firm support from the local organization, the presence of a research team to interact closely with the practical developers, and a mix of developers and managers with different goals, personalities, and responsibilities. We created a consortium of the NASA dynamics group of managers and developers, the contractor (CSC) group of managers and developers, and the research group from the University of Maryland. Everyone participated in all aspects of the laboratory, i.e., managers and developers were part of the research team. The SEL was integrated into the overall activities of the organization and supported by the project budget, not the research budget. The balance created an environment with lots of feedback and collaboration. The original team that remained mostly throughout the SEL's existence were Frank McGarry (NASA), Jerry Page (CSC), Marv Zelkowitz, and myself (UMD).

The SEL lasted for 25 years (1976–2001) during which time we built baselines of various project variables (defects, effort, and project metrics) to better understand the environment and identify where better methods might make a difference. The focus moved to in vivo studies, collecting data from live projects, providing feedback from data collection and measures, and storing and analyzing large amounts of data. The work involved multiple projects and multiple methods in a *single environment and domain,* a strength at the time but a limit for developing broader knowledge across many context variables. The longevity of this work allowed us to demonstrate order of magnitude improvements. Unfortunately, such longitudinal studies are very rare [11].

We learned a great deal not just by experiments, but by trying to understand the problems, applying potential solutions, and learning where they were successful and where they fell short. We ran controlled experiments and performed case studies, but they were done in the context of the larger evolutionary learning process [2].

We learned the importance of understanding the environment (recognizing which context variables in that environment were important), the need to build our own models to understand and characterize that environment (general models were too hard to parameterize for our environment due to the lack of broader context knowledge), the need to model the interactions among many variables (e.g., the environment, projects, processes, products), and that data collection has to be goal driven and well defined [12].

The learning process was more evolutionary than revolutionary. With each learning experience, we tried to package what we had learned into our models of the processes, products, and organizational structure.

The SEL used the university to test high-risk ideas. We built models and tested hypotheses. We developed technologies, methods, and theories as needed to solve a problem, learned what worked and didn't work, applied ideas that we read about or developed on our own when applicable, and all along kept the business going.

The SEL also allowed us to help create an empirical research community. Many students and visiting researchers spent years working in the laboratory, honing their empirical skills, contributing the knowledge and recognizing the need for collaboration. People like David Weiss, David Hutchens, Richard Selby, Dieter Rombach, Lionel Briand, Sandro Morasca, Carolyn Seaman, Filippo Lanubile, William Thomas, Forrest Shull, Manoel Mendonça, Guilherme Travassos, Jyrki Kontio, among others contributed greatly to the research activity.

The most important thing we learned was how to apply the scientific method to the software domain, i.e., how to evolve the process of software development in a particular environment by learning from informal feedback from the application of the concepts, case studies, and controlled experiments [13]. The informal feedback created the opportunity to understand where to focus our case studies and experiments. Informal feedback also, perhaps surprisingly, provided the major insights, i.e., interviews and informal discussion helped us discover important issues such as why a process was difficult to apply.

This work stimulated the realization that we need to package and integrate our experiences by building models and guidelines. Experience needs to be evaluated, tailored, and packaged for reuse so software processes must be put in place to support the reuse of experience. The SEL generated the concept of an experience base of packaged usable experience from the environment that could be used as a decision support system in the development of projects, but the experience packages defined were local to the SEL. The models could not necessarily be reused in other environments but the mechanism for building and packaging the experiences could.

The SEL ran a workshop every year presenting what we had learned that year and requesting papers from others to present their work. This gave us a perspective on the state of the art and practice every year and allowed us all to share our experiences. At its peak, the SEL Workshop had audiences of over 300 attendees.

Summary With respect to our *key variables*, the *kinds of studies* being run involved characterizing an environment via measurement (single environment, single domain), performing evaluations, building predictive models, making improvements. The *set of experimental methods* included more nominal and ordinal data and the use of pre-experimental, quasi-experimental studies and simply learning by the application of an idea. There were parametric models being built to capture and predict variables like cost and schedule [30]. The *publications* mostly consisted of project studies and reviews were mixed. For example, if your study should describe the limitation of some technique, the technique author was miffed, rather than appreciating what could be improved. The *community of researchers* was still small but beginning to grow. There was a metrics community of people trying to define product metrics that would predict defects and assess quality. The *context variables* began to be taken into account. There was no *replication* or *meta-analysis*.

4   Phase III: Tying Studies Together (~1990–1999)

During this time there were attempts to tie studies together. Controlled experiments, case studies, quasi-experiments, qualitative analysis were being used in various combinations, each useful in its own right for varying purposes. Controlled experiments were of value for identifying specific variable relationships while case studies provided the opportunity to scale up. We learned that you could reduce risk by running smaller experiments off-line using the mix of studies to build confidence in a theory based upon multiple treatments. Qualitative analysis began to play a major role in providing deeper insights into what was going on [15]. The major focus was on measuring the relationship between process and product. However, in our field, the kinds of studies performed and the topics studied were still dependent on the opportunities available.

For the 10th anniversary of TSE (1986), Rick Selby, Dave Hutchens, and I defined a framework for experimentation in software engineering and wrote a state-of-the-field paper recognizing that most of the papers in the literature dealt with either experimental studies of programmers in the small doing controlled experiments or data collection on projects in the large [16].

Personal Example Harlan Mills [17] had defined a method for reading code called reading by stepwise abstraction. Based upon our need to improve quality in the SEL we decided to see if the technique would be effective. We made use of the methodology template defined in [16] to study the effects of the approach using different experimental methods. Because the technique was quite new for the SEL environment, we first applied the approach in an advanced software engineering class at the university. We ran a fractional factorial controlled experiment design on 200–300 line code modules to check the effectiveness of the approach when compared to testing. The results were promising in that they showed that for certain types of defects, e.g., interface defects, the approach was more effective in uncovering those defects than functional testing. We found similar results on a replicated experimental design again with students on a 1,000 lines of code project. This encouraged us to try the fractional factorial design with professional programmers on a set of 200–300 line modules. Here the results were even stronger, demonstrating the benefits of the approach. This allowed us to try it in a live project of about 40KLOC using internal NASA developers. The scale-up provided very positive results (e.g., significantly lower defect rates), encouraging us to test the approach on three other projects. The second study was again an internal NASA project of 22KLOC, with similar positive results. The third and fourth studies were larger scale and with the contractor as developer. The 160KLOC project did not show any improvement, so we modified the organizational communication on the fourth project of 140KLOC with positive results again [13]. The problem with the third study was that the contractor was to ask for help when they were confused about applying the approach. In the fourth project, we established bi-weekly meetings in which there was lots of discussion.

The mix of study approaches allowed us to gather information about the effects of the method as well as the effects of context variables (internal vs. contractor) and gain positive evidence about the effectiveness of the approach and how to improve it for a different context. The mix of study types on the same technique allowed us to build evidence that the technique could be effective across a set of context variables (project size, in-house vs. contracted out) and learn how to modify the environment for improvement of the technique [31].

Summary With respect to our *key variables*, all kinds of *studies* continued to be performed on a variety of techniques and we began to see replications of some earlier experiments. There was sufficient research activity to create the Journal of Empirical Software Engineering (started in 1996) with the aim of publishing empirical studies, including replications, which were not previously *publish*able. Empirical research studies were still difficult to publish in a 10-page conference papers, as it was hard to cover all points in that limited page format. Reviewers were looking for more than could possibly be reported in ten conference pages. There was the realization that the evolution of the discipline required a *community of researchers* and teams performing studies. ISERN (started in 1993) created an opportunity for the growing international community of researchers to meet every year with the goal of supporting interaction and collaboration. Their goal was not to defend the need to experiment but to figure out how to do it better. Dieter Rombach created the Fraunhofer Institute for Experimental Software Engineering (1997), which aimed at working with companies to improve the software engineering discipline, allowing Fraunhofer research the opportunity to interact with several different environments. The *set of methods* being used was broad, consisting of a mix of quantitative and qualitative studies, case studies, controlled experiments, and learning by application. *Context variables* were beginning to be taken seriously but not fully recognized as the important set of influencing variables that they are. *Replication* involved building some studies that varied the context, threats to validity; building knowledge across studies about a particular technology.

5   Phase IV: Expanding Studies Across Domains and Environments (∼2000–2009)

This period began to see the expansion of studies across domains and environments and the rise in collaborations. The overall focus became understanding the behavior of various processes in different contexts and environments, allowing for the creation of a decision support system that would provide organizations with support for selecting the right techniques for their particular context, domain, and environment based upon their ability to characterize them. The focus needs to be on specifying the effects of technologies, and experimentally identifying the effects, limits and bounds of techniques. So, technologists need to be more specific about what their techniques do and do not do and we need to evolve empirical evidence about various techniques, gaining new confidence over time by better understanding the effects of influencing variables. We need to concentrate on building a body of knowledge based upon empirical evidence.

This requires the gradual gathering of large amounts of information from different environments and the ability to identify the context variables that influence the outcomes for different environments. Clearly this implies a long-term set of studies, replications, and many collaborations, i.e., different groups need to collaborate to provide a sufficient range of domains and environments developing knowledge about the usefulness of various techniques in context. The work should contribute to an 'experience base' that accumulates the current state of our knowledge over time. Because of the size of the problem, we need to break the task into smaller parts, e.g., limiting the techniques studied or limiting the number of environments and domains, etc. There were several examples of building knowledge for a limited number of techniques in different environments and domains, i.e., studying the effect of context on those specific techniques.

Personal Example I was involved in three such collaborations. The first one was the NSF-sponsored Center for Empirically Based Software Engineering (CeBASE): a consortium of the University of Maryland (UMD), the University of Southern California (USC), Fraunhofer CESE, Mississippi State (MSU), and the University of Nebraska at Lincoln (UNL) [18]. The CeBASE project goal was to enable a decision framework and experience base that would form the basis and infrastructure needed to evaluate and choose among various software development technologies appropriate for the environment. CeBASE concentrated on a limited set of techniques, e.g., defect reduction techniques [14], such as reading, and COTS-based development approaches [19]. It also began to look at agile techniques. The research goal was to create and evolve an empirical research engine for building the research methods that could provide empirical evidence as to what works and under what conditions it works.

It was clear that there was a great deal of research required before we could comfortably build an empirical research engine that could be applied universally to evaluate and provide support for the appropriate use of evaluated methods. This research engine proposed by CeBASE involved defining and improving methods to

- Formulate evolving hypotheses regarding software development decisions
- Collect empirical data and experiences
- Record influencing variables (context)
- Build experience models in the form of lessons learned, heuristics/patterns, decision support frameworks, quantitative models and tools
- Integrate models into a framework
- Test hypotheses by application
- Package what has been learned so far so it can be used and evolved

The results of the work were published in papers and slide presentations. An experience base was built which consisted of our experience with and advice about the use of various defect detection techniques [29] and approaches to dealing with COTS products, in different environments [20]. It also contained the results of e-workshops where concepts were discussed and debated by experts in the areas of interest.

The idea of studying various techniques and maturing them through application to different environments to better understand the influencing context variables was continued as part of the NASA-sponsored High Dependability Computing Project (HDCP). Here the team again consisted of UMD, USC, and Fraunhofer CESE for the empirical work and a variety of universities for the development of the dependability techniques, e.g., Carnegie Mellon University (CMU), University of Washington (UW), Massachusetts Institute of Technology (MIT), University of California Santa Barbara (UCSB).

Because the project was attempting to identify techniques to improve the dependability of the product, we built test beds to study, compare, and mature the techniques for practice. The test beds allowed us to minimize the risk of applying the techniques to live systems. Test beds developed were a simplified MARS Rover and a part of a tactical separation assisted flight environment. For example, the latter test bed was used to identify limits to a method and allow for the method developer to make improvements to the techniques based upon the empirical analysis [21]. The application of the techniques went from test beds to carefully monitored projects to large-scale projects, allowing the techniques to evolve over use and provide the necessary information for the experience base. These test beds became part of the framework and needed to be maintained and evolved, an expensive proposition.

A third example of this knowledge building process is the work performed by the development time working group of the DARPA High Productivity Computing Systems (HPC) project where the domain is high-end computing [22]. The practical focus was improving the time and cost of developing high-end computing (HEC) codes and empirically evaluating the set of competitors for developing a new HPC machine. The research focus was on developing theories, hypotheses, and guidelines that allowed us to characterize, evaluate, predict, and improve how an HEC environment (hardware, software, human) affects the development of high-end computing codes. There was a large research team consisting of MIT Lincoln Labs, MIT, University of California San Diego (UCSD), UCSB, UMD, USC, Fraunhofer CESE, University of Hawaii (UH), MSU, UNL, and the San Diego Supercomputing Center (SDSC). Work proceeded by evolving a series of studies with novices and professionals using controlled experiments (grad students), observational studies (professionals, grad students), case studies (class projects, HPC projects in academia), surveys, and interviews (HPC experts).

Test beds varied from classroom assignments (Array Compaction, the Game of Life, Parallel Sorting, LU Decomposition, ...) to compact applications (Combinations of Kernels, e.g., Embarrassingly Parallel, Coherence, Broadcast, Nearest Neighbor) to full scientific applications (nuclear simulation, climate modeling, ...) being developed at California Institute of Technology (CalTech), Stanford University (SU), University of Chicago (UC), and University of Illinois (UIUC). As new knowledge was discovered, the results were stored in a publically available experience base. The content of the experience base was the empirical evidence collected in terms of the effects of various notations, e.g., MPI, Open MP, for different applications, classifications of high-end computing defects, and test beds. The contents also included experimental packages to support the running of experiments, such as checklists for instructors and experts running studies, instrumentation downloads, and data collection and analysis packages. Results were published in a variety of venues as well as stored in the experience base. But the experience base remained unmaintained. Some of the test beds were used by others for different purposes but they are becoming harder to find.

Each of the projects had a limited lifetime of only about 3 years. Why? Because a funding agency like NSF does not support long-term research endeavors; it felt it needed to continually identify new theories, techniques, and technologies. Unfortunately, there was not even follow-up funding to maintain the experience base that was developed. The CeBASE concepts formed the basis for the HDCP project, but the technique focus changed. Then NASA changed its focus from doing dependability research and again there was no support for maintaining that experience base. DARPA leadership changed and the decision was made that the companies would identify strengths and weaknesses of their own machines. The wiki remains public http://hpcs.cs.umd.edu/ and http://hpcbugbase.org/, but there is no maintenance for it.

In each of the examples, a great deal was learned but there was no support for maintaining the knowledge that was developed in a systematic, shareable, useable form. The evolution of a discipline like software engineering requires an experience base of knowledge on what to use and when across many environments and domains. There has not been sufficient support for maintaining the kind of decision support system that would help organizations build better software more efficiently.

One excellent example of a decision support system was the Clearinghouse project [23], whose goal was to capture experience for the DoD environment. A user would enter the best set of variables that described their environment and project and would be provided with whatever advice was available and the level of evidential support for that information. The project, like my own experiences above, died due to the time limit of the funding.

Summary With respect to our variables, *studies* are being performed to evaluate techniques in multiple contexts and define the relationship between user needs and what's available. Journal and conference *publications* have come to expect some form of analysis from new methods, even if it is only a feasibility study. The community of researchers continues to grow; experimentalists are replicating each other's studies. There are numerous *repetitions* of a few experiments. The *set of methods* available became a rich palate of tools: a full mix of qualitative and quantitative methods, controlled and quasi-experiments, case studies, surveys, folklore gathering, structured interviews and reviews, etc. *Context variables* are being studied and characterized when possible. There are attempts to build knowledge across studies. A good example of the latter is the work of the SNT laboratory at the University of Luxembourg [24], where the focus is on model-based concepts and tools dealing with the set of problems associated with software validation and verification and on the improvement of software validation and verification activities in practice. The laboratory has several organizations as collaborators and a long-term focus.

6   Phase V: Now and the Future

To recapitulate, we can look at the evolution of the research in terms of the interplay of methods, context, and domain. Early work characterized the effects of various methods, (*all study variables fixed*) in isolation to address a particular problem. The desire for understanding broadened and baselines of various project variables (defects, effort, product and project metrics) were built within a single domain and context, identifying where methods might make a difference (*fixed context and domain, varied techniques*) e.g., SEL. Experimental work expanded to applying various experimental designs to examine a specific technique over a limited set of domains and context variables trying to broaden knowledge about the technique and minimize the threats to validity (*fixed technique, varied context and domain*), e.g., reading technique studies. Then the research evolved to consider a limited set of techniques across several contexts and domains (*varied context to study context, fixed technique set*), e.g., CeBASE, and to quantitatively define the effects of various techniques that could solve a particular problem (*evaluate techniques for achieving particular goals and studying the relationships between both*), e.g., HDCP, where we identified the appropriateness and effectiveness of various methods to support the building of dependable systems under varying conditions before transferring them into practice (*introduced test beds (specific contexts) to study techniques*). Finally, there was work on building knowledge in a particular domain, packaging that knowledge in an experience base so it can be used by others, demonstrating the effectiveness of various approaches and learning in what contexts they are effective (*fixed domain, studying techniques and context variables*) HPCS. We now return to a discussion of our key variables.

6.1   Kinds of Studies and Methods

With regard to the study of techniques, we see more papers, both conference and journals, containing a new idea, showing some kind of application, even it is only at the level of a feasibility study. This is in part due to journals and conferences requiring some form of data; i.e., it is clear that no technique should be published without trying it out first. This is a major change in the culture. But it should not end there; the feedback from the application should be used to identify the bounds and limits and open ideas for improvement. Unfortunately, the culture has not changed this much. Techniques need to be experimentally tested to see where they can be improved, even if we only 'learn by applying' as I like to call it [2]. We need to evaluate the bounds and limits of each technique and see how techniques can be integrated with others in the life cycle and what their integration buys you. There are several pockets of this kind of work and they are expanding all the time.

The collection of methods has expanded, including their integration into any particular study. There are many examples of building knowledge about the domain, identifying folklore and theories, doing ethnographic studies, interviews, and observations, building models using grounded theory, case studies, quasi-experiments, controlled experiments, and evolving models supported by evidence. We can find work testing models and hypotheses via studies of all kinds. The door is more open to this kind of research.

6.2   Community of Researchers

We have certainly evolved a community that talks and tries to work with each other. This year will be the 21st ISERN workshop and the number of members continues to grow; more importantly, ISERN keeps track of collaborations and there are many involving the exchange of graduate students and visiting researchers. But we need a more effective community collaboration and communication plan. Most young researchers are primarily interested in establishing themselves and their reputations. Getting a degree in an environment where there is already an established community is a great opportunity for them. Senior (tenured) researchers can afford to build the laboratory structure needed to do this type of work and to build collaborative groups. We need support for a living experience base that represents our combined and integrated experience, evidence, and knowledge at any point in time. This involves a well-defined collaborative research agenda.

I believe the discipline of software engineering will not move forward without such a collaborative research agenda, a community-supported living experience base, and a mature empirical study discipline.

6.3   Publications

The Empirical Software Engineering Journal (EMSE) is in its 18th year and its ISI impact rating has steadily grown. It has achieved an ISI rating of 1.854, second only by a tenth of a point to TSE, the top-rated SE journal. Papers are being submitted from a larger and larger collection of international researchers each year. The ACM/IEEE Empirical Software Engineering and Measurement Symposium ESEM (formally the International Symposium on Empirical Software Engineering ISESE before it joined forces with the Metrics Conference) is in its twelfth year. Journals like TSE welcome experimental work. So there are sufficient venues for publishing empirical research. We have textbooks that specialize in experimentation in the software engineering discipline, most notably, the second edition of 'Experimentation in Software Engineering' [25].

With regard to publications, the guidelines that exist are well defined [26] but are very long, especially for conference papers. So there is a need to supplement reports on a study with technical reports and web-based material that deals with all guideline issues. I believe journals are better than conferences as publication targets due to the feedback and dialog that is associated with the review process. The community needs to identify conference guidelines as to what must be included in the paper and what should be available in the technical report or on-line website. And they must identify ways to use various related publication forms to create an integrated whole.

Papers need to build on prior work. There is now a lot more literature around. Partly due to the history of isolated studies, we do not have a good enough culture of reading, referencing, and assimilating existing material. I admit to having been guilty of not identifying all the related references and integrating my work into the whole tapestry of results. For example, we have been criticized for a large number of studies on "inspections" that do not seem to recognize, build on, or integrate with the past work.

6.4   Context Variables

To me, covering context is the biggest problem and the reason why we need a very large community of researchers. There are too many influencing variables and we do not even know what they are or how to measure for them or the extent of their influence. They represent multidimensional categories such as subject experience, environment, domain, class of SE technologies applied. How many variables are hidden in these? If we are to be successful at building knowledge, we probably need to limit the scope of some of these categories for each research team, like focusing on specific domains, classes of technologies, or environments, expanding out slowly, unifying across the differences when possible. Of course, the problem then becomes integrating the limited scope studies of one group with the others in such a way that we can identify bounds on the extent of influence of the context variables so that a limited, useable set of models can be built.

6.5   Replications and Meta-Analysis

Building theories requires replication, varying the threats, varying the artifacts, and varying the population. These studies require coordination, collaboration, and independence. It takes a team to run an experiment; it is too hard to do it all alone. It involves multiple groups, multiple disciplines, and requires feedback on the design and discussion of the results. Replications require a level of independence, but I do not believe we are at a point where we can run a replication without some form of discussion with the earlier experimenters. We are not yet able to present all that needs to be covered in a conference paper or even a journal. The discussions after the fact are important to understand why the results are different and what that difference exposes about the subject or the study. This is where collaboration and communication are important. A subgroup of the ISERN community is collaborating on replications [27]. There is a workshop on replication (RESER) and there have been several attempts to coordinate studies. One of the original aims of EMSE was to publish replicated results and it has done so. This is real progress.

7   Concluding Remarks

We have come a long way in evolving the discipline of empirical software engineering, but we have a long way to go. Part of the reason for our slow progress has been the lack of an empirical culture within most Computer Science departments. They were mostly spawned by Mathematics departments and mathematics is not an empirical science. So we did not inherit an empirical mind set. The building of our research engine is at its infancy. It needs to be better understood not just by empiricists but by software engineers in general. Theoretical physicists understand and appreciate the work done by experimental physicists and use their results to evolve their own theories. This is not yet true in software engineering. Less than a decade ago, I paraphrased what a software engineer whose work I respect said to me: I am a smart guy and I know my technique is good, so why do I need experimental evidence? *Software engineering requires an empirical research engine that identifies the benefits, limits, and bounds of technologies.*

We need to build a tapestry of models and guidelines that represent our knowledge about the benefits, as well as the bounds and limits of techniques, methods, and life cycle models as well as models representing product characteristics of all kinds. The real question is: If I want a product to have certain characteristics, e.g., schedule achievement, minimum cost, reliability, correctness, safety, security, etc., what are the appropriate techniques, methods, and life-cycle models to achieve those characteristics? *Software engineering needs to codify the relationships between processes and products.*

If we are to make more progress in the discipline of software engineering in general, both in practice and research, that symbiotic relationship between practice and research has to be nourished so both groups can gain and the discipline can evolve. We need many applications of a process, taking place in different environments, each application providing a better understanding of the concepts and their interaction. Over time, all context variables need to be considered. Many of them will not even pop up until we have seen applications of the approach in practice by different people at different sites. *Empirical software engineering needs to balance the symbiotic relationship between theory and practice.*

Research teams need multiple forms of expertise, e.g., domain knowledge, software engineering knowledge, a variety of experimentation capabilities. I am always leery when reading a single-authored empirical paper. The team not only provides different levels of expertise but provides checks and balances on the study itself. *Empirical studies in software engineering need multi-disciplinary teams.*

I believe that replication plays the key role in software engineering. In this case, I do not mean the confirmation that a prior study's results were true or not, which is hard to do since it is hard to replicate the context of the prior study exactly, but 'replication' is needed to expand the context set in which the results may or may not be true and to understand why. This kind of replication requires close interaction between the original study team and the replication team, because we cannot always communicate the original context variables. In a collection of replications of reading studies we did with several groups in Brazil, we found that we had a hard time capturing tacit knowledge in replicating experiments, even when the teams are collaborating [28]. *Replication in software engineering studies should be expanding knowledge rather than confirming it.*

The building of the tapestry of software engineering knowledge is too grand for any one group to perform. Empirical software engineering requires groups who share results in effective ways. They need a repository of evolving models and lessons learned that can be used, added to, and evolved by other researchers. For each group, the focus can be bounded, limiting the context, the domain, the collection of techniques, methods, and life cycle models studied. For example, we can build bodies of knowledge about specific domains. Then we can combine what has been learned from these domains to build larger bodies of knowledge across domains, understanding what is common and what is not. For each domain, this involves folklore gathering, interviews, case studies, controlled experiments, experience bases, etc. *Empirical software engineering needs to build collaborative, communicating communities.*

If we have begun to develop collaborative, communicating communities, what is still missing? First, the need to share results in a truly effective way requires a shared repository of evolving models and lessons learned that can be added to and used by researchers. Second is the requirement for long-term support across organizations and countries of collaborators, not an easy task. Third is the reward system for researchers. Academic researchers are rewarded for creating ideas and sharing them in papers. Sharing and collaborating in the way I am suggesting here takes lots of time, effort, energy, and financial support and may not always result in papers, at least in the beginning. Most disciplines build on each other's work by integrating with the results of work found in journal papers. It is a model that works for physics but I do not believe it works for software engineering. That is because many results of empirical studies are small and evolutionary and can only be truly evaluated based upon the comparison with how it affects the whole. The eventual knowledge base of the discipline is an interconnected and tightly integrated set of process and product characteristics that can only be built by collaborating communities. The result of this can be used as a decision support system integrating process effects with product needs. Medicine has been more successful in working toward this goal. *Empirical software engineering needs to build a decision support system/experience base that provides support of practice and an experience base which represents what we know about the discipline. The internal information is the same but the interfaces are different, geared to different populations.*

We need to understand the different roles of theory and experimentation. Is there one group that develops theory and another that does experimentation, like physics? I do not think so. Their roles are too tightly intertwined in software engineering. The feedback loop from theory to practice to theory is too intertwined and requires rapid response times. There needs to be a desire on both sides to collaborate and a mechanism that supports it.

So building a discipline of software engineering is big science, requiring many collaborations with long-term goals and longitudinal studies, the development of a framework for communicating, coordinating, and integrating experiential models with long-term support that will exist and be available to capture all forms of evidence, like physics. We need methods that support the exploratory nature of this big science. The discipline cannot be understood only by analysis. We need to learn from applying the discipline whether relationships hold, how they vary, and what the limits of various technologies are, so we can know how to configure processes to develop software better. *Software engineering is big science.*

Acknowledgments Most of the work used here as personal examples was developed by many people collaborating as teams at the University of Maryland and its partner organizations. Members of the team are too numerous to mention and have varied over time. But I have had the good fortune to work with many exceptional people who should all be considered as co-authors of this paper. I thank Madeline Diep and Lionel Briand for giving me several suggestions to improve this paper.

References

1. Basili, V.: The past, present, and future of experimental software engineering. J. Braz. Comput. Soc. [online]. **12**(3), 7–12 (2006). ISSN 0104–6500
2. Basili, V.: Learning through applications: the maturing of the QIP in the SEL. In: Oram, A., Wilson, G. (eds.) Making Software. O'Reilly, Sebastopol (2011)
3. Weinberg, G.M.: The Psychology of Computer Programming. Van Nostrand Reinhold, New York (1971)
4. Basili, V., Turner, A.: Iterative enhancement: a practical technique for software development. IEEE Trans. Softw. Eng. **1**(4), 58–66 (1975)
5. Basili, V., Reiter Jr., R.: A controlled experiment quantitatively comparing software development approaches. IEEE Trans. Softw. Eng. **7**(3), 299–320 (1981). IEEE Computer Society Outstanding Paper Award

6. Basili, V., Turner, A.: A transportable extendible compiler. Softw. Pract. **5**(3), 297–298 (1975). July-September
7. Edwards Deming, W.: Out of the Crisis. MIT Press, Center for Advanced Engineering Study, Cambridge, MA (1986)
8. Shadish, W.R., Cook, T.D., Campbell, D.T.: Experimental and Quasi-experimental designs for generalized causal inference. Wadsworth Publishing, Belmont (2001)
9. Basili, V., Zelkowitz, M., McGarry, F., Page, J., Waligora, S., Pajerski, R.: Special report: SEL's software process-improvement program. IEEE Softw. **12**(6), 83–87 (1995)
10. Basili, V., Zelkowitz, M.: Analyzing medium scale software development. In: Proceedings of the Third International Conference on Software Engineering, Atlanta (1978)
11. Basili, V., McGarry, F., Pajerski, R., Zelkowitz, M.: Lessons learned from 25 years of process improvement: the rise and fall of the NASA Software Engineering Laboratory. In: Proceedings of the Twenty-Fourth International Conference on Software Engineering (ICSE), Orlando (2002)
12. Basili, V., Weiss, D.: A methodology for collecting valid software engineering data. IEEE Trans. Softw. Eng. **10**(3), 728–738 (1984)
13. Basili, V., Green, S.: Software process evolution at the SEL. IEEE Softw. **11**(4), 58–66 (1994)
14. Boehm, B., Basili, V.: Software defect reduction top 10 list. IEEE Comput. **34**(1), 135–137 (2001)
15. Seaman, C., Basili, V.: Communication and organization: an empirical study of discussion in inspection meetings. IEEE Trans. Softw. Eng. **24**(7), 559–572 (1998)
16. Basili, V., Selby, R., Hutchens, D.: Experimentation in software engineering. IEEE Trans. Softw. Eng. **12**(7), 733–743 (1986)
17. Linger, R.C., Mills, H.D., Witt, B.I.: Structured Programming: Theory and Practice. Addison Wesley, Reading (1979)
18. Shull, F., Basili, V., Boehm, B., Brown, A.W., Costa, P., Lindvall, M., Port, D., Rus, I., Tesoriero, R., Zelkowitz, M.: What we have learned about fighting defects. In: Proceedings of the Eighth IEEE International Software Metrics Symposium, Ottawa (2002)
19. Basili, V., Boehm, B.: COTS-based systems top 10 list. IEEE Comput. **34**(5), 91–93 (2001)
20. Rus, I., Seaman, C., Lindvall, M., Basili, V., Boehm, B.: A web repository of lessons learned from COTS-Based software development. Crosstalk **15**(9), 25 (2002)
21. Betin-Can, A., Bultan, T., Lindvall, M., Lux, B., Topp, S.: Eliminating synchronization faults in air traffic control software via design for verification with concurrency controllers. Autom. Softw. Eng. **14**(2), 129–178 (2007)
22. Hochstein, L., Nakamura, T., Basili, V.R., Asgari, S., Zelkowitz, M.V., Hollingsworth, J.K., Shull, F., Carver, J., Voelp, M., Zazworka, N., Johnson, P.: Experiments to understand HPC time to development. Cyberinfrastructure Technol. Watch Q. **2**(4A), 24–32 (2006)
23. Shull, F., Turner, R.: An empirical approach to best practice identification and selection: the US department of defense acquisition best practices clearinghouse. In: Proceedings of the ACM/IEEE International Symposium on Empirical Software Engineering (ISESE05), pp. 133–140. Noosa Heads (2005)
24. Briand, L.C.: Embracing the engineering side of software engineering. IEEE Softw. **29**(4), 96 (2012)
25. Wohlin, C., Runeson, P., Hoest, M., Ohlsson, M., Regnell, B., Wesslen, A.: Experimentation in software engineering. Springer, Heidelberg (2012)
26. Kitchenham, B., et al.: Preliminary guidelines for empirical research in software engineering. IEEE Trans. Softw. Eng. (TSE) **28**(8), 721–734 (2002)
27. Natalia, J., Sira, V.: The role of non-exact replications in software engineering experiments. J. Empirical Softw. Eng. **16**, 295–324 (2011)
28. Shull, F., Basili, V., Carver, J., Maldonado, J., Travassos, G., Mendonca, M., Fabbri, S.: Replicating software engineering experiments: addressing the tacit knowledge problem. In: Proceedings of the First International Symposium on Empirical Software Engineering, Nara (2002)

29. Basili, V., Tesoriero, R., Costa, P., Lindvall, M., Rus, I., Shull, F., Zelkowitz, M.: Building an experience base for software engineering: a report on the first CeBASE eWorkshop. In: Proceedings of the Product Focused Software Process Improvement Conference, Kaiserslautern (2001)
30. Boehm, B., et al.: Software Cost Estimation with COCOMO II. Prentice Hall, Upper Saddle River (2000)
31. Maldonado, J., Carver, J., Shull, F., Fabbri, S., Dória, E., Martimiano, L., Mendonça, M., Basili, V.: Perspective-based reading: a replicated experiment focused on individual reviewer effectiveness. Empirical Softw. Eng. Int. J. 11(1), 119–142 (2006)

Moving Toward Evidence-Based Software Production

David M. Weiss, James Kirby Jr., and Robyn R. Lutz

Abstract
Computer software is increasingly critical to the products, infrastructure, and science upon which society depends. However, the production of society's software is known to be problematic. Current understanding of software production, largely based on anecdotes, is inadequate. Achieving the deeper understanding needed to transform software production experiences into software production improvements requires collecting and using evidence on a large scale. This paper proposes some steps toward that outcome, with particular attention to what government can do to stimulate software engineering studies that will advance the capabilities of software production.

1 Introduction

Software is increasingly critical to the products, infrastructure, and science on which we depend. In the words of the U.S. National Research Council, "Software is uniquely unbounded and flexible, having relatively few intrinsic limits on the degree to which it can be scaled in complexity and capability" [1]. Software controlled automation and interoperation of goods and services is increasing. For example,

D.M. Weiss (✉)
Lanh & Oanh Professor of Software Engineering, Department of Computer Science,
226 Atanasoff Hall, Ames, IA 50011, USA
e-mail: weiss@iastate.edu

J. Kirby Jr.
Naval Research Laboratory, Code 5542, Washington, DC 20375
e-mail: james.kirby@nrl.navy.mil

R.R. Lutz
Department of Computer Science, 226 Atanasoff Hall, Ames, IA 50011, USA
e-mail: rlutz@iastate.edu

J. Münch and K. Schmid (eds.), *Perspectives on the Future of Software Engineering*,
DOI 10.1007/978-3-642-37395-4_18, © Springer-Verlag Berlin Heidelberg 2013

work is now advancing on automobiles that are fully controlled by software [2, 3]. Computer software enables and contributes to the improvement of the business processes of the largest industrial [4] and governmental organizations [5]. Both progress in science and the ability to design competitive products with confidence that they will work correctly and reliably is increasingly dependent on simulation-based engineering and science (SBE&S) [6], which is to say that they depend upon complex, large-scale, long-lived computer software. Even products that do not themselves incorporate software may depend upon SBE&S, e.g., automobile tires, engine blocks, beverage cans, golf equipment [6].

As critical as software is to society, the state of its production is problematic. "Software development remains a labor-intensive process in which delays and cost overruns are common, and responding to installed software's errors, anomalies, vulnerabilities, and lack of interoperability is costly to organizations throughout the U.S. economy" [7].

Transformation of software production to better meet society's needs is hampered by our limited understanding of software production, which, being primarily anecdotal, is unsatisfactory. We need evidence, both quantitative and qualitative, to achieve the deeper understanding required to transform software production from hand-craftsmanship to engineering [8]. How do we assess our capability to create and sustain software, and to predict our need for it without some basis in evidence? Our societal, national, and international interests depend on accurate prediction of our software production capabilities and needs. Collecting and using evidence on such a large scale requires stimulation and shaping by government.

The good news is that our dependence on software is so pervasive that small improvements in its production may yield widespread benefits and provide unanticipated opportunities. A U.S. government study estimated that in 2002 the national annual costs of an inadequate infrastructure for software testing ranged between $22.2B and $59.5B. "Over half of these costs are borne by software users in the form of error avoidance and mitigation activities" [9].

This paper makes the case for evidence-based understanding and improvement of software production. It updates our 2010 paper [8] with recent data on software production and steps taken toward evidence-based software production. We propose a strategy for gathering necessary evidence on an international scale and identify some questions on which to focus to turn evidence into understanding that drives improvement. Section 2 gives an example of results achievable with an evidence-based approach and defines software production, the target for evidence collection. As part of an effort to understand the role of software production in an advanced, modern economy, Sect. 3 surveys the employment of software producers in industry. Section 4 defines categories for evidence targeting software production and discusses how to collect it. Section 5 discusses some key hypotheses to be tested using this evidence, and the steps government can take to get started. Section 6 summarizes a broad, evidence-based strategy for software production improvement.

2   Evidence-Based Approaches

Evidence-based approaches have enabled rapid, startling advances in manufacturing, agriculture, medical technology, and other fields. For example, Gawande describes how, in 1900, over 40 % of a family's income in the U.S. went to food. Farming was labor-intensive and engaged almost half the workforce. Productivity was low, and farmers viewed any change in their practices as too risky. The invisible hand of market competition was not improving the situation.

A turning point came when the U.S. Department of Agriculture initiated a pilot project with a single farmer in 1903. Unlike other farmers in the area, he made a profit in what was the worst year for cotton in a quarter century. Experiments, pilot projects and demonstrations followed. Crop forecasting became possible; new hybrids and mechanization techniques moved from research into practice; and radio broadcasts on 163 stations supplied timely information so that farmers themselves could make rational planting decisions.

Gawande describes the resulting transformation: "It shaped a feedback loop of experiment and learning and encouragement for farmers across the country. The results were beyond what anyone could have imagined. Productivity went way up.... Prices fell by half. By 1930, food absorbed just twenty-four per cent of family spending and twenty per cent of the workforce" [10].

While software production is quite different in nature from agriculture, transformation of software production on a national or international scale, at unprecedented speed, is likewise possible. It will require a similar investment in experiments and pilot projects, and in collection, distribution, and analysis of detailed data. It will require better mechanisms to supply industry with information about what works and what doesn't. The transformation of agriculture was not a result of relying on just a few breakthrough ideas, but rather a result of trying many different approaches and selecting those that evidence showed were useful. Achieving improved understanding of software production similarly needs evidence-based investigation of hypotheses.

A key part of enabling the transformation is sharing and dissemination of evidence. The data must be widely collected, and the results of analysis widely disseminated. Once better technology is known, it must be transferred into use. Government has a key role to play here, as it has in other fields (see e.g., [9, 11–13]), to foster data collection, analysis, and dissemination.

We use the term *software production*, instead of *software development*, to emphasize that we refer to three types of activities:

- Software creation, whether starting fresh or reusing existing software,
- Software sustainment, as a system evolves throughout its operational life, and
- Software assurance, which gives confidence that evolving software continues to be safe, secure, and effective, commensurate with the nature of the software and of its use.

We understand the software production of critical interest to be the work of large, multi-disciplinary, geographically distributed, international teams of individuals

Table 1 U.S. Federal Contributions to IT sectors with large economic impact

Research area	University research began	$1B market began	$10B market began	IT market segment
Digital Communications	1965	—	2006	Broadband & Mobile
Computer Architecture	1977	1986	1995	Micro Processors
Software Technologies	1965	1980	1997	Personal Computers
Networking	1968	1983	1999	Internet & Web
Parallel & Distributed Systems	1968	1990	2008	Cloud Computing
Databases	1973	—	1998	Enterprise Systems
Computer Graphics	1965	1977	2003	Entertainment & Design
AI & Robotics	1968	1994	—	Robotics & Assistive Technology

and organizations creating and evolving a variety of artifacts, sometimes over decades. Artifacts may be formal with well-defined semantics such as models, specifications, and code; may be semi-formal with prescribed format and content such as requirements and design documents; or may be informal such as instant messages, wikis, and email.

We are not the first to suggest that evidence is needed, or which methods to use to collect it, but we have not seen elsewhere a call to develop a wide-scale strategy for collecting and using evidence to transform software production [7, 14]. Neither have we elsewhere seen a call to collect detailed data about software production. SIGSOFT's Software Engineering Notes Risks column keeps us informed, entertained, and sometimes aghast at the variety of failures caused by software [15]. Kitchenham et al. discuss how decision makers can use "current best evidence from research" to improve software production [16]. Barr et al. discuss the importance of data sharing and strategies for achieving it [17].

We lack evidence regarding those systemic software production problems that lead to failures, of the distribution of such problems across software systems, industries, and economies. We do not have evidence of the effects of various solutions that have been tried. Nor do we have detailed data on a national or international scale that can lead to the deep understanding of software production that is so critical, given software's centrality to activities throughout society [7]. The consequences of failing to develop a deep understanding of software are that opportunities to transform software production to meet society's needs will not be recognized nor realized.

Investment in information technology research and development has provided significant benefits to the economy. For example, Table 1, containing data drawn from Fig. 1 of [18], shows that beginning in the 1960s and 1970s (mostly U.S. federally funded) university-based research into eight areas of IT contributed to seven $10 billion markets and one $1 billion market. The first column lists the university-based research areas. The last column lists corresponding IT market segments. The table omits industry R&D also illustrated in the figure, some of which was U.S. government-funded. The second column of Table 1 gives the approximate year that university research began; the third and fourth columns give the approximate years that $1B and $10B markets developed, respectively. This great success may have contributed to our current pervasive dependence on computer software. We believe that such investment should be focused as well on improving software production.

Since investment has paid off so significantly in these related areas, it is reasonable to assume that it could also pay off in the improvement of software production. Counterarguments typically assert (1) that software is different from other production industries in that it involves more design and less assembly from reusable, standardized components, (2) that data about software production is proprietary and difficult to obtain, and (3) that software production involves more variables than other production industries, making it more difficult to isolate causative factors. We will discuss these points in more detail in later sections, but for now we note the following:

1. More and more software is produced using standardized reusable components, and work in fields such as software product line engineering is showing continuing success in adopting product line production methods for software. See [19] for some examples.

2. In many industries standardization and regulation have led to open and public availability of data once considered proprietary and incomparable. Reliability of telephone switches is an example. See [20] for a discussion of how such data are collected and used. Companies often use such data as a competitive advantage in advertising the quality or reliability of their products, once measures have become standardized and public. Such organizations have moved from considering the data proprietary and secret to seeing an advantage in publicizing their data.

3. It is very difficult to conduct controlled experiments on software production activities and methods and to isolate single factors as a cause in small datasets, such as studies of production of individual systems. However, the increasing availability of data from large numbers of software repositories, the application of sophisticated data mining techniques, and the use of baseline [21, 22] and A/B studies (also called A/B testing) [23] suggest that there is a basis for finding evidence of differences in productivity, quality, reliability, changeability, and other factors in software production methods, processes, and tools. There are enough positive indications to suggest that this will be a fruitful research area in the future.

With the ever-increasing demand for larger, more complex software-intensive systems and the current potential for improvement in our ability to build them, shaping a "feedback loop of experiment and learning and encouragement" [10] can drive our ability to produce better software more efficiently, much as it did agricultural productivity in a previous century. This feedback loop will also guide better investments in research and education as described below.

3   Software Production in an Advanced, Modern Economy

We use employment of software producers in industry to identify where software production plays a role in an advanced, modern economy. The resulting understanding may facilitate (1) comparing software production across industries and economies and (2) posing questions more precisely than would otherwise be possible. Table 2[1] lists the U.S. employment of selected computer occupations in 2010. The columns list, respectively, standard names for occupations, standard occupational codes, and US employment in the corresponding occupational category. Some categories in the table subsume some categories immediately below them: For instance, the first category, 15-1100 Computer Occupations, subsumes all the categories below it.

We use the employment of 15-1130 Software Developers and Programmers to understand which industries are involved in software production. This broad occupation subsumes the three immediately below it: 15-1131 Computer Programmers; 15-1132 Software Developers, Applications; and 15-1133 Software Developers, Systems Software. Reference [12] defines Computer Programmers as those who write code and may be supervised by Software Developers, Applications, who may "analyze user needs and develop software solutions." Software Developers, System Software "research, design, develop, and test operating systems-level software" for, e.g., "medical, industrial, military, communications, aerospace".

We use the North American Industry Classification System (NAICS) [13], developed by Canada, Mexico, and the U.S., to characterize an economy and its employment of software producers. NAICS provides a hierarchical decomposition of an economy into *sectors*. Figure 1 lists on the left the sectors and corresponding NAICS codes that do not involve agriculture, forestry, fishing, and hunting. Each sector may be decomposed into several *subsectors*, and subsectors into *industry groups* or industries. An industry group is comprised of a number of industries.

In the remainder of this section, we look in more detail at sectors and subsectors employing 50,000 or more software producers. In Fig. 1 employment of software producers (i.e., 15-1130 Software Developers and Programmers) in the corresponding sector labels the bars on the right. Figure 2 illustrates the decomposition of the 147,900 software producers that manufacturing sectors employ into constituent subsectors. The largest employers of software producers in manufacturing are 334 Computer and Electronic Product Manufacturing (93,100) and 336 Transportation Equipment Manufacturing (25,800). The former subsector groups "establishments that manufacture computers, computer peripherals, communications equipment, and similar electronic products, and establishments that manufacture components for such products" [13]. The reference notes that the "Computer and Electronic Product Manufacturing industries have been combined in the hierarchy of NAICS because of the economic significance they have attained."

---

[1]Occupational data for Table 2 and Figs. 1, 2, 3, 4, 5, 6, 7, 8, and 9 comes from [11].

Table 2 Computer occupation employment in U.S. in 2010

Occupation	Occupation code	Employment (thousands)
Computer occupations	15-1100	3,426
Computer and Information Research Scientists	15-1111	28.2
Computer Systems Analysts	15-1121	544.4
Software Developers and Programmers	15-1130	1,276.2
Computer Programmers	15-1131	363.1
Software Developers, Applications	15-1132	520.8
Software Developers, Systems Software	15-1133	392.3
Database and Systems Administrators and Network Architects	15-1140	458
Computer Support Specialists	15-1150	607.1

About the latter subsector, reference [13] notes: "Industries in the Transportation Equipment Manufacturing subsector produce equipment for transporting people and goods. Transportation equipment is a type of machinery [which has its own subsector, 330 Machinery Manufacturing]. An entire subsector is devoted to this activity because of the significance of its economic size in all three North American countries."

Figure 3 illustrates the decomposition of 334 Computer and Electronic Product Manufacturing into its constituent industries. The largest employers of software producers are 3341 Computer and Peripheral Equipment Manufacturing industry (38,000) and 3345 Navigational, Measuring, Electromedical, and Control Instruments Manufacturing (29,900).

Figure 4 decomposes 336 Transportation Equipment Manufacturing into its constituent industries. The largest employer of software producers is 3364 Aerospace Product and Parts Manufacturing industry (23,300).

"The Wholesale Trade sector comprises establishments engaged in wholesaling merchandise, generally without transformation, and rendering services incidental to the sale of merchandise. The merchandise described in this sector includes the outputs of agriculture, mining, manufacturing, and certain information industries, such as publishing" [13]. Figure 5 illustrates the decomposition of the 59,500 software producers employed by the sector. Subsector 423 Merchant Wholesalers, Durable Goods is the largest employer of software producers (45,000). Industries in the subsector buy capital and durable goods on their own account and sell them to other businesses. The contrast with Subsector 425 Wholesale Electronic Markets and Agents and Brokers (8,700 software producers) is that the latter's industries "arrange for the sale of goods owned by others, generally on a fee or commission basis" [13].

Industries in Sector 51 Information (1) produce information and cultural products, (2) provide means for distributing them and data, and (3) process data. Figure 6 illustrates the distribution of the sector's 175,200 software producers among its subsectors. The most significant employers of software producers are sectors 511

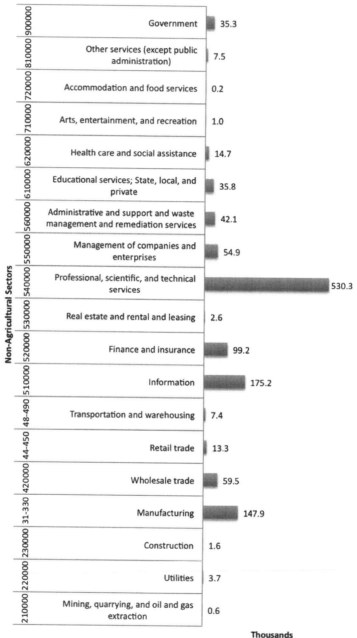

Fig. 1 Employment across U.S. economy

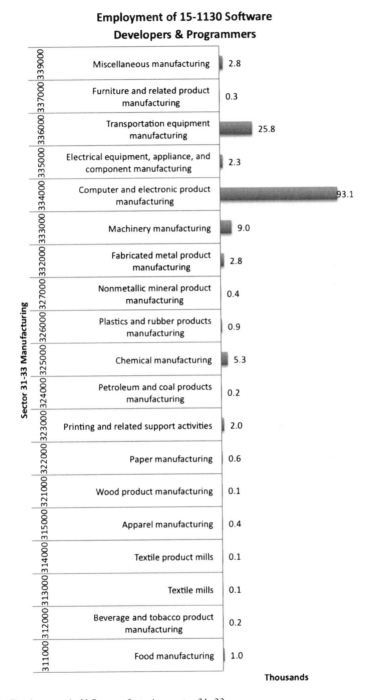

Fig. 2 Employment in U.S. manufacturing sector 31–33

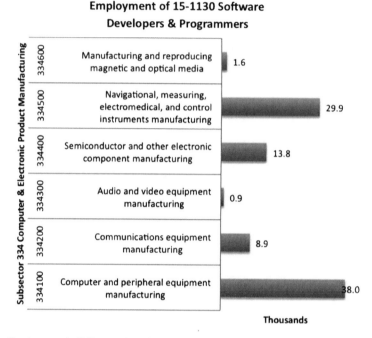

Fig. 3 Employment in U.S. manufacturing subsector 334

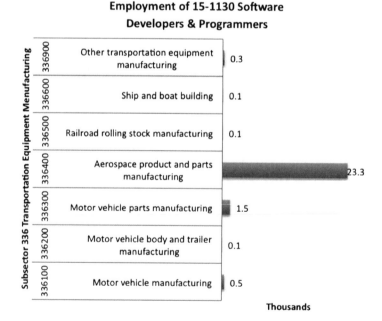

Fig. 4 Employment in U.S. manufacturing subsector 336

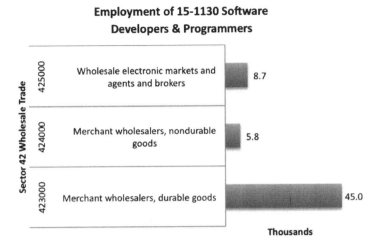

Fig. 5 Employment in U.S. Wholesale Trade sector 42

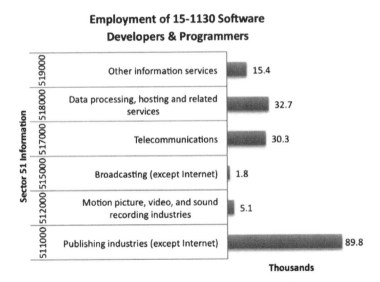

Fig. 6 Employment in U.S. information sector 51

Publishing Industries (89,800), 517 Telecommunications (30,300), and 518 Data Processing, Hosting and Related Services (32,700).

Figure 7 decomposes the 89,800 software producers in Subsector 511 Publishing Industries into 5112 Software Publishers (83,900 software producers) and 5111 Newspaper, Periodical, Book, and Directory Publishers (6,000). Establishments in the former industry may "design, develop, and publish, or publish only" [13]. More

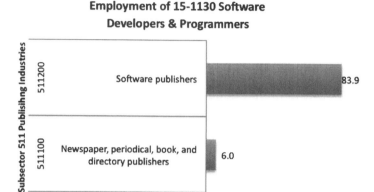

Fig. 7 Employment in U.S. publishing subsector 511

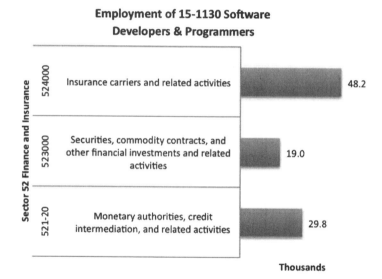

Fig. 8 Employment in U.S. Finance and Insurance Sector 52

detailed data on employment of software producers in 5112 Software Publishers is not available.

Establishments in Sector 52 Finance and Insurance are primarily involved in financial transactions and/or in facilitating financial transactions [13]. Its three subsectors are concerned, respectively, with (1) insurance: 524 Insurance Carriers and Related Activities employs 48,200 software producers, (2) securities and commodities: 523 Securities, Commodity Contracts, and other Financial Investments and Related Activities employs 19,000, and banking: 521–20 Monetary Authorities, Credit Intermediation, and Related Activities employs 29,800 software producers.

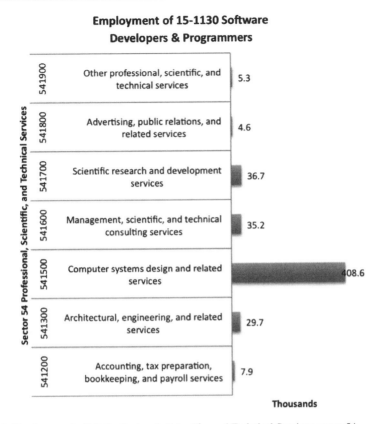

Fig. 9 Employment in U.S. Professional, Scientific, and Technical Services sector 54

Employing by far the largest number of software producers is Sector 54 Professional, Scientific, and Technical Services (530,300). It comprises one subsector 541 Professional, Scientific, and Technical Services, which is decomposed into a number of industries and industry groups (see Fig. 9). One industry, 5415 Computer Systems Design and Related Services, employs over 75 % of the sector total (408,600). Its employment of software producers is not further decomposed. Other industries and industry groups employing significant numbers of software producers are 5413 Architectural, Engineering, and Related Services (29,700); 5416 Management, Scientific, and Technical Consulting Services (25,200); and 5417 Scientific Research and Development Services (36,700).

The remaining sector employing at least 50,000 software producers is 55 Management of Companies and Enterprises (54,900). It is decomposed into one sector of the same name. Employment of software producers in the industries it comprises is not further decomposed. Establishments in this sector hold equity interests in companies and enterprises and/or "administer, oversee, and manage"

Table 3 Industry sectors employing more than 50,000 software producers [11]

Industry sectors		Employment (thousands)
31–330	Manufacturing	147.9
420,000	Wholesale Trade	59.5
51,000	Information	175.2
520,000	Finance and Insurance	99.2
540,000	Professional, Scientific, and Technical Services	530.3
550,000	Management of Companies and Enterprises	54.9

them. These establishments "perform essential activities that are often undertaken in-house by establishments in many sectors in the economy. By consolidating the performance of these activities of the enterprise at one establishment, economies of scale are achieved" [13].

Summary. Table 3 which lists U.S. industry sectors employing more than 50,000 software producers, illustrates the heterogeneous dependence on software production of an advanced, modern economy.

4   Knowledge Basis

Developing an understanding of software production entails examining the decisions and assumptions that artifacts reflect or record. This includes examining the individuals, organizations, disciplines, and mechanisms that make the decisions and create and evolve the artifacts; examining the rationale, assumptions, and mental models and representations underlying the decisions; examining communication and collaboration of individuals and organizations over space and time; and examining the representations of decisions, rationale, and assumptions in various artifacts. We must observe how such forms of knowledge flow among the artifacts, as well as among individuals, disciplines, and organizations. We must study how decisions and assumptions are forgotten, misinterpreted, corrupted, and invalidated over time.

Software production is an information process that is a sequence of representations [24]. A recent white paper on software productivity noted, "At any point in time, the union of the existing artifacts of a software production project constitutes one representation in this information process. The creation of these artifacts, and changes to them over time, demarcate the sequence of representations that forms the software production information process. We can think of this as the state space of software production" [25].

4.1   Acquiring Knowledge

Understanding the development, evolution and expression of three types of knowledge is key to improving software production. First is *domain knowledge*, the knowledge of experts in a particular domain, e.g., pilots and aeronautical engineers in the domain of aircraft, physicians and nurses in the domain of health IT, electrical, acoustic, and optical engineers in the domain of sensor networks. The second type is *software engineering knowledge*, which comprises knowledge of the processes, techniques, and tools used to produce software. We must understand how well society's software producers have mastered both types of knowledge. Estimating the impact of these different factors is known to be a difficult research problem, but some results exist and can be used, such as those underlying [26, 27]. Society's mastery of domain and software engineering knowledge indicates how good we are at building systems in domains of interest. Continuing baseline studies of specific domains will provide us with the evidence needed to make estimates, to identify areas where improvement is needed, and to understand how the knowledge itself is growing and evolving.

The third type of knowledge, *knowledge of a particular software system*, reflects the producers' understanding of the first two types. It includes knowledge recorded in the artifacts discussed earlier and knowledge that defines a particular software system that is being built or modified. We expect developers and sustainers to have this knowledge, but *generational change*, as generations of producers replace their predecessors over decades of operation, often leads to its loss. Key questions are "How much of this knowledge is recorded and kept current?" and "Does the recorded knowledge about the system(s) reflect the (haphazard) history of its development or has it been rationalized, in the sense of [28], to support its future use?"

Whether building a new system or sustaining an existing one, we proceed by making incremental changes to artifacts. Such changes, whose ultimate expression is changes to code, embody changes to decisions and assumptions. The sequence of these changes represents the software production information process. We hypothesize that as knowledge about a system is lost, or becomes corrupted and difficult to understand, the effort required to make a change increases dramatically. System disorder and uncontrolled interdependencies increase the probability of introducing errors when making a change.

We are only beginning the development of standardized, systematic techniques and mechanisms for assembling evidence that translates into knowing how much confidence we can have that we can build a system, or into predicting how well that system will meet its requirements if we do build it. Neither are there mature techniques and mechanisms for collecting evidence about what happens when we try to improve the basis for our confidence that we can build and sustain a particular system. If there were, we could start to think of software engineering as a traditional engineering discipline. We would also have a firm basis for knowing what problems to attack to make substantial progress in improving software engineering, and for estimating the value of particular investments in new software engineering R&D.

A few attempts have been made to establish standardized evidence collection and use within individual organizations, such as [29, 30, 41]. A key research (and technology) issue is how to extend such attempts to cover entire industries and sectors. Could we do this for all software developed for a financial organization? For all software developed for use in the Finance and Insurance Sector? We do not know how homogeneous the software production needs of any sector or industry are. Can improving the software production capabilities of one firm contribute to improving others in its industry or sector? It could be helpful to understand the relationship between domains on the one hand and industries and sectors on the other.

The goal of collecting a broad set of data that will be widely useful is perhaps the most difficult to realize in what we propose. There will be costs to collecting such data, protests against revealing proprietary information, and arguments about how to validate it. The fact that data collection and productive use is accomplished elsewhere gives us some confidence that we can do it for software production, too. CMMI, for example, with government support, has shown that it is possible to get software production organizations to agree on a standard for their comparative evaluation [31]. Indeed, as previously noted, when standardized data becomes publicly available, companies often find a way to use it as a competitive advantage. For example, organizations that are evaluated at a high CMMI level often advertise that fact to suggest that they are better at software development than their competitors.

In summary, *collecting and making available* evidence is a critical contribution of an effort to improve software production.

4.2   Using Knowledge

Using this evidence to reason about the state of software production and what works and what doesn't, e.g., by hypothesis testing, pilot studies, and assembly of examples of successful innovations, is an equally important contribution. *Educating and applying* the resulting new knowledge to improve next-generation workforce skills and production practices is where we can achieve big gains based on evidence. We can transition improved understanding to a wide set of stakeholders via updated course curricula, tutorials at conferences with high attendance by professional developers, and proposals to standards committees. Sponsored industry/academia experimental trials will be critical.

Producing correct, useful software confidently, consistently, and systematically requires explicit definition and statement of the three types of knowledge. Changes in requirements, people, and technology during software production all complicate the job and require that the knowledge not only be made explicit, but be kept current and correct. Iterative development, including the spiral model [32], may be viewed as an attempt to do just that: create what you are sure of first, show it to the stakeholders, especially the customer/user, incorporate feedback, make it explicit (and rational), then proceed to the next iteration. Product line engineering also may be viewed as an attempt to gather, make explicit, and thereby reuse the knowledge needed to produce a family of systems efficiently [33].

We currently have little evidence that such techniques lead to improvements in our ability to produce software. There are few common evidence bases that industry can use to justify the initial investment costs in employing such techniques, or that universities can use to determine what to teach.

4.3   Recognizing Improvement

To gauge improvement in software production, we must characterize a starting point. Many factors make profiling the current state difficult. For example, the unavailability of data because of proprietary concerns is often cited as a major obstacle to empirical research. Consortia have had some past success in reducing the startup cost of data acquisition, and may provide a model of collaboration. Barr et al. discuss the sharing of software engineering research data [17]. Government has a role to play here, both in encouraging and supporting research in data collection and analysis, in making the results of such work publicly available, and in using the results in awarding contracts. As an example, the impetus to achieve high levels of CMMI ratings is often the requirement that organizations bidding on certain types of government contracts must be certified by ISO or at CMMI level 3 or above.

Determining whether a change to existing software production practice yields evidence of improvement requires a reasoned way to derive an identification of the data to be collected from the hypothesis to be investigated [34]. To acquire the data, both product and production process need to be instrumented to make the needed data available. Such instrumentation also enables families of experiments to be run more cost-effectively [21].

5   Achieving Evidence-Based Software Production

Many of the decisions and assumptions that comprise the three types of knowledge are currently recorded imprecisely and informally, in unnecessarily complex ways, and are subject to misinterpretation and misunderstanding. Many are not explicitly recorded. They may exist only in the minds of a small number of individuals for a limited period of time, or may be communicated verbally, in unmaintained notes, or in unpreserved email. Events that invalidate the decisions and assumptions can go unnoticed too readily. Rationale is rarely recorded in a useful manner that can be maintained as software evolves. As an example, every time a programmer writes code, s/he makes decisions about what will be easy to change and what will be hard to change. Sometimes these decisions are made, reviewed, and documented before code is written, but often decisions are made as the code is written and are never documented or reviewed. There are few tools available to assist in preserving, using, and maintaining assumptions and decisions.

Preserving and conveying this knowledge is important both to building and sustaining particular systems and to the systematic, large-scale study of software production across industries and economies. Software producers need to preserve and convey knowledge for future use and reuse. The systematic collection and analysis of the assumptions and decisions that constitute this knowledge can facilitate developing an understanding of the software production information process. Mechanisms to preserve knowledge should be formal enough to allow machine readability so that the knowledge can be automatically maintained without incurring unacceptable cost. Mechanisms to convey knowledge must be available both as "pull" technologies (to query and retrieve stored information) and as "push" technologies (pro-actively to communicate, educate and cause to be remembered needed information) [35].

Making software production an engineering discipline means identifying and standardizing (1) the types of knowledge that we need to produce software, (2) the form in which the knowledge is expressed and preserved, (3) the manner in which the knowledge is communicated, and (4) the way in which future software producers are educated about the knowledge and the process for recording, maintaining, and using it. For each of the preceding points we may formulate questions or form hypotheses to identify what types of knowledge are needed to answer or test them, and collect the appropriate data, as was done for the experiments in agriculture described in [10], and as used in the goal, question, metric approach to software measurement [22, 36, 37].

5.1   Some Initial Hypotheses

Collecting and analyzing detailed data enables us to increase our understanding of software production by testing the following initial hypotheses, implied by the preceding discussion:

1. Decisions are recaptured many times, often in slightly varying forms.
2. Artifacts other than source code are not maintained over time, leading to their disuse, and to source code becoming the definitive artifact.
3. Efforts to rediscover lost decisions, assumptions, and rationale are expensive and ineffective, especially when they must be based on using existing source code for the recovery, and most especially when the originators of that code are not available.
4. Most software production is mostly redevelopment, using existing decisions and assumptions, while changing just a few of them.
5. Most software production does not now include systematic planning for change, especially over long system lifetimes.

Understanding developed from testing these hypotheses may lead to answers to the following questions, which will guide improvement of software production:

1. What knowledge is crucial to sustaining a software system over its expected lifetime?
2. How should that crucial knowledge be kept current? Made available? How should it be represented?
3. How many changes can a software system absorb before it becomes unsustainable, i.e., before a major effort must be mounted to redesign and re-implement it?

Fig. 10 Lag time between
smoking and lung cancer [38]

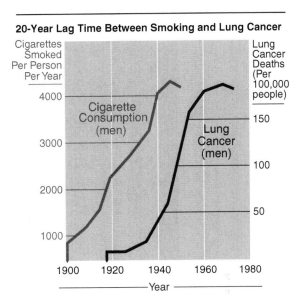

4. How does one reduce the impact of change on large systems and know it?
5. What is the impact of generational change of developers on sustainability?
6. How can one ameliorate the impact of generational change on long-lived systems
   and know it?
7. What factors dominate as the scale of software increases? Size? Complexity?
   Length of expected lifetime?

5.2   Using Evidence to Test Hypotheses

The initial hypotheses are testable through the collection of evidence from software
production from the start of production until the time that the system is retired.
Just as the medical and other communities collect evidence using baseline studies
on large populations in which convincing trends appear, we can perform long-term
baseline studies that show convincing trends in software production. For example,
data showing the correlation of smoking with lung cancer was collected over
decades and became increasingly convincing (see Fig. 10).

Similarly, we can collect data about software artifacts and the organizations and
individuals who create and evolve them that we can use to answer relevant questions
and test relevant hypotheses. We can detect trends, identify correlations, and look
for causal links that we can use to improve our software production capabilities. As
noted before, this has been done on smaller scales than we are proposing [29, 30],
but has not been tried on much larger scales. Standardizing, collecting, maintaining,
making available, and analyzing the data automatically and unobtrusively are not
easy tasks, nor are they tasks that we can do right now. However, other professions
and industries have learned to do this as a matter of course, and our society

benefits from it. There is much that government can do in this regard to encourage academic/industry collaboration [39] and to stimulate software engineering studies that will improve software production.

We thus propose investigation of what sorts of evidence are needed to support claims for improvement in operational systems. Databases of defect, near-miss and accident reports, for example, are a rich source of information about operational experience that have not been adequately incorporated into recommendations for future, similar systems [8].

Note that there are occasions when the software industry does successfully marshal its resources to accomplish similar goals. One example is the reaction to the buffer-overflow problem. Industry recognized buffer-overflow as a widespread, serious problem that could be detected and resolved. Such cases are reactive rather than proactive, however, and we are proposing a widespread proactive approach to identify problems before they become catastrophic and to identify opportunities for significant improvement.

A challenge to implementation of evidence-based software production is that over-generalization of conclusions in the past has bred skepticism about the possibility of knowing anything. We do know that for many software production questions, one size does not fit all. And we know that, judging from employment numbers of software producers in Table 3, software production is important to a number of heterogeneous sectors of the U.S. economy. Whether the use of pair programming, open-source software, modeling tools, or wikis improves software production may depend on variables such as the application domain, the size of the project, the existence of local champions for a technology, the organization's culture, or whether the developers share a motivating goal. As in agriculture or medicine, knowledge of software production accumulates incrementally. Each principled study of a sub-population adds understanding of correlations, of what parameters seem to be relevant and irrelevant, and of what results can be generalized across sub-populations. Increased openness of data builds confidence that the conclusions are not threatened by errors in the collection or analysis of the data. To build understanding and to reach general conclusions, three important contributors are families of experiments, meta-reviews of reported research on a topic, and data availability for sensitivity analysis.

5.3   Benefits

Society's growing dependence on pervasive software—in products and their design, in science, in infrastructure—suggests that even small improvements in its production may yield widespread benefits and provide unexpected opportunity. Shining the light of consistent, standardized, repeatable measurement on software production will itself lead to improvement, perhaps identifying disruptive advancements that [40] calls for. Asking for measures of recorded knowledge requires that there be recording and methods for retrieving what was recorded. Acquiring such knowledge will enable us to exploit advances in computer science, hardware, social media, and software engineering. It will help create software development methods, processes, and tools that are well suited to the goals of organizations engaged in software production, including goals such as reducing total ownership cost, risk, and schedule. We will be better able to take advantage of human strengths and accommodate human weaknesses. Further, as has been demonstrated in so many other fields, an evidence-based approach will provide greater confidence that we have done so.

Some may argue that "imposing" measurement will increase cost and time to develop and sustain systems. It may be true that in some cases, particularly where there is little recording of knowledge now, some initial development costs will be incurred. However, studies of large organizations, such as [29], indicate small overhead in measurement costs, partly because much of the quantitative data collection and analysis is automated.

5.4   Future Steps

Following the agricultural model, we suggest the following initial focus: *(1) Define and execute families of experiments aimed at answering the questions whose answers are judged by experts most likely to have the highest impact on productivity. (2) Ensure that the experimental data are open, to the greatest extent possible in the context, to subsequent researchers and practitioners.*

Some ways in which governments can facilitate this focus are:

- Providing an incentive for the collection of data for large-scale software production
- Funding replication of experiments to increase confidence in results
- Building consortia of industrial, government, and academic partners engaged in software production
- Providing a secure repository for data collections
- Encouraging standards that are evidence-based
- Encouraging standards for evidence collection
- Educating the future work force in evidence-based software production

Government can also play an integral part in helping disseminate results to stakeholders in software production. A natural first step is for it to encourage investigations into better ways of making information more widely available. Understanding which information transfer techniques work and which do not would help inform industrial practitioners more quickly and effectively. New techniques such as crowd-sourcing may offer ways to reach both researchers and industrial practitioners. Fostering these broader, creative collaborations then offers opportunities for new, competitive products.

In addition, government can help by championing evidence-based improvements. In agriculture, field agents from governmental agencies and state universities work directly with farmers to build trust in the evidence. Dissemination via modern social media might speed acceptance of new knowledge in software production, promoting rapid improvement, disruptive advancement, and openness to change.

6   Summary

Because "reliable and robust software is central to activities throughout society" [7], our known problems in software production impose costs throughout society. Transforming software production to reduce those costs and take advantage of the value offered by known best practices requires evidence. We need to put software engineering on an evidence basis, as other fields have done. Our goal is to improve software production based on a better understanding of it. We need to understand the current state of the practice, and the effects of trialed improvements, and to feed back this understanding to the software engineering community. While we need to do this for software production throughout the international economy, we may start on a smaller scale to understand the problems better.

Key questions in implementing this strategy define the steps needed to start collecting and applying evidence:

1. What are the areas of knowledge that are critical to software engineering and how should we measure our effectiveness in defining and using them?
2. How do we standardize the collection of software measurement data across different organizations?
3. What will be the incentives for different organizations to collect the same types of data and provide them for analysis and archiving?
4. Who will be the keeper of the data?
5. How will data be made available to researchers and practitioners who want to use it in different ways?
6. Who will sponsor the research and development needed to answer the preceding questions?

Similar questions have been answered, and the answers used to drive rapid, sustained progress, in fields as diverse as agriculture, genetics, automotive engineering, particle physics, health care, and semiconductor manufacturing. Software production can reap similar rewards.

Acknowledgments Grady Campbell, Jon Bentley, and Rick Buskens provided helpful comments on earlier versions. Peter Meyer provided thoughtful, detailed comments on the present version. Kevin Sullivan brought BLS data to our attention. The second author acknowledges support from ONR and DDR&E/S&T/IS. The work of the third author is supported in part by NSF grant 0916275 with funds from the American Recovery and Reinvestment Act of 2009. The views contained herein do not necessarily represent those of the US Navy nor the US Government.

References

1. National Research Council: Critical Code: Software Producibility for Defense. The National Academies Press, Washington, DC (2010a)
2. Markoff, J.: Google cars drive themselves, in traffic. New York Times, 9 Oct 2010
3. Sherr, I., Ramsey, M.: A Driverless Lexus? Toyota Closer to Automating Cars. Wall Street J. **3** http://online.wsj.com/article/SB10001424127887323374504578220081249592640.html (2013)

4. National Research Council: Measuring and Sustaining the New Economy, Software, Growth, and the Future of the U.S. Economy. The National Academies Press, Washington, DC (2010b)
5. Institute for Defense Analyses.: Assessment of DoD enterprise resource planning business systems (2011)
6. Fast Track Action Committee on Computational Modeling and Simulation, Committee on Technology, National Science and Technology Council.: Simulation-Based Engineering and Science for Discovery and Innovation (2010)
7. President's Council of Advisors on Science and Technology.: Leadership Under Challenge: Information Technology R&D in a Competitive World (2007)
8. Kirby, J., Weiss, D., Lutz, R.: Evidence-based software production. In: Future of Software Engineering Research Workshop, pp. 191–194. Santa Fe (2010)
9. National Institute of Standards & Technology.: The economic impacts of inadequate infrastructure for software testing. Planning report 02–3 (2002)
10. Gawande, A.: How the Senate bill would contain the cost of health care. The New Yorker. 17 Dec 2009
11. U.S. Bureau of Labor Statistics.: Industry-occupation matrix data, by occupation. http:www.bls.gov/emp/ep_table_108.htm (2012)
12. U.S. Bureau of Labor Statistics.: 2010 SOC definitions. http://www.bls.gov/SOC/soc_2010_definitions.pdf (2010)
13. U.S. Bureau of Labor Statistics.: North American Industry Classification System (NAICS) at BLS. http://www.bls.gov/bls/naics.htm (2011)
14. Jackson, D., Thomas, M., Millett, L.I. (eds.): Software for Dependable Systems: Sufficient Evidence? Committee on Certifiably Dependable Software Systems, National Research Council (2007)
15. SIGSOFT Software Engineering Notes. Risks to the public
16. Kitchenham, B., Dyba, T., Jørgensen, M.: Evidence-based Software Engineering. In: Proceedings of the 26th ICSE, Edinburgh, pp. 273–281 (2004)
17. Barr, E., Bird, C., Hyatt, E., Menzies, T., Robies, G.: On the shoulders of giants. In: Future of Software Engineering Research Workshop. Santa Fe (2010)
18. National Research Council: Continuing Innovation in Information Technology. The National Academies Press, Washington, DC (2010c)
19. Software Product Line Hall of Fame. http://splc.net/fame.html
20. Kuhn, D.R.: Sources of failure in the public switched telephone network. IEEE Comput. **30**(4), 31–36 (1997)
21. Basili, V., Caldiera, G., McGarry, F., et al.: The software engineering laboratory: an operational software experience factory. In: Proceedings of the 14th ICSE, Melbourne, pp. 370–381 (1992)
22. Basili, V., Rombach, H.D.: The TAME project: towards improvement-oriented software environments. IEEE Trans. Softw. Eng. **SE-14**(6), 758–773 (1988)
23. Wikipedia.: A/B testing. http://en.wikipedia.org/wiki/A/B_testing (2013)
24. Denning, P.: The great principles of computing. Am. Sci., Sept–Oct 2010
25. Software Design and Productivity coordinating group.: Software Production Data. http://www.nitrd.gov/Subcommittee/sdp/events/September20232011.aspx (2011)
26. Boehm, B.: Software Engineering Economics. Prentice-Hall, Englewood Cliffs (1981)
27. COCOMO.: http://sunset.usc.edu/csse/research/COCOMOII/cocomo_main.html
28. Parnas, D.L., Clements, P.C.: A rational design process: how and why to fake it. IEEE Trans. Softw. Eng. **SE-12**, 251–257 (1986)
29. Hackbarth, R., Palframan, J., Mockus, A., Weiss, D.: Assessing the state of software in a large enterprise. Empirical Softw. Eng. **15**(3), 219–249 (2010)
30. Grady, R., Caswell, D.: Software Metrics: Establishing a Company-Wide Program. Prentice Hall, Englewood Cliffs (1987)
31. CMMI.: Capability Maturity Model. http://www.sei.cmu.edu/cmmi/ (2010)
32. Boehm, B.: A spiral model of software development and enhancement. SIGSOFT SEN **11**(4), 14–24 (1986)
33. Weiss, D., Lai, C.R.T.: Software Product Line Engineering. Addison-Wesley, Boston (1999)

34. Fenton, N.E., Pfleeger, S.L.: Software Metrics: A Rigorous and Practical Approach, 2nd edn. Course Technology (1998)
35. Lutz, R., Lavin, M., Lux, J., Peters, K., Rouquette, N.: Mining requirements knowledge from operational experience. In: Maalej, W., Thurimella, A.K. (eds.) Managing Requirements Knowledge. Springer, New York (2013)
36. Basili, V., Weiss, D.: Evaluating software development by analysis of changes: some data from the software engineering laboratory. IEEE Trans. Softw. Eng. **11**(2), 157–168 (1985)
37. Basili, V., Caldiera, G., Rombach, H.D.: Goal question metric approach. In: Encyclopedia of Software Engineering, pp. 528–532. Wiley (1994)
38. 20-year lag time between smoking and lung cancer. http://en.wikipedia.org/wiki/File:Cancer_smoking_lung_cancer_correlation_from_NIH.svg
39. Rombach, H.D., Achatz, R.: Research collaborations between academia and industry. FOSE 2007, pp. 29–36 (2007)
40. President's Council of Advisors on Science and Technology: Designing a Digital Future: Federally Funded Research and Development in Networking and Information Technology. President's Council of Advisors on Science and Technology (PCAST), Washington, DC (2013)
41. Lutz, R., Mikulski, C.: Empirical analysis of safety-critical anomalies during operations. IEEE Trans. Softw. Eng. **30**(3), 172–180 (2004)

Skating to Where the Puck Is Going: Future Systems and Software Engineering Opportunities and Challenges

Barry Boehm

Abstract

This paper provides an update and extension of a 2005 paper on The Future of Systems and Software Engineering Processes. Some of its challenges and opportunities are similar, such as the need to simultaneously achieve high levels of both agility and assurance. Others have emerged as increasingly important, such as the opportunities and challenges of dealing with smart systems involving ultralarge volumes of data; with multicore chips; with social networking services; and with cloud computing or software as a service. The paper is organized around eight relatively surprise-free trends and two "wild cards" whose trends and implications are harder to foresee. The eight surprise-free trends are:

1. Increasing emphasis on rapid development and adaptability;
2. Increasing software criticality and need for assurance;
3. Increased complexity, global systems of systems, and need for scalability and interoperability;
4. Increased needs to accommodate COTS, software services, and legacy systems;
5. Smart systems with increasingly large volumes of data and ways to learn from them;
6. Increased emphasis on users, social networking services, web applications, and end value;
7. Computational plenty and multicore chips;
8. Increasing integration of software and systems engineering. The two wild-card trends are:
9. Increasing software autonomy; and
10. Combinations of biology and computing.

B. Boehm (✉)
University of Southern California, Los Angeles, CA 90089-0781, USA
e-mail: boehm@usc.edu

J. Münch and K. Schmid (eds.), *Perspectives on the Future of Software Engineering*,
DOI 10.1007/978-3-642-37395-4_19, © Springer-Verlag Berlin Heidelberg 2013

1   Introduction

Wayne Gretzky, who has generally been acknowledged to be the greatest hockey player of all time, has ascribed a good deal of his success to his ability to anticipate where the hockey puck was going, and to skate to where he could capitalize on this knowledge. It is the thesis of this paper that this kind of investment in anticipating where technology, competitors, organizations, and the marketplace are going is increasingly critical to successful systems and software engineering. In contrast, organizations performing continuous process improvement by asking, "How could we have done our last project better?" are actually skating to where the puck has been. Clearly, some such "reflection in action" [1] is good, but if we are living in a world of rapid change, reflection in action needs to be balanced with anticipating the future.

Is the world of systems and software engineering really changing all that fast? This paper is an update of the [2] paper called "The Future of Systems and Software Engineering Processes," and of a follow-on book chapter [3] entitled "Some Future Software Engineering Opportunities and Challenges." One of the predicted 2005 trends was an increase in rates of change in technology and the environment. A good way to calibrate this prediction is to identify how many currently significant trends the 2005 paper failed to predict. These include:

- Use of multicore chips to compensate for the decrease in Moore's Law rates of microcircuit speed increase—these chips will stay on the Moore's Law curve of computing operations per second, but will cause formidable problems in going from efficient sequential software programs to efficient parallel programs [4];
- The explosion in sources of electronic data, such as smart systems and e-commerce, and ways to search and analyze them, such as search engines and recommender systems [5];
- The economic viability and growth in the use of cloud computing and software as a service [6];
- The ability to scale agile methods up to 100-person Scrums of Scrums, under appropriate conditions [7]; and
- The rapid growth of social networking services and web applications [8].

The original paper identified eight relatively surprise-free future trends whose interactions presented significant challenges, and an additional two wild-card trends whose impact was likely to be large, and whose likely nature and realizations would be hard to predict. This paper has revised the eight "surprise-free" trends to reflect the new trends above, but it has left the two wild-card trends as having remained but continuing to be less predictable.

2   Future Software Engineering Opportunities and Challenges

2.1   Increasing Emphasis on Rapid Development and Adaptability

The increasingly rapid pace of systems change discussed above translates into an increasing need for rapid development and adaptability in order to keep up with one's competition. A good example was Hewlett Packard's recognition that their commercial product lifetimes averaged 33 months, while their software development times per product averaged 48 months. This led to an investment in product line architectures and reusable software components that reduced software development times by a factor of 4 down to 12 months [9].

Another response to the challenge of rapid development and adaptability has been the emergence of agile methods [10–13]. Our original [14] analysis of these methods found them generally not able to scale up to larger products. For example, Kent Beck says in [10], "Size clearly matters. You probably couldn't run an XP (eXtreme Programming) project with a hundred programmers. Not fifty. Not twenty, probably. Ten is definitely doable."

However, over the last decade, several organizations have been able to scale up agile methods by using two layers of 10-person Scrum teams. This involves, among other things, having each Scrum team's daily stand-up meeting followed up by a daily stand-up meeting of the Scrum team leaders, and by up-front investments in an evolving system architecture. We have analyzed several of these projects and organizational initiatives in [7]; a successful example and a partial counterexample are provided next.

The *successful example* is provided by a US medical services company with over 1,000 software developers in the US, two European countries, and India. The corporation was on the brink of failure, due largely to its slow, error-prone, and incompatible software applications and processes. A senior internal technical manager, expert in both safety-critical medical applications and agile development, was commissioned by top management to organize a corporate-wide team to transform the company's software development approach. In particular, the team was to address agility, safety, and Sarbanes-Oxley governance and accountability problems.

Software technology and project management leaders from all of its major sites were brought together to architect a corporate information framework and develop a corporate architected agile process approach. The resulting Scrum of Scrums approach was successfully used in a collocated pilot project to create the new information framework while maintaining continuity of service in their existing operations.

Based on the success of this pilot project, the team members returned to their sites and led similar transformational efforts. Within 3 years, they had almost 100 Scrum teams and 1,000 software developers using compatible and coordinated

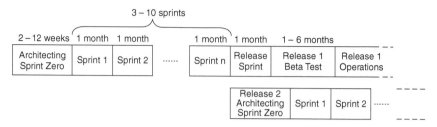

Fig. 1 Example of architected agile process

architected agile approaches. The effort involved their customers and marketers in the effort. Expectations were managed via the pilot project. The release management approach included a 2–12 week architecting Sprint Zero, a series of 3–10 one-month development Sprints, a Release Sprint, and 1–6 months of beta testing; the next release Sprint Zero overlapped the Release Sprint and beta testing. Their agile Scrum approach involved a tailored mix of eXtreme Programming (XP) and corporate practices, 6–12 person teams with dedicated team rooms, and global teams with wiki and daily virtual meeting support—working as if located next-door. Figure 1 shows this example of the Architected Agile approach.

Two of the other success stories had similar approaches. However, circumstances may require *different tailorings* of the architected agile approach. Another variant analyzed was an automated maintenance system that found its Scrum teams aligned with different stakeholders whose objectives diverged in ways that could not be reconciled by daily standup meetings. The project recognized this and has evolved to a more decentralized Scrum-based approach, with centrifugal tendencies monitored and resolved by an empowered Product Framework Group (PFG) consisting of the product owners and technical leads from each development team, and the project systems engineering, architecting, construction, and test leads. The PFG meets near the end of an iteration to assess progress and problems, and to steer the priorities of the upcoming iteration by writing new backlog items and reprioritizing the product backlog. A few days after the start of the next iteration, the PFG meets again to assess what was planned vs. what was needed, and to make necessary adjustments. This has been working much more successfully.

2.2   Increasing Criticality and Need for Assurance

A main reason that products and services are becoming more software-intensive is that software can be more easily and rapidly adapted to change as compared to hardware. A representative statistic is that the percentage of functionality on modern aircraft determined by software increased to 80 % by 2000 [15]. Although people's, systems', and organizations' dependency on software is becoming increasingly critical, the current major challenge in achieving system dependability is that dependability is generally not the top priority for software producers. In the words of the 1999 (U.S.) President's Information Technology Advisory Council (PITAC) Report, "The IT industry spends the bulk of its resources, both financial and human, on rapidly bringing products to market" [16]. Despite some improvements due to cyber security threats, the statement still stands.

This situation will likely continue until a major software-induced systems catastrophe similar in impact on world consciousness to the 9/11 World Trade Center catastrophe stimulates action toward establishing accountability for software dependability. Given the high and increasing software vulnerabilities of the world's current financial, transportation, communications, energy distribution, medical, and emergency services infrastructures, it is highly likely that such a software-induced catastrophe will occur between now and 2025.

Process strategies for highly dependable software-intensive systems and many of the techniques for addressing its challenges have been available for quite some time. A landmark 1975 conference on reliable software included papers on formal specification and verification processes; early error elimination; fault tolerance; fault tree and failure modes and effects analysis; testing theory, processes and tools; independent verification and validation; root cause analysis of empirical data; and use of automated aids for defect detection in software specifications and code [17]. Some of these were adapted from existing systems engineering practices; some were developed for software and adapted for systems engineering.

These have been used to achieve high dependability on smaller systems and some very large self-contained systems such as the AT&T telephone network [18]. Also, new strategies have been emerging to address the people-oriented and value-oriented challenges discussed in Sect. 2.1. These include the Personal and Team Software Processes [19, 20], value/risk-based processes for achieving dependability objectives [21, 22], and value-based systems engineering processes such as Lean Development [23].

Many of the traditional assurance methods such as formal methods are limited in their speed of execution, need for scarce expert developers, and adaptability (often requiring correctness proofs to start over after a requirements change). More recently, some progress has been made in strengthening assurance methods and making them more adaptable. Examples are the use of the ecological concepts of "resilience" as a way to achieve both assurance and adaptability [24, 25]; the use of more incremental assurance cases for reasoning about safety, security, and reliability [26]; the development of more incremental correctness proof techniques [27]; and the use of more systems-oriented assurance approaches [28].

2.2.1 An Incremental Development Process for Achieving Both Agility and Assurance

Simultaneously achieving high assurance levels and rapid adaptability to change requires new approaches to software engineering processes. Figure 2 shows a single increment of the incremental evolution portion of such a model, as presented in the [2] paper and subsequently adapted for use in several commercial organizations needing both agility and assurance. It assumes that the organization has developed:

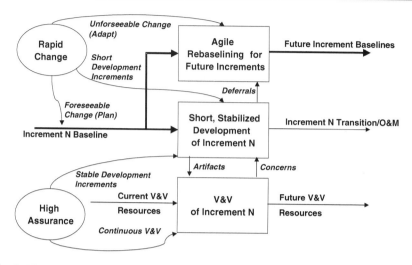

Fig. 2 The incremental commitment spiral process model: increment activities

- A best-effort definition of the system's steady-state capability;
- An incremental sequence of prioritized capabilities culminating in the steady-state capability; and
- A Feasibility Rationale providing sufficient evidence that the system architecture will support the incremental capabilities, that each increment can be developed within its available budget and schedule, and that the series of increments create a satisfactory return on investment for the organization and mutually satisfactory outcomes for the success-critical stakeholders.

In *Balancing Agility and Discipline* [14], we found that rapid change comes in two primary forms. One is relatively predictable change that can be handled by the plan-driven Parnas strategy [29] of encapsulating sources of change within modules, so that the effects of changes are largely confined to individual modules. The other is relatively unpredictable change that may appear simple (such as adding a "cancel" or "undo" capability [30]), but often requires a great deal of agile adaptability to rebaseline the architecture and incremental capabilities into a feasible solution set.

The need to deliver high-assurance incremental capabilities on short fixed schedules means that each increment needs to be kept as stable as possible. This is particularly the case for very large systems of systems with deep supplier hierarchies (often 6–12 levels), in which a high level of rebaselining traffic can easily lead to chaos. In keeping with the use of the spiral model as a risk-driven process model generator, the risks of destabilizing the development process make the development portion of the project into a build-to-specification subset of the spiral model activities. The need for high assurance of each increment also makes it cost-effective to invest in a team of appropriately skilled personnel to continuously verify and validate the increment as it is being developed.

However, "deferring the change traffic" does not imply deferring its change impact analysis, change negotiation, and rebaselining until the beginning of the next increment. With a single development team and rapid rates of change, this would require a team optimized to develop to stable plans and specifications to spend much of the next increment's scarce calendar time performing tasks much better suited to agile teams.

The appropriate metaphor for these tasks is not a build-to-specification metaphor or a purchasing-agent metaphor but an adaptive "command-control-intelligence-surveillance-reconnaissance" (C2ISR) metaphor. It involves an agile team performing the first three activities of the C2ISR "Observe, Orient, Decide, Act" (OODA) loop for the next increments, while the plan-driven development team is performing the "Act" activity for the current increment. "Observing" involves monitoring changes in relevant technology and COTS products, in the competitive marketplace, in external interoperating systems and in the environment; and monitoring progress on the current increment to identify slowdowns and likely scope deferrals. "Orienting" involves performing change impact analyses, risk analyses, and tradeoff analyses to assess candidate rebaselining options for the upcoming increments. "Deciding" involves stakeholder renegotiation of the content of upcoming increments, architecture rebaselining, and the degree of COTS upgrading needed to prepare for the next increment. It also involves updating the future increments' feasibility rationales to ensure that their renegotiated scopes and solutions can be achieved within their budgets and schedules. Often a Kanban approach [31] for change traffic will work well.

A successful rebaseline means that the plan-driven development team can hit the ground running at the beginning of the "Act" phase of developing the next increment, and the agile team can hit the ground running on rebaselining definitions of the increments beyond. This model is similar to the ones used by the major cell phone software developers, who may run several concurrent teams phased to deliver new capabilities every 90 days.

2.3   Increased Complexity, Global Systems of Systems, and Need for Scalability and Interoperability

The global connectivity provided by the Internet provides major economies of scale and network economies [32] that drive both an organization's product and process strategies. Location-independent distribution and mobility services create both rich new bases for synergetic collaboration and challenges in synchronizing activities. Differential salaries provide opportunities for cost savings through global outsourcing, although lack of careful preparation can easily turn the savings into overruns. The ability to develop across multiple time zones creates the prospect of very rapid development via three-shift operations, although again there are significant challenges in management visibility and control, communication semantics, and building shared values and trust. It also implies that collaborative activities such as Participatory Design [33] will require stronger human systems and software engineering processes and skill support not only across application domains but also across different cultures.

A lot of work needs to be done to establish robust success patterns for global collaborative processes. Key challenges as discussed above include cross-cultural bridging; establishment of common shared vision and trust; contracting mechanisms and incentives; handovers and change synchronization in multi-time-zone development; and culture-sensitive collaboration-oriented groupware. Most software packages are oriented around individual use; just determining how best to support groups will take a good deal of research and experimentation. Within individual companies, such as IBM, corporate global collaboration capabilities have made collaborative work largely location-independent, even for large time-zone bridging.

One collaboration process whose future applications niche is becoming better understood is open source software development. Security experts tend to be skeptical about the ability to assure the secure performance of a product developed by volunteers with open access to the source code. Feature prioritization in open source is basically done by performers; this is generally viable for infrastructure software, but less so for competitive corporate applications systems and software. Proliferation of versions can be a problem with volunteer developers. But most experts see the current success of open source development for infrastructure products such as Linux, Apache, and Firefox as sustainable into the future.

Traditionally (and even recently for some forms of agile methods), systems and software development processes were recipes for standalone "stovepipe" systems with high risks of inadequate interoperability with other stovepipe systems. Experience has shown that such collections of stovepipe systems cause unacceptable delays in service, uncoordinated and conflicting plans, ineffective or dangerous decisions, and inability to cope with rapid change.

During the 1990s and early 2000s, standards such as ISO/IEC 12207 [34] and ISO/IEC 15288 [35] began to emerge that situated systems and software project processes within an enterprise framework. Concurrently, enterprise architectures such as the IBM Zachman Framework [36], RM-ODP [37], and the U.S. Federal Enterprise Framework [38], have been developing and evolving, along with a number of commercial Enterprise Resource Planning (ERP) packages.

These frameworks and support packages are making it possible for organizations to reinvent themselves around transformational, network-centric systems of systems. As discussed in [39], these are necessarily software-intensive systems of systems (SISOS), and have tremendous opportunities for success and equally tremendous risks of failure. Examples of successes have been Federal Express; Wal-Mart; and the U.S. Command, Control, Intelligence, Surveillance, and Reconnaissance (C2ISR) system in Iraq; examples of failures have been the Confirm travel reservation system, K-Mart, and the U.S. Advanced Automation System for air traffic control. ERP packages have been the source of many successes and many failures, implying the need for considerable risk/opportunity assessment before committing to an ERP-based solution.

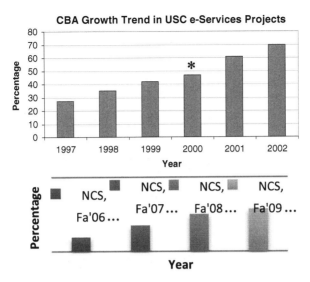

Fig. 3 COTS usage growth in USC e-service projects; recently purchased software services growth

Our work in supporting SISOS development programs has shown that the use of a risk-driven spiral process with early attention to SISOS risks and the use of systems architecting methods [40] can avoid many of the SISOS development pitfalls [41, 42]. A prioritized list of the top ten SISOS risks we have encountered includes several of the trends we have been discussing: (1) acquisition management and staffing, (2) requirements/architecture feasibility, (3) achievable software schedules, (4) supplier integration, (5) adaptation to rapid change, (6) systems and software quality factor achievability, (7) product integration and electronic upgrade, (8) software COTS and reuse feasibility, (9) external interoperability, and (10) technology readiness.

2.4 Increased Needs to Accommodate COTS, Software Services, and Legacy Systems

A 2001 ACM Communications editorial stated, "In the end—and at the beginning— it's all about programming" [43]. Future trends are making this decreasingly true. Although infrastructure software developers will continue to spend most of their time programming, most application software developers are spending more and more of their time assessing, tailoring, and integrating commercial-off-the-shelf (COTS) products. And more recently, the COTS products need to be evaluated with respect to purchased software-as-a-service options.

The left side of Fig. 3 illustrates the COTS trends for a longitudinal sample of small e-services applications going from 28 % COTS-based in 1996–97 to

70 % COTS-based in 2001–2002, plus a corroborative industry-wide 54 % figure (the asterisk *) for COTS-based applications (CBAs) in the 2000 Standish Group survey [44, 45]. COTS software products are particularly challenging to integrate. They are opaque and hard to debug. They are often incompatible with each other due to the need for competitive differentiation. They are uncontrollably evolving, averaging about to 10 months between new releases, and generally unsupported by their vendors after three subsequent releases. These latter statistics are a caution to organizations outsourcing applications with long gestation periods. In one case, we observed an outsourced application with 120 COTS products, 46 % of which were delivered in a vendor-unsupported state [45].

The right side of Fig. 3 shows the corresponding recent growth in the use of purchased software services for a similar longitudinal sample of small e-services applications going from 19 % in 2006–07 to 57 % in 2009–10 [46]. Relative to COTS products, purchased software services have the advantages of eliminating the costs and failure modes of operating one's own server computers, low initial costs, accessibility across more types of user platforms, and getting automatic upgrades. They have the disadvantages of automatic upgrades (no way to keep applications stable by declining upgrades), loss of exclusive control of one's data and speed of performance, and need for Internet access.

Open source software, or an organization's reused or legacy software, is less opaque and less likely to go unsupported. But such software can also have problems with interoperability and continuing evolution. In addition, it often places constraints on a new application's incremental development, as the existing software needs to be decomposable to fit the new increments' content and interfaces. Across the maintenance life cycle, synchronized refresh of a large number of continually evolving COTS, open source, reused, and legacy software and hardware becomes a major additional challenge.

Legacy or Brownfield software is one area in which "it's all about programming" is still largely valid. Today and increasingly in the future, most large software-intensive system (SIS) developments will be constrained by the need to provide continuity of service while migrating their services away from poorly structured and documented legacy software applications. The International Data Corporation has estimated that there are 200 billion lines of such legacy codes in current operation [47]. Yet most SIS process models contain underlying assumptions that an application project can start from scratch in an unconstrained Greenfield approach to developing requirements and solutions. Frequently, such applications will turn out to be unusable when organizations find that there is no way to incrementally undo the Brownfield legacy software in order to phase in the new software.

Recently, several approaches have emerged for re-engineering the legacy software into a service-oriented architecture from which migration to newer software solutions can be accomplished. Examples are the IBM VITA approach [48], the SEI SMART approach [49], and application of the Incremental Commitment Spiral Model [50]. Besides programming, they require a good deal of up-front software systems engineering.

2.4.1   Systems and Software Engineering Process Implications

COTS and software-service economics generally makes sequential waterfall processes (in which the pre-specified system requirements determine the capabilities) incompatible with COTS or service-based solutions (in which the COTS or service capabilities largely determine the requirements; a desired capability is not a requirement if you can't afford the custom solution that would provide it). Some initial software COTS and service-based applications (CBA) development processes are emerging. Some are based on composable process elements covering the major sources of CBA effort (assessment, tailoring, and glue code integration) [45]. Others are oriented around the major functions involved in software CBAs, such as the SEI EPIC process [51]. More recently, decision processes for choosing among COTS-based, services-based, agile, or hybrid processes in different software development situations have been developed and experimentally applied [46].

However, there are still major challenges for the future, such as processes for synchronized multi-COTS refresh across the life-cycle; processes for enterprise-level and systems-of-systems COTS, software services, open source, reuse, and legacy evolution; integrated hardware and software COTS-based system processes; and processes and techniques to compensate for shortfalls in multi-COTS and services usability, dependability, and interoperability. Such COTS and services-oriented shortfalls are another reason why emergent spiral or evolutionary processes are better matches to most future project situations than attempts to pre-specify waterfall and V-model system and software development plans and schedules. For example, consider the following common development sequence:

1. Pick the best set of COTS products or services supporting the system objectives, and
2. Compensate for the selected COTS or services shortfalls with respect to the system objectives.

There is no way to elaborate task 2 (or other tasks depending on it) until task 1 is done, as different COTS or services selections will produce different shortfalls needing compensation.

2.5   Increasingly Large Volumes of Data and Ways to Learn from Them

The growth of the Internet has been matched by the growth of data sources connected to the Internet. Much of the data is in files protected by firewalls, passwords, or encryption, but a tremendous amount is available via people and organizations willing to share the data, or as part of Internet transactions. Another rapidly growing source of data is the emergence of megasensor-empowered smart systems for power grids, buildings, companies, and even cities in such locations as Singapore, Abu Dhabi, South Korea, and Portugal. Also, the increasing economic attractiveness of cloud computing is creating huge data storage and processing complexes that can similarly be used to determine information of interest and economic value. The growing volume of this data has also been matched by the growing sophistication of the technology used to search and reason about the data. Three primary technologies have been search engines, recommender systems, and general data mining techniques.

As one example of the power of search engines, the largest numbers of search matches on Google found in the author's recent (February 10, 2013) informal searching for instances of popular search terms were approximately 13.8 billion for "video," 11.4 billion for "time," 10.6 billion for "news;" 8.2 billion for "music," 6.2 billion for "life," and 5.4 billion for "play." Each of these searches was completed by Google in about 0.3–0.5 s.

This example also points out the challenge of determining which matches out of a billion or so to show that are most likely to be of interest to the viewer or other interested parties. Clearly, some of the interested parties are vendors who would like to advertise their products to people who are interested in the search topic. Their willingness to pay for search providers to highlight their offerings is the main reason for the search providers' economic viability. A good summary of search engine technology is [52].

A good example of recommender systems is the capability developed and evolved by Amazon.com. This began as a way for Amazon to notify someone buying a book on Amazon of the other books most frequently bought by people that had bought the book they were buying. This is an example of collaborative filtering, which can be applied anywhere, as it does not require knowledge of the content of the items bought or accessed. Extensions of collaborative filtering to include item content have also been developed. Another type of recommender system asks users to identify a profile of likes, dislikes, and preferences either among example items or among attributes of items in a given area of interest (restaurants, vacations, music), and provides recommendations or services best satisfying the user's profile. A good summary of recommender systems is [5]. A good example of collaborative-filtering recommender technology is [53], summarizing the approach they used as part of the team that won the $1 million Netflix prize for improving Netflix's recommender system performance by more than 10 %.

Data mining is a more general term for processes that extract patterns from data. It includes recommender systems and other techniques such as clustering algorithms that look for similarities among data elements; association rule learning (such as Amazon.com's rules for most-frequently-bought associated books); classification algorithms such as neural networks and Bayesian classification; and evaluation techniques such as regression and bootstrapping techniques.

Data mining techniques have become a widely-researched area within software engineering. In some cases, such as software cost estimation, the data are too scarce and imprecise for data mining techniques to have made much headway, but a recent issue of IEEE Software [54] includes a number of useful data mining results and prospects for stronger results in the future. These tend to have worked on sufficiently large data repositories in large companies or via the increasing volume of open source software. They include defect-prone module characterization; defect finding via inter-module consistency checking; detection of code churn hot-spots (and correlations with defect frequency) for test planning and remodularization around sources of change; plans-vs.-actuals tracking and dashboarding for early project risk analysis; and social network analysis of interpersonal interaction paths vs. integration failure rates. Another key to the general utility of such data mining results is the availability of metadata on project size, domain, processes used, application criticality, etc., as results often vary significantly across different project types.

2.6   Increased Emphasis on Users and End Value

A 2005 *Computerworld* panel on "The Future of Information Technology (IT)" indicated that usability and total ownership cost-benefits, including user inefficiency and ineffectiveness costs, are becoming IT user organizations' top priorities [55]. A representative quote from panelist W. Brian Arthur was "Computers are working about as fast as we need. The bottleneck is making it all usable." A recurring user-organization desire is to have technology that adapts to people rather than vice versa. This is increasingly reflected in users' product selection activities, with evaluation criteria increasingly emphasizing product usability and value added vs. a previous heavy emphasis on product features and purchase costs. Such trends ultimately will affect producers' product and process priorities, marketing strategies, and competitive survival.

Some technology trends strongly affecting usability and cost-effectiveness are increasingly powerful enterprise support packages, data access and mining tools, social networking applications, virtual reality applications, and increasingly powerful mobile computing and communications devices. Such products have tremendous potential for user value, but determining how they will be best configured will involve a lot of product experimentation, shakeout, and emergence of superior combinations of system capabilities. A further challenge is to track and accommodate changes in user capabilities and preferences; it increasingly appears that the next generation of users will have different strengths and weaknesses with respect to multitasking, attention span, and trial-and-error vs. thought-driven approaches to determining software solutions.

2.6.1   Systems and Software Engineering Process Implications

In terms of future systems and software process implications, the fact that the capability requirements for these products are emergent rather than pre-specifiable has become the primary challenge. Not only do the users exhibit the IKIWISI (I'll know it when I see it) syndrome, but their priorities change with time. These changes often follow a Maslow need hierarchy, in which unsatisfied lower-level needs are top priority, but become lower priorities once the needs are satisfied [56]. Thus, users will initially be motivated by survival in terms of capabilities to process new workloads, followed by security once the workload-processing needs are satisfied, followed by self-actualization in terms of capabilities for analyzing the workload content for self-improvement and market trend insights once the security needs are satisfied. Chapter 1 of the recent *Handbook of Human Systems Integration* [57] summarizes the increased emphasis on human factors integration into systems engineering, and its state of progress in several large government organizations.

It is clear that requirements emergence is incompatible with past process practices such as requirements-driven sequential waterfall process models and formal programming calculi; and with process maturity models emphasizing repeatability and optimization [58]. In their place, more adaptive [12] and risk-driven [59] models are needed. More fundamentally, the theory underlying software process models needs to evolve from purely reductionist "modern" world views (universal, general, timeless, written) to a synthesis of these and situational "postmodern" world views (particular, local, timely, oral) as discussed in [60]. A recent theory of value-based software engineering (VBSE) and its associated software processes [61] provides a starting point for addressing these challenges, and for extending them to systems engineering processes. More recently, Fred Brooks' book, *The Design of Design*, contains a framework and numerous insights and case studies on balancing the modern and postmodern approaches when designing artifacts or systems [62].

A book on VBSE approaches [63] contains further insights and emerging directions for VBSE processes. For example, the chapter on "Stakeholder Value Proposition Elicitation and Reconciliation" in the VBSE book [64] addresses the need to evolve from software products, methods, tools, and educated students strongly focused on individual programming performance to a focus on more group-oriented interdisciplinary collaboration. Negotiation of priorities for requirements involves not only participation from users and acquirers on each requirement's relative mission or business value, but also participation from systems and software engineers on each requirement's relative cost and time to develop and difficulty of implementation.

The aforementioned *Handbook of Human Systems Integration* [57] identifies a number of additional principles and guidelines for integrating human factors concerns into the systems engineering process. In particular, it identifies the need to elevate human factor concerns from a micro-ergonomics to a macro-ergonomics focus on organization, roles, responsibilities, and group processes of collective observation, orientation, decision-making, and coordinated action.

More recently, a major National Research Council study called Human-System Integration in the System Development Process [65] identified some of the inhibitors to effective human-system integration, including hardware-oriented system engineering and management guidance, practices, and processes. It recommended an early version of the Incremental Commitment Spiral Model to be discussed in Sect. 3 as a way to balance hardware, software, and human factors engineering activities, and a set of recommended research areas. Some of its software-related recommendations are:

- Conduct a research program with the goal of revolutionizing the role of end users in designing the system they will use;
- Conduct research to understand the factors that contribute to system resilience, the role of people in resilient systems, and how to design more resilient systems;

- Refine and coordinate the definition of a systems development process that concurrently engineers the system's hardware, software, and human factors aspects, and accommodates the emergence of HSI requirements, such as the incremental commitment model;
- Research and develop shared representations to facilitate communication across different disciplines and life cycle phases;
- Research and develop improved methods and testbeds for systems of systems HSI; and
- Research and develop improved methods and tools for integrating incompatible legacy and external-system user interfaces.

These have led to several advanced environments and practices for stimulating collaborative cross-discipline innovation support. A summary of some of these is provided in [66]. It identified a number of critical success factors, such as including responsible play, focusing on team rewards, using both science and art, making it OK to fail, making it not-OK to not-fail, and competitive multi-sourcing.

2.7   Computational Plenty and Multicore Chips

As discussed in Sect. 1, the use of multicore chips to compensate for the decrease in Moore's Law rates of microcircuit speed increase will keep computing processor technology on the Moore's Law curve of computing operations per second, but will cause formidable problems in going from efficient sequential software programs to efficient parallel programs [4]. The supercomputer field has identified some classes of applications that can be relatively easily parallelized, such as computational fluid dynamics, weather prediction, Monte Carlo methods for modeling and simulation sensitivity analysis, parallel searching, and handling numerous independently-running programs in cloud computing. But for individual sequential programs, computations that need to wait for the results of other computations cannot proceed until the other computations finish, often leaving most of the processors unable to do useful work. In some cases, sequential programs will run more slowly on a multicore processor than on a single-core processor with comparable circuit speed. General solutions such as parallel programming languages (Patterson lists 50 attempts), optimizing compilers, and processor design can help somewhat, but the fundamental problems of sequential dependencies cannot be simply overcome. Two good recent sources of information on multicore technology and programming practices are the March 2010 special issue of IEEE Computer [67] and the summary of key multicore Internet resources in [68].

However, besides processors, the speed, reliability, and reduced cost of other information technologies such as data storage, communications bandwidth, display resolution, and mobile device capabilities and power consumption continue to increase. This computational plenty will spawn new types of platforms (smart dust, smart paint, smart materials, nanotechnology, micro electrical–mechanical systems: MEMS), and new types of applications (sensor networks, conformable or adaptive materials, human prosthetics). When combined with the rapid growth of 3D printing, these have been forecasted to generate a Third Industrial Revolution [69]. These will present process-related challenges for specifying their configurations and behavior; generating the resulting applications; verifying and validating their capabilities, performance, and dependability; and integrating them into even more complex systems of systems.

Besides new challenges, then, computational plenty will enable new and more powerful process-related approaches. It will enable new and more powerful self-monitoring software and computing via on-chip co-processors for assertion checking, trend analysis, intrusion detection, or verifying proof-carrying code. It will enable higher levels of abstraction, such as pattern-oriented programming, multi-aspect oriented programming, domain-oriented visual component assembly, and programming by example with expert feedback on missing portions. It will enable simpler brute-force solutions such as exhaustive case evaluation vs. complex logic.

It will also enable more powerful software, hardware, human factors, and systems engineering tools that provide feedback to developers based on domain knowledge, construction knowledge, human factors knowledge, systems engineering knowledge, or management knowledge. It will enable the equivalent of seat belts and air bags for user-programmers. It will support show-and-tell documentation and much more powerful system query and data mining techniques. It will support realistic virtual game-oriented systems and software engineering education and training. On balance, the added benefits of computational plenty should significantly outweigh the added challenges.

2.8   Increasing Integration of Software and Systems Engineering

Several trends have caused systems engineering and software engineering to initially evolve as largely sequential and independent processes. First, systems engineering began as a discipline for determining how best to configure various hardware components into physical systems such as ships, railroads, or defense systems. Once the systems were configured and their component functional and interface requirements were precisely specified, sequential external or internal contracts could be defined for producing the components. When software components began to appear in such systems, the natural thing to do was to treat them sequentially and independently as Computer Software Configuration Items.

Second, the early history of software engineering was heavily influenced by a highly formal and mathematical approach to specifying software components, and a reductionist approach to deriving computer software programs that correctly implemented the formal specifications. A "separation of concerns" was practiced, in which the responsibility of producing formalizable software requirements was left to others, most often hardware-oriented systems engineers. Some example quotes illustrating this approach are:

- "The notion of 'user' cannot be precisely defined, and therefore has no place in computer science or software engineering," E. W. Dijkstra, panel remarks, ICSE 4, 1979 [70].

- "Analysis and allocation of the system requirements is not the responsibility of the software engineering group but is a prerequisite for their work," CMU-SEI Software Capability Maturity Model, version 1.1, 1993 [58].

As a result, a generation of software engineering education and process improvement goals were focused on reductionist software development practices that assumed that other (mostly non-software people) would furnish appropriate pre-determined requirements for the software.

Third, the business practices of contracting for components were well worked out. Particularly in the government sector, acquisition regulations, specifications, and standards were in place and have been traditionally difficult to change. The path of least resistance was to follow a "purchasing agent" metaphor and sequentially specify requirements, establish contracts, formulate and implement solutions, and use the requirements to acceptance-test the solutions [71, 72]. When requirements and solutions were not well understood or changing rapidly, knowledgeable systems and software engineers and organizations could reinterpret the standards to operate more flexibly, concurrently and pragmatically and to produce satisfactory systems [73, 74]. But all too frequently, the sequential path of least resistance was followed, leading to the delivery of obsolete or poorly-performing systems.

As the pace of change increased and systems became more user-intensive and software-intensive, serious strains were put on the sequential approach. First, it was increasingly appreciated that the requirements for user-intensive systems were generally not pre-specifiable in advance, but emergent with use. This undermined the fundamental assumption of sequential specification and implementation.

Second, having people without software experience determine the software specifications often made the software much harder to produce, putting software even more prominently on the system development's critical path. Systems engineers without software experience would minimize computer speed and storage costs and capacities, which causes software costs to escalate rapidly [75]. They would choose best-of-breed system components whose software was incompatible and time-consuming to integrate. They would assume that adding more resources would speed up turnaround time or software delivery schedules, not being aware of slowdown phenomena such as multiprocessor overhead [75] or Brooks' Law (adding more people to a late software project will make it later) [76].

Third, software people were recognizing that their sequential, reductionist processes were not conducive to producing user-satisfactory software, and were developing alternative software engineering processes (evolutionary, spiral, agile) involving more and more systems engineering activities. Concurrently, systems engineering people were coming to similar conclusions about their sequential, reductionist processes, and developing alternative "soft systems engineering" processes (e.g., [73]), emphasizing the continuous learning aspects of developing successful user-intensive systems. Similarly, the project management field is undergoing questioning about its underlying specification-planning-execution-control theory being obsolete and needing more emphasis on adaptation and value generation [77].

2.8.1 Systems and Software Engineering Process Implications

Many commercial organizations have developed more flexible and concurrent development processes [78]. Also, recent process guidelines and standards such as the Integrated Capability Maturity Model (CMMI) [79], ISO/IEC 12207 for software engineering [34], and ISO/IEC 15288 for systems engineering [35] emphasize the need to integrate systems and software engineering processes, along with hardware engineering processes and human engineering processes. They emphasize such practices as concurrent engineering of requirements and solutions, integrated product and process development, and risk-driven vs. document-driven processes. New process milestones enable effective synchronization and stabilization of concurrent processes [80, 81].

However, contractual acquisition processes still lag behind technical processes. Many organizations and projects develop concurrent and adaptive development processes, only to find them frustrated by progress payments and award fees emphasizing compliance with sequential document-driven deliverables. More recently, though, corporate and professional organizations have been integrating their software and systems engineering activities (e.g., Systems and Software Consortium, Inc., Systems and Software Technology Conference, Practical Systems and Software Measurement). A number of software engineering methods and tools have been extended to address systems engineering, such as the extension of the Unified Modeling Language into the Systems Modeling Language [82]. Recent software engineering Body of Knowledge compendia such as the Graduate Software Engineering 2009 Curriculum Guidelines [83] supported by ACM, IEEE, and INCOSE have strongly integrated software and systems engineering. A similar effort in the systems engineering area, the Systems Engineering Body of Knowledge [84], strongly emphasizes the integration of systems and software engineering. And software process models such as the spiral model have been extended to integrate software and systems engineering, such as the Incremental Commitment Spiral Model to be discussed in Sect. 3.

2.9 Wild Cards: Autonomy and Bio-Computing

"Autonomy" covers technology advancements that use computational plenty to enable computers and software to autonomously evaluate situations and determine best-possible courses of action. Examples include:

- Cooperative intelligent agents that assess situations, analyze trends, and cooperatively negotiate to determine best available courses of action;
- Autonomic software that uses adaptive control techniques to reconfigure itself to cope with changing situations;
- Machine learning techniques that construct and test alternative situation models and converge on versions of models that will best guide system behavior; and
- Extensions of robots at conventional-to-nanotechnology scales empowered with autonomy capabilities such as the above.

Combinations of biology and computing include:

- Biology-based computing, which uses biological or molecular phenomena to solve computational problems beyond the reach of silicon-based technology, and
- Computing-based enhancement of human physical or mental capabilities, perhaps embedded in or attached to human bodies or serving as alternate robotic hosts for (portions of) human bodies.

Examples of books describing these capabilities are Kurzweil's *The Age of Spiritual Machines* [85] and Drexler's books *Engines of Creation* and *Unbounding the Future: The Nanotechnology Revolution* [86, 87]. They identify major benefits that can potentially be derived from such capabilities, such as artificial labor, human shortfall compensation (the five senses, healing, life span, and new capabilities for enjoyment or self-actualization), adaptive control of the environment, or redesigning the world to avoid current problems and create new opportunities.

On the other hand, these books and other sources such as Dyson's *Darwin Among the Machines: The Evolution of Global Intelligence* [88] and Joy's article, "Why the Future Doesn't Need Us" [89], and Crichton's bio/nanotechnology novel *Prey* [90], identify major failure modes that can result from attempts to redesign the world, such as loss of human primacy over computers, overempowerment of humans, and irreversible effects such as plagues or biological dominance of artificial species. From a software process standpoint, processes will be needed to cope with autonomy software failure modes such as undebuggable self-modified software, adaptive control instability, interacting agent commitments with unintended consequences, and commonsense reasoning failures.

As discussed in Dreyfus and Dreyfus' *Mind Over Machine* [91], the track record of artificial intelligence predictions shows that it is easy to overestimate the rate of AI progress. But a good deal of AI technology is usefully at work today and, as we have seen with the Internet and World Wide Web, it is also easy to underestimate rates of IT progress as well. It is likely that the more ambitious predictions above will not take place by 2025, but it is more important to keep both the positive and negative potentials in mind in risk-driven experimentation with emerging capabilities in these wild-card areas between now and 2025.

3 A Scalable Spiral Process Model for Twenty-First Century Systems and Software

3.1 Twenty-First Century System and Software Development and Evolution Modes

In the next 10–20 years, several twenty-first century system and software development and evolution modes will have emerged as the most cost-effective ways to develop needed capabilities in the context of the trends discussed in Sect. 2. The four most common modes are likely to be exploratory development of unprecedented capabilities, business model-based user programming, hardware and software product lines, and network-centric systems of systems. Each is discussed below, along with the primary processes that will most likely best fit their situations.

Exploratory development processes will continue to be used for new products in mainstream organizations and in new areas such as nanotechnology, advanced biotechnology and robotics, virtual reality, and cooperative agent-based systems. They will still focus on highly flexible processes for skill-intensive rapid prototyping. But pressures for rapid transition from prototype to fielded product will increase the emphasis on the concept development phase to meet criteria for demonstrating that the new concepts can be made sufficiently robust, scalable, and cost-effectively producible. The process and associated product capabilities will also need to be selectively open in order to support open-innovation forms of collaborative development with other companies providing complementary capabilities [66, 92].

Business model-based user programming will expand its scope to continue to address the need to produce more and more software capabilities by enabling them to be produced directly by users, as with spreadsheet programs, computer-aided design and manufacturing (CAD/CAM) and website development and evolution. Much of the expanded scope will be provided by better-integrated and more tailorable Enterprise Resource Planning (ERP) COTS packages. As discussed in Sect. 2.7, computational plenty and increased domain understanding will enable more powerful, safer, and easier-to-use user programming capabilities such as programming-by-example with expert-system feedback on missing portions. Larger extensions to the ERP framework may be carried out by in-house software development, but specialty houses with product-line-based solutions will become an increasingly attractive outsourcing solution.

General web-based user programming was just emerging into significance in 2005, and has rapidly burgeoned in the subsequent 5 years. The emergence of new mass-collaboration platforms such as YouTube, Facebook, the iPhone, and computing clouds has created an open marketplace for composable applications and services, and a software engineering area called opportunistic system development [93]. Although there are still composability challenges among these applications and services, technology is emerging to address them [94].

Hardware and software product lines on the hardware side will increasingly include product lines for transportation, communications, medical, construction, and other equipment. On the software side, they will increasingly include product lines for business services, public services, and information infrastructure. Compared to current product lines in these areas, the biggest challenges will be the increasing rates of change and decreasing half-lives of product line architectures, and the increasing proliferation of product line variabilities caused by globalization.

Network-centric systems of systems. As discussed in Sect. 2.6, similar challenges are being faced by organizations in the process of transforming themselves from collections of weakly coordinated, vertically integrated stovepipe systems into seamlessly interoperable network-centric systems of systems (NCSOS). The architectures of these NCSOS are highly software-intensive and, as with the product line architectures above, need to be simultaneously robust, scalable, and evolvable

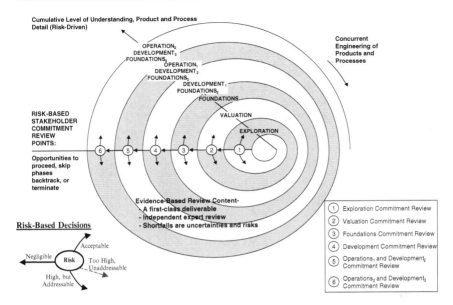

Fig. 4 The incremental commitment spiral model

in flexible but controllable ways. In Sect. 3.2, we describe an emerging scalable spiral process model for developing and evolving twenty-first century product lines and NCSOS.

3.2 Overview of the Incremental Commitment Spiral Model

Based on our experiences in adapting the spiral model to the development of software-intensive systems of systems representative of the twenty-first century trends discussed above, we have been converging on a scalable spiral process model that has shown in several implementations to date to scale well and help projects avoid many sources of project failure, from small e-services applications [95] to superlarge defense systems of systems [41], and multi-enterprise supply chain management systems.

A view of the Incremental Commitment Spiral Model is shown in Fig. 4. As with the original spiral model, its expanding spirals reflect increasing cumulative levels of system understanding, cost, development time, product detail, and process detail. These do not expand uniformly, but as a function of the relative risks of doing too much or too little of product and process definition. Thus, valuation and selection of COTS products may be the highest-risk item and receive most of the early effort, or it might be prototyping of user interfaces, operational concept scenarios, or alternative vehicle platform configurations.

Each spiral will be concurrently rather than sequentially addressing requirements and solutions; products and processes; hardware, software and human factors aspects; and business case analysis of alternative product configurations or product line investments. All of this concurrency is synchronized and stabilized by having the development team collaborate in producing not only artifacts, but also evidence of their combined feasibility. This evidence is then assessed at the various stakeholder commitment decision milestones by independent experts, and any shortfalls in evidence are considered as uncertainties or probabilities of loss, which when multiplied by the relative or absolute size of the prospective loss, becomes its level of Risk Exposure. Any such significant risks should then be addressed by a risk mitigation plan.

The stakeholders then consider the risks and risk mitigation plans, and decide on a course of action. If the risks are acceptable and well covered by risk mitigation plans, the project would proceed into the next spiral. If the risks are high but addressable, the project would remain in the current spiral until the risks are resolved (e.g., working out safety cases for a safety-critical system, or producing acceptable versions of missing risk mitigation plans). If the risks are negligible (e.g., finding at the end of the Exploration spiral that the solution can be easily produced via an already-owned COTS package which has been successfully used to produce more complex applications), there would be no need to perform a Valuation and a Foundations spiral, and the project could go straight into Development. If the risk is too high and unaddressable (e.g., the market window for such a product has already closed), the project should be terminated or rescoped, perhaps to address a different market sector whose market window is clearly sufficiently open. This outcome is shown by the dotted line "going into the third dimension" in the Risk-Based Decisions figure at the lower left of Fig. 4, but is not visible for reasons of simplicity on the numbered circles in the larger spiral diagram.

The Development spirals after the first Development Commitment Review follow the three-team incremental development approach for achieving both agility and assurance shown in Fig. 2 and discussed in Sect. 2.2.1.

3.2.1 Other Views of the Incremental Commitment Spiral Model (ICSM)

Figure 5 presents an updated view of the ICSM life cycle process recommended in the National Research Council "Human-System Integration in the System Development Process" study [65]. It was called the Incremental Commitment Model (ICM) in the study, and given the study's sponsorship by the U.S. Department of Defense (DoD), also showed the DoD Instruction 5000.02 phases and milestones along with their generic ICSM counterparts.

The ICSM builds on the strengths of current process models: early verification and validation concepts in the V-model, concurrency concepts in the Concurrent Engineering model, lighter-weight concepts in the Agile and Lean models, risk-driven concepts in the spiral model, the phases and anchor points in the Rational Unified Process (RUP) [80, 96], and recent extensions of the spiral model to address SoS capability acquisition [97].

In comparison to the software-intensive RUP (the closest widely-used predecessor to the ICSM), the ICSM also addresses hardware and human factors integration.

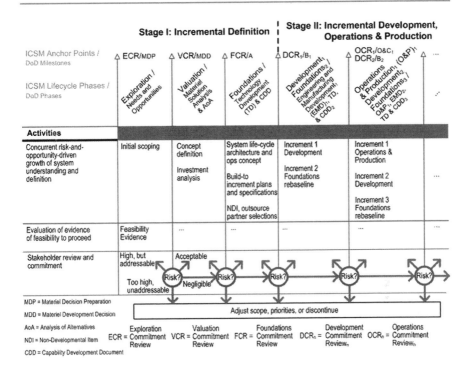

Fig. 5 Phased view of the generic incremental commitment spiral model process

It extends the RUP phases to cover the full system life cycle: an Exploration phase precedes the RUP Inception phase, which is refocused on valuation and investment analysis. The RUP Elaboration phase is refocused on Foundations (a term based on the [40] approach to Systems Architecting, describing concurrent development of requirements, architecture, and plans as the essential foundations for Engineering and Manufacturing Development), to which it adds feasibility evidence as a first-class deliverable. The RUP Construction and Transition phases are combined into Development; and an additional Operations phase combines operations, production, maintenance, and phase-out. Also, the names of the milestones are changed to emphasize that their objectives are to ensure stakeholder commitment to proceed to the next level of resource expenditure based on a thorough feasibility and risk analysis, and not just on the existence of a set of system objectives and a set of architecture diagrams. Thus, the RUP Life Cycle Objectives (LCO) milestone is called the Foundations Commitment Review (FCR) in the ICSM and the RUP Life Cycle Architecture (LCA) milestone is called the Development Commitment Review (DCR).

The top row of Activities in Fig. 5 indicates that a number of system aspects are being concurrently engineered at an increasing level of understanding, definition, and development. The most significant of these aspects are shown in Fig. 6, an

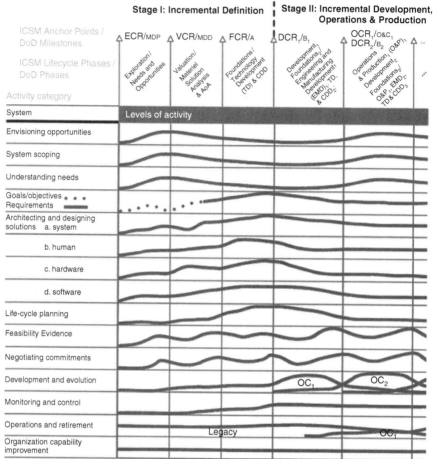

Fig. 6 ICSM activity categories and level of effort

extension of a similar "hump diagram" view of concurrently engineered software projects developed as part of the RUP [96].

As with the RUP version, it should be emphasized that the magnitude and shape of the levels of effort will be risk-driven and likely to vary from project to project. In particular, they are likely to have mini risk/opportunity-driven peaks and valleys, rather than the smooth curves shown for simplicity in Fig. 6. The main intent of this view is to emphasize the necessary concurrency of the primary success-critical activities shown as rows in Fig. 6. Thus, in interpreting the Exploration column, although system scoping is the primary objective of the Exploration phase, doing it well involves a considerable amount of activity in understanding needs, envisioning opportunities, identifying and reconciling stakeholder goals and objectives, architecting solutions, life cycle planning, evaluating alternatives, and negotiating stakeholder commitments.

For example, if one were exploring the initial scoping of a new medical device product line, one would not just interview a number of stakeholders and compile a list of their expressed needs into a requirements specification. One would also *envision and explore opportunities* for using alternative technologies, perhaps via competitive prototyping. In the area of *understanding needs*, one would determine relevant key performance parameters, scenarios, and evaluation criteria for evaluating the prototypers' results. And via the prototypes, one would explore alternative *architectural concepts* for developing, producing, and evolving the medical device product line; *evaluate* their relative feasibility, benefits, and risks for stakeholders to review; and if the risks and rewards are acceptable to the stakeholders, *negotiate commitments* of further resources to proceed into a Valuation phase with a clearer understanding of what level of capabilities would be worth exploring as downstream requirements. For a successful commercial example, see [[65]; Chap. 5] and [84].

Figure 6 indicates that a great deal of concurrent activity occurs within and across the various ICM phases, all of which needs to be synchronized and stabilized (a best-practice term taken from *Microsoft Secrets* [98]) to keep the project under control. To make this concurrency work, the evidence-based anchor point milestone reviews are used to synchronize, stabilize, and risk-assess the ensemble of artifacts at the end of each phase. Each of these anchor point milestone reviews, labeled at the top of Fig. 6, is focused on developer-produced and expert-reviewed *evidence*, instead of individual PowerPoint charts and Unified Modeling Language (UML) diagrams with associated assertions and assumptions, to help the key stakeholders determine the next level of commitment. A tailorable Feasibility Evidence Data Item Description for contract use is provided in [99].

The review processes and the use of independent experts are based on the highly successful AT&T Architecture Review Board procedures described in [100]. Figure 7 shows the content of the Feasibility Evidence Description. Showing the feasibility of the concurrently-developed elements helps synchronize and stabilize the concurrent activities.

The Operations Commitment Review (OCR) is different, in that it addresses the often much higher operational risks of fielding an inadequate system. In general, stakeholders will experience a factor of two-to-ten increase in commitment level in going through the sequence of ECR to DCR milestones, but the increase in going from DCR to OCR can be much higher. These commitment levels are based on typical cost profiles across the various stages of the acquisition life-cycle.

3.2.2 Underlying ICSM Principles

At least as important as the diagrams depicting the ICSM views are its *four underlying principles*. If a project just follows the diagrams without following the principles (as often happened with the original spiral model), the project will have a serious risk of failure. The four principles are [101]:

Feasibility Evidence Description Content

Evidence *provided by developer* and *validated by independent experts* that if the system is built to the specified architecture, it will:

- Satisfy the requirements: capability, interfaces, level of service, and evolution

- Support the operational concept

- Be buildable within the budgets and schedules in the plan

- Generate a viable return on investment

- Generate satisfactory outcomes for all of the success-critical stakeholders

- Resolve all major risks by risk management plans

- Serve as basis for stakeholders' commitment to proceed

Fig. 7 Feasibility evidence description content

1. *Stakeholder value-based system definition and evolution.* If a project fails to include success-critical stakeholders such as end-users, maintainers, or suppliers, these stakeholders will frequently feel little commitment to the project and either underperform or refuse to use the results.
2. *Incremental commitment and accountability.* If success-critical stakeholders are not accountable for their commitments, they are likely to be drawn away to other pursuits when they are most needed.
3. *Concurrent system and software definition and development.* If definition and development of requirements and solutions; hardware, software, and human factors; or product and process definition are done sequentially, the project is likely both to go more slowly, and to make early, hard-to-undo commitments that cut off the best options for project success.
4. *Evidence and risk-based decision making.* If key decisions are made based on assertions, vendor literature, or meeting an arbitrary schedule without access to evidence of feasibility, the project is building up risks. And in the words of Tom Gilb, "If you do not actively attack the risks, the risks will actively attack you."

3.2.3   Model Experience to Date

During the National Research Council Human-Systems Integration study, it was found that the ICSM processes and principles corresponded well with best commercial practices. A good example documented in the study showed its application to a highly successful commercial medical infusion pump development [[65], Chap. 5]. A counterpart well-documented successful government-acquisition project using its principles was the CCPDS-R project described in Appendix D of [74].

A further source of successful projects that have applied the ICSM principles is the annual series of Top-5 software-intensive systems projects published in *CrossTalk* [102]. The "Top-5 Quality Software Projects" were chosen annually by panels of leading experts as role models of best practices and successful outcomes.

Of the 20 Top-5 projects in 2002 through 2005, 16 explicitly used concurrent engineering; 14 explicitly used risk-driven development; and 15 explicitly used incrementally-committed evolutionary, iterative system growth, while additional projects gave indications of their partial use (The project summaries did not include discussion of stakeholder involvement). Evidence of successful results of stakeholder-satisficing can be found in the annual series of University of Southern California (USC) e-Services projects using the Win-Win Spiral model as described in [95]. Since 1998, over 100 user-intensive e-Services applications have used precursor and current versions of the ICSM to achieve a 92 % success rate of on-time delivery of stakeholder-satisfactory systems. Its use on the ultralarge Future Combat Systems program enabled the sponsors to much better identify and deal with the software-intensive program risks, in particular, and identify improved courses of action [41].

A word of caution is that experiences to date indicate that the three teams' activities during evolutionary development are not as neatly orthogonal as they look in Fig. 2. Feedback on development shortfalls from the V&V team either requires a response from the development team (early fixes will be less disruptive and expensive than later fixes), or deferral to a later increment, adding work and coordination by the agile team. The agile team's analyses and prototypes addressing how to accommodate changes and deferred capabilities need to draw on the experience and expertise of the plan-driven development team, requiring some additional development team resources and calendar time. Additional challenges arise if different versions of each increment are going to be deployed in different ways into different environments. The model has sufficient degrees of freedom to address such challenges, but they need to be planned for within the project's schedules and budgets.

4   Implications for Twenty-First Century Enterprise Processes

In working with our commercial and aerospace affiliates on how they can best evolve to succeed as twenty-first century enterprises, we have found several twentieth century process-related institutions that need to be significantly rethought and reworked to contribute to success. We will discuss two leading examples below: acquisition practices and human relations. In the interest of brevity, some other important institutions needing rethinking and rework but not discussed in detail are continuous process improvement (repeatability and optimization around the past vs. adaptability and optimization around the future); supplier management (adversarial win-lose vs. team-oriented win-win); internal R&D strategies (core capability research plus external technology experimentation vs. full-spectrum self-invention); and enterprise integration (not-invented-here stovepipes vs. enterprise-wide learning and sharing).

4.1   Adaptive Versus Purchasing-Agent Acquisition

The twentieth century purchasing agent or contracts manager is most comfortable with a fixed procurement to a set of pre-specified requirements; selection of the least-cost, technically adequate supplier; and a minimum of bothersome requirements changes. Many of our current acquisition institutions—regulations, specifications, standards, contract types, award fee structures, reviews and audits—are optimized around this procurement model.

Such institutions have been the bane of many projects attempting to deliver successful systems in a world of emerging requirements and rapid change. The project people may put together good technical and management strategies to do concurrent problem and solution definition, teambuilding, and mutual-learning prototypes and options analyses. Then they find that their progress payments and award fees involve early delivery of complete functional and performance specifications. Given the choice between following their original strategies and getting paid, they proceed to get paid and marry themselves in haste to a set of premature requirements, and then find themselves repenting at leisure for the rest of the project (if any leisure time is available).

Build-to-specification contract mechanisms still have their place, but it is just for the stabilized increment development team in Fig. 2. If such mechanisms are applied to the agile rebaselining teams, frustration and chaos ensues. What is needed for the three-team approach is separate contracting mechanisms for the three team functions, under an overall contract structure that enables them to be synchronized and rebalanced across the life cycle. Also needed are source selection mechanisms more likely to choose the most competent supplier, using such approaches as competitive exercises to develop representative system artifacts using the people, products, processes, methods, and tools in the offeror's proposal.

A good transitional role model is the CCPDS-R project described in [74]. Its US Air Force customer and TRW contractor (selected using a competitive exercise such as the one described above) reinterpreted the traditional defense regulations, specifications, and standards. They held a Preliminary Design Review: not a PowerPoint show at Month 4, but a fully validated architecture and demonstration of the working high-risk user interface and networking capabilities at Month 14. The resulting system delivery, including over a million lines of software source code, exceeded customer expectations within budget and schedule.

Other good acquisition approaches are the Scandinavian Participatory Design approach [33], Checkland's Soft Systems Methodology [73], lean acquisition and development processes [23], and Vested Outsourcing contracting mechanisms and award fee structures [103, 104]. These all reflect the treatment of acquisition using an adaptive-system metaphor rather than a purchasing-agent metaphor.

4.2   Human Relations

Traditional twentieth century human relations or personnel organizations and processes tend to emphasize individual vs. team-oriented reward structures and monolithic career paths. These do not fit well with the team-oriented, diverse-skill needs required for twenty-first century success.

In *Balancing Agility and Discipline* [14], we found that "plan the work and work the plan" oriented people are drawn toward organizations that thrive on order. People there feel comfortable and empowered if there are clear policies and procedures defining how to succeed. On the other hand, agility people are drawn toward organizations that thrive on chaos. People there feel comfortable and empowered if they have few policies and procedures, and many degrees of freedom to determine how to succeed. In our USC Balancing Agility and Discipline Workshops, we found that most of our affiliates had cultures that were strongly oriented toward one of these poles, with the challenge of evolving toward the other pole without losing the good features of their existing culture and staff. More recently, these workshops have surfaced the Architected Agile approach summarized in Sect. 2.1 [7].

The three-team approach presented in Sect. 2.2.1 provides a way for organizations to develop multiple role-oriented real or virtual skill centers with incentive structures and career paths focused both on excellence within one's preferred role and teamwork with the other contributors to success. Some other key considerations are the need for some rotation of people across team roles or as part of integrated product teams to avoid overspecialization, and the continual lookout for people who are good at all three team roles; they will be strong candidates for project-level or organization-level management or technical leadership careers.

A good framework for pursuing a human relations strategy for twenty-first century success is the People Capability Maturity Model [105]. Its process areas on participatory culture, workgroup development, competency development, career development, empowered workgroups, and continuous workforce innovation emphasize the types of initiatives necessary to empower people and organizations (such as the purchasing agents and departments discussed above) to cope with the challenges of twenty-first century system development. The P-CMM book also has several case studies of the benefits realized by organizations adopting the model for their human relations activities. The Collins *Good to Great* book [106] is organized around a stepwise approach characterizing the 11 outstanding performance companies' transformation into cultures having both an ethic of entrepreneurship and a culture of discipline. It begins with getting the right people and includes setting ambitious but achievable goals and constancy of purpose in achieving them.

5   Conclusions

The surprise-free and wild-card twenty-first century trends discussed in Sect. 2 provide evidence that significant changes in and integration of systems and software engineering processes will be needed for successful twenty-first century enterprises.

Particularly important are changes that emphasize value generation and enable dynamic balancing of the agility, discipline, and scalability necessary to cope with the twenty-first century challenges of increasing rapid change, high dependability, and scalability to globally-integrated, software-intensive systems of systems.

Section 3 presents an incremental commitment spiral model (ICSM) process framework and set of product and process strategies for coping with these challenges. They are proving to be effective as we evolve them with our industry and government affiliate organizations. The product strategies involve system and software architectures that encapsulate sources of rapid unpredictable change into elements developed by agile teams within a framework and set of elements developed by a plan-driven team. The process strategies involve stabilized increment development executed by the plan-driven team and verified and validated by a V&V team, along with concurrent agile, pro-active change assessment and renegotiation of stable plans and specifications for executing the next increment, as shown in Fig. 2.

However, process and architecture strategies are only necessary and not sufficient conditions for enterprise success. Section 4 identifies and describes some of the complementary organizational initiatives that will be necessary to enable the product and process strategies to succeed. These include rethinking and reworking acquisition contracting practices, human relations, continuous process improvement, supplier management, internal R&D strategies, and enterprise integration.

Another consideration is that the future of software engineering will be in the hands of students learning software engineering over the next two decades. They will be practicing their profession well into the 2040s, 2050s and probably 2060s. The pace of change continues to accelerate, as does the complexity of the systems. This presents many serious, but exciting, challenges to software engineering education and practice, including:

- Anticipating future trends (e.g., via collection and analysis of empirical data) and preparing students to deal with them;
- Capitalizing on information technology to enable the delivery of just-in-time and web-based education;
- Monitoring current principles and practices and separating timeless principles from outdated practices;
- Participating in leading-edge systems and software engineering research and practice, and incorporating the results into project practice and the curriculum;
- Packaging smaller-scale educational experiences in ways that apply to large-scale projects;
- Helping students learn how to learn, through state-of-the-art analyses, future-oriented educational games and exercises, and participation in research; and
- Offering lifelong learning opportunities for systems and software engineers who must update their skills to keep pace with the evolution of best practices, and individuals entering the software engineering field from outside disciplines, who need further education to make the transition successfully.

Underlying and strengthening all of these critical success factors are commitments to and investments in evidence-based systems and software engineering.

Stakeholders' use of feasibility evidence to determine the risks of deciding to go forward at key project decision milestones, as discussed in Sect. 3.2.1, is critical to project success, as shortfalls in feasibility evidence are uncertainties or Probabilities of Loss, which when multiplied by their counterpart Sizes of Loss, become Risk Exposures.

Once developed, such feasibility evidence becomes an extremely valuable database that can be analyzed for trends in an organization's critical project success factors. As an example, the data collected in Fig. 3 on the growth of COTS (and later, cloud services) intensiveness of our web service applications enabled us to develop and evolve methods, processes, and tools for COTS-based systems assessment, tailoring, and integration, at a time that a leading software engineering journal was telling its readers that software engineering success was all about programming.

As a final conclusion, it is appropriate to recognize the seminal contributions to empirical evidence-based software engineering of Prof. Dieter Rombach. These began with his contributions at the University of Maryland with Prof. Victor Basili and others to such key empirical methods and the Goal-Question-Metric and Experience Factory approaches [107, 108], followed by his leadership of the Fraunhofer Institute for Experimental Software Engineering, widely recognized as the premier role model organization in successfully researching, developing, and applying empirical software engineering methods, processes, and tools for industrial application [109], and in contributions to its underlying concepts and theories [110].

References

1. Schon, D.: The Reflective Practitioner. Basic Books, New York (1983)
2. Boehm, B.: The Future of Software and Systems Engineering Processes, Technical Report USC-CSE-2005-507 (2005)
3. Boehm, B.: Some future software engineering opportunities and challenges. In: Sebastian Nanz (ed.) The Future of Software Engineering, pp. 1–32. doi:10.1007/978-3-642-15187-3_1, Springer, Berlin/Heidelberg (2011)
4. Patterson, D.: The trouble with multicore, IEEE Spectrum. 28–32, 52–53 (2010)
5. Adomavicius, G., Tuzhilin, A.: Toward the next generation of recommender systems: a survey of the state-of-the-art and possible extensions. IEEE Trans. Knowl. Data Eng. **17**(6), 734–749 (2005)
6. Cusumano, M.: The Business of Software. Free Press/Simon & Schuster, New York (2004)
7. Boehm, B., Lane, J., Koolmanojwong, S., Turner, R.: Architected Agile Solutions for Software-Reliant Systems, Proceedings, INCOSE (2010)
8. Wikipedia: "Social networking service;" "Web application" (2013)
9. Grady, R.: Successful Software Process Improvement. Prentice Hall, Upper Saddle River (1997)
10. Beck, K.: Extreme Programming Explained. Addison Wesley, Harlow (1999)
11. Cockburn, A.: Agile Software Development. Addison Wesley, Boston (2002)
12. Highsmith, J.: Adaptive Software Development. Dorset House, New York (2000)
13. Schwaber, K., Beedle, M.: Agile Software Development with Scrum. Prentice Hall, Upper Saddle River (2002)
14. Boehm, B., Turner, R.: Balancing Agility and Discipline. Addison Wesley, Boston (2004)
15. Ferguson, J.: Crouching dragon, hidden software: software in DOD weapon systems. IEEE Softw. **18**(4), 105–107 (2001)

16. PITAC (President's Information Technology Advisory Committee): Report to the President: Information Technology Research: Investing in Our Future (1999)
17. Boehm, B., Hoare, C.A.R. (eds.): Proceedings, 1975 International Conference on Reliable Software. ACM/IEEE (1975)
18. Musa, J.: Software reliability engineering. McGraw Hill, New York (1999)
19. Humphrey, W.: Introduction to the Personal Software Process. Addison Wesley, Reading (1997)
20. Humphrey, W.: Introduction to the Team Software Process. Addison Wesley, Reading (2000)
21. Gerrard, P., Thompson, N.: Risk-Based E-Business Testing. Artech House, Boston (2002)
22. Huang, L.: A value-based process achieving software dependability. Proceedings, Software Process Workshop 2005 (2005)
23. Womack, J., Jones, D.: Lean Thinking: Banish Waste and Create Wealth in Your Corporation. Simon & Schuster, New York (1996)
24. Hollnagel, E., Woods, D., Leveson, N. (eds.): Resilience Engineering: Concepts and Precepts. Ashgate Publishing, Burlington (2006)
25. Jackson, S.: Architecting Resilient Systems. Wiley, Oxford (2009)
26. ISO (International Standards Organization): Systems and Software Engineering – Systems and Software Assurance – Part 2: Assurance Case (ISO/IEC 15026) (2009)
27. Yin, X., Knight, J.: Formal Verification of Large Software Systems, Proceedings, NASA Formal Methods Symposium 2 (2010)
28. Leveson, N.: Engineering a Safer World. MIT Press, Cambridge (2011)
29. Parnas, D.: Designing software for ease of extension and contraction. Trans. Softw. Eng., IEEE, SE-5, (1979)
30. Bass, L., John, B.E.: Linking usability to software architecture patterns through general scenarios. J. Syst. Softw. 66(3), 187–197 (2003)
31. Anderson, D.: Kanban. Blue Hole Press (2010)
32. Arthur, W.B.: Increasing returns and the new world of business. Harvard Business Review 74, 100–109 (1996)
33. Ehn, P. (ed.): Work-Oriented Design of Computer Artifacts, Lawrence Earlbaum Assoc. (1990)
34. ISO (International Standards Organization): Standard for Information Technology – Software Life Cycle Processes. ISO/IEC 12207 (1995)
35. ISO (International Standards Organization): Systems Engineering – System Life Cycle Processes. ISO/IEC 15288 (2002)
36. Zachman, J.: A framework for information systems architecture. IBM Syst. J. 26(3), 276–292 (1987)
37. Putman, J.: Architecting with RM-ODP. Prentice Hall, Upper Saddle River (2001)
38. FCIO (Federal CIO Council): A Practical Guide to Federal Enterprise Architecture, version 1.0. (2001)
39. Harned, D., Lundquist, J.: What transformation means for the defense industry. The McKinsey Q. 57–63 (2003)
40. Rechtin, E.: Systems Architecting. Prentice Hall, Englewood Cliffs (1991)
41. Blanchette, S., Crosson, S., Boehm, B.: Evaluating the Software Design of a Complex System of Systems, CMU/SEI Tech Report CMU/SEI-2009-TR-023, (2010) January
42. Boehm, B., Brown, A.W., Basili, V., Turner, R.: Spiral acquisition of software-intensive systems of systems. CrossTalk 17(5), 4–9 (2004)
43. Crawford, D.: Editorial pointers. Comm. ACM 5 (2001)
44. Standish Group: Extreme Chaos. http://www.standishgroup.com (2001)
45. Yang, Y., Bhuta, J., Port, D., Boehm, B.: Value-based processes for COTS-based applications. IEEE Softw. 22, 54–62 (2005)
46. Koolmanojwong, S.: The Incremental Commitment Model process patterns for rapid-fielding projects, Qualifying Exam Report. Also TR USC-CSSE-2009-526 (2009)
47. Price, H., Morley, J.: Create, apply, and amplify: a story of technology development. SEI Monit. 2 (2009)

48. Hopkins, R., Jenkins, K.: Eating the IT Elephant: Moving from Greenfield Development to Brownfield. IBM Press, Upper Saddle River (2008)
49. Lewis, G., Morris, E.J., Smith, D.B., Simanta, S.: SMART: Analyzing the Reuse Potential of Legacy Components on a Service-Oriented Architecture Environment, CMU/SEI-2008-TN-008 (2008)
50. Boehm, B.: Applying the Incremental Commitment Model to Brownfield Systems Development, Proceedings, CSER 2009 (2009)
51. Albert, C., Brownsword, L.: Evolutionary Process for Integrating COTS-Based Systems (EPIC): An Overview. CMU/SEI-2003-TR-009. Software Engineering Institute, Pittsburgh (2002)
52. Büttcher, S., Clarke, L., Cormack, G.: Information Retrieval: Implementing and Evaluating Search Engines. MIT Press, Cambridge (2010)
53. Koren, Y., Bell, R., Volinsky, C.: Matrix factorization techniques for recommender systems. IEEE Comput. **42**, 30–37 (2009)
54. Nagappan, N., Zimmermann, T., Zeller, A. (eds.): Special issue on mining software archives, IEEE Softw. (2009)
55. Anthes, G.: The future of IT. Computerworld. 27–36 (2005)
56. Maslow, A.: Motivation and Personality. Harper and Row (1954)
57. Booher, H. (ed.): Handbook of Human Systems Integration. Wiley, Hoboken (2003)
58. Paulk, M., Weber, C., Curtis, B., Chrissis, M.: The Capability Maturity Model. Addison Wesley, Reading (1994)
59. Boehm, B.: A spiral model for software development and enhancement. IEEE Comput. **21**, 61–72 (1988)
60. Toulmin, S.: Cosmopolis. University of Chicago Press, Chicago (1992)
61. Boehm, B. and Jain, A.: An initial theory of value-based software engineering. In: Aurum, A., Biffl, S., Boehm, B., Erdogmus, H., Gruenbacher, P. (eds.): Value-Based Software Engineering. Springer (2005)
62. Brooks, F.: The Design of Design. Addison Wesley, Upper Saddle River (2010)
63. Biffl, S., Aurum, A., Boehm, B., Erdogmus, H., Gruenbacher, P. (eds.): Value-Based Software Engineering. Springer (2005)
64. Gruenbacher, P., Koszegi, S., Biffl, S.: Stakeholder value proposition elicitation and reconciliation. In: Aurum, A., Biffl, S., Boehm, B., Erdogmus, H., Gruenbacher, P. (eds.) Value-Based Software Engineering. Springer (2005)
65. Pew, R., Mavor, A. (eds.): Human-System Integration in the System development Process: A New Look. National Academies Press, Washington (2007)
66. Lane, J., Boehm, B., Bolas, M., Madni, A., Turner, R.: Critical Success Factors for Rapid, Innovative Solutions, Proceedings, ICSP 2010 (2010)
67. IEEE Computer: Special Issue on Multicore Programming (2010)
68. Doernhofer, M.: Multicore and multithreaded programming. ACM Sofw. Eng. Notes. 8–16 (2010)
69. Markillie, P.: A third industrial revolution, The economist special report (2012) April 21
70. Dijkstra, E.: Panel remarks. Software Engineering: As It Should Be. ICSE 4 – See also EWD 791 at http://www.cs.utexas/users/EWD (1979)
71. U.S. Department of Defense, MIL-STD-1521B: Reviews and Audits (1985)
72. U.S. Department of Defense, DOD-STD-2167A: Defense System Software Development (1988)
73. Checkland, P.: Systems Thinking, Systems Practice, 2nd edn. Wiley, Chichester (1999)
74. Royce, W.E.: Software Project Management. Addison Wesley, Reading (1998)
75. Boehm, B.: Software Engineering Economics. Prentice Hall, Englewood Cliffs (1981)
76. Brooks, F.: The Mythical Man-Month, 2nd edn. Addison Wesley, Reading (1995)
77. Koskela, L., Howell, L.: The Underlying Theory of Project Management is Obsolete, Proceedings, PMI Research Conference, pp. 293–302. (2002)

78. Womack, J.P., Jones, D.T., Roos, D.: The Machine that Changed the World: The Story of Lean production. Harper Perennial, New York (1990)
79. Chrissis, M.B., Konrad, M., Shrum, S.: CMMI. Addison Wesley, Boston (2003)
80. Boehm, B.: Anchoring the software process. Software. 73–82 (1996)
81. Kroll, P., Kruchten, P.: The Rational Unified Process Made Easy: A Practitioner's Guide to the Rational Unified Process. Addison Wesley, Boston (2003)
82. OMG (Object Management Group): OMG SysML v.1.2, http://www.sysml.org/specs.htm (2010)
83. Pyster, A., et al.: Graduate Software Engineering 2009 (GSwE2009) Curriculum Guidelines, Stevens Institute (2009)
84. Pyster, A., Olwell, D., Hutchison, N., Enck, S., Anthony, J., Henry, D., Squires, A. (eds.): Guide to the Systems Engineering Body of Knowledge (SEBoK) version 1.0.1. The Trustees of the Stevens Institute of Technology, Hoboken (2012). Available at: http://www.sebokwiki.org
85. Kurzweil, R.: The Age of Spiritual Machines. Penguin, New York (1999)
86. Drexler, K.E.: Engines of Creation. Anchor, Garden City (1986)
87. Drexler, K.E., Peterson, C., Pergamit, G.: Unbounding the Future: The Nanotechnology Revolution. William Morrow & Co., New York (1991)
88. Dyson, G.B.: Darwin Among the Machines: The Evolution of Global Intelligence. Helix Books/Addison Wesley, Reading (1997)
89. Joy, B.: Why the Future Doesn't Need Us: Wired (2000)
90. Crichton, M.: Prey. Harper Collins, New York (2002)
91. Dreyfus, H., Dreyfus, S.: Mind over Machine. Macmillan, New York (1986)
92. Chesbrough, H.: Open Innovation. Harvard Business School Press, Boston (2003)
93. Ncube, C., Oberndorf, P., Kark, A. (eds.): Special Issue on Opportunistic System Development, IEEE Softw. (2008)
94. Boehm, B., Bhuta, J.: Balancing opportunities and risks in component-based software development. IEEE Softw. 15(6), 56–63 (2008)
95. Boehm, B., Egyed, A., Kwan, J., Port, D., Shah, A., Madachy, R.: Using the WinWin spiral model: a case study. IEEE Comput. 31, 33–44 (1998)
96. Kruchten, P.: The Rational Unified Process. Addison Wesley, Boston (1999)
97. Boehm, B., Lane, J.: Using the incremental commitment model to integrate system acquisition, systems engineering, and software engineering. CrossTalk 20(10), 4–9 (2007)
98. Cusumano, M., Selby, R.: Microsoft Secrets. Harper Collins, London (1996)
99. Boehm, B., Lane, J., Koolmanojwong, S., Turner, R.: An Evidence-Based Systems Engineering (SE) Data Item Description, Proceedings, CSER (2013)
100. Maranzano, J.F., Rozsypal, S.A., Zimmerman, G.H., Warnken, G.W., Wirth, P.E., Weiss, D.M.: Architecture reviews: practice and experience. IEEE Softw. 22(2), 34–43 (2005)
101. Boehm, B., Lane, J., Koolmanojwong, S., Turner, R.: Principles for Successful Systems Engineering, Proceedings, CSER (2012)
102. CrossTalk: "Top Five Quality Software Projects," (January 2002), (July 2003), (July 2004), www.stsc.hill.af.mil/crosstalk
103. Vitasek, K., Ledyard, M., Manrodt, K.: Vested Outsourcing. Palgrave Macmillan, New York (2010)
104. Vitasek, K., Crawford, J., Nyden, N., Kawamoto, K.: The Vested Outsourcing Manual. Palgrave Macmillan, New York (2011)
105. Curtis, B., Hefley, B., Miller, S.: The People Capability Maturity Model. Addison Wesley, Boston (2002)
106. Collins, J.: Good to Great. Harper Collins, New York (2001)
107. Basili, V., Caldeira, G., Rombach, H.D.: Goal question metric paradigm. In: Marciniak, J.J. (ed.) Encyclopedia of Software Engineering, pp. 528–532. Wiley, New York (1994)
108. Basili, V., Caldeira, G., Rombach, H.D.: Experience factory. In: Marciniak, J.J. (ed.) Encyclopedia of Software Engineering, pp. 469–476. Wiley, New York (1994)

109. Rombach, H.D.: IESE overview. In: Marciniak, J.J. (ed.) Encyclopedia of Software Engineering, 2nd edn. Wiley, New York (2002)
110. Endres, A., Rombach, D.: A Handbook of Software and Systems Engineering: Empirical Observations, Laws, and Theories. Addison Wesley, New York (2003)

Formalism and Intuition in Software Engineering

Michael Jackson

Abstract
A major and so far unmet challenge in software engineering is to achieve and act upon a clear and sound understanding of the relationship between formalism and intuition in the development process. The challenge is salient in the development of cyber-physical systems, in which the computer interacts with the human and physical world to ensure a behaviour there that satisfies the requirements of the system's stakeholders. The nature of the computer as a formally defined symbol-processing engine invites a formal mathematical approach to software development. Contrary considerations militate against excessive reliance on formalism. The non-formal nature of the human and physical world, the complexity of system function, and the need for human comprehension at every level demand application of non-formal and intuitional knowledge, of insight and technique rather than calculation. The challenge, then, is to determine how these two facets of the development process—formalism and intuition—can work together most productively. This short essay describes some origins and aspects of the challenge and offers a perspective for addressing it.

1 Introduction

Dieter Rombach's work has been admirably characterised by a resolve to pay attention to the reality of software engineering practice and to the multitude of intuitive and informal insights that have been offered [1] to clarify its challenges and support its improvement. This short paper follows his excellent example, addressing a specific challenge in software development practice: the proper relationship between formalism and intuition.

M. Jackson (✉)
Department of Computing, The Open University, Milton Keynes MK7 6AA, United Kingdom
e-mail: jacksonma@acm.org

J. Münch and K. Schmid (eds.), *Perspectives on the Future of Software Engineering*,
DOI 10.1007/978-3-642-37395-4_20, © Springer-Verlag Berlin Heidelberg 2013

Intuition is the faculty of recognition, understanding and action in the world on the basis of experience, insight and knowledge, with little or no appeal to conscious reasoning. The strength of intuition is that it is unbounded: in exercising our intuition we are not restricted to a limited set of observations and considerations decided a priori, but we draw whatever presents itself to us from the situation in hand. When we read an intuitive description the words are not opaque: we are looking at the subject matter through the medium of the description. This is how human oral and written communication works: as I hear or read your words I experience or enact through them, in my imagination, what you are saying about the world.

Some extreme examples of human intuition dispense with conscious use of language altogether. Studying how firefighters decide how to tackle a fire leads one researcher [2] to define intuition as "the way we translate our experiences into judgments and decisions ... by using patterns to recognize what's going on in a situation." Another researcher [3] describes how operators in military, air traffic control, and other critical environments rely on maintaining an integrated cognitive map drawn from diverse inputs: they call it 'having the bubble'. The map allows them to maintain and act on a single picture of the overall situation and operational status without conscious description, analysis or reasoning.

Formalism, by contrast, relies entirely on conscious description, analysis, and reasoning. Its use is not an innate human faculty, but a skill that must be learned. Formalism is an intellectual artifact that evolved from the development of mathematics in ancient civilisations. Its essence is abstraction. Arithmetic and geometry emerged from practical needs: counting shepherds' flocks, measuring farmers' land, paying taxes, and laying out the structures of large buildings. The Greeks saw that mathematics had an intrinsic intellectual interest. Numbers, planes, points and lines could be completely separated from their practical utility. Plato's rule that no-one ignorant of geometry should enter his Academy in Athens was not an expression of welcome to land surveyors or estate agents: it expressed the conviction that knowledge of the material world was inferior to knowledge of mathematics. Only in the abstract world of mathematics could the conclusions of reasoning be proved correct beyond all doubt.

In modern times some mathematicians have expressed the essentially abstract nature of formalism uncompromisingly. In an address [4] at the University of Pennsylvania, the German mathematician Hermann Weyl said:

> We now come to the decisive step of mathematical abstraction: we forget about what the symbols stand for. [The mathematician] need not be idle; there are many operations he may carry out with these symbols, without ever having to look at the things they stand for.

Weyl's doctoral advisor was David Hilbert, whom he reported [5] as saying:

> It must be possible to replace in all geometric statements the words point, line, plane, by table, chair, mug.

For Weyl and Hilbert, the symbols used in a formal description are arbitrarily chosen: any reference to the material world is a mischievous and misleading irrelevance.

Extreme forms of pure intuition or pure formalism are unlikely to appear in any practical enterprise, and certainly not in software development. In practice, formalism is more like applied than like pure mathematics: application to the material world is never very far away, and intuition plays a significant part. In practice, intuition finds expression in semi-formal documents and discourse: some lightweight formal notions may be introduced to avoid obvious potential confusions, and sound reasoning is recognised—though not always achieved—as a desirable goal. How the two should be balanced and combined, both in the large and in the small, is still an open question.

2   Some Software History

Two streams may be distinguished in the evolving modern practice of software development since it began in the 1940s. One may be called the formal stream. Programs are regarded as mathematical objects: their properties and behaviour can be analysed formally and predictions of the results of execution can be formally proved or disproved. The other stream may be called the intuitive stream. Programs are regarded as structures inviting human comprehension: the results of their execution can be predicted—not always reliably—by an intuitive process of mental enactment combined with some informal reasoning.

Both streams have a long history. A talk by Alan Turing in 1949 [6] used assertions over program variables to construct a formal proof of correctness of a small program to compute the factorial function. Techniques of program structuring, devised and justified by intuition, came to prominence in the 1960s with the control structures of Algol 60 [7], Conway's invention of coroutines [8], and the class concept of Simula67 [9]. Dijkstra's advocacy of restricted control flow patterns in the famous GO TO letter [10] rested on their virtue of minimising the conceptual gap between the static program text and its dynamic execution: the program would be more comprehensible. In further developments in structured programming the two streams came together. A structured program text was not only easier to understand: the nested structure of localised contexts allowed a structured proof of correctness based on formal reasoning.

At this stage the academic and research communities made an implicit choice with far-reaching consequences. Some of the intellectual leaders of those communities were encouraged by the success and promise of formal mathematical techniques to focus their attention and efforts on that stream. They relaxed, and eventually forsook, their interest in the intuitive aspects of program design and structure. For those researchers themselves the choice was fruitful: study of the more formal aspects of computing stimulated a rich flow of results in that particular branch of logic and mathematics.

For the field of software development as a whole this effective separation of the formal and intuitive streams was a major loss. The formal stream flowed on, diverging further and further from the concerns and practices of realistic software development projects. The intuitive stream, too, flowed on, but in increasing isolation. Systems became richer and more complex, and the computer's role in them became increasingly one of intimate interaction with the human and physical world. Software engineering came to be less concerned with purely symbolic computation and more concerned with the material world and with the economic and operational purposes of the system of which software was now only a part. Development projects responded increasingly to economic and managerial imperatives and trends rather than to intellectual or scientific disciplines.

In recent decades advocates of formal methods have made admirable efforts to reconnect the two streams to their mutual advantage; but the very necessity of these efforts is an indictment of the present state of software development practice and theory as a whole. Formalism and intuition are still too often seen as competing adversaries. Some formalists believe that their work offers powerful solutions that practitioners have wilfully ignored. Some practitioners believe that formalists have simply ignored the real problems and difficulties of software engineering. The purpose of this essay is to offer a little relationship counselling to the parties, and to address the implicit challenge: How can we combine the undoubted benefits of formal techniques with the more intuitive and informal aspects that have always been an integral part of the practice of traditional branches of engineering?

3   Software Engineering

Structured programming was ideally suited to what we may call *pure programming*. The archetypical expository examples of pure programming are calculating the greatest common divisor of two integers, sorting an array of integers, solving the travelling salesman problem, or computing the convex hull of a set of points in 3-space. These problems proved surprisingly fertile in stimulating insights into program design technique, but they were all limited in a crucial way: they required only computation of symbolic output results from symbolic input data. The developer investigates the problem world, identifies a symbolic computational problem that can usefully be solved by computer, and constructs a program to solve it. The user captures the input data for each desired program execution and presents it as input to the machine. The resulting output is then taken by the same or another user and applied in some way to guide action in the problem world. The process is shown in the upper part of Fig. 1.

A realistic program of this kind may be designed to solve a general mathematical problem—for example, to solve a set of partial differential equations. It may or may not embody some more specialised theory of the problem world. For example, an early use of electronic computing was to print tables of calculated trajectories for artillery under test at the Aberdeen Proving Grounds in Maryland, USA [11]. The programs may have explicitly embodied a substantial ballistic theory, or they may have been programmed only to solve general systems of partial differential equations. In either case, the machine executing a pure program is isolated from the problem world by the operators who prepare and present the machine's inputs and collect and use its outputs.

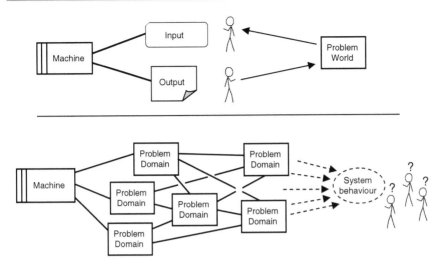

Fig. 1 A pure program and a software engineered cyber-physical system

By contrast, the lower part of Fig. 1 shows a *cyber-physical* system, whose development is a task, not of pure programming but of *software engineering*. In such a system the *machine*—the computing part—is introduced into a material *problem world* to serve specific purposes. The problem world consists of interconnected *problem domains*. Some of these domains are physical parts of the world such as mechatronic devices, other computer systems, parts of the built environment, parts of the natural world, and objects such as credit cards that encode lexical information in physical form. Additionally, some other problem domains are human beings participating in the system behaviour, interacting with each other and with the other domains, in both active and passive roles as users, operators, patients, subjects, passengers, drivers, and so on. All of these problem domains have their own given properties and behaviours.

The function of the machine is to ensure a certain desired behaviour in this world, by monitoring and controlling the parts of the world to which it is directly interfaced. The desired behaviour in the world is not limited to these directly interfaced parts, but also embraces other more remote parts which are monitored and controlled through their interactions with other, neighbouring, parts and thus, indirectly, with the machine. The purpose of this desired behaviour is to satisfy the needs of the system's *stakeholders*. Some stakeholders, such as operators, patients and users, are not mere observers but also participate as problem domains in the system behaviour. Others, such as safety regulators and business managers, observe the system behaviour only from a distance. All stakeholders legitimately expect the system behaviour, seen in particular projections from their individual perspectives, to satisfy their needs and purposes.

4   The Development Task

The behaviour of a cyber-physical system is governed by the interacting behaviours of the machine and the problem domains. Within the limits of the hardware and operating system, the machine's behaviour can be freely defined by the software developed for the system. The behaviour of each problem domain is constrained by its given properties; superimposed on these is the effect of its interactions with other parts of the system. To achieve the desired overall system behaviour the machine must both respect and exploit the given properties and behaviours of all the problem domains.

The overall system behaviour must satisfy the needs of the stakeholders. It is a mistake to suppose that this behaviour is understood in advance by the stakeholders, either individually or collectively, and is waiting only to be discovered and documented. The stakeholders do have various needs and desires, but they may be only dimly perceived. A major part of the development task—explicitly recognised in the past 20 years as *requirements engineering*—is designing behaviour projections that will satisfy the needs of each stakeholder, and combining these projected behaviours into a design for the overall system behaviour. Each desired projected behaviour, and the complete system behaviour that somehow combines them all, must be *feasible*: that is, it must be achievable by the machine, suitably programmed and interacting with the problem domains.

The development task, then, has many facets and parts. The properties of each problem domain must be studied, described and analysed; the many projections of the desired system behaviour must be designed, described and presented to the stakeholders for their critical approval; the combination of these projections must itself be designed; and the behaviour of the machine must be designed and specified at its interface to the problem world. The resulting system is a complex artifact. Before examining the sources and nature of its complexity we will first look briefly at the ubiquitous intellectual activity of software engineering: describing a material reality and reasoning about its properties and behaviour.

5   Describing and Reasoning

Figure 2 outlines the general process of forming a description and reasoning about it to draw useful conclusions about the machine or the problem world, expressed in a modified or new description.

Description A is constructed first. Phenomena of the reality, relevant to the concern in hand, are selected and named, the mapping between names and phenomena being given by the interpretation. The meaning of the description—what it says about the world—depends on the interpretation and on the language in which the description is expressed. Given description A, it is then possible to reason about the world on the basis of that description, deducing a conclusion in the form of

Fig. 2 Describing a material
reality and reasoning about it

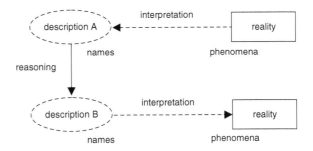

description B. This conclusion has a meaning in the reality, which can be understood by reading the derived description in the light of the interpretation.

This simplified account allows us to recognise the difference between formal and non-formal description and reasoning. In a formal setting the chosen language of description is a formal language, rigorously specified. The selected phenomena must then be regarded as elements of types supported by the language. For example: in the language of propositional calculus each relevant phenomenon must be an atomic uninterpreted truth-functional proposition; in the language of predicate calculus it must be a predicate, a function, or an individual. The grammar of the language also includes a small set of connectives, such as logical operators, allowing meaningful statements to be made in the language and combined in various ways. Descriptions are assembled from these elements according to rigid syntactic rules. The advantage purchased by this linguistic rigidity is a formal calculus of reliable reasoning. All or part of the initial description can be treated as a premiss from which conclusions can be derived and proved with mathematical certainty.

The diagram applies equally well to the structure of intuitive or informal description and reasoning. An informal description must be expressed in some language. The language has symbols, and the symbols have some interpretation—that is, they denote some phenomena of the described reality. Yet the content, character and virtues of the intuitive process are quite different from the formal. Symbol choices are very significant in informal description, especially if the descriptions are expressed in natural language: they remind us to look across from the description to the reality it describes and to check continually whether the description remains valid. The logic of informal description is unconstrained: it is nearly true to say that in a rich natural language like English we can say anything whatsoever. We can even define and use new linguistic features within one description. The price for this linguistic freedom is some imprecision in description, and unreliability in both the process and the results of reasoning. Nonetheless, intuition and informality are not merely degraded and incompetent cousins of formalism. Imprecision and unreliability bring major compensating benefits.

In practice the activity of describing and reasoning is rarely perfectly formal or perfectly informal. Rejecting Hilbert's maxim, most formalists usually choose symbols intended to remind the reader of the phenomena they denote in the reality; and many intuitive practitioners use natural language description with careful definitions of the meanings of names, or include embedded formal notations such as finite state machines where greater precision seems necessary.

6   Formalism and System Complexities

Cyber-physical systems exhibit complexity in more than one dimension. The functional complexity of a realistic system is immediately obvious. Typically a system has many functional features whose purposes are not harmonious or even consistent. The individual features may be intrinsically complex, and the complexity of the whole system is greatly increased by their interactions. Some features may be mutually exclusive in time, but during system operation multiple features may be simultaneously active. Further, many systems are required to operate essentially continuously, scarcely ever reaching a quiescent state in which the system can be removed from service, isolated from the rest of the world, and returned to a well-understood initial state before resuming operation. So the system may be required to achieve smooth transitions between different functional behaviours adjacent in time. For an avionics system, for example, there are transitions from taking-off to climbing, from landing to taxiing, and so on; and a lift control system must maintain user safety and reasonable convenience in the transition from normal lift service to firefighter operation.

One effect of this functional complexity is that there are few or no invariant properties of the required system behaviour. For example, it might be thought that in a system to control the movement of railway trains over a region of track a safety invariant must hold: no two trains must ever be present in the same track segment. But in reality this cannot be a required invariant: it would make it impossible to assemble a train from two trains, or for a breakdown train to deal with the aftermath of a collision or to rescue a locomotive that has lost tractive power. An access control system might seem to demand that no person is ever present in a room for which they have no access authorisation. But this property would restrict escape routes from the building in case of fire, and in that context would be forbidden by fire regulations. In a lift control system an apparent safety invariant stipulates that the lift car doors are never open unless the lift is in home position at a floor. But a firefighter who is in the lift at a high floor must not be prevented from descending even if the doors refuse to close.

The given properties and behaviours of a problem domain—those that it possesses independently of the behaviour of the machine—exhibit a similar dynamic complexity. The given properties and behaviours are determined by four factors, at least two of which are dynamic. A fifth factor determines which properties are of interest at any time.

The first determining factor is *scientific law*—for example, the laws of physics. At the granularity relevant to most software engineering these laws are constant and well understood.

The second factor is what we may call the *constitution* of the domain. This is its shape and material, and the designed, evolved or otherwise determined configuration of its constituent parts. For example, within the bounds set by physics, a person's body weight, physical strength and reaction speed are determined by human physiology in general and the individual's physiology in particular. The maximum acceleration of a lift car rising in its shaft is determined not only by the laws of physics but also by the design of the motor, the power supply and the lift car and counterweight. This second factor, constitution, is more or less constant for each particular problem domain, and is open to study and analysis.

A third, time-varying, factor is the *condition* of the domain. Engineered devices degrade over time, especially if they are not properly maintained or subjected to misuse or to excessive loads. A human operator becomes tired in an extended session of participation in the system; and, in the contrary direction, an operator's speed and skill may increase with practice over a number of similar sessions.

A fourth factor is variation of the *environment* over time. Carefully engineered devices assume an acceptable operating environment, specifying such conditions as wind speed, ambient temperature, air purity and atmospheric pressure. Human behaviour, too, depends on such environmental conditions. If the environment changes the domain may exhibit changed properties.

Broadly, we may say that the first two of these four factors—scientific law and domain constitution—can be investigated and analysed at system design time. The third and fourth—condition and environment—vary during system operation.

The fifth factor, *domain role*, is of a different kind. At any particular time, a problem domain has a large set of potentially observable properties subject to the first four factors, but only a small subset are significant for the system behaviour. The domain itself participates only in some of the system's functions, and in those it plays only a limited role exhibiting only a subset of its given properties. For example, the aerodynamic properties of a car body are highly significant while it is being driven at high speed on a motorway, but irrelevant to its desired behaviour in automatically assisted parking, in the aftermath of a collision, or while undergoing maintenance in the workshop.

These considerations may be summarised by saying that the rarity of required invariants of system behaviour is parallelled by the rarity of invariants of problem domain properties.

7   Contexts of Domains and Behaviours

There is an important interplay between the variation of domain properties and the variation of the active set of system functional behaviours. For each domain the properties of current significance varies according to its role in each system behaviour of the currently active set. They vary also with changes in the environment, and some of those changes will naturally demand different system behaviours. For example, a power failure in the lift control system seriously affects the properties of the mechatronic equipment, which is now running on emergency power supplies of limited capacity; at the same time it also requires transition to a special parking behaviour in which passengers are brought safely to the nearest available floor.

The most obvious examples of this interplay of domain properties and system behaviour are found in fault-tolerance. In the lift control system, to provide normal lift service the machine must directly control the motor power and direction, and monitor the floor sensors to detect the arrival and departure of the lift car at each floor. This behaviour is possible only if the relevant problem domains of the lift equipment are in healthy condition: this is therefore a *local assumption*, on which the behaviour will rely [12]. It then becomes necessary to develop another system behaviour whose specific purpose is to monitor the health of the lift equipment by observing its run-time behaviour. These are therefore at least three distinct system functional behaviours: one to provide normal lift service; a second to detect and perhaps diagnose equipment faults; and at least one other to provide the appropriate behaviour in the presence of a fault. The domain properties of the equipment on which they rely are quite different: one relies on fault-free behaviour; the second relies on the estimated probabilities of different equipment faults and on their consequences in observable phenomena; the third relies on the residual functionality of the faulty equipment.

This restriction of each projection of system behaviour to a particular context in which particular assumptions hold is only a finer-grain version of the inevitable restriction on the whole system's operating conditions. No system, however critical, can aspire to operate dependably in every circumstance that is logically or physically possible. Tall buildings are designed to withstand high wind speeds, but only up to a limit of what is reasonably plausible in each building's particular location. Passenger aircraft are designed to fly in the earth's atmosphere, but not in air of unlimited turbulence or in a high density of volcanic ash. Even when we choose to extend the proposed operational conditions to allow graceful degradation of system function, we must still accept some limitations. We can aim only to choose reasonable limits on the circumstances our system will be designed to handle, and to design with adequate reliability within those limits.

The resolutions of functional and domain complexity come together in the assumed *context* of each projected functional behaviour. Each projected functional behaviour can then be represented as shown in the lower part of Fig. 1. In each projection the impediments to successful application of appropriate formalism have been greatly diminished. How and why this is so is discussed in the following section.

8   Structure, Invention and Proof

The great French physicist and mathematician Henri Poincaré wrote [13]:

> For the pure geometer himself, this faculty [intuition] is necessary; it is by logic one demonstrates, by intuition one invents. To know how to criticize is good, to know how to create is better. You know how to recognize if a combination is correct; what a predicament if you have not the art of choosing among all the possible combinations. Logic tells us that on such and such a way we are sure not to meet any obstacle; it does not say which way

leads to the end. For that it is necessary to see the end from afar, and the faculty which teaches us to see is intuition. Without it the geometer would be like a writer who should be versed in grammar but had no ideas.

Poincaré is speaking of mathematics, but what he says applies no less to software engineering. It is worth understanding what he says.

The key point is the distinction between demonstration or proof on one side, and invention or discovery on the other side. The primary role of formalism is proof. Before engaging in proof we must know what we wish to prove and the exact context and subject matter for which we wish to prove it. Then we are able to choose an appropriate formal language for our description, knowing that its supported types can represent the relevant phenomena of the reality, and that its logic allows the kind of reasoning on which we are embarking.

In inventing and discovering, on the other hand, we do not know exactly what we wish to invent or discover: if we did we would already have it in our hand. In Poincaré's words, it is necessary to see the end from afar, and the faculty that teaches us to see is intuition. By this we do not mean that we should leap foolishly to a wild guess, impatient of careful thought and reasoning. Rather, invention and discovery are learning processes of a particular kind, in which we need to explore a space of possibilities, sketching our thoughts and perceptions at each resting place that seems promising. For this kind of intellectual activity we need freedom to record our perceptions while they are inchoate, imprecise and even inconsistent. We need a loose structuring of our descriptions and reasoning in which we can reconsider any step without invalidating every other part of what we have done so far. We need to be able to add modal statements about time or obligation to a description that so far contains nothing alien to classical logic. We need to be able to offer temporary accommodation to counterexamples to ensure that they will not be forgotten, without undermining or erasing the imperfectly general but still valuable observation or conclusion that they disprove.

Formalism militates strongly against these purposes. Even if we eschew Hilbert's insistence on extreme mathematical abstraction, the very formality of the chosen language focuses our attention on its abstract logical content and distracts us from attending to the reality described. We are compelled to choose the descriptive language at the outset, when we know least about the terrain to be explored and the flora and fauna we will find there. Worse, a formalism encourages the construction of a single mathematical structure whose virtue is founded on its internal consistency. A single counterexample or a discovered contradiction is a complete disproof: from the contradiction every truth and every falsehood follows without distinction, and the whole edifice becomes discredited.

By contrast, an informal process of discovering properties of the problem world and of the stakeholders' requirements allows the invention of instances of a conceptual structure such as the assemblage of system behaviours sketched in the preceding section. Within such a structure it is possible to separate distinct projections of the system behaviour. Each such projection rests on explicit assumptions of problem domain properties in the context for which the behaviour is designed, and is accompanied by an informal design of the relevant projection of the machine behaviour relying on those assumptions.

Within each of these limited projections formalism can then play its most effective role. The operational context, the problem domain properties, and the desired functionality are restricted: within those restrictions, uniform and relatively simple assumptions can be captured in axioms and a well-chosen formalisation can achieve a good approximation to the problem world reality. The informal design explains how the projected system behaviour is to be achieved, and this explanation can then be made precise and subjected to formal analysis to detect any logical errors. Formalism is deployed locally within each part of the structure. The structure itself, and the substance of its parts, are the product of an intuitive and informal approach.

9   Envoi

To a committed formalist, advocacy of intuition in software engineering may seem a heretical denial of the value of formalism and rigour. Not so. The point is that formalism has its proper place. Its place is not in the early stages of exploration and learning, where it is premature and restrictive, but in the later stages, where we need to validate our informal discoveries, designs and inferences by submitting them to the rigour of formal proof. Its place is not in the processes of conceiving, designing and forming large structures, but in the later stage of constructing and checking the smaller parts for which those structures provide their carefully defined and restricted contexts, and the relationships among those parts. The essential point is that at every level informal and intelligent use of intuition must precede application of formalism. It must shape the large structure of the whole set of development artifacts; and within that structure it must guide the process of learning, understanding, inventing and documenting the given and desired properties and behaviours of the problem domains. Only then can these descriptions be profitably formalised and their formal consequences verified.

Acknowledgements This essay owes much to years of cooperation and stimulating discussion with many people, especially Anthony Hall, Ian Hayes, Daniel Jackson, Cliff Jones, Thein Than Tun and Yijun Yu. Since none of them has yet seen even a draft of the essay, they cannot be held responsible for its deficiencies.

References

1. Endres, A., Rombach, D.: A Handbook of Software and Systems Engineering. Addison-Wesley (2003)
2. Klein, G.: Intuition at Work. Doubleday (2003)
3. Rochlin, G.I.: Trapped in the Net: The Unanticipated Consequences of Computerization. Princeton University Press (1997)

4. Weyl, H.: The Mathematical Way of Thinking; address given at the Bicentennial Conference at the University of Pennsylvania (1940)
5. Weyl, H.: David Hilbert and his mathematical work. Bull. Am. Math. Soc. **50**, 612–654 (1944)
6. Turing, A M.: Checking a large routine. In: Report on a Conference on High Speed Automatic Calculating Machines, pp. 67–69. Cambridge University Mathematical Laboratory, Cambridge (1949). Discussed in: Jones, C.B.: The Early Search for Tractable Ways of Reasoning about Programs; IEEE Annals of the History of Computing, vol. 25(2), pp. 26–49. 2003
7. Backus, J.W., Bauer, F.L., Green, J., Katz, C., McCarthy, J., Perlis, A.J., Rutishauser, H., Samelson, K., Vauquois, B., Wegstein, J.H., van Wijngaarden, A., Woodger, M. Naur, P. (eds.): Report on the Algorithmic Language ALGOL 60. Commun. ACM. **3**(5), 299–314 (1960)
8. Conway, M.E.: Design of a separable transition-diagram compiler. Commun. ACM **6**(7), 396–408 (1963)
9. Dahl, O-J., Hoare, C.A.R.: Hierarchical program structures. In: Dahl, O-J., Dijkstra, E.W., Hoare, C.A.R. (eds.) Structured Programming. Academic (1972)
10. Dijkstra, E.W.: A case against the go to statement; EWD 215, published as a letter to the Editor (Go To Statement Considered Harmful). Commun. ACM. **11**(3), 147–148 (1968)
11. Dickinson, E.R.: Production of Firing Tables for Cannon Artillery; Report No 1371, US Army Materiel Command, Ballistic research Laboratories, Aberdeen Proving ground, Maryland (1967)
12. Hayes, I.J., Jackson, M.A., Jones, C.B.: Determining the specification of a control system from that of its environment. In: Araki, K., Gnesi, S., Mandrioli, D. (eds.) Formal Methods: Proceedings of FME2003, Springer. Lecture Notes in Computer Science, vol. 2805, pp. 154–169. (2003)
13. Poincaré, H.: Science et Méthode; Flammarion 1908; English translation by Francis Maitland, Nelson, 1914 and Dover 1952, 2003

Education of Software Engineers

Marvin V. Zelkowitz

Abstract
The field of software engineering had its beginnings in the 1960s, almost 50 years ago. Since that time you would expect that significant progress has been made in understanding the models, methods, and techniques that lend themselves to proper software development. However, we are still making some of the same mistakes that were supposedly "solved" in the 1960s and 1970s. Industry still doesn't understand the critical importance that correct programs have in the proper functioning of society today. In this paper, several examples are given in how we are still "reinventing the wheel" as well as describing new challenges that will impact software engineers in the near future.

1 Introduction

As I was reading the *New York Times* at the end of 2010, the headline of a news article suddenly hit me—"A Pinpoint Beam Strays Invisibly, Harming Instead of Healing—A Radiation Setting Is Wrong, and Patients are Harmed" while undergoing SRS (stereotactic radiosurgery) treatment in a hospital. As American baseball player Yogi Berra once said, "It's déjà vu all over again." When the story first appeared, it was not clear if the cause was software-related, but it sure read a lot like the Therac-25 disaster of the mid-1980s [1]. The Therac-25 was an earlier medical device where some patients were given fatal instead of therapeutic doses of radiation. A short time later I did read that the problem was in the programming

M.V. Zelkowitz (✉)
University of Maryland, College Park, MD, USA

Fraunhofer Center for Experimental Software Engineering, 5825 University Research Court, Suite 1300, College Park, MD 20740-3823, USA
e-mail: mvz@cs.umd.edu

J. Münch and K. Schmid (eds.), *Perspectives on the Future of Software Engineering*, DOI 10.1007/978-3-642-37395-4_21, © Springer-Verlag Berlin Heidelberg 2013

of the SRS machine and involved passing information among three incompatible computers [2]. We apparently never learn.

In the case of the Therac-25, the problem was that the erase character key was not handled correctly, so if the code to switch between radiation and x-ray treatment was typed incorrectly and the backspace key was depressed, the machine would go into the wrong state. However, the real message of the Therac-25 was not that there was a software bug. Those happen all the time in programs and are generally fixed. However, in this case the software engineers designing the Therac-25 missed a key engineering principle in designing that device.

Any competent designer should be able to build software that detects a failure and either corrects it or responds in a safe manner. Fault detection and correction is standard fare for a competent software tester. The problem with the Therac-25 was that a single error was compounded with a second error. That is, the error in switching between radiation and x-ray modes was compounded by the error in the backspace key. The device was not designed to handle multiple points of failure. Hardware engineers know how to build products having multiple failure modes, but this is something that is still new to most software designers.

Software failures are well-documented in the literature. On June 4, 1996 on its maiden flight, an Ariane 5 rocket blew up 38 s after launch [3]. In this case, a software register overran its limit and caused an incorrect value, interpreted by the control software as the rocket being out of control. Control was switched to the backup computer, running the same software. Since it, too, overran its limit because of the same software problem, the control program could only interpret that the problem was indeed true and had the rocket blow up.

Again, software was the cause, but that was not the real lesson from this experience. The designers of the Ariane 5 thought they were being smart by using the same code, which worked correctly on the older Ariane 4 rocket. However, the environment in which the Ariane 4 code was executing was different from that of the Ariane 5, and reusing the same code when its specifications changed without a thorough study of those specifications is a prescription for disaster. In this case the problem was compounded by eliminating sufficient testing, since performance of the computer was an issue and "the code was correct" from the earlier Ariane 4 rocket. Such shortcuts are never a good idea. As a result of the failure, we again have that well-worn truism—"You don't have the money to do it right, but you do have the money to do it again."

I don't mean to just pick on the European Space Agency. NASA is also guilty of similar fiascos. Almost everyone knows of the Mars Climate Orbiter that crashed into Mars on November 10, 1999 due to a mix-up between Imperial measurement units and metric measurement units between two different components of software. A simple dimensional analysis between parameters and arguments in a subroutine would have revealed the problem.

2   Future Software Engineering Needs

The messages learned from such examples as these are critical for producing quality software. Software is a critical component of just about every device sold today. Even non-safety-critical software has problems. The PC I am using to write this paper downloads a new "critical update" to some piece of software on my machine almost daily. Every day when I turn on my smartphone, two or three applications on the phone download a revised version of themselves—usually to fix a problem. Applications on my Windows 7 operating system seem to fail regularly. What have we learned about producing good software? My general impression seems to be "Not much." As for the SRS accident I mentioned at the beginning of this paper, I could find no reference anywhere in the *New York Times* article to any similarities to the Therac-25 incidents of the early 1980s. Since that happened almost 30 years ago, I assume it was well before most current professionals (both journalists and computer personnel) were plying their trade and the incident is rapidly moving into the realm of ancient history. I have been a computer science researcher since the late 1960s, and there are few of us still around compared to the multitudes of programmers working today.

So how are we in the USA responding to these problems? I assume much of what goes on in the USA is similar in other countries. As described by the US Bureau of Labor Statistics, the largest growth in the computer field will "all require substantial training beyond the basic skills of an operator but not the scientific education of a computer hardware engineer. *It isn't necessary to have a Bachelor of Science degree to be considered a software engineer.*" [Emphasis added.] [4] I can't imagine any agency saying, for example, "Electronics are easy to fix today since you simply replace a bad component with a new one, so it is no longer necessary for electrical engineers to have college degrees." For some reason we haven't been able to get the message across to non-computer people that building software is actually hard.

My interpretation of the Bureau of Labor Statistics statement is that a continual "dumbing down" of the ability of most software engineers is in store for the future. While there are certainly talented professionals in the field, new employees will not be as competent as the present generation of engineers. Management seems to be looking for inexpensive solutions to solve the personnel problem rather than what is needed to eliminate the problem itself.

For years Dave Parnas has been at the forefront in trying to get the field to regard software engineering as an engineering discipline, in deed as well as in name, by emphasizing good engineering principles in the curriculum of a computer science or related program [5]. However, even if successful, it makes little difference if most of the next generation of software engineers does not even have a Bachelor of Science degree.

What are we teaching the next generation of software engineers? When I taught classes in software engineering, I have always used the lessons of the Therac-25, the Ariane 5, the Mars Climate Orbiter, as well as other examples, as important concepts in system design. Testing, debugging, verification, and coding programs are important tools in any software engineering toolbox. But what are programmers actually using? " . . . , there are people who find debuggers to be an inferior tool and who prefer to use in-program logging, or *printf*, statements to find out where their program is going wrong" [6]. With all of the research in debugging systems and new testing tools filling conference proceedings, is anyone actually using that technology? As another quote, consider the following: "Investing in a large amount of software testing can be difficult to justify, particularly for a startup company" [7]. What does this statement mean? A startup company is allowed to sell inferior code because testing a program is expensive? Would a new aircraft or a new automobile manufacturer ever make a statement like that? Are we allowing such products to be regularly sold? If software engineering were a true engineering discipline, those comments would be grounds for removing the licenses of all those involved in developing and selling such products.

Those are concepts whose negative impact was well understood and taught about in the 1970s. Haven't we learned anything since then?

3   Technology Saves the Day (So Far)

3.1   Moore's Law

What has saved the software engineer up until now is "Moore's Law." For over 50 years computers have been doubling in speed about every 2 years, while at the same time becoming cheaper to purchase. However, the general public, and most computer experts, do not really understand what Gordon Moore really said in 1965. He claimed component density on a chip would double every 18 months with each component taking up less space. At first this size shrinkage roughly translated into increased speed. But faster circuit speeds also meant more heat being produced, meaning more energy needed to power the chip.

For 40 years this has allowed inefficient and poorly designed programs to survive. But the days of ever cheaper and faster machines is rapidly ending. Heat generation and power usage have radically slowed down the production of ever faster processors since around 2005. To limit heat and power, most processors are no longer produced at clock speeds greater than 3 GHz. With users increasingly using smartphones and tablet computers, lightweight machines with long battery life is the driving force. The goal is to make machines smaller and faster using less energy per cycle. By limiting computation speed, but increasing the number of cores in each processor we continue to get the benefits of "Moore's Law" without generating increased heat. Thus the number of separate processors on each CPU chip now doubles according to "Moore's Law" every 2 years or so. Essentially each core is a separate CPU and 4 and 8 core processors are becoming common.

However, multiple cores make programming harder, not easier, in order to use these multicore processors effectively [8]. The complex algorithms developed over the last few decades that were part of the High Performance Computing (HPC) community's need to achieve petascale performance (i.e., 10^{15} floating point operations per second) must now be applied to the ordinary desktop machine.

Although the top ranking of the currently fastest machines is now 17.59 petaflops,[1] this speed was achieved on a highly specialized set of benchmark programs. While such petascale machines have been produced, in reality they run at only 10 % or so of peak performance most of the time since programming such parallelism is extremely difficult.

What will be needed for many future applications are not under-qualified computer technicians, but better qualified software engineers who understand the implications of parallel processing in addition to all the other technologies that have arisen in the quest for effective trustworthy software.

3.2   Massive Open Online Courses

There are now two competing forces acting upon the university that have the possibility to greatly alter the landscape. On the one hand, society is pushing back on the high costs of running a university. Universities, especially in the United States, have to do more with less money, so the need for increased revenue other than from student tuition or from the state is great. On the other hand, the World Wide Web has become the great equalizer and is location independent. If you visit a website, it really doesn't matter if it is in the same building as you, across the street, or across the world. From the user's perspective, they are all the same.

Universities have embraced the web with massive open online courses (MOOC). Once a course is broadcast on the web, it really doesn't add to the cost of running the course to have more students access the course website. Initially, some universities let non-paying students audit classes that local university students were taking for credit. In one early case, Canadian school Athabasca University offered a course to 25 tuition paying students and free to 2,300 others. However, the floodgates opened when Stanford University offered a course on artificial intelligence in the fall of 2011 to over 160,000 online students. Most were just auditing, but the issue that became apparent was how does a university commercialize such courses? If students want to take the course for credit, having them pay for it will solve most of the financial part. But how does the university handle the learning and evaluation part of any course? The number of teaching assistants needed to address 100,000 students in one course would overwhelm any university. (Assuming an optimistically high number of 1,000 student enrollees per teaching assistant, a single MOOC would require over 100 graduate students for this single course. This permits only 20 min per student per course, a very low number if course grading and some advising is included in this total.)

This is where software engineering gets involved in this discussion. For some classes, automated tests can work. The technology to automatically grade short answer and multiple choice tests is available. But what about a course in software engineering? Software engineering is a group engineering laboratory activity. It requires group interactions and group decision making. What experience can a

---

[1] http://www.top500.org, November 2012.

student get from working alone in a home office on a computer connected to the web? Do we know what can be done in order to make the MOOC concept work?

4   Evolution of Computer Technology

As a programmer since 1962 and a professor of computer science since 1971 I have tried to instill the ideals of the field in my students. But I find it very frustrating when we are still talking about the same debugging techniques that were "old" when I started teaching in 1971. It would be like in astronomy where each new generation of PhDs would have to first learn how to grind their own lenses as Galileo did 400 years ago before beginning their studies. How could physics and astronomy have progressed as much as they did if so restricted? Yet we seem to still be stuck reinventing the 1970s. I would hope that we can do better.

One of the causes of this "reinvention of the wheel" in software engineering is that each generation of computer technology has been the product of a new generation of developers. In the 1960s and 1970s we saw the development of the large scale mainframes with large multiuser operating systems such as IBM's OS/360. System crashes were quite high at first, but eventually we learned how to make such systems reliable. UNIX, building on the research of the 1960s was initially released in 1970 and has been highly reliable [9].

While computer professionals were working on large mainframes perfecting complex code, the next generation of machines in the 1970s was being developed initially by computer hobbyists. The Apple II by Steve Jobs and Steve Wozniak in the mid-1970s and the MS-DOS software for the IBM PC by Microsoft founder Bill Gates in the early 1980s were essentially new developments, not built upon the foundation we learned about in the 1960s.

This trend continued through multiple generations of machines. The Android operating system developed by Google for the smartphone was generated by yet another generation of developers. While Android is a powerful operating system, applications seem to be updated regularly to fix errors. Only Apple seems to have done it right. In 2002 they released the forerunner of their latest operating system, OS X. This is based upon a UNIX kernel, which already was a thoroughly solid foundation in which to build a system.

Looking at all of these new generations of software and hardware and at the various failures described earlier, the solution cannot be less knowledgeable software engineers, but higher standards necessary for all.

5   A Strategy for Software Design

In order to address the problem of bad software, let me reinvent and describe a technique common in the 1970s, which seems to have been lost in today's development cycle. It is a form of fault tree analysis for software that makes many of the errors described earlier easier to find.

Fault tree analysis (FTA) analyzes a system design for failure by looking for program states that indicate an error. It is a common technique in safety or reliability engineering to determine the probability of a safety accident. FTA is not generally applied to software designs. Let me describe a system I built in the early 1970s which used similar techniques in order to achieve high reliability from failure.

PLUM was an error correcting PL/I compiler I developed in the early 1970s [10]. PL/I was a mildly popular programming language initially developed by IBM in the 1960s and 1970s which had a structure that had aspects of both Fortran and Pascal. PLUM's distinguishing feature was that if it found a compilation error, it would generate an error message and "correct" the error. By correction I mean that it would change the input at the point of the error to something that represented a correct program. It might not be (and usually wasn't) the program that the user thought he was writing, but it was semantically and syntactically correct.

This feature was designed during the days when programs were submitted on punched cards and with most compilers, if there was a syntactic error, there would be no useful output and the user would have to wait a day before submitting a corrected program. Using this error correction strategy, even if the correction was not the right one, the process enabled the program to continue to process the program and find other potential problems. And sometimes the compiler even made the correct assumption and did compile the program the user thought he had written.

However, the side benefit of this strategy gave a process for greatly improving the reliability of the resulting program. At the University of Maryland computer center, the staff kept a large file of bad programming cards collected from trash baskets. (This was the early 1970s and keypunches were still being used to type in programs.) This nonsense collection consisting of mistyped Fortran, MAD, COBOL, Assembler and data cards was fed as the input to every commercial compiler on the university system. All crashed! Not only did they fail to find all errors, but they were unable to terminate normally. But not only did PLUM find all the errors in these cards, it even "executed" the program. (We have to take the word "execution" loosely here. For the most part the bad cards were replaced by labels and PLUM simply executed a series of null statements.)

However, what is important here is that PLUM never had a problem scanning for multiple failure modes. Because of PLUM's error correction philosophy, every error found by PLUM was replaced by a sequence of correct PL/1 code. Thus every error was the "first" fault in the program and once it was corrected the program had no remaining faults up to that point in the program. This eliminates the problems described earlier in the SRS and Therac-25 cases. There is never a need for multiple failure modes since every error is the first. And programmers are usually pretty good at fixing initial errors. It is only when keeping track of multiple errors simultaneously that complexity gets out of hand.

6   Challenges

There shouldn't be a need to justify the importance of computers for the future. Every facet of our society depends upon computer technology. However, I have concerns about how we are currently training the next generation of software engineers and how that will evolve in the future. I don't have the answers, so instead I'll give my view of the question. *What do we need to do to get a well-trained workforce in software engineering?* Specifically, how will we address the following concerns in the future, based upon the issues I presented earlier?

1. How to make society realize the importance of software engineering?

As stated earlier, a U.S. government agency does not believe software engineers need to be engineers, yet we have evidence that programs are still hard to write, we continue to make errors, and the increased use of multicore processors will only increase the complexity of future systems. Yet much of society still views programming as just a trade that anyone can do.

A simple anecdote—I have a friend who is an engineer who manages a team that writes systems for astronomers to use. There is also a separate technical support group who manage the computers for the entire institute. Many of the astronomers cannot tell them apart since from the professional astronomer's point of view, both simply make the machines work. However, the technicians' role is to monitor the machines, perform backups, and fix system-wide hardware and software problems. They are responsible for the institute-wide applications that are obtained from outside vendors, including such products as database systems, word processing and other desktop applications, security products, etc. However, the programming staff has the role of designing, building, and testing new application software specifically for the astronomers. Both groups are necessary, but their roles are very different.

A second anecdote—From 1976 through 2002 Victor Basili and I were involved in the NASA Goddard Space Flight Center Software Engineering Laboratory [11]. What I learned over 25 years was that software was never high on a project team's priority list. Spacecraft were designed and then software was considered. Software people were rarely, if ever, part of important decision making panels. The impression I had was that the software people were like plumbing in a building. They were important for the proper functioning of the organization, but were never visible to management.

2. How to create software tools that people really care about?

As a compiler writer, tool builder, and experimentalist over 40 years, I still have my doubts about how successful we have been. The typical conference proceedings today in software engineering contains numerous papers of the form

How <my acronym>, using <this new theory of mine>,
is useful for the testing of <application domain>
and is able to find <class of errors> better than existing tools.

While this all sounds nice, the tool is never mentioned again in other publications and is quickly forgotten. Few end up as commercial products.

In one study, Dolores Wallace from the National Institute of Standards and Technology in Gaithersburg, Maryland and I looked at various methods used to validate a new technology [12]. We compared the academic researcher and the industrial user. Both groups seemed to have different goals in determining which validation method would be most effective. The researcher wanted scientific validity. That meant controlled replicated studies where most variables could be controlled. That necessarily meant that most such studies were relatively small and that they were done in a laboratory setting and not in the "real world."

On the other hand, the industrial user wants to check out a new technology in a relevant environment. That means large case studies where few of the conflicting variables can be controlled. Replication is rare due to the size and costs of each such development. From the research perspective, these studies are of less value since they are simply anecdotal and do not indicate major trends.

Thus the industrial user and the academic researcher have differing goals in understanding what is needed when validating a new technology. It is no wonder that many of the academic conference papers do not make it into industrial practice.
3. How do we train future software engineers?

In this paper I gave several examples of how systems have failed. How do we build a relevant curriculum? The long standing dispute of whether software engineering is a separate field or part of computer science has not been settled. While there are some separate software engineering departments, few are part of engineering schools with full engineering credentials for its graduates. Concepts like parallel and multicore programming, fault tree analysis, project management economics, and measurement and prediction need to be part of the curriculum in addition to the standard concepts of requirements analysis, design, coding, and testing methods.
4. MOOCs?

Finally, we need to address the impact of the massive online open course. Software engineering is basically a laboratory subject, so how to adapt it for an online environment will not be easy. But I believe we must. The economics are forcing the issue and credit courses in an MOOC environment are going to happen. How do we utilize this technology without losing control of the educational process?

All of these questions, except this last one, have been around for years; however, I do not believe they have been solved. We must solve them. Computers control all aspects of our technological world. We must be able to appropriately control the computers.

7   In Conclusion

Finally, in a paper I recently read from December, 2012: "The developer sets a breakpoint, runs the program, and then sequentially steps through the code from the breakpoint, verifying the state changes as expected" [13]. This is a crude primitive technique which I was able to eliminate in my dissertation in 1971 using a prototype implementation on a 2 megabyte IBM mainframe. Today's machines can have tens of gigabytes to work with. Haven't we learned anything in 40 years?

References

1. Leveson, N.G., Turner, C.S.: An investigation of the Therac-25 accidents. Computer (IEEE) **26**(7), 18–41 (1993)
2. Neumann P. G. and contributors: Risks to the public. ACM Softw. Eng. Notes **36**(2), 19–27 (Page 21, Comment by Jeremy Epstein) (2011)
3. Nuseibeh, B.: Ariane 5: who dunnit? IEEE Softw. **14**(3), 15–16 (1997)
4. Grier, D.A.: The migration to the middle. IEEE Comput. **44**(1), 1214 (2011)
5. Parnas, D.L.: Inside risks: risks of undisciplined development. Commun. ACM **53**(10), 25–27 (2010)
6. Neville-Neil, G.V.: Kode Vicious: literate coding. Commun. ACM **53**(12), 37–38 (2010)
7. Ortega, R.: How much software testing is enough? Commun. ACM **53**(9), 9 (2010)
8. Sutter, H.: The free lunch is over: a fundamental turn toward concurrency in software. Dr. Dobb's J. **30**(3) (2005)
9. Dennis, R., Thompson, K.: The UNIX time-sharing system. Commun. ACM **17**(7), 365–375 (1974)
10. Zelkowitz, M.V.: Automatic program analysis and evaluation. In: Second International Conference on Software Engineering, pp. 158–163, San Francisco (1976)
11. Basili, V., McGarry, F., Pajerski, R., Zelkowitz, M.: Lessons learned from 25 years of process improvement: the rise and fall of the NASA Software Engineering Laboratory. In: IEEE Computer Society and ACM International Conference on Software Engineering, pp. 69–79. Orlando (2002)
12. Zelkowitz, M.V., Wallace, D.R.: Validating the benefit of new software technology. Softw. Qual. Pract. **1**(1) (1998)
13. Spear, A., Levy, M., Desnoyers, M.: Using tracing to solve the multicore system debug problem. IEEE Comput. **45**(12), 60–64 (2012)

Integrated Software Process and Product Lines

Dieter Rombach

Abstract

Increasing demands imposed on software-intensive systems will require more rigorous engineering and management of software artifacts and processes. Software product line engineering allows for the effective reuse of software artifacts based on the pro-active organization of similar artifacts according to similarities and variances. Software processes—although also variable across projects—are still not managed in a similar systematic way. This paper motivates the need for Software Process Lines similar to Product Lines. As a result of such organization, processes within an organization could be organized according to similarities and differences, allowing for better tailoring to specific project needs (corresponds to application engineering in product lines). The vision of SPPL (integrated product and process line) engineering is presented, where suitable artifacts and processes can be chosen based on a set of product & process requirements and project constraints. The paper concludes with some resulting challenges for research, practice, and teaching.

1   Introduction

Increasing demands imposed on software-intensive systems will require more rigorous engineering and management of software artifacts and processes. For example, software embedded in automobiles exceeds 10 million lines of code already today and has to satisfy extreme safety requirements. Such developments can only be mastered with highly modular architectures enabling the reuse of

D. Rombach (✉)
University of Kaiserslautern & Fraunhofer IESE, Kaiserslautern 67663, Germany
e-mail: dieter.rombach@iese.fraunhofer.de

J. Münch and K. Schmid (eds.), *Perspectives on the Future of Software Engineering,*   359
DOI 10.1007/978-3-642-37395-4 12. The previous version of this paper was published
in Lecture Notes in Computer Science 3840 Springer 2005, ISBN 3-540-31112-2.

verified and validated components and the checking of safety requirements at the system integration level. The processes used will highly depend on the degree of safety or reliability to be achieved and on other project characteristics. Choosing trustable components and performing needed module adaptations and additionally required verification & validation, and checking adherence to safety or reliability requirements at the system integration level with the appropriate processes are the key engineering decisions.

Software product line engineering allows for the effective reuse of software artifacts based on the pro-active organization of similar artifacts for a given domain according to similarities and variances. Software processes—although also variable across projects—are still not managed in a similar systematic way. It must not only be the objective to establish software process lines in order to choose the appropriate and proven processes, but to establish integrated software process & product lines (SPPL) in order to systematically choose both artifacts and processes needed for a given project.

This paper motivates the need for Software Process Lines similar to Product Lines.

As a result of such organization, processes within an organization could be organized according to similarities and differences allowing for better tailoring to specific project needs (corresponds to application engineering in product lines). The vision of SPPL (integrated product and process line) engineering is presented, where suitable artifacts and processes can be chosen based on a set of product and process requirements and project constraints. The paper concludes with some resulting challenges for research, practice, and teaching.

2   Motivation for Proactive Reuse

Engineering requires reuse of proven artifacts. In software engineering, the major challenge to reuse stems from the fact that such artifacts typically have to be changed and tailored to the needs of unique projects. One approach to support such adaptation in a systematic way is to differentiate between commonalities and variations across all systems to be developed within a given domain, and to pre-define limits for variations that can be supported.

2.1   Mature Software Engineering

Mature software engineering requires, among other things, a focus on all engineering and management processes, the application of techniques, methods and tools suitable for practical engineering, and effective reuse.

2.2 Reuse Challenges

Assumptions for successful reuse include the following [1]:

– All experience can be reused: Traditionally, the emphasis has been on reusing concrete objects of 'source code'. This limitation reflects the traditional view that software equals code. It ignores the importance of reusing all kinds of software-related experiences including artifacts at all levels of abstraction ranging from requirements to test cases, processes, and other knowledge, such as reliability, cost or resource models.

– Reuse typically requires some modification: Under the assumption that software developments are typically different in some way, modification of reuse candidates from previous projects must be anticipated. The degree of modification depends on how many, and to what degree, existing characteristics of a reuse candidate differ from the ones needed in the target system.

– Reuse must be integrated into (tailored to) the target projects: Reuse is intended to make software development more effective. In order to achieve this objective, we need to tailor reuse practices to the respective development processes.

The question is how we can minimize the tailoring actually needed and how we can systematically guide the actual tailoring.

2.3 Commonality and Variation

Software systems within any domain can be characterized by their

– Commonalities: These are functionalities that are contained in all (or at least a large number of) systems within that domain.

– Variabilities: These are functionalities that are unique to one (or some number of) system(s) within some domain.

These commonalities and variabilities are then implemented via an architecture of components with

– Fixed commonalities: Such components can be reused across all (or at least a large number of) systems of a domain without change.

– Controlled variabilities: Such components can be reused with limited and controlled change. Examples include parameterized components or components with optional or modifiable functionalities (e.g., via conditional compilation at the code level, via decision models at the UML modeling level). Modifiable functionalities may be defined in a binary way (include or not include!) or in a continuous way (e.g., ranges of parameters such as reliability [0.9 ... 0.99]).

– Adhoc variabilities: Such components may be unique to one system and will have to be developed from scratch. However, in order to prevent architecture erosion, the interfaces for the inclusion of such components should be well defined, and they should not address nonfunctional requirements (e.g., reliability, performance or safety), as such requirements are known to carry the risk of architecture discontinuities.

A good architecture should

- Maximize the percentage of components with fixed commonalities and controlled variation, and
- Be stable across the entire family of systems within a domain.

3   Product and Process Lines

Software product line (SPL) engineering' represents the most promising approach to proactive reuse based on pre-designed commonalities and controlled variabilities across a family of systems. This chapter briefly summarizes the state-of-the-art and—practice in SPL engineering, motivates why processes would also benefit from similar treatment as artifacts, and suggests the expansion of SPL engineering to 'Software Process Line engineering'. Based on the hypothesis in Sect. 2.2—that effective reuse must comprise all experiences (artifacts and processes)—the vision of 'integrated software process & product line engineering' (SPPL) is created.

3.1   Software Product Lines

Software Product Line (SPL) engineering has been proposed by the Software Engineering Institute (SEI) at Carnegie Mellon University. However, the underlying ideas of differentiating between the development of experiences reusable across projects and the project-specific development of a software system by means of reusing available experiences have been formulated as early as the 1980s under the label 'experience factory' [2].

The main characteristics of SPL engineering include:

- Two (2) separate development processes: One distinguishes between the domain engineering process, by which artifacts for reuse are being created, and the application engineering process, by which project-specific systems are being developed.
- An artifact repository: Reusable artifacts at all abstraction levels—from requirements to test cases—are made available.
- A systematic reuse process: For each predefined choice of variabilities, the choice of components is pre-defined (e.g., via 'product maps').
- A systematic artifact management process: For each exception (e.g., an unintended change to a component of a supposedly controlled variability) it will be decided whether this exception will be factored into the component or not.

The objectives of using SPL engineering are—as in the case of all reuse approaches—increased quality, reduced cost and time, and reduced risk. Especially a reduction of cost can be achieved only if the requirements engineering process within the domain engineering process is based on sound 'scoping'. Scoping attempts to maximize the common functionalities and controlled variabilities so that they can be addressed with one stable architecture and domain engineering effort can be amortized over the number of possible applications.

Several real-world implementations of SPL engineering exist and show remarkable results. Especially time to market reductions by orders of magnitudes and reduced quality risks are reported. One example includes the company Market Maker which produces stock trading software for professionals and non-professionals, and which recently reported about such experiences from 5 years of product line engineering [ICSE 2005]. Fraunhofer IESE assists companies in establishing SPL engineering based on PuLSE—an SPL approach supporting effective scoping, providing tools for variability specification and management at all abstraction levels, and providing means for incremental build-up of product lines. Example implementations exist at Bosch (automotive supply company), Ricoh (printer business) and Market Maker (stock trading).

The artifacts created with an SPL development organization can be organized according to an 'is_a' relationship. Each component created from a domain artifact (without or with controlled change) is in an 'is_a' relationship with the reused domain artifact. This direct relationship (instead of the multiple derivation sequences in non-SPL settings, where application $N+1$ is derived from application N) avoids all the configuration management problems we know from release- or variant-based developments.

3.2 Problems with Software Processes

Today we can distinguish mainly two kinds of software processes—the prescriptive company processes and the processes actually executed in projects. The former are typically phase-based, serve to control projects company-wide wrt. cost and time, and allow synchronization with other processes, such as system engineering processes (combining development of mechanical, electronic and software components in embedded system domains) or non-engineering processes, such as acquisition or distribution. However, such processes provide little guidance for software developers. The latter processes are the processes by which software systems have been developed. Mostly they are implicit and have an unclear relationship with the company-wide prescriptive processes.

Some of the problems resulting from this current situation include:
- Lack of guidance for software developers from a process that is too generic.
- Problems with measurement due to the lack of process adherence to the process for which metrics have been defined.
- Problems with feedback due to the fact that the lessons learned during projects cannot be related to the company-wide process.

What is missing is a clear relationship between a generic company process and the actual instantiations (either for a specific business unit or for a concrete project). It is unclear what the commonalities and controlled variabilities are across all process instances. The commonalities should be captured in the company-wide process; the controlled variabilities should be specified and guidelines for tailoring should exist. The discriminators for the 'is_a' relationship between processes would be

- Product & process requirements: Examples could include degree of reliability or certain sets of functionalities and effort distributions or time.
- Project characteristics: Examples could include the experience of developers.

3.3   Software Process Lines

Software process lines would be based on the same principles described in Sect. 3.1. That means we would, by means of a domain engineering process, create a generic (set of) process(es) that capture the commonalities and controlled variabilities across a domain. The variabilities—and thereby the discriminators for process instances—in the case of processes are product and process goals as well as project characteristics. The knowledge about these variabilities—as well as their instantiation into concrete processes—comes from empirical studies on the impact of processes on goals under given project characteristics (often referred to as context).

For example, we might have a generic inspection process associated with a certain development milestone. Variabilities of the developments could be different degrees of reliability (highly reliable, normally reliable) of the software under development, and the experience of the inspectors (high, medium). In this case we might create—and by means of empirical studies validate—the following hypotheses:

- Perspective-based reading is best suited for software with high reliability requirements and medium experience.
- Ad-hoc reading is best suited for software with normal reliability requirements and highly experienced inspectors.
- Checklist-based reading is most suitable for all other combinations.

Here we would have three 'is_a' relationships between ad-hoc/checklist-based/perspective-based inspections and a generic inspection process.

The main characteristics of software process line engineering would be similar to the ones listed in Sect. 3.1:

- Two (2) separate development processes: One distinguishes between the domain engineering process, by which processes for reuse are being created, and the application engineering process, by which project-specific processes are being developed.
- A process repository: Reusable processes at all abstraction levels are made available.
- A systematic reuse process: For each predefined choice of variabilities, the choice of process components is pre-defined (e.g., via empirically justified 'project maps').
- A systematic process management process: For each exception (e.g. an unexpected behavior of the process occurs) it will be decided whether this exception will be factored into the generic process or not.

The objectives of using software process line engineering are—as in the case of all reuse approaches—increased predictability, reduced cost and time, and reduced risk. The way to build such process hierarchies is either bottom-up or top-down. Top-down establishment reflects the typical standardization process. Bottom-up approaches look at commonalities and variabilities across a number of projects, perform a commonality analysis [3], and model the process in terms of commonalities and controlled variances.

Several real-world implementations of software process lines have been started. Examples include the process architecture (created bottom-up) at NASA Goddard Space Flight Center's SEL, and the newly proposed and top-down developed V-Model XT for public development sub-contracts in Germany [http://www.v-model-xt.de].

3.4   Integrated Software Process and Product Lines

There exists a strong correlation between process and products in the sense that the product goals are achieved as a function of executing some process under certain project characteristics. It would be desirable to establish a focus on reusing experience like software artifacts and processes. Such an organization would be called a 'Software Process & Product Line (SPPL)". Here artifacts and processes are captured and organized according to discriminators combining product and process requirements, and project characteristics.

It might be obvious that such an organization could also be viewed as a 'comprehensive Experience Factory' implementation. The interesting vision would be that one wants to start a project by characterizing it and submitting a query (e.g., in the form of a set of GQMs [4]) to the repository. Then a combined set of artifacts and processes would be provided to plan and run a project with.

4   Future Work

Process lines and even integrated process and product lines can be built today. However, efforts in research, practice, and education & training are needed in order to support the establishment of SPPLs.

4.1   Research

The most important research tasks needed include:
- The design of process modeling languages with features for variability specification: Example languages with features for variability specification MVP-L.
- More effective methods for creating empirically grounded 'process -7 product' models. Here the research thread on 'evidence-based software engineering' or 'value based software engineering' as well as portals for evidence on process effectiveness and efficiency such as 'CeBASE' or 'VSEK', or even books like [5].

- Theoretical & engineering foundations for process lines (especially organizing) and integrated SPPLs. Discrepancies will be handled separately.

4.2   Practice

The most important practice changes include:
- Acceptance of the importance of processes and the need to manage them.
- Empirical model building based on studies imposed upon projects.
- Wide-spread adoption of SPL.
- Expansion of the SPL idea to the SPPL vision.

4.3   Education and Training

In the case of embedded systems:
- Higher focus on process, more specifically on the appropriate use of process
- Training of new methods in laboratory settings
- Role-based education & training. Especially in the product line context, we have to separate developers (top-down problem solvers) from domain engineers (bottom-up abstractors).

5   Conclusions

Delivery of increasingly complex software systems in more and more customer variations requires effective (pro-active) reuse in the form of product lines. In these product lines, all kinds of experience (mostly artifacts and processes) need to be stored and managed. We call such product lines 'software process and product lines'. This paper suggests an expansion of the well-defined and proven principles of software product line engineering to processes, and an integration of both based on the ideas of the 'Experience Factory'.

References

1. Basili, V.R., Rombach, H.D.: Support for comprehensive reuse. IEE Br. Comput. Soc. Softw. Eng. J. **6**(5), 303–316 (1991b)
2. Basili, V.R., Caldiera, G., Rombach, H.D.: The experience factory. In: Marciniak, J.J. (ed.) Encyclopedia of Software Engineering, vol. I, pp. 469–476. Wiley (1994)
3. Ocampo, A., Bella, F., Münch, J.: Software process commonality analysis. Int. J. Softw. Process Improv. Pract. **10**(3), 273–285 (2005)
4. Basili, V.R., Caldiera, G., Rombach, H.D.: Goal question metric paradigm. In: Marciniak, J.J. (ed.) Encyclopedia of Software Engineering, vol. 1, pp. 528–532. Wiley (1994)
5. Endres, A., Rombach, H.D.: A Handbook of Software and Systems Engineering – Empirical Observations, Laws and Theories. Pearson Addison Wesley, Harlow/New York (2003)

Printed by Publishers' Graphics LLC
LMO130627.15.14.32